Faith in the New Millennium

Faith in the New Millennium

The Future of Religion and American Politics

Edited by

MATTHEW AVERY SUTTON

AND DARREN DOCHUK

OXFORD
UNIVERSITY PRESS

OXFORD
UNIVERSITY PRESS

Oxford University Press is a department of the University of
Oxford. It furthers the University's objective of excellence in research,
scholarship, and education by publishing worldwide.

Oxford is a registered trademark of Oxford University Press
in the UK and in certain other countries.

Published in the United States of America by
Oxford University Press
198 Madison Avenue, New York, NY 10016, United States of America

© Oxford University Press 2016

"Questionnaire," copyright © 2010 by Wendell Berry, from *Leavings*.
Reprinted by permission of Counterpoint.
Lines from "National Brotherhood Week" from *That Was the Year That Was*,
© 1964 Tom Lehrer, reprinted by permission of Tom Lehrer.

Library of Congress Cataloging-in-Publication Data
Faith in the new millennium: the future of religion and American politics / edited by
Matthew Avery Sutton and Darren Dochuk.
pages cm
ISBN 978-0-19-937270-6 (pbk.: alk. paper)—ISBN 978-0-19-937269-0
(hardback: alk. paper)
1. Religion and politics—United States—History—21st century.   2. United States—
Politics and government—21st century.   3. Obama, Barack—Political and social views.
4. Obama, Barack—Religion.   I. Sutton, Matthew Avery,   II. Dochuk, Darren.
BL2525.F343 2016
322′.10973—dc23
2015005460

3 5 7 9 8 6 4 2
Printed in Canada
on acid-free paper

To Paul Harvey, Amanda Porterfield,
and Philip Goff

Contents

III. *Religion*

Acknowledgments

THE IDEA FOR this book was conceived by Amanda Porterfield and Edward J. Blum, who hoped to continue work begun in 2007 by that year's class of Young Scholars in American Religion. The project evolved from there. The editors gratefully acknowledge the many people and institutes that made this project possible. Philip Goff and the Center for the Study of Religion and American Culture at Indiana University-Purdue University Indianapolis provided support with funding from the Lilly Endowment for a group of early career scholars to begin thinking about how their research on religion intersected across space and time. In 2012, many of those scholars, joined by a handful of others, met at the campus of Southern Methodist University (SMU) to share drafts of the essays that appear here. SMU's Center for Presidential History and especially its director Jeffrey A. Engel were excellent hosts and provided substantial support. The conference also received significant support from the John C. Danforth Center on Religion and Politics at Washington University in St. Louis and its director R. Marie Griffith. At Oxford University Press, we are grateful to Theo Calderara, Gina Chung, and their team for their countless contributions to this volume. Finally, we dedicate this book to Paul Harvey, Amanda Porterfield, and Philip Goff, who trained a generation of Young Scholars in American Religion to see the relevance of their research for the modern world.

List of Contributors

Edward J. Blum is professor of history at San Diego State University. He is the co-author of *The Color of Christ: The Son of God and the Saga of Race in America* and author of *Reforging the White Republic: Race, Religion, and American Nationalism, 1865–1898*.

Anthea Butler is associate professor of religion and Africana studies at the University of Pennsylvania. She is the author of *Women in the Church of God in Christ: Making a Sanctified World*.

Mark A. Chancey is professor of religious studies at Dedman College of Humanities and Sciences at Southern Methodist University. His most recent books are *The Bible in the Public Square: Its Enduring Influence in American Life*, co-edited with Carol Meyers and Eric M. Meyers, and *Alexander to Constantine: Archaeology of the Land of the Bible*, co-authored with Eric M. Meyers.

Darren Dochuk is associate professor of history at the University of Notre Dame. He is the author of *From Bible Belt to Sunbelt: Plain-folk Religion, Grassroots Politics, and the Rise of Evangelical Conservatism*.

Kate Carté Engel is an associate professor of history at Southern Methodist University. She is the author of *Religion and Profit: Moravians in Early America* and a forthcoming work on transatlantic religion and the American Revolution.

J. Spencer Fluhman is associate professor of history at Brigham Young University. He is author of *"A Peculiar People": Anti-Mormonism and the Making of Religion in Nineteenth-Century America* and editor of *Mormon Studies Review*.

Rebecca Anne Goetz is associate professor of history at New York University. She is the author of *The Baptism of Early Virginia: How Christianity Created Race.*

Jennifer Graber is associate professor of religious studies at the University of Texas at Austin. She is the author of *The Furnace of Affliction: Prisons and Religion in Antebellum America.*

Alison Collis Greene is assistant professor of history at Mississippi State University. She is author of *No Depression in Heaven: The Great Depression, the New Deal, and the Transformation of Religion in the Delta.*

Matthew S. Hedstrom is associate professor of religious studies and American studies at the University of Virginia. He is the author of *The Rise of Liberal Religion: Book Culture and American Spirituality in the Twentieth Century.*

Charles F. Irons is associate professor of history at Elon University. He is the author of *The Origins of Proslavery Christianity: White and Black Evangelicals in Colonial and Antebellum Virginia.*

Steven P. Miller is the author of *The Age of Evangelicalism: America's Born-Again Years* and *Billy Graham and the Rise of the Republican South.*

Amanda Porterfield is the Robert A. Spivey professor of religion and history at Florida State University. Her most recent book is *Conceived in Doubt: Religion and Politics in the New American Nation.*

Andrew Preston is professor of American History at Cambridge University where he is a fellow of Clare College. His most recent book is *Sword of the Spirit, Shield of Faith: Religion in American War and Diplomacy.*

Arlene M. Sánchez-Walsh is professor of religious studies at Azusa Pacific University. She is the author of *Latino Pentecostal Identity* and the forthcoming *Pentecostalism in America.*

Kevin M. Schultz is an associate professor of history, Catholic studies, and religious studies at the University of Illinois at Chicago. He is the author of *Tri-Faith America: How Catholics and Jews Held Postwar America to its Protestant Promise* and *Buckley and Mailer: The Difficult Friendship that Shaped the Sixties.*

Matthew Avery Sutton is the Edward R. Meyer Distinguished Professor of History at Washington State University. He is the author of *American Apocalypse: A History of Modern Evangelicalism* and *Aimee Semple McPherson and the Resurrection of Christian America.*

Faith in the New Millennium

Introduction

Matthew Avery Sutton and Darren Dochuk

FUTURE GENERATIONS OF Americans will likely look back on the time between September 11, 2001, and the end of the Obama presidency as a period of substantial transformation. The global economy crashed and then began to rebound, but only tentatively, and with new crises seemingly always on the horizon. Innovative technologies from the iPhone to Twitter have changed the way people communicate. China is now challenging the United States for economic supremacy. Global warming is stoking fears for the future. Terrorists in search of weapons of mass destruction threaten the world's peace and security. Politics in the United States has become dysfunctional, with apparently insurmountable divides between "red" states and "blue" states. Fracking is now a topic for dinner-table debate. Americans' sense of community and commitment to the greater good have waned. The US military is deployed around the world in conflicts that never seem to end. Cuba is opening up. Newspapers are closing down. Global pandemics from Ebola to the bird flu inspire fear and dread. Gays and lesbians are securing rights long denied.

And in concert with all of these transformations, the nature and practice of religion and its impact on American political culture is shifting in equally profound ways. On one level, the tumult in this realm should surprise no one. After all, the fusion of religion and politics in the United States has always generated energy, controversy, and dramatic change, baffling many Americans (and much of the world) at each striking turn. The nation's unique political structure is partly responsible for the sustained potency of the "God factor." At its very founding, the United States helped pioneer the separation of church and state, yet in the process paradoxically created one of the most religiously charged political cultures in the modern West. Rather than facilitate, or even encourage, religious indifference or apathy or secularism, disestablishment did just the opposite. It democratized religion and freed peoples of different faiths to influence society and state indirectly but ultimately more effectively.

Unfettered by formal government control and uninhibited by rigid structures of established church authority, religious Americans have shaped the nation in many ways: through voluntary associations, the free promotion of their values and opinions, active lobbying on behalf of their moral concerns, fierce competition in the market of ideas, and countless grassroots crusades for reforms they deemed essential to the life of their communities and their country. Alexis de Tocqueville famously declared that "religion in America takes no direct part in the government of society, but it must be regarded as the first of their political institutions." What Tocqueville bore witness to in the early nineteenth century we still see in the early twenty-first: an entwining of religion and politics that fuels societal change and makes any attempt to distinguish one from the other nearly impossible.[1]

The God factor's dizzying effects on our early twenty-first-century moment are also exceptional. In the new millennium, faith is not exactly what it was before, particularly where politics is concerned. Evidence certainly abounds that the politicization of religion, which burst into the open as early as the precedent-setting Jefferson-Hamilton 1800 presidential campaign, has continued to intensify in American life.

This has been a bipartisan affair. Since the rise of the Moral Majority in the late 1970s, Republican Party leaders have claimed that Judeo-Christian values lie at the heart of their party and their policies. Tea Party activists have recently delivered these claims with a force that has shattered the peace in the heartland and on Capitol Hill. Although Democrats have embraced the God revolution more slowly and somewhat more reluctantly than their GOP counterparts, by the beginning of the new century they too had made the Almighty a central part of their campaigns. In the last couple of decades, all of the major presidential candidates have talked about the role of faith in their lives and have shared their religious beliefs and church commitments with the media and voters.

That is, until recently. During the 2012 campaign, Barack Obama minimized the role of religion in his administration and in his life. This provided a stark contrast with 2008, when Obama emphasized how his Chicago church had nurtured him as a person, a community organizer, and a politician. Highlighting faith, however, had backfired when incendiary messages preached by his liberationist pastor Jeremiah Wright went viral. Since then, Obama has not made religion an overt part of his presidency.

Notable shifts are underway in the GOP as well. Indeed, the Republican Party has faced a different kind of problem in recent years. The founders of the Religious Right, the men and women most responsible for making God-talk a part of mainstream politics, have faded from the spotlight. Jerry Falwell is dead, Pat Robertson's influence has waned, James Dobson and Billy Graham have retired, and Phyllis Schlafly can no longer move mass numbers of people to action. Furthermore, when Mormon Mitt Romney ran as the GOP candidate in 2012, party operatives recognized that the less they said about religion the better. Since many Americans remain suspicious of the Church of Jesus Christ of Latter-day Saints, the campaign did its best to avoid shining a spotlight on religion.

And yet, even as religion seems to be losing some traction in the two parties, there are new signs that it is merely recalibrating and reloading, and gaining fresh ground on broader political terrain. Religious affiliation, for example, continues to be an important predictor of voting behavior. The results of the 2014 midterm elections revealed that white evangelicals and white Catholics are voting as strongly as ever for the GOP. Meanwhile, the majority of those who claim no religious affiliation—the so-called nones—seem to vote mostly Democratic. The close relationship between religious affiliation, race, and voting habits, which begs for deeper analysis, at the very least suggests that matters of belief and unbelief are important considerations in the way Americans elect their politicians.

There are numerous other signs that religion is both adjusting and maintaining its grip on American politics, even as it is being pushed and pulled in new directions by the political exigencies of our time. Although the generation that launched the culture wars is fading into history, the spirit of the Religious Right continues to spark grassroots battles over education, gender, sexuality, taxation, and global warming. Young evangelicals, meanwhile, may be shunning the hard-edged conservatism of their parents, but they are every bit as earnest in channeling their theological convictions into action on behalf of political causes such as environmental protection and economic justice—and they are not ceding any ground on the issue of abortion.

In the political center and on the left, a new, substantially more diverse population—in terms of ethnicity, sexual orientation, and religious affiliation (and non-affiliation)—has entered politics in different ways by championing immigration reform, internationalism, gay marriage, and—most recently—policing and incarceration reform. All of which is to say that religion appears to be at a crossroads in its political career and America itself at a point of departure. Yet as we assess this country and its shifting patterns of faith and politics in the new millennium, it seems equally apparent that the religious energy Tocqueville saw at work in American politics remains unabated, its influence as pervasive today as it was two centuries ago.

Considering the upheaval of our moment, and the apparent shifts in this nation's religious and political character, it is imperative that scholars take the long view and offer careful assessment of how faith is functioning in the new millennium. Americans—students, scholars, and an informed public—need to better understand how issues of faith and issues of policy now intersect, differently from and similarly to what came before, with anticipation of what may likely come next.

This volume's sixteen authors have taken on this task. Each essay examines a contemporary issue, controversy, or policy through a deep historical lens. In our current twenty-four-hour-news-cycle media environment, where complexity is often buried under bluster, these essays make a powerful case for understanding the stories behind the news.

We asked each participant to write an essay that explores how her or his own research sheds light on an issue in contemporary American religious life and politics. The result is a series of essays that address major controversies and questions related to the intersections of religion and immigration, civil rights, race, ethnicity, foreign policy, the environment, and much more.

Together, these essays reveal how faith is shaping modern America and how modern America is shaping faith.

Note

1. Alexis de Tocqueville, *Alexis De Tocqueville on Democracy, Revolution, and Society: Selected Writings*, ed. John Stone and Stephen Mennell (Chicago: University of Chicago Press, 1980), 93.

I

Politics

I

The Founding Fathers in Modern America

Kate Carté Engel

ON SATURDAY, AUGUST 2, 2014, the fall election cycle got underway in a small town in western Kentucky at the annual Fancy Farm Picnic, where national attention was fixed on the tight Senate race between Democrat Alison Grimes and thirty-year incumbent Republican Mitch McConnell, the Senate minority leader. Before the main acts made their speeches, Democrat Charles Hatchett, a candidate for the US House from Kentucky's first congressional district, took the stage. Hatchett, a real estate broker and auctioneer from Paducah, Kentucky, launched quickly into his main theme: the nation's Founding Fathers and the importance of Christianity to America.[1]

"Let me tell you exactly what happened with our country in the first beginning," Hatchett cried, straining to speak over the noisy crowd. He started to recount George Washington's ordeal at Valley Forge, arguably the most important moment of the Revolutionary era for twenty-first-century conservative Christian retellings of the nation's founding. Although that story takes different forms in different Christian venues, Hatchett focused on the most providential version, highlighting simultaneously God's favor toward the United States and Washington's personal devotion and leadership. "Alright," he began, trying to keep control of his audience, "there was so many people that had been lost, you know, in other words, they were killed in battle, that George Washington was about to give up." Lest he be interpreted as saying that Washington was cowardly, he quickly added, "I'm talking to you about the man," emphasizing that all men, all

Christians, have internal struggles. But, Hatchett explained, Washington responded in the way of a true Christian, and so God provided.

> What [Washington] did was, he prayed in Jesus name for them to have a miracle, and the miracle they needed was they were out of food. . . . Well, what Washington prayed for was provisions to feed them, nine thousand people was in that army, and a miracle happened, fish—it was in wintertime—fish had swum up the . . . river, and they took out, with forks and shovels, and threw them on the bank[. It was] a miracle where they were fed.[2]

God's favor for his chosen nation was evident in his direct intervention to support the suffering troops and their devout leader. Crucial to that intervention was the piety and prayer of the nation's leader, George Washington. Hatchett reiterated his message: "God needs to go back into this country, and Christ-like manners needs to go too!"

The religious overtones of Hatchett's speech were impossible to miss. His invocation of divine intervention at Valley Forge fit awkwardly into his political agenda, but it served important purposes nonetheless. Personally, it established him as a man of faith who saw the world through Christian eyes. Politically, it demonstrated his attachment to a patriotism that paints the United States as a sacred entity with a special, covenantal relationship with a Christian God. These bone fides, he hoped, lent credibility to his negative assessment of his Republican competitors.

Although Hatchett's depiction of the nation's founding was unusual in its explicit reliance on religion, key elements from his reading—repackaged into a secular form—appear in numerous other venues. Christian nationalism, the belief that the United States has a special relationship with a Christian God and a divine or even prophetic place in Christian history, has long played an important role in national political and cultural conversations. The intertwining of patriotism and religion has been labeled "civil religion," by Robert Bellah and others, but that concept is most often used to explain broad cultural celebrations like Thanksgiving or the singing of "God Bless America" at baseball games since September 11, 2001.[3] Hatchett's blending of Christianity and US history, on the other hand, is representative of a more specific, conservative discourse that has risen to prominence since the 1970s, when fears of global communism and the stagnation of American greatness led to calls for renewal, framed in a particular narrative of the nation's past.[4] In 1981, theologian

Francis A. Schaeffer issued *A Christian Manifesto*, arguing that "the basic problem of the Christians in this country in the last eighty years or so" had been the decline of faithfulness, which had been present at the nation's illustrious start. "This linkage of Christian thinking and the concepts of government," he explained, "were not incidental but fundamental."[5] Schaeffer's blending of history and demand for moral reform resonated widely, and in the twenty-first century it found its most vocal spokesman in Texas businessman David Barton. Barton, an amateur historian who combined a love of primary sources with a keen political activism, produced a small mountain of historical works and a large empire of speaking tours and media appearances that shared the nation's "true" Christian history with a generation that had been denied its heritage by liberal teachers.[6]

Though David Barton has been the most prominent practitioner of conservative Christian readings of the nation's past—even after one of his books was disavowed by its own publisher for rampant factual errors—it would be a mistake to view the histories produced by Barton and his colleagues only within the lens of political struggle, as many scholars and pundits have done.[7] The sheer quantity and repetitive nature of these materials, appearing as books, blogs, articles, and sermons, suggest that the consumers of conservative Christian narratives of US history are reading and listening for some *other* reason than to glean information about the past. Instead, I argue that conservative Christians have turned the act of retelling the nation's founding into a religious practice, one that continually reaffirms their vision of the nation's moral purpose and serves as a call to action to rebuild what has been lost. The pages that follow explore this distinctive religious practice. After first situating conservative Christian retellings of the founding era in wider popular interest, this chapter details the nature of the ritual retelling of the nation's founding and the meanings that conservative Christians draw from that history. It then turns to the histories themselves to examine which subjects are included. Finally, the conclusion suggests how this religious practice shapes public life in the United States.

Popular Interest in the Founding of the United States

Before an examination of how conservative Christians understand, structure, and study the founding era, a brief note about the wider cultural obsession with the American Revolution is warranted, because distinctively Christian readings of the era intertwine with a great deal of general interest in the subject. Americans have been engaged in the process of narrating their own past for political ends since the founding era itself.[8] Interest in the American Revolution as a foundational event permeates our political and cultural discourse. Lincoln's Gettysburg Address began with an iconic reference to the nation's "fathers," and the phrase "Founding Fathers" is itself at least a century old.[9] In their interest in the American Revolution, conservative Christians are not diverging from the interests of the general public but rather participating in a popular act of national historical interpretation that has elevated the founding era to a higher level of historical significance than the eras that came before and after it.

Popular interest in the Revolution has tended to follow a biographical and narrative line. Since the turn of the twenty-first century, the phenomenon known as "Founders Chic" has fed a deep interest in the lives of a small pantheon of leaders who are generally accepted as Founders.[10] John Adams, Thomas Jefferson, James Madison, Benjamin Franklin, and above all George Washington have all received numerous biographical treatments from academicians with Ivy League pedigrees and from ministers, pundits, and interested writers. The juggernaut biography of John Adams written by David McCullough in 2001 led to a multipart HBO series, and published collections of the letters exchanged by John and Abigail Adams have also hit the bestseller lists. These works are undoubtedly hagiographic in the general sense of the term, and, like most popular histories, they are carefully situated to appeal to many audiences, whether devout or hostile to religion. McCullough's Adams is pious, but his religious beliefs and practices do not intrude on the biography's core narrative.[11] For Christians who take pride in having a biblical worldview that differs from the American mainstream, such easy reads are entertaining and noncontroversial.

Christians too have been active consumers of material on the Revolutionary era. Yet interest in the Revolution within Christian circles differs from that which drives popular histories, like those produced by David McCullough. Wheaton College historian Robert Tracy McKenzie explores this territory regularly in his blog *Faith and History: Thinking Christianly about the American Past*. He summarized the issue shortly before Independence Day in 2014. "As I have spoken to churches, Christian schools, and Christian home-schooling groups over the years, the question of whether America was founded as a Christian nation has regularly been the single most common question that I am asked," McKenzie recounted. The central thrust of these questions remains consistent, he continued. "If they are interested in history at all, the Christians that I meet outside the Academy keep coming back to the same basic question: Was the United States founded as a Christian country, by Christian statesmen, guided by Christian principles?"[12]

The search for core principles of the founding era plays a key role in conservative Christian histories of the Revolution, a topic that this chapter explores in detail, but Christian communities are not monolithic, so it is important to remember that the conservative Christian historical reading discussed below coexists with a second, more conventional interest in the period as a time of important change. Serious scholars within the diverse Christian community answer questions about the meaning of the Revolutionary era in ways that follow academic and secular scholarship, and there is ample evidence that their responses find a willing audience. Indeed, self-consciously Christian historians carefully mediate between academic historians and a deeply interested Christian general public.[13] A survey of some major evangelical publications, such as *Christianity Today* and its subsidiaries, suggests that Christian readers seek out both titles aimed particularly at them and also more "secular" titles. In *Christianity Today*, Robert Tracy McKenzie reviewed Matthew Stewart's decidedly nonreligious *Nature's God: The Heretical Origins of the American Republic*, faulting it not for its perspective on religion or its thesis but for its lack of historical subtlety. Jonathan Yeager, an academic scholar of the eighteenth century, glowingly reviewed literary scholar Vincent Caretta's biography of Phyllis Wheatley for *Books & Culture*, and the periodical *Christian History* includes extensive bibliographies that highlight works of academic scholarship. These works, along with the academic productions of evangelical scholars such as Mark Noll, John Fea, and Thomas Kidd, ensure that intellectually inquisitive Christians who are seeking historical information about the nation's origins can quite easily find sources that scholars would champion.

Christian booksellers also bring together works of scholarship on religion and the founding era, as well as on Puritan New England, with explicitly devotional materials intended to guide individuals and families in their spiritual lives. Focus on the Family's online store has a "Church History" book section, which itself has an "American Religious History" section. Here one finds works by Amanda Porterfield, Paul Harvey, and

Anthea Butler, to name only a few. Focus on the Family partners with the online retailer Christianbook.com, and at that site one finds Robert Gingrich's *Faith & Freedom: The Founding Fathers in their Own Words*, a book produced for a Christian audience, listed as a bestseller. One also finds books by scholars George Marsden and Anthea Butler on the first page, alongside culture warriors David Barton and Peter Marshall. This diverse body of materials gathered in a single place provides a caution against oversimplifying the broad category of Christian readers and authors, yet it also provides a comparative context for the distinctive readings examined below.

In order to understand the religious practice of reading the American foundling, it is necessary to distinguish the widespread interest among Americans, including Christian Americans, in the nation's founding, on the one hand, and the kind of engagement that a Charles Hatchett exhibits, on the other. The two discussions are almost entirely separate. Where the work of Christian scholars like Fea, Marsden, and McKenzie draw widely from academic and popular works, those who participate in the religious practice of retelling the founding era use texts that exist in a tight circle of internal references.[14] Whatever their nonreligious reading habits, when conservative Christians engage the religious practice of historical narrative, the voices of popular authors and academics, Christians or non-Christians, disappear. As a result, their reading exists as a separate discussion that operates under its own logic.

A *Christian Hermeneutic for the American Revolution*

Conservative Christians have arrived at their version of US history by applying some of the same hermeneutical strategies to history that they are familiar with from studying scripture.[15] This parallel provides the basis of seeing the conservative Christian discussion about the American Revolution as a religious practice. Biblically minded Protestants apply the concept of a harmonious meaning to the entirety of scripture in order to manage passages that would otherwise be difficult or contradictory. The concept that "scripture interprets scripture" suggests that, in the words of megachurch pastor Rick Warren, "the Bible is its own best commentary," a point Warren lists as the second of six principles for interpreting scripture.[16] The concept is repeated widely in various guides for understanding that complex text, and it is linked to the Protestant concept of *sola scriptura* or "by scripture alone." If the Bible is the one source of truth, then it must provide all the tools necessary for its own interpretation, and the overall meanings of the entire text must harmonize. As a tool for reading scripture, this method allows the faithful to systematize the vastly different types of texts that appear within the canon. The legal prescriptions of the Hebrew Bible must harmonize with teachings of Jesus and his disciples, and the letters of Paul must offer a similar meaning as the Psalms.[17]

The idea that scripture interprets scripture is a method of historical analysis as well as a form of textual reading. Some moments, events, and passages are far more important than others. The interpreter determines what these moments and events are through his or her knowledge of the principles and meanings of the whole. The American Revolution is not so much an era of profound and sequential change but rather a text with a cohesive meaning. Performing this reading requires a three-step process. First, the text is defined. Certain aspects of the era are included in the canon and others are excluded. Because the messiness of canonization is distracting, this selection process is largely invisible in the final retellings, and it becomes clear only when the narratives in question are juxtaposed to outside knowledge. Rather than continually reengage the process of canonization, writers, ministers, and bloggers generally draw from a shared corpus of texts that reinforce their version of what matters. The second step in the process is generally the first one visible to readers: the writer introduces the era with a clear sense of its guiding meaning. Having that meaning in mind, authors perform their analysis (the third step), looking both backward and forward in their historical reasoning. The process of historical analysis is successful if the best illustrations of the identified principles are explained. Difficult or contradictory moments fall from view as less important and problematic historical narratives or events become heretical readings.

The practice of interpreting the nation's founding as having identifiable principles that are consistent across the era has enormous consequences for conservative Christian readings of the period. It changes the texture of who is an appropriate spokesperson and which moments and events are consequential. Rather than applying (or desiring) an academic historical lens, in which historical events and figures are measured by their importance to subsequent events, this strategy of reading history as a body of scripture challenges the historian to find those moments that *best* represent the "meaning" of the period. Perhaps most importantly, an era that has been canonized may be treated as a text to be edited and rearranged without concern for sequence or consequence. The readings of the nation's founding produced through this method follow a distinctive pattern, but as important as identifying the pattern is considering the process of creating and revisiting this past as a ritualistic religious reading practice. By employing the same strategies to interpret history as are used to read scripture, the study of history becomes a religious act.

The Principles of the American Revolution

Conservative Christian readings of the American founding begin and end with principles, not just in interpretation but usually also in structure. In this they participate in a wider national discussion about what "American values" are and what "our Founding Fathers believed"—both well-worn phrases that no one is surprised to hear from any politician or pundit. Conservative Christian approaches are notable, however, in their essential project of distilling from the founding era specific, often quantified principles that authors then depict as representing the entirety of the era from 1750 to 1800, and often even the period from 1620 to 1800. Nearly two centuries of colonial history are swept into the meaning of "founding."

For some writers, the principles are a matter of the culture wars; for others, they are purely educational. But in both cases the key idea is the restoration of an essential and true character and meaning of the founding era. Michael Novak's *On Two Wings: Humble Faith and Common Sense at the American Founding* introduces his two principles (and his book's titular metaphor) by saying "one wing of the eagle by which American democracy took flight has been quietly forgotten." Novak here refers to what he calls "humble faith," the principle that, along with "plain reason," led to the greatness of "American democracy." He makes his case in a very brief introduction at the start of his second chapter. *"On two wings the American eagle rose into the sky. On plain reason and humble faith.* Plain reason is not so hard to understand. But how did the Founders think of faith? And what, in their minds, did faith add to reason?"[18] His italicized sentences, which appear to be his own words and are not cited, are reminiscent of biblical texts, including Isaiah 40:31 ("They shall mount up with wings as eagles"). Novak, a Catholic, later discusses a passage written by Pope John Paul II that says, "Faith and reason are like two wings on which the human spirit rises to the contemplation of truth."[19] Even more important than the indirect reference is Novak's choice of writing style.

He adopts a bible-esque tone, implying, through its simple assertion, that this interpretation is a True Fact, indeed, a statement of principle. Finally, his interrogative framing, by which the question sets up the range of possible answers, guides the reader in the investigation of principle, the purpose of studying this history.

As might be expected, pedagogical texts forefront principles in equally stark ways. *America's Providential History*, by Mark A. Beliles and Stephen K. McDowell, has a list of "Seven Principles of Liberty" in the conclusion.[20] A similar structure appears in *The American Patriot's Bible*, published by Thomas Nelson Press in 2009. It begins with "The Seven Principles of the Judeo-Christian Ethic," which readers are told were the core beliefs of "our nation's Founding Fathers." When those men "gave us documents such as the Declaration of Independence, the Constitution, the Bill of Rights, and others, they had to lean upon a common understanding of law, government, social order, and morality." It is not necessary that these principles be uniformly representative of revolutionary public opinion or even of the Founders, as the authors are quick to point out. The important element is that they are guiding principles, in both the past and present. "Whether each of the Founding Fathers was a Christian is not the issue. Their writings, their statements, and their votes evidence that the majority of them embraced these great principles as the basis for a civilized nation."[21] The seven itemized principles are not the same ones Novak—or other authors—outlines, but the diversity of founding principles ultimately reinforces the idea that it is the repeated and slightly varying practice of searching for principles that matters, not the particular outcome.[22]

Guided by a focus on principle, conservative Christian historians are generally more comfortable writing in a thematic vein, rather than using a chronological approach. Themes match well with teaching principles in history, and they help handle apparently contradictory evidence. Thus Peter Lillback's massive biography of Washington discusses the "early life of George Washington" but then moves through Washington as he appeared in a number of roles, such as "Low Churchman," "Vestryman," and "Soldier." The primary goal here is undoubtedly to focus on Washington's individual character, but the consequence is to take the man out of time. Washington's and, by extension, other Founders', youthful experiences in religious establishments, and then eventual governance of a nation that disavowed religious establishment, is never directly touched upon. The practice of taking evidence from varied historical contexts and applying it to a single principle is normalized. Michael Novak uses a similar strategy when he frames "Ten Questions about the Founding," and David Barton's *Wallbuilders* website also avoids narrative in favor of narrow topical investigations that leapfrog between time periods.[23] Though they vary in specifics, these works collectively interpret a cohesive early American era to mean that "Founding Fathers" were devout Christians and that the era had as its central meaning the promotion of liberty and conservative Protestant Christianity. That meaning is seen as both universal and readily transferable to the present.

Reading the Founding Era through Principle

How does the nation's founding look when viewed through the filter of the conservative Christian search for principle? Writers emphasize the importance of Protestant devotion and institutions, God's covenant with the American people, the powerful flowering of an undefined liberty, and the faithfulness of the Founding Fathers. The story begins with the Pilgrims and the Puritans, and then, as it moves to the Americans' conflict with Great Britain, focuses on two points: the importance of public prayer and the piety of particular leaders. The crisis endured by Washington's forces at Valley Forge is the pivotal event in this narrative. From that terrible winter in 1777–1778, writers turn quickly to the Revolution's fulfillment in the Constitution ten years later, or to topically organized analyses of their chosen principles.

The prominence of the Puritans to the American founding emerges from many sources. The *American Patriot's Bible*, in its section entitled "Christianity in Colonial America," uses nearly all of its text to describe the Pilgrims' arrival in 1620, the Puritans' arrival in 1630 (with a mention of John Winthrop's invocation of the "city on a hill," a biblical reference that for many is synonymous with Ronald Reagan), and then tells of the 1638 founding of New Haven colony. "When these colonial settlers arrived in America, the influence of the Bible on their lives came with them," the text asserts.[24] Passing reference to other places and peoples in North America imply that they pale in comparison to the importance of the "real" Founders in New England. The *Patriot's Bible*, of course, does not purport to chronicle all of American history. More instructive is *America's Providential History*, a textbook aimed at homeschooled children. It summarizes the confusion of colonial origins succinctly. "We can see a consistent Christian dominance in the settlement of every single colony," the authors write. The Puritans then provide their best evidence. "A joint statement made by all the Northern Colonies in the *New England Confederation* of 1643 would just as well have been made by all 13 colonies. It stated: 'We all came into these parts of America with one and the same end and aim, namely, to advance the kingdom of our Lord Jesus Christ, and to enjoy the liberties of the Gospel in purity with peace.'" This purpose of government, in which "civil government is a reflection or a proiduct of church government," is the meaning of the colonial era.[25]

Peter Marshall and David Manuel's enormously influential 1977 work, *The Light and the Glory*, uses roughly half of its pages to describe the Pilgrims and the Puritans. The story regularly shifts in time between the authors' search for meaning and a richly elaborated narrative, including details such as the color of the wake behind the Mayflower, the facial expressions of historical figures, and even fictionalized dialogue. The reader is invited to lose herself in the drama of the past, and yet reminded that the purpose of the reading is to discern the meaning of momentous events. This continual telescoping between past and present, between knowable and unknowable details creates readable prose, but it also obscures the temporal elision between the early seventeenth century and the late eighteenth. Describing the Mayflower Compact, Marshall and Manuel write that the Pilgrims drafted a document that was "pragmatic, realistic, and expedient." Yet it also "embodied the same principles of equality and government by the consent of the governed which would become the cornerstones of American Democracy."[26] The authors then immediately amend their analysis with a paranthetical that reaches much farther back in time. They note that the origin of the Compact's principles can be found with the ancient Hebrews, before skating forward in time to cite the Declaration of Independence's opening lines. In the space of one page, the authors demonstrate the centrality of the Pilgrim's document to a history that stretches from biblical times to the Revolution, and through the enduring importance of Jefferson's words, to our own time. Interestingly, the Compact itself—and the question of what specifically is meant by "principles of equality" amid language that stresses obedience and the sovereignty of the King—is not parsed. The exegetical point has already been made.

The Great Awakening serves as an essential transition between Puritan society and the Revolution in many Christian retellings, and for Marshall and Manuel it also explains the Revolution's great success. "Through the almost universal, almost simultaneous experience of the

Great Awakening, we began to become aware of ourselves as a *nation*, a body of believers which had a national identity as a people chosen by God for a specific purpose: to be not just 'a city on a hill,' but a veritable citadel of Light in a darkened world." At the end of the chapter, George Whitefield dramatically gasps his last and expires, but his mission has been fulfilled: "His dream had come true: America was a nation now—one nation under God." On the next page, the account of the Revolution begins with the line: "When does tyranny become tyranny?"[27]

It is easy, of course, to pick apart such heavily fictionalized retellings, but the ways that Marshall and Manuel's moment casts its history are instructive. Whitefield, the quintessential transatlantic religious figure, never left the Church of England. Moreover, he died in 1770, far too early in the Revolutionary crisis to assume inevitable independence, and the key movers in New England's patriot movement were quite removed from the growing evangelical camp. But these details are not significant to a reading that self-evidently connects evangelicalism and revolutionary fulfillment. "America was a nation now—one nation under God," Manuel and Marshall stress. "America" here functions more as an idea than a geographic or political term. The meaning conveyed is not "thirteen colonies of British North America that rebelled against Parliamentary authority and founded their own nation through violence" but rather the realization of an ideal, summed up in the phrase "one nation under God." The whole moment implies that the words of the 1954 pledge of allegiance *could have been* uttered (there is no suggesting from Marshall and Manuel that they were) by George Whitefield. The narrative extracts from the era as a whole a key meaning: the United States is a blessed nation under the careful watch of an evangelical God.[28]

In the conservative Christian narrative, the war years have two primary characteristics: first, a culture that valued public prayer and its clergy and second, leaders who valiantly and successfully struggled as men to live up to the great responsibilities God had given them. Michael Novak, in his *On Two Wings*, lists "Seven Events that Revealed the Power of the Second Wing." Each is a demonstration of public observations of Christianity meant, in Novak's argument, to show that faith was a primary motivator of the Revolution. For this analysis to work, one must remember that what is being motivated is not specific historical action, such as anger over the passage of the Boston Port Act, but rather the American founding in its greatest terms. Novak's first event is the Continental Congress's request to Anglican minister Jacob Duché to lead prayers in 1774. The second, fourth, and seventh events likewise suggest the importance of ministers and public prayer through the declaration of Fast Days. The third event, Novak argues, was "the prayer written as a sub-text of the Declaration itself," as "the very form of the Declaration was that of a traditional American prayer, a compact not unlike the Mayflower Compact." These, "only the latest in a long series of local and regional covenants," should be seen (and here Novak quotes political scientist Donald Lutz) as "a public elaboration, almost a celebration, of a people's fundamental values." Values, like principles, become actors in history. Novak here telescopes back to the Mayflower Compact in the same way that Marshall and Manuel telescoped forward. In light of the fundamental principles they discuss, this creates a cohesive narrative.[29]

Clergy play a major role in other retellings as well, representing the point that revolutionary Americans followed a biblical worldview. The *American Patriot's Bible* argues that when the Declaration referred to "laws of nature and of nature's God," colonists expressed the "principle upon which the Founders stood." More explicitly, *"laws of nature* were understood to mean the will of God for man as revealed to man's reason. However, because man is fallen and his reason does not always comprehend this law, God gave His law in the Bible to make it absolutely clear." The authors then draw a direct line to the clergy. "Thus, it was the Churches that became the primary source that stirred the fires of liberty, telling the colonists that the English government was usurping their God-given rights." On the next page, the *Patriot's Bible* recounts an apocryphal story about Peter Muhlenberg, a minister in Virginia, throwing off his clerical robes mid-sermon to join Washington's troops.[30]

The principles taught in these works about events that took place between 1775 and 1781, the period of active fighting, emphasize leadership and personal character. George Washington, the ultimate Founder, offers perfect material. Because Washington was intentionally silent on most subjects of religion, authors are forced to read his faith through his actions, and they comfortably impute to Washington what they hope to see. The *American Patriot's Bible* has a brief section discussing Washington's character, but rather than offer examples of his words, the authors focus on the dilemma of how a man of such greatness can even be known, including glowing retellings from after his death.[31] *The Light and the Glory* introduces Washington in similar terms. "Because of [his] humility and [his] popularity, and because of a truly supernatural gift of wisdom, he evoked jealousy from his colleagues in Congress and in the military. But the affection of the people never wavered."[32] Charles Hatchett's portrayal of Washington as a man who doubted fits in this context. The test is not a problem. Rather, the reader learns that the Founder overcame through faith and asked his sturdy soldiers to do the same.[33]

Having constructed a devout and sober leader in Washington, Valley Forge—interpreted as his greatest test—becomes the climax and the conclusion of the Revolutionary era. It brings together the character lessons embedded in the teaching about Washington, the importance of prayer, and the key role of faith in difficult times.[34] After the wretched descriptions of the soldiers' miseries, readers might wonder how the army persevered. "Most historians agree that the reason ... can be attributed to their love of liberty and to their General George Washington, and his amazing quality of leadership," write the authors of *America's Providential History*.[35] Marshall and Manuel recount a story, familiar to many Americans, of Washington bowing his head in prayer in Valley Forge. Though the great man sought privacy, he was seen by a neighboring Quaker, who spread the word.[36] The portrait painted (literally, in patriotic works of art) of the general kneeling in the snow at Valley Forge is of a man who, in a time of crisis, turned to his faith and his Bible to act decisively. After this emotional peak, conservative Christian narratives turn to the Constitution, usually returning to a thematic rather than narrative approach. Marshall and Manuel move from Valley Forge to the end of the war in less than ten pages. *America's Providential History* briefly covers the battles of Trenton and Yorktown, then the rest of the book proceeds thematically. In many ways, with Valley Forge, the Revolution is complete.

Conclusion

When conservative Christians apply scriptural interpretive strategies to the American founding, they create religious readings of the past. These readings enter the political discourse stripped of their essential intellectual underpinnings. Pundit Stanley Kurtz recently wrote in the *National Review* about the Advanced Placement US History standards, for example, using the key elements of a Christian reading of the Revolution:

> What is the core of the American story? What is American history about? For a long time ... the heart of the American story was said to be the Founding, with its principles of liberty and equality.[37]

Kurtz would probably have little patience for Charles Hatchett, but Kurtz's reading owes a great debt to the religious practices of conservative Christians and their historians who have canonized the founding era and described it as a period replete with moral meaning. The principles that can be derived, studied, and prayerfully implemented provide the purpose for studying the era. The ritual and repetitive circularity of this process is no more problematic than when it is applied to devotional reading of Christian scripture. This is history as religious practice.

Two implications can be drawn from this investigation. First, understanding a significant religious practice is valuable in its own right, for it helps to explain the place of the United States in the soul of conservative Christianity and the means by which members of that community continually reaffirm the importance of their political ties. Moreover, it helps explain the impasse that occurs when both liberals and academic historians (not completely overlapping groups) argue with Christian conservatives. From the academic perspective, the apparent flaws in historical reasoning in the works of someone like David Barton damn them beyond use. For conservatives, factual errors are less meaningful than principles, and they see no reason to question the underlying principles of the era, regardless of Jefferson's personal faith or the fact that Washington owned slaves. Unless both sides understand the hermeneutical approach Christians are using, each will simply continue to tread the same ground.

Potentially defusing the tiresome culture wars is a lofty enough goal in itself, but a second, more fundamental implication of this work is the identification of a significant way in which religious practice inhabits the public realm. Political speech drawing on the conservative Christian reading of the nation's founding is a mainstay of national rhetoric, from Ronald Reagan's 1983 "Evil Empire" speech to, with very different inflections, Barack Obama's second inaugural address in 2012. Identifying the ways that religion exists, and often masks itself, in moments like those reveals powerful undercurrents in the political life of the United States. In this case, when political figures participate in a minority religious practice, they elevate that practice to a position of power, and the disproportionate political influence of conservative Christian modes of reading the nation's founding stands in stark contrast to the trend of increasing religious acceptance that Kevin Schultz has so convincingly presented in this volume. The conservative Christian hermeneutical approach to the nation's history thus suggests that religion continues to be present in unexpected ways in American politics.

Notes

1. I would particularly like to thank my SMU colleague Mark Chancey for his help and expertise in shaping this project. Hatchett's Fancy Farm speech is available in video at http://www.ket.org/fancyfarm/.

2. For the circulation of this story elsewhere, see, for example, http://www. news-press.com/story/news/local/lehigh/2014/09/24/first-president-gave-glory-god/16131355/.

3. Robert Bellah, "Civil Religion in America," *Daedelus* 96 (1967): 1–21.

4. Scholars who have examined Christian uses of American history include Randall J. Stephens and Karl W. Giberson, *The Annointed: Evangelical Truth in a Secular Age* (Cambridge, MA: Belknap Press, 2011), and Braden Anderson, *Chosen Nation: Scripture, Theopolitics, and the Project of National Identity* (Eugene, OR: Cascade Books, 2011).

5. Francis A. Schaeffer, *A Christian Manifesto* (Wheaton, IL: Crossway, 2005 [1981]), 17, 31–32.

6. Barton's activities can be assessed at his website, wallbuilders.com. For more on Barton, see Stephens and Giberson, *The Annointed*, 83–96, and a *New York Times* profile from 2011 at http://www.nytimes.com/2011/05/05/us/politics/05barton. html?ref=us&_r=0.

7. See, for example, Michelle Goldberg, *Kingdom Coming: The Rise of Christian Nationalism* (New York: Norton, 2006), and Steven P. Miller, *The Age of Evangelicalism: America's Born-Again Years* (New York: Oxford University Press, 2014). The controversy over David Barton's book, *Jefferson Lies* (Nashville: Thomas Nelson Press, 2012), brought the disagreement among Christians over readings of the American past to the public eye. For scholarly discussions of the controversy, see, for example, Jared Burkholder at http:// pietistschoolman.com/2014/04/25/should-christian-scholars-be-watchdogs-an-interview-with-david-barton-critic-warren-throckmorton/ and Paul Harvey at http://religiondispatches.org/david-barton-falling-from-grace/.

8. Early Americanists have produced an extensive literature on the creation of American national identity. See, for example, David Waldstreicher, *In the Midst of Perpetual Fetes: The Making of American Nationalism, 1776–1820* (Chapel Hill: University of North Carolina Press, 1997), and Sarah Purcell, *Sealed with Blood: War, Sacrifice and Memory in Revolutionary America* (Philadelphia: University of Pennsylvania Press, 2002).

9. Rachel Bradshaw, "How the Signers Became 'Founding Fathers,'" *Constitution Daily* (blog), June 19, 2011, http://blog.constitutioncenter.org/2011/06/how-the-signers-became-founding-fathers/.

10. For an exploration of this moment in terms of cultural, but not religious, politics, see David Waldstreicher, "Founders Chic as Culture War," *Radical History Review* 84, no. 2 (2002): 185–194.

11. McCullough's treatment of Adams asserts that the man was "both a devout Christian and an independent thinker," but his narrative skips some key moments in the Christian retelling of the era. David McCullough, *John Adams* (New York: Simon and Schuster, 2002).

12. Robert Tracy McKenzie, "From My Commonplace Book: Chesterton on Patriotism and History," *Faith and History* (blog), June 11, 2014, http://faithandamericanhistory.wordpress.com/2014/06/11/from-my-commonplace-book-chesterton-on-patriotism-and-history/.

13. In addition to McKenzie's work, Mark Noll and Thomas Kidd, among others, have been vocal advocates of scholarly readings of the nation's past. See, for example, Mark Noll et al., *The Search for a Christian America* (Colorado Springs: Helmers and Howard, 1989), and John Fea's *Was America Founded as a Christian Nation?* (Louisville, KY: Westminster John Knox Press, 2011).

14. John Fea, *Was America Founded as a Christian Nation?*, 72–73.

15. Critics speaking from a secular or progressive perspective have pointed out the tendency for conservative Christians to "proof-text" history. See http://www.rightwingwatch.org/content/proof-texting-insight-how-david-barton-constructs-his-pseudo-history.

16. http://rickwarren.org/devotional/english/six-principles-for-interpreting-scripture

17. See, for example, http://hermeneutics.stackexchange.com/questions/79/what-does-it-mean-that-scripture-interprets-scripture and http://theresurgence.com/2013/08/08/7-key-principles-for-interpreting-the-bible. See also James I. Packer, *Fundamentalism and the Word of God* (Grand Rapids, MI: Eerdmans, 1958), 101–114, and Gerald Bray, *Biblical Interpretation: Past and Present* (Danvers Grove, IL: InterVarsity Press, 1996), 480–482. Bray situates this form of biblical interpretation within the context of conservative reactions to cultural criticism.

18. Michael Novak, *On Two Wings: Humble Faith and Common Sense at the American Founding* (New York: Encounter Press, 2002), 1, 27.

19. Novak, *On Two Wings*, 91. I am grateful to Mark Chancey for his help with this passage.

20. Mark A. Beliles and Stephen K. McDowell, *America's Providential History* (Charlottesville, VA: Providence Foundation, 1989). *America's Providential History* takes its cues from the system promoted by the Foundation for American Christian Education, which itself forefronts the importance of the "Principle Approach." Rosalie Slater's work and FACE are discussed in Darren Dochuk, *From Bible Belt to Sunbelt: Plain-Folk Religion, Grassroots Politics and Evangelical Conservatism* (New York: W. W. Norton, 2010), 207–208.

21. *American Patriot's Bible* (Nashville: Thomas Nelson, Inc., 2009), front matter.

22. The *American Patriot's Bible* lists as its seven principles: the dignity of human life, the traditional monogamous family, a national work ethic, the right to a God-centered education, the Abrahamic covenant, common decency, and personal accountability to God.

23. Peter Lillback with Jerry Newcombe, *George Washington's Sacred Fire* (Bryn Mawr, PA: Providence Forum Press, 2006); http://www.wallbuilders.com/libissuesarticles.asp?id=24548 and http://www.wallbuilders.com/LIBissuesArticles.asp?id=100766.

24. *American Patriot's Bible*, I-5–I-8.

25. *America's Providential History*, quote 91. The various quotations highlighted by these works often recirculate around web sources in reconfigured form, attesting to the broad influence of these texts. See also http://www.timetracts.com/was%20america%20a%20christian%20nation.htm.

26. Peter Marshall and David Manuel, *The Light and the Glory* (Old Tappan, NJ: Fleming H. Revell, 1977), 120.

27. Marshall and Manuel, *The Light and the Glory*, 251. This last line is frequently quoted and plagiarized around the Internet. See also http://www.creators.com/lifestylefeatures/inspiration/kids-talk-about-god/why-did-the-early-colonists-come-to-america.html, http://www.redletterchristians.org/problem-national-day-prayer/, and http://www.washingtonubf.org/Resources/Leaders/GeorgeWhitefield.html.

28. For some, Whitefield's role in the Revolution is such that he should be seen as a Founding Father. See Stephen Mansfield, *Forgotten Founding Father* and http://biblicalawakening.blogspot.com/2011/08/george-whitefield-and-his-impact-on.html.

29. Novak, 13–24.

30. *American Patriot's Bible*, I-14–I-15. This story is also reprinted in *America's Providential History*, 144–145, Peter A. Lillback's *George Washington's Sacred Fire*, 1063, n. 19. See also http://www.reclaimamericaforchrist.org/lettertopatriotpastors.htm, http://www.youtube.com/watch?v=MP03SjqOhMI (for Barton).

31. *American Patriot's Bible*, 64.

32. Marshall and Manuel, *The Light and the Glory*, 283.

33. See also Lillback, *George Washington's Sacred Fire*, 377–402.

34. See also, Newt Gingrich et al., *Valley Forge: George Washington and the Crucible of Victory* (New York: St. Martin's Press, 2010). The possibility that Washington prayed, or did not pray, at Valley Forge is one that has received a fair amount of discussion. Many conservative Christians are comfortable saying merely that Washington "probably" prayed.

35. Beliles and McDowell, *America's Providential History*, 154–155.

36. Marshall and Manuel, *The Light and the Glory*, 222–223.

37. Stanley Kurtz, "Why the College Board Demoted the Founders," *The Corner* (blog), September 9, 2014, http://www.nationalreview.com/corner/387464/why-college-board-demoted-founders-stanley-kurtz.

2

Slavery and Religion in (Not Just) a Christian Nation

Edward J. Blum

INSTEAD OF HOLDING her torch in one hand and tablet in the other, this Statue of Liberty replica used both hands to cover her face and eyes. Depicted on roadside billboards in 2010 by a group of "deeply concerned" Minnesotans, this new Lady Liberty shielded her eyes from the towering yellow words beside her that highway drivers could not possibly avoid: "We are no longer a Christian nation." Underneath in white lettering was the name of the man who had spoken them, the nation's current president, Barack Obama.[1]

He had uttered this line four years earlier. As the keynote speaker at a 2006 conference hosted by left-leaning evangelical Protestants, then Senator Obama had stated, "Whatever we once were, we are no longer a Christian nation, at least not just."[2] Transcripts published later in the *New York Times* and other media outlets slightly rearranged his words. "Just" now preceded the phrase "Christian nation" so that the sentence read: "Whatever we once were, we are no longer just a Christian nation."[3]

One word was pivotal. The placement, migration, or deletion of the word "just" influenced how Americans viewed Obama and presented their own opinions on religion and politics in the nation. During the 2008 campaign season, Fox News repeatedly aired this particular portion of the 2006 video as part of their anti-Obama reporting. Individuals from Texas and California mailed strikingly similar letters to local newspapers about watching "in horror" how Obama had stated "with pride" that "we are no longer a Christian nation." Blogs and websites buzzed with discussions of whether eliminating the word "just" altered his original meaning. In 2012, during Obama's drive for re-election, an affiliate of Focus on the Family included these words on pamphlets urging Iowa voters to rally against him. All of the fuss over just one word led the nonpartisan political watchdog group FactCheck.Org to investigate whether attacks involving it were part of an "organized effort" of misinformation.[4]

There are several reasons this particular sentence has had such a malleable and contentious afterlife. The first reason has to do with Obama himself. Originally voiced at a small convention by a first-term junior senator, these words became attached to one of the most polarizing political figures in American history. He symbolized "hope" for millions, while many others considered his administration an "Obama-nation."[5]

Second, Obama did not reference just any topic. When he spoke the words "Christian nation," he engaged an enduring and vexed theme in American history. For generations, it is one that has touched emotional, educational, political, and legal nerves. Discussions of the nation as Christian, challenges to that idea, and debates surrounding it have factored in everything from the American Revolution to the writing of the Constitution, from the Civil War to the Civil Rights Movement, and from twentieth-century Supreme Court decisions to twenty-first-century culture wars.[6]

Third, the new digital and technological era in which Obama's presidency has taken place has transformed how information is created, publicized, located, altered, displayed, and discussed. With relative ease, Obama's statement—as well as many others by or about him—has been resurrected and redesigned, cut and pasted, linked to and toggled from. One did not have to be at the 2006 convention to hear his speech. It was posted on YouTube. One did not have to travel to Minnesota in 2010 to see the Statue of Liberty blocking her eyes. One could view photographs of the billboards online, read responses to them, and comment publicly.

The digital revolution has affected not only contemporary politics but also knowledge about and uses of the past.[7] This is particularly important when considering the topic Obama addressed: Christian nationalism. Debates about it turn repeatedly to the writings of the nation's founding generation. Historians, educators, those invested in matters of religion and government, and even the FBI scrutinize, among other works, the writings and letters of Thomas Jefferson, the Declaration of

Independence, and the Constitution.[8] Digitization and sharing on the World Wide Web have made it possible for virtually anyone to locate these sources, search the documents for key words and phrases, and curate particular texts for their own purposes.

Two documents from the 1770s not only combine Christian nationalism, the founding generation, and the role of digitization, but also add slavery and race to the mix. In 1774 and again in 1777, a handful of Massachusetts African American men sent antislavery petitions to white local political leaders. These two petitions were part of a broader antislavery campaign emerging from black Bostonians who were joining together under the leadership of figures like Prince Hall and poet Phyllis Wheatley. Attempting to speak for enslaved women and men in Boston and throughout Massachusetts, the petitioners called upon the colonial governor and the new revolutionary legislature to free them, their families, and anyone else held in bondage. Their goal was the total abolition of slavery in Massachusetts. Their petitions, in combination with the revolutionary ethos of the War of Independence; the lawsuits of other African Americans within the state; and the antislavery labors of white lawyers, jurists, and legislators ultimately led Massachusetts in 1783 to become the first state in the new United States to end slavery.[9]

Notably, the authors of the 1774 and 1777 petitions framed their perspectives on religion, politics, law, and civil society within the concept of Christian nationalism. The petitions show not only that discussions of Christian nationalism should take race seriously but also that these African American writers engaged issues far beyond the problem of slavery in a Christian nation.

To unpack the meanings within these late eighteenth-century petitions and to understand how the ideas of the authors compared and contrasted with those of their contemporaries, this chapter combines the close textual analysis of traditional humanities scholarship with the "distant reading" approaches advocated by literary scholars like Frank Moretti. Such approaches use digital platforms and tools to locate, correlate, and connect words and phrases across vast terrains of space and time. Digital-age historians can do more than locate sources online; they can employ digitization for new insights. This chapter heeds the call of digital humanities scholarship that urges the search for new perspectives through—as one touchstone work puts it—the "conjunctions between the micro and the macro, general surface trends and deep hermeneutic inquiry, the global view from above and the local view on the ground."[10]

By scrutinizing the petitions' particular language, contextualizing their key concepts with digital platforms and tools that allow for massive data mining, and finally tracing the history of the petitions from material artifacts to website features, this chapter makes three overall claims. First, although the petitioners were legally enslaved and their main goal was emancipation, they nonetheless participated creatively in their era's broad re-envisioning of civil society. This included struggles over key concepts, such as religion, the country, and law, which have continued to influence American politics from their time to the Obama presidency. Second, as the petitioners invoked religious concepts to end enslavement, they linked beliefs, bodies, actions, and words in unique configurations that contrasted sharply with the perspectives of many of their contemporaries. Zooming in on the petitions' language and then zooming out to the massive corpus of eighteenth-century writings shows how the petitioners' perspectives worked within and simultaneously troubled other standpoints. Third, a brief history of the petitions from handwritten paper documents to transcribed pages in print publications and then to multiformatted digitized texts highlights the importance of information production and dissemination. It also returns us to Obama's 2006 speech. Analyzing his address with close and distant reading techniques reveals that the emphasis on just one sentence hid other critical elements. Beyond the statement about the United States no longer being a Christian nation, or at least not just one, Obama challenged the way many Americans combine religion, politics, and law. In this way, he had much in common with the Massachusetts petitioners of the 1770s. They and he were not just interested in whether or not the United States is a Christian nation. They and he were primarily interested in whether the nation, its laws, and the Christians within it are just.

Joining Bodies and Beliefs

In January 1777, just six months after American revolutionaries declared independence, a group of black Bostonians sent a revision of their earlier 1774 petition to the newly formed Massachusetts Bay state legislature. They complained that they were "detained in a State of Slavery in the Bowels of a free & Christian Country." They and others had been "Unjustly Dragged" to this "Land of Liberty" where they were "sold Like

Beast of Burthen." This all happened "among A People Profesing the mild Religion of Jesus." Their "Life of Slavery" was so bad that it was "far worse than Nonexistence."[11]

In both documents, the petitioners referenced living in a "Christian country." Although "country" and "nation" have been and are oftentimes used interchangeably to refer to political and civil societies, "Christian country" seemed more common in the eighteenth century than "Christian nation." The results of placing both phrases into the Google Books Ngram Viewer, a digital graphing program that indicates how often words or phrases are used relative to the more than eight million digitized English works, suggest broad shifts in language and meaning (see figure 2.1). Before 1860, writers used "Christian country" three times more often than "Christian nation." The two phrases then ran parallel from 1860 to 1980, but after that, "Christian nation" rose in prominence. By 2006, when Obama employed the phrase, "Christian nation" was used twice as often as "Christian country."[12]

The shift in nomenclature points not only to the rise of "nations" as foundational "imagined political communities" of affiliation that claim to transcend time, space, and geography, but also to a loosening of associations between Christianity and geography. According to the logic of nationalism, a person can be an "American" and a "Christian" regardless of location. For the petitioners who lamented that many had been dragged from their "country" to this "land," "Christian country" may have been as much about civil society as it was about distinctive notions of geographical space.[13]

Using the phrase before the American Revolution, the petitioners disclosed that this concept existed before the "United States of America" did

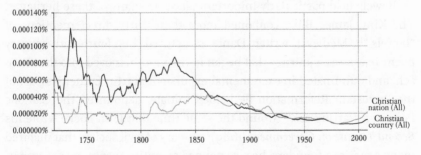

FIGURE 2.1 Courtesy of Google Books Ngram Viewer, http://books.google.com/ngrams

as a country or nation. In fact, the idea that Great Britain was a "Christian country" had its own political history. When the American Revolution began, "Great Britain" was just seventy years old. After England, Scotland, and Wales joined politically in the 1707 Act of Union, Protestant Christianity helped create a shared sense of nationhood that bound people in each region. When the Massachusetts petitioners used this phrase in 1774, there was nothing particularly "American" about it. It was a transatlantic, Anglo-American concept.[14]

While the petitioners acknowledged living generally in a "Christian Country," they located themselves particularly in its "Bowels." In this way, the writers presented civil society as a body, and their use of corporeal language fit squarely within Christian, medieval, and Enlightenment traditions of analogizing civil societies with bodily imagery.

Bodily analogies had biblical precedent. In 1 Corinthians, the Apostle Paul told believers, "By one spirit are we all baptized into one body, whether we be Jews or Gentiles, whether we be bond or free." This body of hands and feet, eyes and ears, "is not one member, but many." While bodies are made of many parts, the pieces are equally valued and valuable within the one body of the faith family.[15]

Discussions of civil society also turned to bodies during the medieval period and the Enlightenment. European kings were thought to have two bodies. Their physical bodies would decay, but the "body politic" that they symbolized was understood to be timeless, immutable, and composite.[16] The visual frontispiece for Thomas Hobbes's Leviathan (1651) figured the body of the sovereign, or at least his top half, as the aggregation of hundreds of individual bodies. These constitute the body politic as they are absorbed into it and put into motion by the sovereign. It was a case of bodies within a body.[17]

Bowels held particularly important places in many of these heritages. The King James Bible contained more than thirty direct mentions of "bowels."[18] Medieval writer Dante structured his fourteenth-century poem Inferno as a journey that began in the mouth, moved into the stomach, and culminated in excremental expulsion. Martin Luther, as part of the Protestant Reformation he helped initiate, denounced the Catholic Pope as a "farting ass." Around the same time that John Locke wrote his Second Treatise on Government (1689), a theory of civil society that inspired many American founders, he also penned an entire chapter on the importance of "going to stool regularly" for his work Some Thoughts Concerning Education (1690).[19]

The Apostle Paul's list of body parts did not include the bowels and *Leviathan*'s frontispiece featured the sovereign from the waist up, but Hobbes pressed the bowels rhetorically into his theory of civil society. When discussing "those things that weaken" a commonwealth, Hobbes lashed out at "the great number of Corporations," by which he meant towns, "which are as it were many lesser commonwealths in the bowels of a greater, like wormes in the entrayles of a natural man."[20]

While the reference to bowels emphasized body parts, the mention of being sold "like Beast of Burthen" accentuated what was done to and with bodies. Linguistic strategies, such as slave naming, and physical activities, such as whipping and selling, bordered on equating the enslaved with domesticated animals. In response, generations of African Americans damned their treatment as analogous to that of animals.[21]

Beasts of burden were noteworthy entities in British law and history. They were generally recognized as able to perform two functions: carry loads on their backs and haul weighty objects behind them. English poor laws created a hierarchy of poverty by differentiating those who traveled with one horse, mule, or "beast of burden," and those who traveled "with more."[22] Others roped in the phrase to discuss interactions among humans. When Scottish minister and historian William Robertson wrote a history of the Americas, he denounced Native American men for treating their wives as "no better than ... beast[s] of burden."[23]

Beasts run from start to finish in the King James Bible. The book of Genesis describes how "God formed every beast of the field." In the Book of Isaiah, too heavy a burden was placed on cattle when they were forced to carry idols. Later, in Daniel, there are four terrifying "Beasts." By the Book of Revelation, "the Beast" is a leading figure, a character discussed by some American colonial and revolutionary ministers. All told, the King James Bible mentions "beast" or "beasts" more than three hundred times.[24]

Discussions of beastliness and its relationship to slavery had a specific history in colonial Massachusetts. Earlier in the eighteenth century, church leader Cotton Mather had viewed the humanity of slaves as a contested point that needed to be defended. In a pamphlet titled *The Negro Christianized*, Mather maintained that humane regard for the enslaved was both right Christian theology and effective domestic policy. Christianizing slaves, he wrote bluntly, will make them "Better Servants." These masters will have "more work done for them, and better done, than those *Inhumane* Masters, who have used their Negroes worse than their Horses." To the question of whether "Negroes have Rational Souls," Mather exploded: "Let that Bruitish insinuation be never Whispered any more . . . They are Men, and not Beasts." Inhumanity and beastliness characterized slaveholders behaving and believing badly. Animality was not an innate element of those enslaved.[25]

By seeking to make legal and social change with language and frameworks from the Bible, medieval traditions, and relatively new Enlightenment concepts, the petitioners joined other Revolutionary-age writers that included Thomas Jefferson, Tom Paine, Benjamin Franklin, and John Adams. As many scholars have shown, the founders drew heavily, in ideological and textual regards, from these various backgrounds.[26]

Yet these Massachusetts writers combined what some other founders wished to separate. Thomas Jefferson, for instance, was a master of division. In the Declaration of Independence, he disassociated ideology from social and embodied realities when he wrote that "all men are created equal." Later in *Notes on Virginia*, he maintained that if Virginians decided to free their slaves, they should be physically separated from whites through a process of colonization. Years later, Jefferson used a razor to remove passages from the Gospels, and when Jefferson defined religion, he did so by divorcing it from elements of human connection. To him, religion was "a matter which lies solely between Man & his God."[27]

What Jefferson divided, these petitioners united. As part of their cry against slavery in a Christian country, they approached religion as a topic that joined humans to other humans, linked ideas to social realities, and combined bodies with beliefs. These approaches were perhaps nowhere better exemplified than in a distinctive rhetorical construction they crafted for the 1777 petition when they wondered how they could be treated these ways among "a people professing the mild Religion of Jesus."

Professing the "Mild Religion of Jesus"

This line was not just unique to the 1777 petition. It was singular for its age. A search for the exact phrase at the corpus of digitized works published between 1600 and 1850 at books.gogle.com produced zero results.[28] Unpacking the words and juxtaposing them against similar phrases uncovers several more examples of how they combined complex legal, political, and theological issues into a tight rhetorical package.

"Professing" a faith was a crucial concept in Anglo-American societies. When in the middle of the eighteenth century the British Parliament debated whether to offer citizenship rights to Jewish residents, the bill they discussed was titled, "An Act to Permit Persons Professing the Jewish Religion to be Naturalized by Parliament." British officials used the same language in reference to Roman Catholicism in Ireland. "Professing" suggested that legally for the British, one was part of a religious community not because of biology or heritage, but because one consented verbally or contractually.[29]

In the colonies, professions took place within broad oath-taking cultures where individuals voiced their identities and loyalties. These oaths could be to a sovereign, a church, or an organization like the Sons of Liberty, which required a verbalized secret oath for membership. In order to hold some political offices, individuals often had to pledge to abide by specific faith tenets or laws. To speak or profess publicly was part and parcel of being a member of a group.[30]

During and after the Revolution, several leading Americans challenged professions of religion in law and governance. In 1779, Thomas Jefferson wrote for a new statute of religious freedom in Virginia that "all men shall be free to profess . . . their opinions on matters of religion, and that the same shall in no wise . . . affect their civil capacities." In 1786, this line concluded Virginia's statute for religious freedom. One year later, the newly written federal Constitution called for elected presidents to take an "Oath" or "Affirmation" to protect the Constitution. Article 6, however—the only piece of the original Constitution to use the word "religious"—stated that "no religious Test shall ever be required as a Qualification to any Office or public Trust under the United States." The Constitution thus did not reject all oaths, only those directly identified as religious.[31]

The Massachusetts petitioners attached profession to the "religion of Jesus," a common phrase in the eighteenth century. Jacob Duché, a leading pastor in Philadelphia, titled one of his sermons "The Religion of Jesus, the Only Source of Happiness."[32] When George Washington addressed the Delaware Nation in 1779, he implored his listeners "to learn our arts and ways of life and above all—the religion of Jesus." Then one decade later, when a group of Presbyterians cheered that Americans had elected Washington to be their first president, they hoped that he and the new government would help "restore true virtue, and the religion of Jesus to their deserved throne in our land."[33]

The modifier "mild" distinguished the petition. Neither "mild religion of Jesus," nor the less specific "mild religion," produces hits when searched at Founders Online, a National Archives digital collection of 151,000 documents from and to George Washington, Benjamin Franklin, John Adams, Alexander Hamilton, James Madison, and Thomas Jefferson. A search for "mild religion of Jesus" at books.google.com for the years 1700 to 1830 yields fewer than thirty results.[34]

The general mildness of Jesus, however, could be heard with increasing frequency within the American colonies. Most noteworthy, colonists sang it from Charles Wesley's hymn "Gentle Jesus, Meek and Mild." Written ostensibly for children, it was first published in 1742 and repeatedly thereafter in hymnals. Charles and his brother John Wesley also referred to the spirit of God's love and the dove sent from God as "mild."[35]

The Wesley brothers did more than help establish a new and powerful Protestant group eventually named Methodism. They facilitated sweeping changes in colonial and early national culture. Their hymns swept across the American landscape. Methodism emphasized personal piety and encouraged a shift to more emotional and sentimental forms of Christianity. It also played a significant role in turning attention from the seemingly distant, authoritarian father God to the personalized human Jesus. Methodism's emphasis on action, feeling, and close intimacies with Jesus appealed to many African Americans.[36]

While the component parts and the phrase "professing the mild religion of Jesus" touched upon this large array of matters, they also reveal how the petitioners differed from their contemporaries. In terms of mildness, legions of Americans in and around 1777 found both Jesus and Christianity to be quite the opposite. The people were at war, and some church leaders had been fanning the flames for years. One Connecticut chaplain, for instance, composed a prayer in 1775 for patriot soldiers: "And may I prove myself a faithful follower of Jesus Christ, whom all the armies of heaven follow; fight the good fight of faith; and have my present conflicts against the world, the flesh and the devil crowned with victory and triumph!" When historian James Byrd charted uses of the Bible during the revolutionary period, he found that pastors invoked martial metaphors and violent biblical passages more than any other themes.[37]

The petitioners entered widespread discussions of the links among religion, politics, law, war, and society. They emphasized mildness as others called for war. In a society discussing the legal merits of religious oaths, they asked Americans to consider the relationships between what they said and what they did. While some founders prepared to distance religion and politics—or at least churches and governments—through the Constitution's First Amendment, the petitioners used biblical language and concepts for legal ends.

Until recent decades, however, their inventions and insights have gone largely unnoticed. For two centuries, their petitions suffered a fate close to what the petitioners viewed as better than enslavement: "nonexistence." Only through twentieth-century social movements and technological transformations of the digital age have the petitions become widely available so that they can give voice to African American perspectives on Christian nationalism during the founding generation. How and where these once-forgotten petitions entered public domains returns us to the twenty-first century and the digital age that facilitated and structured responses to Obama's speech in 2006.

Conclusion: From Paper Petitions to Digital Data

In the eighteenth century, these petitions were handwritten on pieces of paper and only people in and around Boston could read them. Today, the petitions can be viewed on computer monitors and tablet screens by anyone with access to the World Wide Web. The history of the petitions in terms of material culture, geography, and publication highlights both the role of the digital age for historical knowledge and the value of close and distant reading for providing new perspectives.[38]

In the late eighteenth century, the petitions circulated throughout Massachusetts and into other New England states. The writers, signers, and their allies placed consistent pressure on local political and judicial leaders, and in 1783, the state's court declared slavery unconstitutional. The petitioners, their families, their friends, and anyone else held in bondage in Massachusetts were now legally free. African Americans there went on to play pivotal roles in campaigns against slavery throughout the entire nation.[39]

The fate of the petitions was far less dramatic. State officials kept at least one copy and held it within their Boston archives from the early nineteenth century to the present. Historian William Cooper Nell located it there and reprinted a transcription of it in 1855 as part of his broader work on African Americans during the revolution.[40] Another copy made its way into the library of the Massachusetts Historical Society, founded in 1791 in Boston. In 1878, the society printed transcriptions of both petitions in a volume of documents related to slavery in Massachusetts. Almost ten years later, a group of African Americans in Boston did likewise.[41]

Seventy years later, Herbert Aptheker, a white scholar long committed to civil rights in the United States, included them in the first volume of his *A Documentary History of the Negro People in the United States*. First published in 1951, this volume was then reprinted every year from 1962 to 1969 as the modern Civil Rights Movement led many citizens and institutions to be interested in African American history.[42]

The petitions did not receive widespread scholarly notice until featured on digital historical projects. As librarians and historically engaged Americans of the 1990s began transcribing and scanning documents from the past, some digitized the petitions in various forms and housed them on their websites. These included the Massachusetts Historical Society, PBS's *Africans in America* website (which also included the four-part documentary from the late 1990s), and George Mason University's *History Matters*.[43] Digitization seemed to have direct outcomes in scholarship. Before 1995, scholars rarely mentioned the petitions in articles or books. Since then, they have been quoted with increasing frequency.[44]

Digital platforms and tools have made it possible for these petitions to move from a state of virtual nonexistence to multiple existences in the virtual realm. As they begin to enter contemporary discussions of Christian nationalism, they seem to trouble contemporary political agendas. The petitioners referenced the nation explicitly as "Christian," a point many conservatives cherish and liberals downplay. But the men of Boston invoked Christianity not to applaud the country but to criticize it. Their emphasis on racial justice, moreover, links them to contemporary liberals.

Handling the petitions in contemporary debates is tricky. For instance, when the conservative think tank the Heritage Foundation created a webpage for the 1777 petition, they included an introduction stating, "The Founders were united in their unequivocal denunciations of slavery." Later, the introduction emphasized the petitioners' use of biblical language, which connects them from "Frederick Douglass to Martin Luther King and Clarence Thomas." It would not take much thinking to challenge the claim about the founders or to wonder about the ties that bind Douglass, King, and the conservative Supreme Court justice Clarence Thomas.[45]

The same combination of close and distant reading with digital tools may offer insights about Obama's 2006 speech that were not vigorously debated in blog discussions or posted on Minnesota billboards. A quantitative analysis of the speech's almost 4,600 total words suggests that religion was the dominant theme, with Christianity right behind it. Obama spoke the word "religious" thirty-one times and "religion" fourteen times. He mentioned some variant of "Christ" or "Christian" more than twenty-five times and the "Bible" eight times. Alternatively, Obama used the word "Muslim" five times, some form of "Jew" four times, and "Hindu" once. At no point did he mention the Koran or any other foundational written work from a religious tradition.[46]

Visual representation of Obama's speech can also be telling. While those in Minnesota lifted one portion of a sentence and placed it alongside a digitally altered Statue of Liberty, the digital program Wordle™ provides another way of viewing his speech. Limiting his word usage to the thirty most used words, the Wordle™ graphic emphasizes religion, faith, and Christianity. This visualization gives the impression that Obama stressed Christianity as the nation's primary religion (see figure 2.2).

Text-based data mining and digital displays, however, alter the meaning of Obama's words as much as billboards. Reading Obama's comments about Christianity closely, we see that he parsed the concepts of "Christianity" and "the Bible" in order to address broader issues of education, law, and military affairs. His strategy took the form of rhetorical

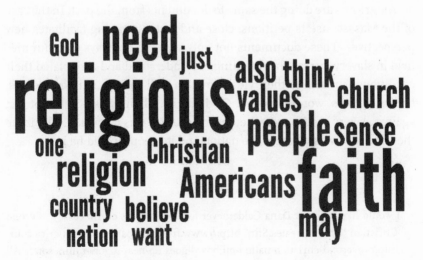

FIGURE 2.2 Courtesy of Wordle.net

questions that relied upon audience knowledge of and debates about both American history and the Bible.

"Whose Christianity would we teach in the schools?," he asked. "Would we go with James Dobson's, or Al Sharpton's?" This juxtaposition necessitates that one be or become familiar with the politically conservative evangelical James Dobson and the liberal civil rights activist Al Sharpton. Then, Obama considered the Bible and law, "Which passages of Scripture should guide our public policy? Should we go with Leviticus, which suggests slavery is ok and that eating shellfish is abomination?" In this case, Obama cherry-picked particular laws from a lengthy biblical text to contest the ways some Americans wished to incorporate biblical texts for contemporary law. Finally, Obama brought the Bible to bear on the nation's military choices, "Or should we just stick to the Sermon on the Mount—a passage that is so radical that it's doubtful that our own Defense Department would survive its application?" Even biblical passages that seemed universally admired could be problematic when pressed into service for twenty-first-century matters.[47]

Obama concluded this portion of his speech by emphasizing the need to read: "So before we get carried away, let's read our bibles. Folks haven't been reading their bibles." Whether Americans were reading the Bible or not, they were certainly paying attention to Obama. Supporters and opponents listened to him, read him, represented his words, and elected him to the nation's highest office. In the case of this speech, Americans took part of one sentence, reformatted it, transformed it, and debated it for years.

Americans are doing the same to documents from the past. In the case of the Massachusetts petitions, close and distant reading facilitates new perspectives. These documents not only speak to the ways communities held in slavery during the founding era understood and articulated their conditions, but also to their viewpoints on civil society, religion, beliefs, bodies, actions, words, law, and Christianity. Theirs was a fight not just against slavery or just over whether the country was Christian. The issue then and now was whether the nation and its people could be just.

Notes

1. I would like to thank Dana Caldemeyer for her insights on this essay. "Second 'Christian Nation' Creates Stir," http://www.freedomboardsacrossamerica.com/ 2010/09/second-christian-nation-billboard-goes-up-near-rogers-minnesota/. All footnoted websites accessed on November 29, 2014.

2. "Obama: We are no longer a Christian nation": https://www.youtube.com/watch?v=tmC3IevZiik.

3. "Obama's 2006 Speech on Faith and Politics," *New York Times*, June 28, 2006, http://www.nytimes.com/2006/06/28/us/politics/2006obamaspeech.html.

4. Peter Hamby, "Anti-Obama Mail Piece: 'We Are No Longer a Christian Nation,'" CNN.com, October 31, 2012, http://politicalticker.blogs.cnn.com/2012/10/31/anti-obama-mail-piece-we-are-no-longer-a-christian-nation/; "Obama and the 'Christian Nation' Quote," FactCheck.Org, August 26, 2008, http://www.fact-check.org/2008/08/obama-and-the-christian-nation-quote/.

5. Hal Elliott Wert, *Hope: A Collection of Obama Posters and Prints* (Minneapolis: Zenith Press, 2009); Jerome R. Corsi, *The Obama Nation: Leftist Politics and the Cult of Personality* (New York: Simon and Schuster, 2008).

6. John D. Wilsey, *One Nation Under God?: An Evangelical Critique of Christian America* (Eugene, OR: Pickwick Publications, 2011); Isaac Kramnick and R. Laurence Moore, *The Godless Constitution: A Moral Defense of the Secular State* (New York: W. W. Norton and Co., 2005 [1996]).

7. Toni Weller, ed., *History in the Digital Age* (New York: Routledge, 2013); Jack Dougherty and Kristen Nawrotzki, eds., *Writing History in the Digital Age* (Ann Arbor: University of Michigan Press, 2013).

8. Randall J. Stephens and Karl W. Giberson, *The Anointed: Evangelical Truth in a Secular Age* (Cambridge, MA: The Belknap Press of Harvard University Press, 2011), chapter 2.

9. Christopher Cameron, *To Plead Our Own Cause: African Americans in Massachusetts and the Making of the Antislavery Movement* (Kent, OH: Kent State University Press, 2014), chapter 3.

10. Franco Moretti, *Distant Reading* (London: Verso, 2013); Matthew L. Jockers, *Macroanalysis: Digital Methods and Literary History* (Urbana: University of Illinois Press, 2013); Anne Brudick, Johanna Drucker, Peter Lunenfeld, Todd Presner, and Jeffrey Schnapp, eds., *Digital_Humanities* (Cambridge, MA: MIT Press, 2012), 39.

11. *Collections of the Massachusetts Historical Society: Volume 3, Fifth Series* (Boston: The Society, 1878), 432–437. Cameron, *To Plead Our Own Cause*, chapter 3.

12. Search of "Christian nation" and "Christian country" at Google Books Ngram Viewer, https://books.google.com/ngrams/, case-insensitive checked, custom range between 1750 and 2008, smoothing of 3. Jean-Baptiste Michel, et al., "Quantitative Analysis of Culture Using Millions of Digitized Books," *Science* 331, no. 6012 (January 2011): 176–182; Chris Gratien and Daniel Pontillo, "Google Ngram: An Intro for Historians," *Hazine: A Guide to Researching the Middle East and Beyond*, January 11, 2014, http://hazine.info/google-ngram-for-historians/.

13. Benedict Anderson, *Imagined Communities: Reflections on the Origin and Spread of Nationalism*, rev. ed. (Verso: London, 1991); Maurizio Viroli, *For Love of*

Country: An Essay on Patriotism and Nationalism (New York: Oxford University Press, 1995).

14. Linda Colley, *Britons: Forging the Nation, 1707–1837* (New Haven, CT: Yale University Press, 1992), chapter 1; J. C. D. Clark, "Protestantism, Nationalism, and National Identity, 1660–1832," *The Historical Journal* 43, no. 1 (March 2000): 249–276.

15. 1 Corinthians 12:12–24, King James Bible.

16. Ted A. Smith, *Weird John Brown: Divine Violence and the Limits of Ethics* (Stanford: Stanford University Press, 2014); Ernst H. Kantorowicz, *The King's Two Bodies: A Study in Medieval Political Theology* (Princeton, NJ: Princeton University Press, 1997).

17. "Thomas Hobbes, Leviathan (London: Andrew Crooke, 1651)," Special Collections, St. John's College, University of Cambridge, http://www.joh.cam. ac.uk/library/special_collections/early_books/pix/leviathan.htm.

18. Aggregate search results for "bowel" and "bowels" at "1611 King James Bible," http://www.kingjamesbibleonline.org/1611-Bible/.

19. See Kyla Wazana Tompkins, *Racial Indigestion: Eating Bodies in the 19th Century* (New York and London: New York University Press, 2012), 116; Lawrence P. Buck, *The Roman Monster: An Icon of the Papal Antichrist in Reformation Polemics* (Kirksville, MO: Truman State University Press, 2014), 168; John Locke, *Some Thoughts Concerning Education* (London: Sherwood, Neely, and Jones, 1809 [1690]), 28–31.

20. Thomas Hobbes, *Leviathan, Parts I and II* (New York: Macmillan, 1985), 261.

21. David Brion Davis, *The Problem of Slavery in the Age of Emancipation* (New York: Alfred A. Knopf, 2014), chapter 1; Mia Bay, *The White Image in the Black Mind: African-American Ideas about White People, 1830–1925* (New York: Oxford University Press, 2000), chapter 4.

22. Richard Burn, *The History of the Poor Laws: With Observations* (London: H. Woodfall and W. Straham, 1764), 277.

23. *The Works of William Robertson, D.D.* (London: Frederick Westley and A. H. Davis, 1835), 822.

24. James P. Byrd, *Sacred Scripture, Sacred War: The Bible and the American Revolution* (New York: Oxford University Press, 2013), chapter 6; aggregate search results for "beast" and "beasts" at "1611 King James Bible," http://www. kingjamesbibleonline.org/1611-Bible/.

25. Cotton Mather, *The Negro Christianized* (Boston: B. Green, 1706), 13–15.

26. Henry F. May, *The Enlightenment in America* (New York: Oxford University Press, 1976); Frank Lambert, *The Founding Fathers and the Place of Religion in America* (Princeton, NJ: Princeton University Press, 2003).

27. Edwin S. Gaustad, *Sworn on the Altar of God: A Religious Biography of Thomas Jefferson* (Grand Rapids, MI: William B. Eerdmans Publishing Company, 1996);

Edward J. Blum and Paul Harvey, *The Color of Christ: The Son of God and the Saga of Race in America* (Chapel Hill: University of North Carolina Press, 2012), 72.

28. Search for "professing the mild religion of Jesus" custom date range Jan 1, 1600—Dec 31, 1850 at Books.Google.Com.

29. Paul R. Mendes-Flohr and Jehuda Reinharz, eds., "The Jew Bill," *The Jew in the Modern World: A Documentary History* (New York: Oxford University Press, 1995), 27–28; Edmund Keene, *Considerations on the Bill to Permit Persons Professing the Jewish Religion to be Naturalized by Parliament* (London: R. Baldwin, 1753); *The State of His Majesty's Subjects in Ireland Professing the Roman Catholic Religion* (Dublin: H. Hitzpatrick, 1800).

30. Charles Evans, "Oaths of Allegiance in Colonial New England," *American Antiquarian Society* (October 1921): 377–438; Jay Fliegelman, *Declaring Independence: Jefferson, Natural Language, and the Culture of Performance* (Stanford, CA: Stanford University Press, 1993).

31. Frank Lambert, *Separation of Church and State: Founding Principle of Religious Liberty* (Macon, GA: Mercer University Press, 2014); Kramnick and Moore, *The Godless Constitution*, 29.

32. Jacob Duché, *Discourses on Various Subjects* (London: J. Phillips, 1779), 41–58.

33. George Washington, "Address to the Delaware Nation, 12 May 1779"; "From George Washington to the Presbyterian Ministers of Massachusetts and New Hampshire, 2 November 1789," addendum. Both sources located through search for "religion of Jesus" at Founders Online: http://founders.archives.gov/. The search listed nine other examples.

34. Search for "mild religion of Jesus" custom date range January 1, 1700–December 31, 1830 at books.google.com.

35. John Wesley and Charles Wesley, *Hymns and Sacred Poems* (Bristol: Felix Farley, 1742), 12, 33, 194–195, 274.

36. John H. Wigger, *Taking Heaven by Storm: Methodism and the Rise of Popular Christianity in America* (New York: Oxford University Press, 1998); Richard S. Newman, *Freedom's Prophet: Bishop Richard Allen, the AME Church, and the Black Founding Fathers* (New York: New York University Press, 2008).

37. James P. Byrd, *Sacred Scripture, Sacred War: The Bible and the American Revolution* (New York: Oxford University Press, 2013), especially chapter 3; Thomas S. Kidd, *God of Liberty: A Religious History of the American Revolution* (New York: Basic Books, 2010), 119–120.

38. For the importance of materiality and publishing in religious history, see Sonia Hazard, "The Material Turn in the Study of Religion," *Religion and Society* 4, no. 1 (2013): 58–78.

39. Cameron, *To Plead Our Own Cause*, 64–65; Margot Minardi, *Making Slavery History: Abolitionism and the Politics of Memory in Massachusetts* (New York: Oxford University Press, 2010).

40. William C. Nell, *The Colored Patriots of the American Revolution* (Boston: R. F. Wallcut, 1855), 44–46.

41. *Collections of the Massachusetts Historical Society*: Volume 3: Fifth Series (Boston: The Society, 1878); *Proceedings of the One Hundredth Anniversary of the Granting of Warrant 429 to African Lodge, at Boston* (Boston: Franklin Press, 1885), 12.

42. Herbert Aptheker, *A Documentary History of the Negro People in the United States: Volume 1, From Colonial Times through the Civil War* (Secaucus: Citadel Press, 1951), 5–12. For other editions, see worldcat.org search for "Documentary History of the Negro People in the United States."

43. "Petition for freedom (manuscript copy) to the Massachusetts Council and the House of Representatives, [13] January 1777," Massachusetts Historical Society Collections Online, http://www.masshist.org/database/557; "Petition 1/13/1777," Africans in America, http://www.pbs.org/wgbh/aia/part2/2h32.html; "Natural and Inalienable Right to Freedom," History Matters, http://historymatters.gmu.edu/d/6237/.

44. Searches conducted at books.google.com, scholar.google.com, jstor.org, and muse.jhu.edu.

45. The Heritage Foundation, "Slave Petition for Freedom to the Massachusetts Legislature," http://www.heritage.org/initiatives/first-principles/primary-sources/slave-petition-for-freedom-to-the-massachusetts-legislature.

46. Data from "Obama's 2006 Speech on Faith and Politics," *New York Times*, June 28, 2006, http://www.nytimes.com/2006/06/28/us/politics/2006obamaspeech.html.

47. "Obama's 2006 Speech on Faith and Politics," *New York Times*, June 28, 2006, http://www.nytimes.com/2006/06/28/us/politics/2006obamaspeech.html.

3

Religion and the "Outsider" Candidates

Charles F. Irons

JOHN KERRY ENCOUNTERED stiff headwinds from some of his fellow Roman Catholics during the 2004 presidential campaign. Kerry supported a woman's right to an abortion and thereby ran afoul of official Catholic teaching. Less than five months before the election, the US Conference of Catholic Bishops issued a stern reminder that lawmakers bore a sacred "obligation in conscience to work toward correcting morally defective laws" such as legalized abortion, "lest they be guilty of cooperating in evil and in sinning against the common good." The conference stopped short of officially sanctioning Kerry or other pro-choice politicians and instead deferred to individual bishops the decision of whether or not to bar any politician from communion. Just one month before the election, three Southern bishops joined Archbishop Raymond Burke from St. Louis in taking this dramatic step. They proclaimed that pro-choice politicians would only be able receive the sacrament "after reconciliation with the church has occurred, with the knowledge and consent of the local bishop, and public disavowal of former support for procured abortion."[1]

In November 2007, interviewers from the Pew Forum on Religion and Public Life invited Kerry to reflect on his experiences in the campaign and on the role of faith in politics more generally. The defeated Democratic nominee wrestled with "the distinction between an appropriate discussion of [faith and values] versus a violation of the line we've drawn in our country of the, quote, 'separation between church and state.'"[2] In his analysis, Kerry drew a sharp line between private devotional practice and the "secular" work of governance, suggesting limits on the types of advocacy he considered acceptable from religious practitioners and on the types of statements he felt candidates should make. If, for example, a reporter had asked him about the greatest sin in his life, Kerry insisted, "My instant answer would have been, that's between God and me and you have no business asking such a stupid question." Significantly, Kerry professed the same reticence to offer confessional statements that might help in the polls, explaining that "those kinds of questions you ought to, by and large, just deny."

Kerry went on to articulate his conviction that the distinctive work of religion happened within the walls of the individual psyche, and that confessional differences melted away when people of faith chose to work for the common good. "And it doesn't have to be a religion, per se," he suggested, in a nod to the growing diversity of faith traditions within the United States. "It can be a philosophy, a way of life, Confucianism, Buddhism, Hinduism. There are many different ways in which people choose to have a guiding set of values within their life, and for many it is organized religion; for many it is not." Kerry posited it as an article of political faith that "no matter what philosophy or religion, organized or otherwise, people adopt, they almost all have a golden rule within them. And if you are legitimately practicing almost any of them and you are practicing them well, you will tend to be a pretty good citizen and a pretty good person."[3]

Scholars have long argued that Protestants, with their emphasis on conversion, first created the possibility of a "secular" public sphere by privatizing religious experience and that the separation of church and state to which Kerry appealed is one manifestation of this process. Recently, however, scholars have begun to question whether the secularism that developed from "European and Christian origins is, in fact, universal and fully separate from Christianity." This chapter accepts as its starting place the contention that what appears universal in the US context actually "constitutes a specifically Protestant form of secularism," referred to here as "Protestant secularism."[4] Within Protestant secularism, as several scholars have noted, politicians and others have tended to distinguish between "good" and "bad" religion by how effectively practitioners within the tradition honor the boundaries between internal transformation and external action. Adherents to "good" traditions may have dogmas of their own, in this model, but they translate them into reasonable argument or more universal "values" when engaging those outside of their tradition.

Adherents of "bad" religion, in contrast, do not register a change in key between domains. As Tracy Fessenden put it, " 'good' religion is good in the measure that it tends toward invisibility, or at least unobtrusiveness," protecting or preserving an ostensibly neutral space in which converted and unconverted, insiders and aliens may do the work of commerce and governance.[5]

I argue here that candidates from outside of the white Protestant main-stream, such as Kerry, have ironically been even more intentional and successful at reinforcing Protestant secularism than have their Protestant rivals. Instead of fundamentally challenging Protestant privilege, outsider candidates have ossified a potentially more fluid concept with memorable rhetoric, policy choices, and campaign precedents. The strength of this consensus has been especially clear in the 2004–2012 election cycles, which boasted an unusual number of candidates outside of Protestant tra-ditions. Besides the Catholic Kerry, Mitt Romney, a Mormon, ran as the 2012 Republican nominee. When Jeremiah Wright preached about God damning America, he underscored some of the differences between black and white Protestant traditions and compelled Barack Obama as well to assume the mantle of a minority religious candidate. The proportion of Americans who insisted that Obama was a Muslim—roughly 12 percent at the time of the 2008 election—only exacerbated the forty-fourth pres-ident's outsider status, a phenomenon Rebecca Goetz explores in more detail later in this volume.[6] Kerry, Romney, and Obama differ in their faith convictions, but as candidates they sounded remarkably similar notes about the relationship between private belief and public action. Together they helped further marginalize public expressions of doctrinally specific religious belief.

Protestants—especially evangelicals—have benefited both culturally and politically by defining secularism in their own terms. Most fundamen-tally, when Americans accept the idea that engagement with the divine is a private, interior act, they are adopting a Protestant taxonomy of religion and a Protestant understanding of conversion.[7] Moreover, they are accept-ing as a matter of faith that "true religion" will grow most quickly under the "voluntary principle," without any support from the state.[8] Finally, by cordoning off as "bad" those religions in which practitioners violate one or another of the central tenets of Protestant secularism (demanding state sponsorship of religious activity, arguing from revelation, etc.), Western Protestants have made the privatization of religious practice a key char-acteristic of "modernity" and a formidable trope with which to stigmatize

domestic or foreign religious outsiders as foes of progress.[9] Some conservative Christians now worry the separation between private faith and
public life may be too severe, but Protestant churchgoers have reaped a
great harvest over two centuries by embedding their understanding of the
nature of religious experience in the ground rules for political engagement. As Kerry, Romney, and Obama promoted Protestant secularism,
they to some extent worked against their own religious interests and reinforced the conditions white Protestants consider most desirable.

Thomas Jefferson set the pattern for candidates outside of white
Protestant traditions, though he shared more in common with his evangelical fellow citizens than most historians are prepared to acknowledge.
Jefferson is already the towering figure in nearly every account of church/
state relations in the United States, since he penned some of the most
important documents scholars and jurists use to understand the origins of the First Amendment, namely the Virginia Statute for Religious
Freedom and a famous 1802 letter to the Danbury Baptist Association
in Connecticut. It is not simply semantics to say that Jefferson was also
a principal architect of Protestant secularism. The riddle in Jefferson's
case is how someone who did not self-identify as a Protestant could nonetheless give words and legal form to the core conventions generations of
Protestants have embraced as their own.

The Sage of Monticello mocked specific Christian dogmas in his public
and private writings and was unremitting in his hostility to Presbyterian
and Roman Catholic "priestcraft," leading many scholars to characterize him as somehow more "secular" or "modern" than his peers. While
Jefferson was certainly no orthodox Christian, he was nonetheless an early
adherent to Scottish Common Sense Realism and therefore anticipated
the epistemological posture of early nineteenth-century evangelicals.[10] On
matters of morality, Jefferson accepted the idea of a moral sense, "as much
a part of man as his leg or arm," through which any individual could
discern fundamental ("self-evident") moral truths. Similarly, on matters
of religion (distinguished from morality by its truth claims about natural
philosophy), Jefferson depicted reason as a divinely appointed tool with
which any individual could evaluate theological propositions.[11]

Jefferson's confidence in his fellow citizens' ability to use reason to
unseat all false gods *and to enshrine true religion* had enormous implications for the relationship of the religious and the secular as constituted in
the United States. As evangelicals would do later in the nineteenth century, he advocated what we now conceive of as "secularism" not to destroy

Christianity but instead to protect the liberty of the individual to exercise his or her reason to discover "Nature's God." "Jefferson believed that by erecting a wall between church and state," as one recent scholar put it, "he could protect free inquiry and, by doing so, aid the process by which a purified Christianity housed in reason rather than faith would become America's civil religion." Jefferson went on to articulate another central tenet of the American version of secularism: the belief that truly free minds will discover only such religious sentiments as will render them more useful as citizens. Anticipating Kerry's belief that all good religions lead to the golden rule, Jefferson anticipated "the progress of those senti-ments which tend to restore to man all his natural rights [in this case, free exercise], convinced he has no natural right in opposition to his social duties."[12]

As a political candidate, sitting president, and retired statesman, Jefferson left plenty of evidence of his obsession with crafting a response to Christianity that both conformed to reason and inculcated good citizen-ship. His opponents in the 1800 election, including many New England Congregationalists, had seized upon Jefferson's published remarks in *Notes on the State of Virginia* to argue that the candidate was dangerously indifferent to the maintenance of Protestant Christianity as the de facto national religion. In fact, Jefferson had used rather strong language to make his point that "the legitimate powers of government extend to such acts only as are injurious to others," almost taunting supporters of state-level religious establishments that "it does me no injury for my neighbor to say there are twenty gods, or no god." After the election, Jefferson was person-ally smarting from the criticism he had received for his heterodox beliefs and also desperate to find common ground between bitterly antagonistic Federalist and Democratic-Republican factions. This was the context in which he not only wrote the Danbury letter but also set about in private to answer for himself how far reason could take him toward Christianity as then taught by Protestant divines. He worked up a "Syllabus ... of the merit of the doctrines of Jesus" which he mailed to Benjamin Rush in April 1803, confessing in his cover letter to be a "Christian, in the only sense [Jesus] wished any one to be; sincerely attached to his doctrines, in preference to all others; ascribing to himself every *human* excellence; & believing he never claimed any other."[13]

While there is more to say about Jefferson's battles with New England Congregationalists and his personal struggles to harmonize religious com-mitment and sound citizenship, the essential insight here is that Jefferson, the father of the separation of church and state in a US context, personally endorsed and lent his pen to support a version of secularism that was anything but neutral. Instead, he protected space for specifically Protestant kinds of "religious" activity—namely, engagement with texts, an inner transformation, and voluntary association in communities of the faithful. Moreover, Jefferson strove to make "reasonableness" a gauge of "good" or permissible religion, and struck out violently against any attempts, even private ones, to constrain another's conscience. In a September 1800 letter to Rush, Jefferson laid out this proposition most clearly, pledging to use all of his power if elected president to fight attempts to introduce a religious establishment. Referring to Congregationalist and Episcopalian fears that a President Jefferson would enforce the anti-establishment clause of the First Amendment, the Virginian warned, "They believe rightly; for I have sworn upon the altar of god, eternal hostility against every form of tyranny over the mind of man." Jefferson immediately qualified his animosity toward these Protestant denominations, assuring Rush "this [i.e., opposition to establishment] is all they have to fear from me," and making it clear that he would support Protestant practice so long as Protestant leaders did not try to use the state to enforce their will.[14] When subsequent candidates have found themselves in Jefferson's shoes—as members or representatives of minority religious traditions in an overwhelmingly Protestant country—they have followed his pattern of advocating for space at the table in a way that has further entrenched Protestant secularism.

Two centuries separate Jefferson's retirement from public office in 1809 and Barack Obama's inauguration. During this time, Protestants confirmed their hold on political power. Few outsider religious candidates earned a major party's nomination during that interval, though those who did reinforced Jefferson's positions. Joseph Smith made a brief run in 1844, for instance, and Al Smith became the first Roman Catholic nominee of a major party when he accepted the Democratic nomination in 1928. The most important interloper was John F. Kennedy, who tackled his Roman Catholicism head-on and breathed new life into Jefferson's precepts. Before the Greater Houston Ministerial Association on September 12, 1960, Kennedy systematically affirmed all the major characteristics of Protestant secularism. He denounced religious coercion repeatedly, proclaiming his belief in an America "where no Catholic prelate would tell the president (should he be Catholic) how to act, and no Protestant minister would tell his parishioners for whom to vote." He urged attention to issues and not dogma, reminding the Texans that "side by side with Bowie and Crockett died McCafferty and Bailey and Carey. But no one knows whether they were Catholic or not, for there was no religious test at the Alamo." He made his case expansive, including other minority traditions on his coattails. "For while this year it may be a Catholic against whom the finger of suspicion is pointed," he cautioned, "in other years it has been, and may someday be again, a Jew—or a Quaker or a Unitarian or a Baptist." Finally, he stressed that his religious views were "his own private affair" and underscored that he did "not speak for [his] church on public matters," and that the church did not speak for him.[15] In a narrow sense, this appeal to Jefferson and the founding principles of Protestant secularism (Kennedy referenced Jefferson's Statute for Religious Freedom twice) served Roman Catholics well and paved the way for Kennedy's election. In a larger sense, however, the victory also further normalized a distinctly Protestant accommodation between church and state.[16]

In more recent years, John Kerry, Mitt Romney, and Barack Obama have used strikingly parallel language to affirm the Protestant secularism embedded within American law and culture. They have used the bully pulpit (or at least their relatively privileged spots on the campaign trail) to define "good" religion in Jeffersonian terms as that which produces internal transformation, involves only voluntary association, is consistent with reason, and does not presume to enforce any distinctive moral code. Under fire or suspicion from Protestant voters, Kerry, Romney, and Obama have each delivered at least one landmark "religion speech" in which they have described religion as a private exchange which translates into politics primarily by expanding the believer's sense of the public good. Moreover, they have offered nearly identical definitions of "good" and "bad" religions which are slightly more capacious than Jefferson's but just as politically charged as those of prior generations, since they are now related so closely to questions about terrorism and public safety.

Kerry addressed his religious commitments most directly on October 24, 2004, at a time when he and George W. Bush were deadlocked in the polls at 49 percent each. Kerry chose to give his speech in Broward County, Florida, ground zero for Al Gore's defeat in the 2000 election and therefore a site of immense symbolic significance—and on Sunday, no less. The Democratic nominee announced his intention "to talk about the foundations of belief and commitment that brought me to public service, that have sustained me in the best and worst of times, and that I will carry with me every day as president." In the remarks that followed, he walked a delicate tightrope, quoting scripture repeatedly but underscoring at every turn that the distinctive experience was only internal, and that more profound impulses toward the common good were the only external markers of his Catholic faith. At the rhetorical center of the address he quoted from the Book of James, saying, "It is not enough, my brother, to say you have faith when there are no deeds . . . Faith without works is dead." Kerry used this verse, which encapsulates the classic Catholic contention that faith *and* works (rather than faith alone) are necessary for salvation, as the great pivot from a discussion of his religious heritage to a discourse on his political principles. "For me," he went on, "that means having and holding to a vision of a society of the common good, where individual rights and freedoms are connected to our responsibility to others. It means understanding that the authentic role of leadership is to advance the liberty of each of us and the good that can come to all of us, when we work together as one united community."

Kerry further explained that Roman Catholics were obliged to live "moral" lives but not to attempt to enact on others the specific policy positions advocated by their church leaders. Reminding his auditors of the communion controversy that had commanded so much ink over the summer, he said, "I know there are some Bishops who have suggested that as a public official I must cast votes or take public positions—on issues like a woman's right to choose and stem cell research—that carry out the tenets of the Catholic Church." Then, trying to adhere to the boundaries of "good" religion by refusing to constrain another's conscience, Kerry demurred. "I love my Church; I respect the Bishops; but I respectfully disagree." He continued, "My task, as I see it, is not to write every doctrine into law. That is not possible or right in a pluralistic society."[17] Kerry's precise motive in refusing to follow his tradition's teaching remains unclear. Certainly the decision was expedient, since 33 percent of registered Democrats in 2004–2005 believed abortion should be legal in all circumstances, and an additional 53 percent thought it should be allowed at least some of the time.[18] Whether Kerry sought political advantage from his posture is immaterial; regardless, he reinforced the Protestant secularism that has characterized American presidential politics since Jefferson.

Republicans, too, nominated a candidate from outside the traditional Protestant fold when they put Mitt Romney up for the highest office in 2012. Romney would revisit his faith several times during the campaign, but he had made his signature statement during the Republican primary more than four years earlier. Facing a primary field that included Mike Huckabee, a charismatic Baptist, and well aware of the cycle of anti-Mormon exposés Spencer Fluhman discusses in Chapter 12 of this book, Romney attempted to lay to rest concerns about his membership in the Church of Jesus Christ of Latter-day Saints (LDS) in December 2007. He did so not by defending Mormonism per se (indeed, he refused to address "his church's distinctive doctrines") but by reaffirming a model of Protestant secularism and firmly placing the Latter-day Saints in the category of "good" religions. Romney may have deployed different anecdotes and aligned more closely with conservative religious perspectives, but he otherwise echoed Kerry's Broward County speech.

Romney inverted Kerry's sequencing and led off by assuring the American people he would never allow religious authorities to dictate policy positions. No listener could have missed the homage to Kennedy's 1960 speech. "Let me assure you," he leveled, "that no authorities of my church, or of any other church for that matter, will ever exert influence on presidential decisions. Their authority is theirs, within the province of church affairs, and it ends where the affairs of the nation begin." Romney solemnly declared that he would guard against any legislation rooted too closely in the distinctive doctrines of any one tradition. "I will put no doctrine of any church above the plain duties of the office and the sovereign authority of the law," he promised.

Romney went on to insist that specific religious doctrines were irrelevant to political debates, that religious conviction was a private affair, and that many different religious practices could lead to a stronger commitment to the common good. In a complicated rhetorical move, Romney signaled solidarity with conservative Mormons, Jews, and Christians while nonetheless holding to the tenets of Protestant secularism. He joined the culture wars on behalf of conservatives, for instance, proclaiming that God "should remain on our currency, in our pledge, in the teaching of our history, and during the holiday season, nativity scenes and menorahs should be welcome in our public places." Romney then retreated to a much more familiar script, proclaiming that the primary purpose of faith was enlarging believers' sense of the common good, dramatically downplaying specific religious beliefs, and welcoming within the fold of "good religion" all those traditions willing to forbear from advancing sectarian positions through the ballot box. "I believe that every faith I have encountered draws its adherents closer to God," Romney declared, before cataloging what he saw as the most winsome features of Catholicism, evangelicalism, Lutheranism, Judaism, and Islam. "It is important to recognize that while differences in theology exist between the churches in America, we share a common creed of moral convictions," he assured listeners. "And where the affairs of our nation are concerned, it's usually a sound rule to focus on the latter—on the great moral principles that urge us all on a common course."[19] Romney largely succeeded with his "Faith in America" speech in defusing his religious background as a campaign issue, both for 2008 and 2012. Significant numbers of white evangelical Republicans (36 percent) confessed in 2008 that they would be less likely to vote for a Mormon, but most maintained that LDS affiliation would make no difference at the ballot box. In 2012, only a few Southern evangelical Republicans said they would rather stay home than vote for a Mormon in the general election.[20]

On the road against Obama in 2012, Romney had several occasions on which to reiterate his defense of Protestant secularism. At a town hall meeting in Wisconsin, Ron Paul supporter Bret Hatch tried to put Romney in the awkward position of either renouncing his faith or owning prejudice against black Americans:

ROMNEY: "Why don't you give me a question?"

HATCH: "Ok, well, in the Mormon book it says there were a blackness came upon all the children of Canaan that they were despised."

ROMNEY: "I'm sorry we're just not going to have a discussion about religion in my view, but if you have a question, I'll be happy to answer your question."

HATCH: "I guess my question is do you believe it's a sin for a white man to marry and procreate with a black?"

ROMNEY: "No." [Turning to face the other side of the room.]

Rather than exegete away any of Hatch's concerns, Romney pulled down the veil between private belief and public policy. He could not quite let the issue go, however, and returned to Hatch moments later. "This gentleman wanted to talk about the *doctrines* of my religion. I'll talk about the *practices* of my faith," Romney said (emphasis added). He then recounted his work as what he called a "lay minister." "And one of the reasons I'm running for president of the United States is I want to help people, I want to lighten that burden," he concluded, emphasizing the practical ethic of service over and above any particular teaching of his church.[21]

Barack Obama, despite his membership in Trinity United Church of Christ in Chicago, also found himself portrayed as an outsider to the Protestant mainstream, both because of his father's faith in Islam and because of his identification with a black Protestant strain within the United Church of Christ (UCC), which had an institutional and theological history distinct from white-controlled denominations. As a result, Obama has spent considerable energy discussing his own religious views and aligning with the patterns characteristic of Protestant secularism. From the outset, Obama has maintained a posture both analytical and confessional, attempting to delineate with precision what he has called "rules of engagement" between religiously motivated and more humanistic citizens. His first major statement in 2006 was the most nuanced, and his 2008 speech, "A More Perfect Union," represented a second ambitious attempt to deal with his religious heritage, this time in tandem with an explicit discussion about race.

As a freshman senator from Illinois, Obama took on the question of faith and politics in June 2006 at the Call to Renewal's "Building a Covenant for a New America" conference. Protestant liberal Jim Wallis of Sojourners had helped to organize a bipartisan network of over six hundred "churches, faith-based organizations, and individuals working to overcome poverty in America," and the conference organizers boasted that their program would conclude with Obama's "first-ever major address on the intersection of politics and his faith."[22] The young politician did not disappoint. He opened with an account of the inner turmoil his opponent in his senate race had caused when he charged that "Jesus Christ would not vote for Barack Obama." Initially, Obama recounted, he "answered with what has come to be the typically liberal response in such debates—namely, I said that we live in a pluralistic society, that I can't impose my own religious views on another." In truth, Obama did not modify his position materially upon further reflection, but he did deploy more sophisticated language to describe it, drawing even more deeply on Jefferson's example than had Kerry or Romney. Many Americans, as Edward Blum indicates in Chapter 2, did not pay attention to the finer points of the speech but instead jousted over the proper placement of the word "just" in one of Obama's statements and argued whether or not Obama had denigrated the country's Christian heritage. Those attentive to the language of Protestant secularism, however, heard Obama emphasize in a forceful way the role of reason and elucidate why he believed people of faith were obligated to translate their convictions into universal values before engaging in political speech.

Obama came to a celebration of reason through a series of confessional moments—about his run-in with Alan Keyes, his own conversion to Christianity, and an epistolary encounter with a pro-life physician. Whereas Jefferson reluctantly tolerated totalizing religious commitments so long as those who professed them resorted to reason in public debate, Obama was more generously inclined to those with intense faith commitments but made the same plea that reason be the lingua franca of political conversation. "Democracy demands that the religiously motivated translate their concerns into universal, rather than religion-specific, values," he explained. "It requires that their proposals be subject to argument, and amenable to reason." In a retelling of the story of Abraham and Isaac, in which Abraham almost sacrifices his only son, Obama acknowledged the possibility that people of faith might see and hear things inaccessible to others—but held that reason and evidence nonetheless provided the only possible rules of engagement in public life. "It's fair to say that if any of us leaving this church saw Abraham on a roof of a building raising his knife, we would, at the very least, call the police and expect the Department of Children and Family Services to take Isaac away from Abraham," Obama observed. "We would do so because we do not hear what Abraham hears, do not see what Abraham sees, true as those experiences may be. So the best we can do is act in accordance with those things that we all see, and that we all hear, be it common laws or basic reason." Even when he argued for partnerships between people of many or no faiths, Obama required that the terms of their cooperation be forged in mutually accessible language, what his correspondent the physician called "fair-minded words."[23]

In his landmark speech, "A More Perfect Union," Obama fully identified with the black Protestant tradition even as he reiterated his commitment to keeping some of that tradition's distinctive qualities from the public sphere. Drawing upon the testimony of his first visit to Jeremiah Wright's church recorded in *Dreams from My Father*, he lingered in his description of the services on precisely those elements that outside observers might characterize as the *least* rational. "Like other black churches, Trinity's services are full of raucous laughter and sometimes bawdy humor," he said. "They are full of dancing and clapping and screaming and shouting that may seem jarring to the untrained ear." After identifying with some of the distinctive elements of black Protestantism, however, Obama channeled this heritage into universal political values. "In the end, then," he summarized, "what is called for is nothing more and nothing less than what all the world's great religions demand—that we do unto others as we would have them do unto us. Let us be our brother's keeper, scripture tells us. Let us be our sister's keeper. Let us find that common stake we all have in one another, and let our politics reflect that spirit as well."[24]

Kerry, Romney, and Obama—on different sides of the political spectrum and with different religious backgrounds—have each articulated a Jeffersonian vision of Protestant secularism. They have also agreed to a large extent on what makes "bad religion" in the twenty-first century. In his time, Jefferson believed that American Calvinists were suspect because they believed things impossible to prove by reason (for example, the existence of the Trinity), aspired to enforce belief in those things through a religious establishment, and refused to translate their political concerns into universal values.[25] Uniformly, the candidates briefly profiled above have placed Islamic terrorists into the equivalent category for the twenty-first century. In the text of his most important speech on religion, for example, Romney reckoned jihadists as beyond the pale, as much for their violations of Protestant secularist conventions as the actual violence done to Americans. "Infinitely worse is the other extreme, the creed of conversion by conquest: violent Jihad, murder as martyrdom ... killing Christians, Jews, and Muslims with equal indifference. These radical Islamists do their preaching not by reason or example, but in the coercion of minds and the shedding of blood. We face no greater danger today than theocratic tyranny, and the boundless suffering these states and groups could inflict if given the chance."[26]

Obama has also condemned Islamic terrorists while defending Islam in general, though his efforts have essentially boiled down to a defense of Protestant secularism against the "fanatical" efforts of those who would use *either* politics *or* violence to advance religious goals. In a September 24, 2014, address to the United Nations, he pleaded, "We have reaffirmed again and again that the United States is not and never will be at war with Islam. Islam teaches peace. Muslims the world over aspire to live with dignity and a sense of justice. And when it comes to America and Islam, there is no us and them, there is only us—because millions of Muslim Americans are part of the fabric of our country." The problem is misguided "extremists who cannot build or create anything, and therefore peddle only fanaticism and hate."[27]

Presidents and presidential candidates are not the only actors in our national life who advocate for Protestant secularism. They do, however, endure media scrutiny more intense than that directed at any celebrity and therefore have exceptional platforms from which to shape political discourse. This is especially true of the religious outsiders who have stood for the highest office and who have had to explain to a dwindling but still powerful Protestant majority that their faith is compatible with American democracy. Kerry, Romney, and Obama have not only played by the Jeffersonian rules in making their respective cases before the American people, but they also have helped to heighten anxieties about where free exercise crosses the line into political oppression. Each man has encouraged Americans to limit the public expression of their distinctive religious commitments to the lowest-common denominator of the golden rule. When men and women read the imperatives of that rule differently, as in the case of the rights of women or the unborn, for example, they run a greater risk than ever of being branded with the label of fanaticism that politicians of both parties have placed so confidently on Islamic terrorists.

Notes

1. United States Conference of Catholic Bishops, Taskforce on Catholic Bishops and Catholic Politicians, "Interim Report: Catholics in Political Life," June 15, 2004, http://www.usccb.org/issues-and-action/faithful-citizenship/church-teaching/interim-reflections-tf-bishops-politicians.cfm; Kristen Wyatt, "Communion Barred to Abortion Supporters," AP Online, August 4, 2004, Newspaper Source Plus.

2. "Faith and the Public Dialogue: A Conversation with Sen. John Kerry," moderated by E. J. Dionne, Pew Research: Religion and Public Life Project, November 1, 2007, http://www.pewforum.org/2007/11/01/faith-and-the-public-dialogue-a-conversation-with-sen-john-kerry/.

3. Ibid.

4. Janet R. Jakobsen and Ann Pellegrini, Secularisms (Durham, NC: Duke University Press, 2008), 3.

5. Tracy Fessenden, Culture and Redemption: Religion, the Secular, and American Literature (Princeton, NJ: Princeton University Press, 2007), quotation p. 2; also, for example, Robert Orsi, Between Heaven and Earth: The Religious Worlds People Make and the Scholars Who Study Them (Princeton, NJ: Princeton University Press, 2005); and R. Marie Griffith and Melani McAlister, "Introduction: Is the Public Square Still Naked?" American Quarterly 59, no. 3, Religion and Politics in the Contemporary United States (2007): 527–563.

6. Michael Dimock, "Belief That Obama is Muslim is Durable, Bipartisan—but Most Likely to Sway Democratic Votes," Pew Research Center, July 15, 2008, http://www.pewresearch.org/2008/07/15/belief-that-obama-is-muslim-is-durable-bipartisan-but-most-likely-to-sway-democratic-votes/.

7. Influential works highlighting the constructed nature of the concept of religion include Talal Asad, *Genealogies of Religion: Discipline and Reasons of Power in Christianity and Islam* (Princeton, NJ: Princeton University Press, 1993) and Timothy Fitzgerald, *The Ideology of Religious Studies* (New York: Oxford University Press, 2003).

8. The phrase "voluntary principle" is Robert Baird's; for an excellent discussion of Baird's work and the origins of "Evangelical Secularism," see John Lardas Modern, *Secularism in Antebellum America* (Chicago: University of Chicago Press, 2011), 77–85.

9. Webb Keane, *Christian Moderns: Freedom and Fetish in the Mission Encounter* (Berkeley: University of California Press, 2007).

10. Indeed, Jefferson traveled a similar route to what Modern calls "Evangelical Secularism" several decades before the protagonists in Modern's account did so, and without the additional stimulus of a world of new machines. On Jefferson and the moral sense, see Allen Jayne, *Jefferson's Declaration of Independence: Origins, Philosophy, and Theology* (Lexington: University Press of Kentucky, 1998).

11. Jefferson to Peter Carr, August 10, 1787, in *Jefferson: Writings* (New York: Library of America, 1984), 900–906; see also, Jefferson, "Query XVII: Religion," in *Notes on the State of Virginia*, ed. William Peden (Chapel Hill: University of North Carolina Press, 1954 [1785]), 159.

12. Johann Neem, "Beyond the Wall: Reinterpreting Jefferson's Danbury Address," *Journal of the Early Republic* 27, no. 1 (2007): 139–154, quotations 142 and 153.

13. Jefferson, "Query XVII: Religion," 159; Jefferson to Benjamin Rush, April 21, 1803, in *Writings*, 1122–1126. The best introduction to these documents and to Jefferson's motivation and editorial process remains *Jefferson's Extracts from the Gospels: "The Philosophy of Jesus" and "The Life and Morals of Jesus,"* ed. by Dickinson Adams, intro by Eugene R. Sheridan (Princeton, NJ: Princeton University Press, 1983).

14. Jefferson to Benjamin Rush, September 23, 1800, in *Writings*, 1080–1082.

15. John F. Kennedy, "Address to Protestant Ministers," online at *National Public Radio*, September 12, 1960, http://www.npr.org/templates/story/story.php?storyId=16920600.

16. Kevin M. Schulz captures some of the tensions inherent in this postwar accommodation in *Tri-Faith America: How Catholics and Jews Held Postwar America to Its Protestant Promise* (New York: Oxford University Press, 2011). In one example (chapter 7), Protestants and Jews deepened the privatization of religious belief by prohibiting the federal government from compiling any statistics on adherence, but "Catholics overwhelmingly rejected the idea of religious privacy, seeing religion as profoundly social as well as transcendent."

17. John Kerry, "Remarks at the Broward Center for the Performing Arts in Fort Lauderdale, Florida," curated online by Gerhard Peters of the University of

California Santa Barbara, *American Presidency Project*, October 24, 2004, http://www.presidency.ucsb.edu/ws/index.php?pid=29748.

18. Frank Newport and Lydia Saad, "Religion, Politics Inform Americans' Views on Abortion," *Gallup*, April 3, 2006, http://www.gallup.com/poll/22222/religion-politics-inform-americans-views-abortion.aspx.

19. Mitt Romney, "Faith in America," online at *National Public Radio*, December 6, 2007, http://www.npr.org/templates/story/story.php?storyId=16969460.

20. Scott Keeter and Gregory Smith, "How the Public Perceives Romney, Mormons," *Pew Research*, December 7, 2004, http://www.pewforum.org/2007/12/04/how-the-public-perceives-romney-mormons/; "Bias against Mormonism May Not Keep Romney out of White House," *Research News @ Vanderbilt*, January 18, 2012, http://news.vanderbilt.edu/2012/01/mormon-bias/; John-Charles Duffy, "What Happened to Romney's 'Evangelical Problem'?" *Religion and Politics: Fit for Polite Company*, July 9, 2012, http://religionandpolitics.org/2012/07/09/what-happened-to-romneys-evangelical-problem/.

21. Emily Friedman, "Mormon Question Sparks Tense Moment during Mitt Romney Town Hall," ABC News, April 2, 2012, http://abcnews.go.com/blogs/politics/2012/04/mormon-question-sparks-tense-moment-during-mitt-romney-town-hall/.

22. "Religious Leaders to Unveil 'Covenant for a New America,'" press release *Faith in Public Life*, June 23, 2006, http://www.faithinpubliclife.org/newsroom/press/religious_leaders_to_unveil_co/.

23. Barack Obama, "Keynote at the Call to Renewal's Building a Covenant for a New America Conference," *New York Times*, June 28, 2006, http://www.nytimes.com/2006/06/28/us/politics/2006obamaspeech.html?pagewanted=all&_r=1&.

24. Barack Obama, "A More Perfect Union," *National Public Radio*, March 18, 2008, http://www.npr.org/templates/story/story.php?storyId=88478467.

25. See Peter S. Onuf, "Jefferson's Religion: Priestcraft, the Enlightenment, and the Republican Revolution," in *The Mind of Thomas Jefferson* (Charlottesville: University of Virginia Press, 2007), 139–168.

26. Romney, "Faith in America."

27. Barack Obama, "Remarks by President Obama in Address to the United Nations General Assembly," White House Briefing Room, September 24, 2014, http://www.whitehouse.gov/the-press-office/2014/09/24/remarks-president-obama-address-united-nations-general-assembly.

4

African American Religious Conservatives in the New Millennium

Anthea Butler

THREE DAYS AFTER the 2009 inauguration of the first African American US president, Alveda King, niece of Dr. Martin Luther King Jr. and a member of the pro-life group Priests for Life, led a group of antiabortion protestors to the White House for what she called the Birmingham Letter Project. Timed to coincide with the annual pro-life marches commemorating *Roe v. Wade*, the group placed 1,400 flowers on the lawn, symbolizing the abortion of 1,400 African American children each day in America. King read an extended passage from Ezekiel 34 before chastising the president:

> Although we rejoice with President Obama's historic win as the first African American elected President of the United States, we are deeply troubled by his radical support of abortion. His embracing of prenatal murder is a tragedy and travesty of social justice and the principles of Dr. Martin Luther King and the scriptures. By supporting policies which have resulted in the deaths of over 50 million innocent American Lives, President Obama overlooks the eternal truth of loving your neighbor as yourself.[1]

The protest posed a dilemma for conservative black Christians who consider themselves pro-life: what do you do when the first black president is pro-choice?

Fast-forward three years to May 2012. In an interview with Robin
Roberts of ABC's *Good Morning America*, President Obama announced
his support for same-sex marriage. Explicitly linking his decision to his
faith, the president explained his and first lady Michelle Obama's support:

> We are both practicing Christians and obviously this position may
> be considered to put us at odds with the view of others, but you
> know, when we think about our faith, the thing at the root that we
> think about is, not only Christ sacrificing himself on our behalf,
> but it's also the Golden Rule, you know, treat others as you would
> want to be treated. And I think that's what we try to impart to our
> kids and that's what motivates me as president and I figure the
> more consistent I can be in being true to those precepts, the better
> I will be as a dad and husband, and hopefully, the better I will be
> as president.[2]

The president's announcement, greeted with elation on the left and
disdain on the right, received a mixed response from African American
clergy. In a conference call after the announcement, black religious leaders expressed their dismay. The Reverend Delbert Coates, who participated in the call, told the *New York Times* that the pastors "were wrestling
with their ability to get over his theological position. Gay marriage is contrary to their understanding of scripture. There are people who are really
wrestling over this." Pastor Jamal Harrison Bryant declared that he felt
"jilted" by President Obama.[3]

The election of Barack Obama as the United States' first black president was an important moment for Americans, but especially for African
Americans. Many described the 2008 election as a watershed moment
for race relations and civil rights. But one segment of the voting population was not wholly supportive of Obama: black conservatives. Some
disapproved of Obama's support for abortion, LGBT rights, and—more
recently—same-sex marriage (SSM). For a small yet vocal group of black
conservatives, abortion and SSM not only violate their sincerely held religious beliefs but erode the black family. Black conservatives see family values in much the same way white conservatives do, but with an important
difference: their conservative beliefs are linked with the history of slavery
and the struggle for civil rights.

There has always been a strain of conservative thought in African
American Christianity similar to that found among white evangelicals

and fundamentalists. Political scientists and other scholars tend to ignore this fact, simply focusing on white evangelicals who vote for candidates with matching views on moral and social issues. Mainstream media outlets seldom use the word "evangelical" to describe African Americans with conservative viewpoints, despite the fact that they fit neatly into the evangelical definition. Voting habits, rather than religious affinities and affiliations, are the reason many black churchgoers who vote Democrat are considered to be moderates.[4] Yet African American voters often hold strong beliefs about moral issues such as homosexuality, premarital sex, and SSM. So what really constitutes a black conservative voter in the age of Obama? Are their numbers growing?

Although black conservatives may hold on to moral issues rooted in their evangelical Christian beliefs, many support Democrats and liberal causes out of pragmatism. Historian Mark Noll has pointed out that although black and white conservative Christians agree on moral issues, they often vote differently based on political issues.[5] What then, of the other black conservatives, the ones that are not only morally conservative but fiscally conservative, and have chosen to ally themselves with religious organizations run primarily by white conservatives?

These black conservatives find common cause among white conservative Christians and, for the most part, have alienated themselves from other morally conservative African Americans. Dr. Ben Carson famously chastised President Obama over the Affordable Care Act in a speech at the 2013 National Prayer Breakfast, linking the biblical principle of tithing to healthcare. Carson, a pediatric neurosurgeon, had long been admired by both African Americans and whites alike for his story of uplift in his book *Gifted Hands*. Since his stand against President Obama, Carson has become a darling of white religious conservatives. Carson exemplifies this dilemma: how do conservative black Democrats and Republicans negotiate their moral concerns differently in the age of Obama?

In a recent book entitled *Black Conservative Intellectuals in Modern America*, Michael L. Ondaajte states that "when one considers the extent to which American conservatism has been conditioned by racist notions of black inferiority, the existence of powerful conservative black spokespeople is astonishing."[6] Ondaajte gives little attention to religion, instead focusing on figures like John McWhorter and Shelby Steele. But there is another stream of black conservatism, one that is specifically Christian and concerned with "respectability." African Americans' quest for "respectability" has been a key part of their efforts to blend into American society. As defined by Evelyn Brooks Higginbotham, respectability has to do with deportment. It requires the embrace of traditional values of modesty, family, and marriage. Respectability is rooted in critiques of African American lives in the Reconstruction era and beyond.

While Ondaajte's book attempts to explain the existence of black conservatives in spite of the racial bias endemic to American conservatism, one cannot understand black conservatives without understanding how notions of religiosity and respectability inform their conservative beliefs. These black conservatives appeal to broader "American" values—usually conflated with conservative religious values—to promote a homogenous conservatism, and they only refer to race as something they have transcended or overcome. And while they don't often share white conservatives' racial politics, they do share their religious beliefs about family. Conserving these values helps them to locate themselves within the broader conservative view of how America was and should be.

By taking respectability and conservative biblical beliefs seriously, we can discern a different genealogy for black conservatives, one that begins in the nineteenth century. According to historian Charles P. Henry, a more "organic conservatism" paralleling the twentieth-century black rights movement can be seen in the establishment of the American Moral Reform Society in the 1830s.[7] William Whipper, the founder, believed that African Americans should reject calls for emigration by focusing on uplift and morality.[8] While some of Whipper's beliefs about racial institutions were ignored by other African Americans, one thing was clear both for Whipper and those—such as Booker T. Washington, Kelly Miller Smith, and John Jackson, president of the National Baptist Convention of the 1960s—who followed in his footsteps: embracing a white standard for black moral worth was the key to success, assimilation, and respect.[9]

While Henry's analysis of the genealogy of black conservatism is sound, some other factors account for the power of black conservatives in the post-civil rights era. Some black churches have shifted from a prophetic focus to an embrace of prosperity and respectability. The burning of inner-city communities like Watts and Detroit, the Moynihan Report, and the rise of the black middle class have all contributed to that shift. These churches have also shifted their focus from the structural sin of racism to individual sins, quieting their prophetic voice in the public square. They speak about personal morality, decrying the sins of their children, and society. The fusion of morality and prosperity has fueled the growth of black conservatism.[10]

For black conservatives in the age of Obama, respectability and religion inform their advocacy. Obama fits their narrative of respectability in certain respects, but his economic policies and liberal stances on LGBT issues and abortion do not. It is this dissonance that has pushed black conservatives' engagement with President Obama to the forefront of media discourse, and put them into a quandary: How do they press their agenda on the issues that they care about, in this case, abortion and SSM? Should they frame them as issues that everyone should care about or as issues that affect the African American community specifically? What effect does the election of America's first black president have on their alliances? Should they fight for their ideal of black family from within the African American community, or do they partner with white evangelicals and other conservatives? The small subset of black conservatives who have formed alliances with white conservatives are able to fight for issues specific to black families and broader evangelicalism but are cut off from the larger community of black conservatives who vote Democratic. Their conservative political leanings have alienated them from the broader African American religious community, leaving them with little choice but to assimilate with white conservative evangelicals.

African American Conservatives and Abortion

Both black conservatives and black nationalists have used the term "genocide" to describe abortion and other population control methods. While nationalists are not the major focus of this essay, it is important to remember that the shared narrative of slavery and racism creates interesting alliances. Each group is concerned with the numbers of African American women who have received abortions. The use of the term "genocide" with regard to abortion and family planning has entered black conservative discourse. At a meeting of black antiabortion leaders in Orlando, Florida, Sr. Patricia Marie, a black nun representing the Franciscan Handmaids of the Most Pure Heart of Mary, remarked that "the black anti-abortion movement is small because blacks 'think it is a white thing'" and that "abortion providers take advantage of black women and their babies in a lucrative business that prunes the black population." Such sentiments have had widespread appeal.[11]

This mythos of the reduction in the black population through abortion arises from a misappropriation of a 1939 quote by Margaret Sanger, founder of Planned Parenthood. The Negro Project, started by Sanger in 1939, was designed to bring healthcare to black women in the South. According to Sanger, both a black physician and black minister would be needed in order for the project to succeed and gain the trust of the community. Sanger wanted a minister to debunk claims, *if they arose*, that the program was designed to "exterminate" the community.[12] The distortion of Sanger's statement by pro-life activists provides a link from Sanger and Planned Parenthood to eugenics and genocide. Given the history of the Tuskegee Project and forced sterilization of African American women, it is easy for many to believe that Sanger was aiming to destroy the African American community.

Pro-life activists also invoke slavery to promote the idea that abortion rights activists and pro-abortion laws treat black people as less than human. Pro-life activists, including African Americans, claim that much as the Dred Scott decision robbed enslaved Africans of their rights, *Roe v. Wade* did the same to the unborn. A fetus under *Roe* is not a person and therefore can be harmed or mistreated. Justice Antonin Scalia actually made this argument at the close of his dissenting opinion in *Planned Parenthood v. Casey* (1993).[13] Frank Pavone, former director of Priests for Life, the organization Alveda King often represents, has argued that the language of the Civil Rights Movement lends itself seamlessly to the anti-abortion cause and that after visits to Ebenezer Baptist Church and visits with the King family, "the message is exactly right. Nothing has to change except to include one more group of people: the unborn."[14]

Comparing abortion to slavery and genocide is a common tactic in pro-life circles. It gained momentum during the 2008 presidential campaign. Rod Parsley, an Ohio megachurch pastor with a large African American congregation and television following, was instrumental in bringing votes to George Bush in Ohio in 2004. In February of 2008, he began to preach a series on how abortion was "black genocide." Within a week, he had publically endorsed John McCain's presidential campaign.[15] While McCain would later jettison Parsley from his roster of supporters, the rhetoric surrounding abortion as black genocide didn't subside. Black conservatives like Day Gardner, then president of the black National Pro-Life Union, issued a statement after Super Tuesday denouncing Obama's position on abortion:

The man who wants to be President never mentioned the racism of an organization that purposefully plants abortion facilities firmly in black and minority neighborhoods and urban communities. We have lost more than 15 million black children since 1973—targeted and slaughtered by abortion and Obama doesn't utter a word or bat an eye.[16]

Gardner and other black pro-lifers used this kind of rhetoric in order to get more press and hopefully appeal to some black voters. With financial and public-relations help from white pro-lifers, they strategized in order to piggyback on Obama's campaign events. In April 2008, black conservatives affiliated with Gardner's organization rallied outside of a Planned Parenthood office in Washington, DC. As signs proclaiming "black genocide" were held up, Gardner declared, "Black America must wake up and stand up to this racist organization."[17] A similar event was held during the Democratic National Convention in Denver in August 2008. So when Alveda King and others showed up soon after the inauguration of President Obama, it marked the continuation of these efforts.

Those efforts came with an assist from predominately white pro-life organizations that had long struggled to make inroads into the black community. By changing their messaging strategy to focus on black genocide, they were able to rally conservative African Americans to their cause. They used both films and billboards highlighting the genocide meme to carry their message. On June 18, 2009, a film called *Maafa 21: Black Genocide in 21st Century America* premiered in the US Capitol visitor's center. Produced and funded by white antiabortion activist Mark Crutcher, founder of Life Dynamics, *Maafa 21* claims that eugenicists and Planned Parenthood targeted black communities.[18] The word "Maafa" is Swahili for "tragedy" or "disaster." Featured in the film is black pro-life activist Reverend Clenard Childress, who openly uses the word "conspiracy" because he thinks it will attract African Americans. "In the African American Community, if you shout conspiracy they'll listen because of the history they've had in this country. I come from the conspiracy tone whenever I'm speaking, especially to African Americans, so they'll understand you have to do some digging, you'll have to go beneath the veneer."[19]

The film uses the same tactics, depicting Planned Parenthood as an organization committed to killing off black people. DVDs of *Maafa 21* were made available to churches and individuals, and a compelling trailer appeared on YouTube. Slick and well produced, the movie was shown at historically black colleges and universities, and black conservative right-to-life leaders used it as a tool. Catherine Davis, minority outreach coordinator for Georgia Right to Life, began traveling to colleges and churches in the area to show the film. The Georgia organization coupled the showing with more than eighty billboards placed around Atlanta that proclaimed "Black Children are an endangered Species." The billboards directed people to a website, toomanyaborted.com.[20] Nancy Smith, director of Georgia Right to Life, told the *New York Times*, "We were shocked when we spent less money and had more phone calls to the hot line."[21]

Similar billboards also appeared across the country in 2011, including in Chicago and New York, sponsored by Pastor Stephen Broden, African American pastor of Fair Park Bible Fellowship in Dallas and a founder of Life Always. On the south side of Chicago, the billboards featured a picture of President Obama alongside the caption, "Every 21 minutes, our next possible leader is aborted."[22] Many of the billboards were vandalized, and social workers in Chicago covered two of them with cloth banners reading "In 21 minutes, this sign should be down" and "Abort Racism." Billboards in New York City depicting a young black girl with the caption, "The Most Dangerous place for an African American is in the Womb," met the same fate after criticism from various sources, including public advocate and future mayor, Bill de Blasio.[23] Broden, a rather colorful figure who ran unsuccessfully for congress as a Republican in 2010, is touted on the National Black Pro-Life Coalition website as saying, "The practice of abortion is a genocidal plot to decimate the demography of our community and black leaders are silent! Their silence is egregious and tantamount to approval."[24]

While to outsiders these stories seem disconnected, they are united by several factors. Black conservatives involved in the pro-life movement start organizations but often require assistance of white conservative groups in order to get a broader hearing and raise funds. Speakers like Day, King, and other black pro-lifers receive invitations to major conservative events such as the Values Voters Summit, giving them legitimacy in the wider movement and, often, access to other funding streams. While these pro-lifers may be unknown in many black religious circles, they are well known among conservative white evangelicals. By framing the abortion discussion as part of the narrative of genocide, these black conservatives can make some inroads into the broader community of moderates and black conservatives. While they have not been effective in swaying many African American Christians to vote Republican simply out of a desire to see *Roe v. Wade* repealed, the issue of SSM, however, has the potential to do so.

Black Conservatives Rally Against
Same-sex Marriage

Opposition to SSM is more widespread among African American Christians. A Pew Center research poll in 2013 showed a scant 2 percent decrease in the number of black Protestants opposed to SSM on grounds of religious belief between 2003 (66 percent) and 2013 (64 percent).[25] African Americans have been very conservative on the issue, and despite the tendency to vote for other liberal causes, their position on SSM has held firmly over time. While the opposition comes primarily from evangelical readings of scripture, some of it is a reaction to LGBT activists' equating the fight for SSM and LGBT rights with the civil rights struggle. Leaders such as the late Fred Shuttlesworth and Bernice King have made it clear that the fight for SSM should not be equated with the Civil Rights Movement.

Their beliefs on marriage are rooted in conservative interpretations of the Bible. Michael G. Long recounts in his book *Martin Luther King Jr, Homosexuality, and the Early Gay Rights Movement* that Shuttlesworth laid out his position clearly in an interview with *Ebony Magazine*.

> Despite what many in this world may argue, I cannot waiver from the God-established principle that marriage is a union meant to be shared between a man and a woman; and no matter how "open-minded" people of this earth become, God's word cannot be changed and should not be ignored! . . . God created men to be husbands of wives, and women to be wives of husbands.[26]

Bernice King—unlike her mother, Coretta Scott King, who supported LGBT rights and SSM—said of her famous father, "I know deep down in my sanctified soul that he did not take a bullet for same sex unions."[27] King, for years an associate pastor at New Birth, a megachurch run by Bishop Eddie Long, angered many in 2004 when she and Long held a march against SSM that started at Martin Luther King Jr.'s gravesite. Since leaving the church, King has articulated a more tolerant approach toward the LGBT community, although she has not come forward to support SSM.

In the 2008 presidential campaign, SSM played a role in bringing out African American voters in California. While the Obama campaign had already mobilized many of these voters, they were explicitly blamed (along with conservative Mormons) for the passage of Proposition 8. But this narrative was proven false. More interestingly, the president would finally come out in support of SSM in May of 2012, and articulate his change of mind in biblical terms. Because of that, the conservative black pastors who had supported his 2008 bid were very, very troubled.

The announcement of President Obama's support for SSM in an interview with Robin Roberts of *Good Morning America* came as a surprise. At the time of the 2008 election, Obama said that he believed marriage was for a man and a woman, yet he was opposed to Proposition 8. Before 2008, Obama had articulated several positions on SSM, including "yes," "undecided," supporting the repeal of the Defense of Marriage Act (DOMA), and supporting civil unions.[28] So while Obama evolved in his thinking, the announcement still took many Americans, including black religious conservatives, by surprise. After the announcement, Obama held a conference call with black pastors that was described as amicable, but that was perhaps because only eight pastors were on the call.[29]

That number is telling. While Obama has enjoyed support from many in the African American community, he has distanced himself from many black pastors, in part because of his estrangement from the Reverend Jeremiah Wright during the 2008 election. Wright, a preacher in the prophetic civil rights tradition, aroused the ire of many conservatives when his infamous "God damn America" sermon seemed to be playing on an endless loop during the 2008 primary.[30] Not wanting to invite that type of scrutiny of his religious beliefs again, Obama's subsequent visits to African American churches were carefully planned and choreographed. With the decision to support SSM, even more choreography was scripted.

The National Association for the Advancement of Colored People (NAACP) announced a few days later that they supported the president's statement. The double blow put black conservative leaders on the defensive. Two of the most vocal pastors opposed to Obama's announcement were Reverend Jamal Bryant of Empowerment Temple in Baltimore and Reverend William Owens, president of the Coalition of African American Pastors (CAAP). Bryant, a prosperity preacher who said that "sanctified sissies" were ruining the church, expressed his dismay at the president's decision.

> My response was shock and disappointment. And what many clergy are trying to discern is that is this a decision made out of political expediency or moral conviction? The timeliness of this whole matter does not makes sense given what has happened in

North Carolina. So my question is, is he exchanging one minority for another? It has been speculated that the president is taking the black vote for granted, so did he think he could do this without any losses from his black supporters? The President has not been able to find one credible black pastor of note to stand with him on this issue. That's saying something.[31]

Bryant appeared all over the media in the following days, and gathered a group of black pastors to discuss their next move. Other noted black conservatives like Bishop Harry Jackson and Bishop Larry Palmer joined white evangelicals at "The Defense of Marriage Summit" on May 24, 2012, in Washington DC, to "confront" the president on SSM. In an interview with CBN News, Bishop Palmer remarked, "I don't think [SSM] is relevant to a civil rights fight at all. It's a fight between right and wrong. This happens to be wrong."[32]

The most vocal and out-front pastor was CAAP president Owens. A boisterous preacher, Owens has claimed that he marched in the Civil Rights Movement in Nashville, a claim that could not be verified by any other Civil Rights Movement leaders.[33] Owens, however, took advantage of the backing he had from the National Organization for Marriage (NOM) and began to blast the president at every opportunity. While calling for thousands of pastors to sign his petition against SSM, Owens was collecting $20,000 a year from NOM to help them to drive a "wedge" between black voters and the president. Owens seemed to be speaking for invisible pastors as he appeared at events throughout the summer of 2012. Generating smoke but no heat, his blustering about President Obama bordered on incoherent. His campaign, funded by NOM, was really a bust.

While Owens may not have generated much of substance, denominations did reiterate their beliefs on SSM. The Church of God in Christ reissued to the press their statement against SSM from 2004 soon after the president's announcement.[34] The AME Zion Church also reaffirmed its belief that marriage is between a man and a woman but made a distinction between the rights of the state and the rights of the church.[35] Most importantly, the statement noted that the positions of the president are "consistent with the interests of our congregational members" and pleaded that "the issues, not *an* issue become the nexus of our consideration" (emphasis mine).[36]

Despite all of this, many of these morally conservative churches encouraged their parishioners to support President Obama over Mitt Romney in

2012. Even Jamal Bryant registered voters at his church and urged his congregation to vote for President Obama. But he also advocated that they oppose Referendum 6, on the ballot in Maryland, which would legalize SSM.[37] After a pitched battle between black pastors and churches on either side of the referendum, it passed. The flight of African American voters from Obama because of his support of SSM did not occur; Obama received more than 90 percent of the African American vote.[38]

What are we to make of these two issues, abortion and SSM, with regard to two distinct groups of black conservatives? Despite the visibility of both groups in recent years, the manner in which they engaged the issues of abortion and SSM varied. Small but vocal subsets of black conservatives working with white organizations on both abortion and SSM were able to amplify their voices in the media. White antiabortion organizations benefited from black conservative faces and voices, helping to further their cause. The case against SSM, however, did not fare well, with increasing numbers of states approving SSM, and African Americans slowly becoming more accepting of it. All of these stories however, raise an important question: Are African Americans true "conservatives" if they vote for liberal Democrats and causes, while holding to strict biblical morality codes? Or are true black conservatives those who in addition to adhering to strict morality codes are also proponents of limited government and fiscal responsibility? Most importantly, are they willing, like William Whipper, to make themselves respectable in order to assimilate?

It is clear that, in order to be successful, the leaders of abortion and marriage interest groups like Value Voters, Defense of Marriage, NOM, and Right to Life, need to find like-minded people of all ethnicities. For black conservatives, crossing over to vote Republican or placing moral issues above economic and other concerns of the community may alienate them from other black Christian voters who are conservative in their personal moral beliefs, but moderate when it comes to economic issues, education, and other issues. The fact that Barack Obama is black has certainly made it more difficult for some black conservatives to oppose him, just as it has allowed others, who have decided to oppose the president on moral grounds, to make names for themselves. One thing is certain: in order to ascertain what makes a black conservative, we need to understand the divide between morally oriented black conservatives who vote Democratic and those who buy into the full conservative program. Continuing to unpack these differences may hold a key to how to begin to truly consider African Americans as part of American evangelicalism.

Notes

1. Priests for Life, "Alveda King's Appeal to President Obama," Priestsforlife.org, January 23, 2009, http://www.priestsforlife.org/africanamerican/appeal-to-obama.htm.
2. Rick Klein, "Obama: I think Same Sex Couples Should Be Able to Get Married," May 12, 2012, ABC News, http://abcnews.go.com/blogs/politics/2012/05/obama-comes-out-i-think-same-sex-couples-should-be-able-to-get-married/.
3. Peter Baker and Rachel Swarns, "After Obama's Decision on Marriage, a Call to Pastors," *New York Times*, May 13, 2012, http://www.nytimes.com/2012/05/14/us/politics/on-marriage-obama-tried-to-limit-risk.html?pagewanted=all&_r=1&.
4. On blacks and the Democratic Party, see http://www.factcheck.org/2008/04/blacks-and-the-democratic-party/.
5. Mark Noll, interview on "The Jesus Factor," *Frontline*, December 10, 2003, http://www.pbs.org/wgbh/pages/frontline/shows/jesus/interviews/noll.html.
6. Michael Ondaajte, *Black Conservative Intellectuals in Modern America* (Philadelphia: University of Pennsylvania Press, 2010), 1.
7. Charles P. Henry, "Herman Cain and the Rise of the Black Right," *Journal of Black Studies* 20 (2013): 3.
8. Ibid.
9. Ibid.
10. Anthea Butler, "From Prophecy to Prosperity," *Dissent Magazine* (Winter 2014): 38–41.
11. *National Catholic Reporter*, September 2, 1994, 3.
12. Jean H. Baker, *Margaret Sanger, a Life of Passion* (New York: Hill and Wang, 2011), 251.
13. Jamin Ben Rankin, "Roe v. Wade and the Dred Scott Decision: Justice Scalia's Peculiar Analogy in Planned Parenthood v. Casey," *American University Journal of Gender, Social Policy & the Law* 1 (1993): 61.
14. Kathryn Joyce, "Abortion as Back Genocide: An Old Scare Tactic Re-emerges," *The Public Eye*, April 29, 2010, http://www.publiceye.org/magazine/v25n1/abortion-black-genocide.html.
15. Alan Johnson, "Huckabee, McCain Keep Rivalry in Motion," February 27, 2008, http://www.dispatch.com/content/stories/local/2008/02/27/GOP27.ART_ART_02-27-08_A1_IS9FKJU.html.
16. Special Report, "The Patriot Pastors War against Hell," *People for the American Way*, August 2006, 4–5.
17. David Brody, "Planned Parenthood Accused of Racism," CBN News, April 25, 2008, http://www.cbn.com/CBNnews/363785.aspx?option=print.
18. Crutcher's Life Dynamics was founded in 1992 in order to provide litigation support for women who sue abortionists and to provide strategy for pro-life crisis pregnancy centers. See Media Matters for America, "Who is Mark

Crutcher?," February 1, 2011, http://mediamatters.org/research/2011/02/01/who-is-mark-crutcher/175838.

19. Kathryn Joyce, " Is Abortion Black Genocide?," *The Public Eye* 25, no. 2 (Summer 2010): 5.

20. Shaila Dewan, "To Court Blacks, Foes of Abortion Make Racial Case," *New York Times*, February 27, 2010, A1.

21. Ibid.

22. http://chicago.cbslocal.com/2011/04/04/south-side-anti-abortion-billboards-covered-up/

23. Li Robins, "Billboard Opposing Abortion Stirs Debate," *New York Times*, February 23, 2011, http://cityroom.blogs.nytimes.com/2011/02/23/billboard-opposing-abortion-stirs-debate/?module=ArrowsNav&contentCollection=N.Y.%2FRegion&action=keypress&region=FixedLeft&pgtype=Blogs.

24. http://www.blackprolifecoalition.org/speakers/stephenbroden.html

25. David Masci, "March for Marriage Rally Reflects Steadfast Opposition to Gay Marriage among Evangelical Christians," June 19, 2014, http://www.pewresearch.org/fact-tank/2014/06/19/march-for-marriage-rally-reflects-steadfast-opposition-to-gay-marriage-among-evangelical-christians/.

26. Michael G. Long, *Martin Luther King Jr. Homosexuality and the Early Gay Rights Movement* (New York: Palgrave McMillan, 2012), 56.

27. Andrew Clark, "Martin Luther King's Daughter Bernice Takes up Mantle as US Civil Rights Leader," *The Guardian*, November 1, 2009, http://www.theguardian.com/world/2009/nov/01/bernice-king-sclc-female-leader.

28. Madonna Lebling and Lucy Shackelford, "Timeline of Obama's Gay Marriage Views," *Washington Post*, May 9, 2012, http://www.washingtonpost.com/politics/timeline-of-obamas-gay-marriage-views/2012/05/09/gIQArlQPEU_story.html.

29. Dylan Stableford, "Obama Calls Pastors to Explain Same Sex Marriage Support," ABC News, May 14, 2012, http://abcnews.go.com/Politics/OTUS/obama-calls-pastors-explain-gay-marriage-support-black/story?id=16342670.

30. Richard Thompson, "Project Trinity: The Perilous Mission of Obama's Church," *The New Yorker*, April 7, 2008, http://www.newyorker.com/magazine/2008/04/07/project-trinity.

31. Andrew Showell, "Obama's Stance on Same Sex Marriage and the Black Church," BET.com, May 11, 2012, http://www.bet.com/news/politics/2012/05/11/obama-s-stance-on-same-sex-marriage-and-the-black-church.html.

32. Jennifer Wishon, "Minority Pastors: Gay Rights not a Civil Right," CBN News, June 6, 2012, http://www.cbn.com/cbnnews/politics/2012/June/Minority-Pastors-Gay-Marriage-Not-a-Civil-Right/.

33. Adam Serwer, "NOM Thinks This Black Preacher Will Convince You to Oppose Gay Marriage," *Mother Jones*, August 10, 2012, http://www.motherjones.com/politics/2012/08/nom-newest-anti-gay-marriage-front-man-william-owens.

34. "COGIC Takes a Stand against Same Sex Marriage, *Charisma Magazine,* May2,2012,http://www.charismanews.com/us/33464-cogic-takes-stand-against-same-sex-marriage.

35. "TheA.M.E.ZionBoardofBishops'OfficialStatementonSameSexMarriage," *The Star of Zion,* October 3, 2012, http://thestarofzion.com/the-ame-zion-board-of-bishops-official-statement-on-same-sex-marriage-p209-1.htm.

36. http://thestarofzion.com/the-ame-zion-board-of-bishops-official-statement-on-same-sex-marriage-p209-1.htm?

37. http://www.bloomberg.com/news/2012-10-19/black-shift-on-maryland-gay-marriage-pits-clergy-against-naacp.html

38. Thom File, "The Diversifying Electorate Voting Rates by Race and Hispanic Origin in 2012 (and Other Recent Elections)," Current Population Survey Reports, P20-569 (Washington, DC: US Census Bureau, 2013).

5

Barack Hussein Obama

AMERICA'S FIRST MUSLIM PRESIDENT?

Rebecca Anne Goetz

THERE ARE APPROXIMATELY three million Muslims in the United States—an unofficial estimate since the US Census does not count the population by religious affiliation.[1] Muslim Americans, like every other religious group in the country, are a diverse group. They follow a variety of Islamic traditions: they are Sunni, Shi'a, Ismaili, Ahmadi, or American sects such as the Nation of Islam. Muslim Americans are also racially and ethnically diverse: they are African American; of South Asian, southeast Asian, Arab, or West African descent; and Latino or white.[2] Until September 11, 2001, Muslim Americans lived in relative obscurity, largely escaping the notice of historians, sociologists, and policy makers. The advent of the War on Terror catapulted Muslim Americans into the public eye. These communities went from being demographic curiosities to perceived threats. In the aftermath of September 11, state surveillance of Muslim communities and student organizations increased.[3] Hate crimes against Muslims and mosques increased, and tens of thousands of South Asian and Middle Eastern Muslims were deported for minor infractions under post-9/11 "special registration" procedures. Muslim citizens were detained, sometimes for months.[4] The election of Barack Hussein Obama in 2008 further spurred the notoriety of Muslim Americans. Obama's middle name, his Kenyan father, and his childhood spent partly in the majority-Muslim nation of Indonesia fueled speculation that Obama himself was a secret Muslim. Despite the long history of Islam in the United States and despite the enormous diversity of Muslim beliefs and practices in the country, both 9/11 and Obama's election have proved to be focal points for critiques of Islam.

The ideas that Muslims are foreign and that Islam is incompatible with American values have a long genealogy that has informed and directed post-9/11 discourse. This Islamophobic discourse persists alongside a deep and sustained interest and engagement with Islam in the United States. In many ways, September 11 enhanced the cultural practice of excluding Muslims from the American narrative. Yet Islam and Muslims have been present in this American space for over five hundred years. This chapter examines this sustained Muslim presence—first among enslaved people, and later among free blacks and Muslim immigrants from Asia, Africa, and the Middle East—as well as European and American ideas and stereotypes about Islam. The long history of Muslims in America and the long engagement of Americans with stereotypes about Islam collided after 9/11 in ways that both denied the Americanness of Islam and revealed deep-rooted Islamophobic narratives.

Islam and Christianity arrived on the North American continent at the same time. Christopher Columbus's crew included *conversos*, that is, Muslims and Jews who had been coerced into converting to Christianity in order to escape death or exile. Early in the sixteenth century, enslaved Muslims accompanied conquistadores in their *entradas* all over the Americas. Estebanico was an enslaved North African from Azamor in Morocco who accompanied Pánfilo de Narváez's *entrada* into Florida. Estebanico's captors might not have thought of him as Muslim and likely forced him to convert to Christianity after his capture (when he would have acquired his new name, Stephen). Between 1527 and 1536, Estebanico and three other Spanish survivors of Narváez's expedition walked from present-day Texas to the Pacific coast of Mexico. Estebanico was no stranger to cultural fluidity; his remarkable linguistic abilities helped pilot the survivors of Narváez's expedition across North America. In 1539, Estebanico accompanied another *entrada* into the American Southwest, using his knowledge of native cultures, languages, and diplomatic customs to help guide Spanish conquistadores. (He was killed near Sonora in 1540.)[5] Did Estebanico identify as Muslim? It is a question that is impossible to answer, but Spanish officials were suspicious of Muslim converts to Christianity (forced or otherwise). Officially the New World was off limits to *conversos*, who were barred from making the journey unless they were "black or other slaves born under the tutelage of Christians."[6] Estebanico was not born Christian and thus his presence in the Americas suggests that this was a rule honored in the breach. The Spanish continued to use enslaved African Muslims as key parts of their colonization schemes; the settlement at St. Augustine almost certainly sheltered many enslaved Malinke Muslims in the late sixteenth century.[7] In other words, there were enslaved Muslims in North America long before permanent English settlement began at Jamestown in 1607.

Most Muslims who came to the Americas before 1850 arrived as Estebanico did, as enslaved people mostly from West and West Central Africa, but also in small numbers from North Africa. Enslaved Muslims of the New World remain largely opaque in the scholarship on slavery, though Sylviane Diouf thought that of the 12.5 million enslaved people brought to the Americas from West Africa at least several hundred thousand were likely Muslim. Many enslaved people arriving in North America would have been familiar with Islam even if they did not identify as Muslim themselves; Michael Gomez has noted that around 50 percent of enslaved people coming to mainland North America came from areas of West Africa where Islam was either state sponsored or associated with a culturally significant minority, reflecting the cosmopolitan religious lives of West Africans who combined Christianity, Islam, and traditional West African practice in novel ways.[8] The general problem remains that enslaved Muslims were an even more invisible minority within the "invisible institution" of slave religion.[9] As Edward Curtis has noted, "when whites observed African American Muslim rituals, they often did not understand what was taking place right in front of their eyes."[10] Nevertheless, Diouf pressed historians to recognize that enslaved Muslims were everywhere, that sources written by Europeans occasionally acknowledged their presence (especially in Latin America and the Caribbean), and that "Islam was indeed a diasporic religion."[11]

Though the lives of the vast majority of enslaved Muslims remain unseen, scholars know a great deal about a few individuals. In 1788, soldiers from another ethnic group captured Abd al-Rahman Ibrahima and sold him to European slave traders. Abd al-Rahman lived as an enslaved man in New Orleans for decades, marrying an African American Baptist woman named Isabella, before writing a letter to his relatives in Africa in Arabic in 1826 asking for his freedom. (The letter eventually made its way to the Sultan of Morocco, who asked President John Quincy Adams to intercede.) Abd al-Rahman was eventually freed, and he toured the United States displaying himself to large audiences to raise money to buy freedom for his wife and his children. In Washington DC, Abd al-Rahman

stood before a painting of Niagara Falls for eight hours dressed in a tur-
ban and carrying a scimitar, signing autograph albums and reciting passages of the Koran to audiences eager to experience his foreignness.[12]
Newspapers around the country chronicled his travels and his life story.
Colonization enthusiasts hoped that Abd al-Rahman, who was celebrated
as a "Moorish prince," would aid them in establishing diplomatic ties
between the infant colony of freed people of Liberia and nearby African
kingdoms as well as helping convert West Africans to Christianity.[13]
In 1829 he journeyed to Liberia with his wife, though he was unable to
fulfill the hopes of his captors/sponsors in the United States—he died
shortly after his arrival there. We know about Abd al-Rahman in part
because he was literate and was able to advocate for himself and his family. He used American curiosity about Muslims and desire to convert
them to Christianity to gain his freedom. Yarrow Mamout, an educated
West African who was enslaved in 1752, gained his freedom after forty-
five years as a slave to a Maryland family. He moved to Washington, DC,
where he owned property until his death in 1823. Unlike Abd-al-Rahman
and Yarrow, Omar ibn Said was not so lucky. Though he wrote his mem-
oirs in Arabic in 1831, he was never able to parlay his literacy into freedom. He passed away in 1863, still enslaved by a Confederate general.
Nevertheless, his autobiography is now considered an important contri-
bution to American literature.[14]

Abd al-Rahman, Yarrow, and Omar had compelling biographies that
often stand in for stories of enslaved Muslims, but the fact remains that
most enslaved Muslims were either not literate or did not otherwise have
the means to make their stories known. Most enslaved Muslims worked
to keep their faith intact in less dramatic ways, even in the face of persecution, passing on their names, rituals (including prayer mats and beads),
and prayers to their descendants. Frederick Douglass's family name of
Bailey might have been a corruption of the Muslim name Bilal or Bilali,
for example.[15] As Michael Gomez has noted, scholars can see hints of
enslaved Muslims in slave advertisements from the middle of the eighteenth century on: the names and ethnic identities of runaways suggest
the presence of enslaved Muslims in ways that slaveholders could not recognize.[16] Retaining Islam as enslaved people was both a form of resistance
and a method of self-preservation. While the biographies of individuals
like Abd al-Rahman and Yarrow Mamout suggest how enslaved Muslims
lived, the devotion of most of these people went unrecognized and unre-
membered by the Americans who owned them.

The numbers of enslaved Muslims in the United States probably rose in the last decade before the close of the transatlantic slave trade. Beginning in 1804, a series of jihads swept across the African continent from Senegambia to the Red Sea. During the course of the fighting, many Muslims were enslaved and shipped to the United States, which had drastically increased importations of enslaved people in anticipation of the closing of the trade in 1808 (other enslaved Muslims were shipped to Brazil, Cuba, and Trinidad).[17] Sometimes these enslaved Muslims were apparent even to white Americans. Writing in 1842, Presbyterian clergyman Charles Colcock Jones noted that "the Mohammedan Africans remaining of the old stock of importations, although accustomed to hear the Gospel preached, have been known to accommodate Christianity to Mohammedanism. 'God,' say they, 'is Allah, and Jesus Christ is Mohammed—the religion is the same, but different countries have different names.'"[18] On Jones's Georgia plantation, West African traditions and practices were alive and well, and Jones apparently had read enough about Islam at Princeton and Andover Theological Seminary to recognize some rituals. Nevertheless, Jones's observations signal some discomfort with African American spirituality, a discomfort echoed over a century and a half later in Americans' skepticism about Barack Obama's Christianity.

Even after the United States and Great Britain closed their transatlantic slave trades, many parts of Latin America continued to import enslaved Africans. Enslaved Muslims were instrumental in a slave revolt in Bahia in Brazil in 1835. The slaves wore amulets with Arabic lettering. These talismans were an important part of popular Muslim devotion in West Africa. Literate enslaved men wrote in Arabic to one another while planning that rebellion.[19] Muslim rebels were thus able to overcome a problem many enslaved people encountered—the lack of a common language and culture to help facilitate rebellion.

Despite the visibility of African Muslims such as Abd al-Rahman and Yarrow Mamout, the religion of most enslaved Muslims remained invisible to their captors. This was the beginning of an erasure; the presence of enslaved Muslims was opaque to their captors and thus remains largely opaque to historians. This is also in part due to historian Albert Raboteau's insistence that the Middle Passage destroyed slave religiosity. Though historians have now abandoned this historiographical position, it remains difficult to recover the experiences of enslaved Muslims, and it remains equally easy to overlook them, thus writing them out of American history.

Refusal to recognize this part of the Muslim American past contributes to an ideology in which Islam is foreign to the United States.

African Americans have remembered Muslims pasts in ways that shaped African American and American culture to the present. Edward Blyden, who was born in the Danish West Indies and attempted to get an education in the United States (but was denied admission to several theological seminaries because of his race), wrote a hugely influential collection of essays that concluded that Islam was better for people of African descent than Christianity. Islam, Blyden wrote, found its black converts "at home in a state of freedom and independence of the teachers who brought it to them. When it was offered to them they were at liberty to choose for themselves." On the other hand, Christianity came with slavery, and taught black people "their utter and permanent inferiority and subordination to their instructors, to whom they stood in the relation of chattels."[20] After launching the United Negro Improvement Association in 1914, Marcus Garvey also presented Islam as an African religion that could link African Americans with their pasts and help foster resistance in the present. Both Blyden and Garvey were enormously influential in African American communities and helped spur interest in Islam. At the turn of the century, thousands of African Americans joined the Ahmadiyya movement, a branch of Islam that sent missionaries from India to the United States. Other African Americans joined homegrown Islamic movements such as Noble Drew Ali's Moorish Science Temple (founded in 1925) and the Nation of Islam (founded in 1930). Though these new sects were heterodox in nature, they were instrumental in building community across racial and sectarian lines, especially in the Great Migration cities of the upper Midwest.[21] The long history of Islam in the United States, then, is one that is deeply entwined with the African American experience.

If white Americans did not learn about Islam from enslaved people, they did learn about it through their own experiences. European Christians and North African and Ottoman Muslims came into extended contact with one another in the context of warfare, violence, piracy, enslavement, and travel. The English privateer and adventurer Francis Drake carried some enslaved Turks away with him after his siege of Cartagena de Indias in 1586. ("Turk" was an all-purpose English descriptor of any Muslim person from North Africa or the Ottoman East.) One of these men, a Turk named Chinano, converted to Christianity before the English sent him back to Constantinople, where they hoped he would facilitate conversions from Islam to Christianity (their hopes were unfounded). The way the

English treated Chinano displayed both their discomfort with Muslims (Meredith Hanmer, the minister who baptized him, referred to him as "the silly Turk") and their sense that their English Protestantism had acquired a rival.[22]

Englishmen saw Islam as a threat and competitor for one simple reason: English sailors, merchants, mercenaries, and travelers in the Mediterranean were under constant risk of being captured, enslaved, and converted to Islam. An estimated one million Europeans were enslaved between 1400 and 1800 in North Africa and the Ottoman Empire, and some of these people (mostly men) converted to Islam in order to gain their freedom. Others hoped that relatives would ransom them (they wrote letters to family and charitable organizations in England, often at the insistence of their owners, in hopes of redemption).[23] North African piracy threatened American shores as well; in 1690, Virginia resident Daniel Tyler was reported "unhappily taken by the Turkes & carryed to Algeir [Algiers] & hath not for at least 7 years past been heard of soe that he is esteemed dead."[24] Tyler's disappearance into slavery was not at all unusual among European sailors; in 1622, English sailor John Rawlins found himself enslaved in Algiers as well. In an eerie mirror image of what enslaved African Muslims must have experienced in the New World, Rawlins wrote of his experience in captivity: "We had heavy hearts and looked with sad countenances, yet many came to behold us, sometimes taking us by the hand, sometimes turning us round about, sometimes feeling our browns [muscles] and naked arms, and so beholding prices written in our breasts, they bargained for us accordingly, and at last we were sold."[25] Unlike Daniel Tyler, Rawlins made it back to England and was able to tell his story. The experience of captivity defined Islam for early modern Europeans.[26]

William Strachey, a Virginia colonist, used his experience as a clerk for the Levant Company in Constantinople to draw comparisons between Ottoman Muslims and native North Americans. Some of Strachey's observations were relatively neutral. He noted, "[t]heir [the Indians'] drinck is (as the Turkes) cleere water," and "they [the Indians] spredd a Matt (as the Turks doe a carpet) for him [a werowance] to sit upon."[27] Strachey's comparisons were less sanguine when discussing Indians' marital habits. Strachey wrote that Wahunsonacock, the paramount chief of Tidewater Virginia, followed a polygamous practice, but did not keep all his wives "as the Turke in one Saraglia or howse." He also theorized that these "sensual helpes (as the Turkes)" weakened the Indians' body politic.[28] Though

Strachey used other comparisons as well (describing a game young Indian boys played as similar to one described in Virgil, for example), Islam was more than merely another point of reference for him. Strachey's experience of Islam in the Ottoman Empire was both an idiom for comprehending the strangeness of native people and a way of expressing disdain for native customs, such as polygamy, that the English knew of primarily from Muslim countries.

Islam operated in English discourses about the New World generally as a point of negative comparison. Between the seventeenth and nineteenth centuries, the Islamic world occupied a key place in Anglo-American polemics against political tyranny, seemingly senseless violence, slavery, and other questionable practices. Timothy Marr has called this practice, present in Strachey's writings, "Islamicism"—an orientalism that both described the "intractable difference" of Islam while simultaneously upholding Anglo-American identity.[29] The identification of political violence and tyranny with Islamic practice generally and Muslim peoples in particular is thus a centuries-long rhetorical tradition. For example, one late seventeenth-century account of Bacon's Rebellion described the rebel Englishman Nathaniel Bacon as "lookeing as demurely as the great Turks Muftie, at the reading [of] some holy sentence, extracted forth of the Alchron [Koran]." The writer of this particular polemic also referred to Bacon's followers as "Janissaries" and Bacon himself as "in imitation of the great Sultan."[30] The anonymous writer knew his readers would understand the insult intended by comparing Bacon to the Ottoman Sultan and his followers to the famous slave-soldiers of the Ottoman Empire. To call a political opponent "Turkish" was to intimate both tyranny and the potential for violence.

Using Islamicist comparisons became an effective way of critiquing American society, especially Americans' attachment to slavery. Writing in 1790 and shortly before his death, Benjamin Franklin's final satire, in the tradition of Silence Dogood, examined the United States' affection for slavery and the slave trade from the perspective of a North African sultan. In the voice of the fictional Muslim leader, Franklin asked,

> If we cease our cruises against the Christians, how shall we be furnished with the commodities their countries produce, and which are so necessary for us? If we forbear to make slaves of their people, who in this hot climate are to cultivate our lands? Who are to perform the common labors of our city, and in our families? Must we

not then be our own slaves? And is there not more compassion and more favor due to us as Musselmen than to these Christian dogs?[31]

Franklin even satirized the oft-used argument that enslavement benefited the enslaved by bringing them to Christianity: "Here they are brought into a land where the sun of Islamism gives forth its light, and shines in full splendor, and they have an opportunity of making themselves acquainted with the true doctrine, and thereby saving their immortal souls."[32] By asking white Americans to imagine their own enslavement at the hands of Muslims they already believed to be political and religious despots, Franklin exposed slavery as an institution more appropriately associated with a religious and cultural Other than with liberty-loving Americans. Though his was an effective rhetorical gesture, Franklin also reinforced the long-standing association of Islam and tyranny. American Islamicism was thus a complicated interplay of actual human experiences with the Muslim Other and rumor, stereotypes, and the ever-present threat of violence.

In the nineteenth century, Americans used Islamicist discourses to understand Thomas Jefferson's wars with the North African states. While many Americans saw military actions against Tripoli and Algiers as necessary responses to despotic and piratical Muslim states, they were also interested in viewing North African Muslims. As Abd al-Rahman would be displayed a few decades later to satisfy American Islamicist curiosity, so too were Tripolitan prisoners of war displayed in New York City theaters in 1805.[33] American prisoners in Tripoli were similarly displayed there, and newspaper reports carried descriptions of the prison in which some Americans were confined: it was "black and dreary . . . more fit to be the abode of demons, than of mortals."[34] Though the United States eventually claimed victory in its wars with North African states, these conflicts reinforced narratives of captivity and political tyranny that had circulated in the Anglophone Atlantic since the seventeenth century.

Nineteenth-century American observers of Islam linked their understanding of a politically tyrannical Islam to an emergent idea of Islam that was also tyrannical in the home, especially to women, emphasizing the strangeness of sexuality and femininity in Muslim states. Nineteenth-century plays and other fictional works show an intense fascination with both political tyranny and the mythology of the harem. American fascination with Muslim women translated into a "near consensus that Muslim women [were] oppressed, and by Islam specifically, and that they [could] be saved only by outside intervention."[35] Over the course of the nineteenth century, the American missionary presence in the Middle East focused their commentary on the status of Muslim women, creating and reinforcing an idea of Islam as a fundamental antithesis to American Christian femininity.

Of particular (and often prurient) interest was the Muslim practice of polygamy, which Americans saw as both an invitation to political tyranny and an intentional oppression of women.[36] Nowhere was this more apparent than in the American critiques of the Latter-day Saints (Mormons). One commentator wrote, "Turkey is in our midst. Modern Mohammedanism has its Mecca at Salt Lake, where Prophet Heber C. Kimball speaks of his wives as 'cows.' Clearly the Koran was Joseph Smith's model, so closely followed as to exclude even the poor pretension of originality of his foul 'revelations.' "[37] Seeing Mormons, who practiced polygamy until 1890, as American "Muslims" was part and parcel of the nineteenth-century critique of the Latter-day Saints and of Islam. Critics charged the Latter-day Saints with tyrannical despotism and misogyny, thus effectively creating Mormons as infidels who were just as decadent and theologically bankrupt as Muslims. While Americans had difficulty seeing enslaved Muslims in their midst, they had no such trouble understanding Islam as inherently tyrannical or misogynistic—two tropes that persist in the twenty-first century.

Though the numbers of Muslim immigrants to the United States remained low through the first half of the twentieth century, small communities of Muslims formed their own American Islamic faith in pockets around the country. It was not until after Lyndon Baines Johnson signed the Hart-Celler Act in 1965 that larger numbers of Muslims immigrated to the United States from Asia, Africa, and the Middle East.[38] Though there was some anxiety over the presence of new Muslim Americans during the Iranian Revolution, for the most part these communities remained unremarkable to other Americans until after September 11, 2001. In the post-9/11 atmosphere of suspicion, both the denial of Islam's long history in the Americas and the equally long Islamicist tradition of American understandings of Islam and Muslims as inherently violent, tyrannical, and misogynistic came together to create new and deeply damaging Islamophobic discourses.

After his emergence as a serious candidate for the presidency, Barack Obama became a focal point for American commentary on Islam. The Reverend Franklin Graham, son of the famed evangelist Billy Graham, remarked to CNN's John King, "I think the president's problem is that he was born a Muslim, his father was a Muslim. The seed of Islam is passed through the father like the seed of Judaism is passed through the mother. He was born a Muslim, his father gave him an Islamic name." Though Graham later backpedaled, claiming he had no reason to believe Obama was not in fact Christian, some of Graham's prior comments about Islam were also controversial. In December 2009 Graham told CNN that "true Islam cannot be practiced in this country [the United States]. You can't beat your wife. You cannot murder your children if you think they've com-mitted adultery or something like that, which they do practice in these other countries." Graham echoed nineteenth-century critiques of Islam as misogynistic and violent. Graham's comments, coming as they did from a well-known and mainstream evangelical leader, also gave voice to reservations that many Americans had about Obama's religious beliefs even as they frightened Muslim Americans.[39] Graham's comments are certainly not unique and are deeply rooted in a thoroughly American dis-course on Islam that is not limited to one end or the other of the political spectrum.[40] Both American liberals and conservative evangelicals share a penchant for ahistorical engagement with Islam that centers on critiques rooted in shared notions about Islam as inherently violent, misogynistic, anti-American, and anti-Christian.

One of the key problems in understanding American attitudes toward Islam and Muslims is that there is a general reluctance to recognize that Muslim Americans are often the victims of racial animus. This reluc-tance stems from a belief that religious affiliation is a voluntary, cultural attribute, whereas racial identity is not a choice but an uncontrollable quirk of biology.[41] Yet religion and race have historically been intricately entwined categories.[42] Ideas about the heritability and immutability of religious belief and belonging formed in the early modern period, but their power and longevity echo uncomfortably in the early twenty-first century. When Graham comments on the "seed of Islam" as a heritable, unchangeable quality, he is attaching modern Islamophobic discourses to intellectual genealogies of religion and race that extend centuries into the American past.

Most anti-Muslim comments are invariably accompanied by protesta-tions that such comments are not racist. If we define Islamophobia as a form of racism that not only encourages irrational fears about Muslims but also insists that all or most Muslims are adherents of a violent, misog-ynistic religion, then comments such as Graham's reflect American

Islamicist discourses dating back to the early modern period. Comments about spousal abuse, misogyny, honor killings, genital mutilation, the heritability of Islam, and the sincerity of converts point to a conflation of religion and race intended to convince Americans that Muslims are fundamentally and irredeemably un-American. In some ways these discourses would be familiar to eighteenth- and nineteenth-century Americans, who understood Islam as dangerously tyrannical. But the events of September 11 fundamentally altered this familiar critique from one that was Islamicist to one that is Islamophobic. Barack Obama thus became a focal point of Islamophobic commentary in the United States. This is a discourse that denies the actual existence and complex histories of Muslim Americans, an erasure that especially marginalizes the experiences of African American Muslims in slavery and freedom. Much of this discourse racializes religious affiliation, allowing modern American commentators across the political spectrum to describe Islam and Muslims as irredeemably violent, tyrannical, misogynistic, and above all, unable to be truly American. This kind of rhetoric has a long history, as we have seen, but it has had the effect of marginalizing and "othering" Muslim Americans. Reconstituting marginalized Muslim Americans as critically important parts of the American narrative would transform the nation's origin stories and Americans' sense of who belongs in this American space.

Notes

The author would like to thank Manan Ahmed Asif, Gaiutra Bahadur, Edward J. Blum, Benedikt Brunner, Darren Dochuk, Salman Adil Hussain, Charles Irons, and Matthew Sutton for their comments on this essay.

1. Kambiz GhaneaBassiri, *A History of Islam in America* (Cambridge: Cambridge University Press, 2010), 2, n. 2. GhaneaBassiri's book is the best one-volume history of Islam and Muslims in America currently available.
2. Hjamil A. Martínez-Vásquez, *Latina/o y Musulmán: The Construction of Latina/o Identity among Latina/o Muslims in the United States* (Eugene, OR: Pickwick Press, 2010).
3. Matt Apuzo and Joseph Goldstein, "New York Drops Unit that Spied on Muslims," *New York Times*, April 15, 2014, http://www.nytimes.com/2014/04/16/nyregion/police-unit-that-spied-on-muslims-is-disbanded.html?_r=0.
4. See especially Moustapha Bayoumi, *How Does It Feel to Be a Problem? Being Young and Arab in America* (New York: Penguin Books, 2009).

5. Andrés Reséndez, *A Land So Strange: The Epic Journey of Cabeza de Vaca* (New York: Basic Books, 2007), 55–56.

6. Rolena Adorno and Patrick Charles Pautz, eds., *Alvar Núñez Cabeza de Vaca: His Account, His Life, and the Expedition of Pánfilo de Narváez* (Lincoln: University of Nebraska Press, 1999), II, 17. Cabeza de Vaca also noted that a prophecy by a Muslim woman in Hornachos, Spain, predicted the failure of the expedition. I, 273, n. 3; 274–275.

7. Michael A. Gomez, *Exchanging Our Country Marks: The Transformation of African Identities in the Colonial and Antebellum South* (Chapel Hill and London: University of North Carolina Press, 1998), 67.

8. Michael A. Gomez, "Muslims in Early America," *Journal of Southern History* 60, no. 4 (November 1994): 671–710.

9. The "invisible institution" was a phrase coined by the historian Albert J. Raboteau in his seminal book *Slave Religion: The "Invisible Institution" in the Antebellum South* (New York: Oxford University Press, 1978).

10. Edward E. Curtis IV, *Muslims in America: A Short History* (Oxford and New York: Oxford University Press, 2009), 14. Kidd agrees on this point; see Thomas S. Kidd, *American Christians and Islam: Evangelical Culture and Muslims from the Colonial Period to the Age of Terrorism* (Princeton, NJ: Princeton University Press, 2008), 1.

11. Sylviane Diouf, *Servants of Allah: African Muslims Enslaved in the Americas*, 15th anniversary edition (New York and London: New York University Press, 2013). For her discussion of the demographic problems, see 68–70; on Islam as a diasporic religion, see 6.

12. Curtis 6–10; Jill Lepore, *A is for American: Letters and Other Characters in the Newly United States* (New York: Alfred A. Knopf, 2002), 111–112.

13. "Norfolk Colonization Society," Richmond Inquirer [Virginia], January 15, 1829, 3.

14. Ala Alryyes, "'Arabic Work,' Islam, and American Literature," in *A Muslim American Slave: The Life of Omar Ibn Said*, edited by Ala Alryyes (Madison: The University of Wisconsin Press, 2011), 3–46.

15. Jason Young, "African Religions in the Early South," *Journal of Southern Religion* 14 (2012), http://jsr.fsu.edu/issues/vol14/young.html.

16. Gomez, *Country Marks*, 68–70.

17. Paul E. Lovejoy, *Transformations in Slavery: A History of Slavery in Africa*, 2nd ed. (Cambridge: Cambridge University Press, 2000), 191–225; Diouf, 53–55; Gomez, *Country Marks*, 65–66.

18. Quoted in Raboteau, 47.

19. Diouf, 186–191. There has been some suggestion that enslaved Muslims thought of their rebellion as a jihad. Diouf, 13; João José Reis, *Slave Rebellion in Brazil: The Muslim Uprising of 1835 in Bahia*, translated by Arthur Brakel (Baltimore: Johns Hopkins University Press, 1995).

20. Edward J. Blyden, *Christianity, Islam and the Negro Race (1887)*, edited by Christopher Fyfe (Edinburgh: University of Edinburgh Press, 1967), 11–12.

21. Sally Howell, *Old Islam in Detroit: Rediscovering the Muslim American Past* (New York: Oxford University Press, 2014). For a brief overview of African American Islamic movements, see Curtis, 29–44; see also Edward E. Curtis, *Islam in Black America: Identity, Liberation, and Difference in African American Islamic Thought* (Albany: State University of New York Press, 2002), and Michael Gomez, *Black Crescent: The Experience and Legacy of African Muslims in the Americas* (Cambridge: Cambridge University Press, 2005).

22. On Chinano, see Rebecca Anne Goetz, *The Baptism of Early Virginia: How Christianity Created Race* (Baltimore: Johns Hopkins University Press, 2012), 18; Nabil Matar, *Turks, Moors, and Englishmen in the Age of Discovery* (New York: Columbia University Press, 1999), 21; on Islam as a threat to Christianity, see Kidd, xii. "Christians have long seen Islam as one of their major competitors—sometimes their primary competitor—for souls on the global stage."

23. Nabil Matar, "England and Mediterranean Captivity, 1577–1704," in *Piracy, Slavery, and Redemption: Barbary Captivity Narratives from Early Modern England*, edited by Daniel J. Vitkus (New York: Columbia University Press, 1999), 21. Matar notes that some Britons felt lucky to have been in Turkish hands, because French, Spanish, and Italian galleys were often considered worse—conversion would not result in freedom, nor did families back home organize to redeem captives who remained in European hands.

24. York County Court Records [Virginia], vol. VIII, fol. 441–442, May 26, 1690, "Daniell Tyler Taken by ye Turkes."

25. John Rawlins, *The Famous and Wonderful Recovery of a Ship of Bristol, Called the Exchange, from the Turkish Pirates of Argier [Algiers]* (London, 1622) reproduced in Vitkus, ed., 103.

26. Lisa Voigt, *Writing Captivity in the Early Modern Atlantic: Circulations of Knowledge and Authority in the Iberian and English Imperial Worlds* (London and Chapel Hill: University of North Carolina Press, 2009), 47.

27. William Strachey, *The Historie of Travell into Virginia Britania (1612)*, edited by Louis B. Wright and Virginia Freund (London: The Hakluyt Society, 1953), 81, 84.

28. Ibid., 61, 116.

29. Timothy Marr, *The Cultural Roots of American Islamicism* (Cambridge: Cambridge University Press, 2006), 9.

30. [John and/or Ann Cotton], [*The History of Bacon's and Ingram's Rebellion, 1675–1676*], Virginia Historical Society, Mss2 C8295 a 1.

31. Benjamin Franklin writing as Historicus, *The Federal Gazette*, March 23, 1790, in *A Benjamin Franklin Reader*, edited by Walter Isaacson (New York: Simon and Schuster, 2003), 372–376.

32. Ibid., 374.
33. Robert J. Allison, *The Crescent Obscured: The United States and the Muslim World, 1776–1815* (New York and Oxford: Oxford University Press, 1995), xv, xvi, 33.
34. Quoted in Allison, 117.
35. Elora Shehabuddin, "Gender and the Figure of the 'Moderate Muslim': Feminism in the Twenty-First Century," in *The Question of Gender: Joan W. Scott's Critical Feminism*, edited by Judith Butler and Elizabeth Weed (Bloomington: Indiana University Press, 2011), 102–142; quote on 105.
36. Marr, 187.
37. Frances Willard quoted in Marr, 207. See also J. Spencer Fluhman, *"A Peculiar People": Anti-Mormonism and the Making of Religion in Nineteenth-Century America* (Chapel Hill and London: The University of North Carolina Press, 2011) and Fluhman's essay in this volume.
38. See Curtis, *Muslims in America*, 47–71.
39. "Graham: Obama Born a Muslim, Now a Christian," CNN Politics, August 19, 2010, http://politicalticker.blogs.cnn.com/2010/08/19/graham-obama-born-a-muslim-now-a-christian/. Graham was not alone among American evangelicals in his opinions about Islam. Many other evangelical leaders have espoused similar ideas. See, for example, Nathan Lean, *The Islamophobia Industry: How the Right Manufactures Fear of Muslims* (London: Pluto Press, 2012), esp. 79–118. For a look at the complicated ways in which American evangelicals think about Islam, see Kidd, *American Christians and Islam*. As Kidd notes, many evangelicals have used the terror attacks of September 11, 2001, to both critique Islam and renew evangelizing efforts.
40. On this point, see Deepa Kumar, "Islamophobia: A Bipartisan Project," *The Nation*, July 2, 2012, http://www.thenation.com/article/168695/islamophobia-bipartisan-project#.
41. On this problem generally, see Nasar Meer and Tariq Modood, "Refutations of Racism in the 'Muslim Question,'" *Patterns of Prejudice* 43, nos. 3–4 (2009): 335–354.
42. On this point, see Goetz, *The Baptism of Early Virginia*; George M. Fredrickson, *Racism: A Short History* (Princeton, NJ: Princeton University Press, 2002); Junaid Rana, *Terrifying Muslims: Race and Labor in the South Asian Diaspora* (Durham and London: Duke University Press, 2011).

II

Policy

6

From Drone War to Indian War

PROTECTING (AND LIBERATING) INNOCENT WOMEN AND CHILDREN

Jennifer Graber

Questionnaire

by Wendell Berry

> *How much poison are you willing*
> *to eat for the success of the free*
> *market and global trade? Please*
> *name your preferred poisons.*
>
> *For the sake of goodness, how much*
> *evil are you willing to do?*
> *Fill in the following blanks*
> *with the names of your favorite*
> *evils and acts of hatred.*
>
> *What sacrifices are you prepared*
> *to make for culture and civilization?*
> *Please list the mountains, shrines,*
> *and works of art you would*
> *most willingly destroy.*
>
> *In the name of patriotism and*
> *the flag, how much of our beloved*
> *land are you willing to desecrate?*
> *List in the following spaces*

the mountains, rivers, towns, farms
you could most readily do without.

State briefly the ideas, ideals, or hopes,
the energy sources, the kinds of security;
for which you would kill a child.
Name, please, the children whom
you would be willing to kill.[1]

"Name, please, the children"

Noor Aziz, eight years old; Abdul Wasit, seventeen years old; Noor Syed, eight years old. So begins a list of Pakistani and Yemeni children killed by American drones since the beginning of the War on Terror.[2] The list contains 118 names. It includes two Yemeni girls, Khadije Ali Mokbel Louqye and Shafiq Hussein Abdullah Awad, both of whom were one year old when they died as a result of US drone strikes.

In April 2013, religious studies professor and progressive Muslim leader Omid Safi published an essay about children killed in contemporary global conflicts.[3] He reflected on the Boston Marathon bombing and its youngest victim, eight-year-old Martin Richard. Safi argued that Americans who grieved Richard's death shared feelings of anger and pain with parents of children killed by American drone strikes. At the end of his piece, Safi named the marathon bombing's three victims along with the 118 Pakistani and Yemeni children. Worried that Americans failed to sympathize with foreign civilians harmed by drone attacks, Safi wondered, "How do we urge our fellow Americans to expand the circle of their concern, and see our suffering HERE as being connected to the suffering THERE?"

While Safi is right about failures to recognize certain situations of global suffering, he also overlooks Americans' historic concern for foreign women and children. Since the founding era, Americans have decried rumors of infanticide and foot binding in China, widow burning in India, harems in the Middle East, and abandoned orphans in Central America.[4] They have also expressed concern for the "foreigners" within US boundaries, including Native American women in nomadic encampments and immigrant children working in urban factories.[5] Americans have long argued that foreign women's and children's situations demand not only attention and sympathy but also saving action.

Literary critic Amy Kaplan has called this saving impulse "imperial domesticity."[6] In her study of antebellum home manuals and magazines, Kaplan found that female writers focused on problems besetting women and children around the world. These writers offered civilizing visions of domestic life to the "savages" in the United States and abroad.[7] To extend Kaplan's argument, I contend that the discourse of imperial domesticity is especially powerful in times of war. Because women and children are typically considered noncombatants during conflict, both supporters and opponents of various wars have argued for their protection. At the same time, articulations of imperial domesticity affirm that foreign women and children lead troubled lives and require liberation from their male relations and religious cultures. For example, when First Lady Laura Bush stepped in to offer the presidential weekly radio address soon after the 2001 invasion of Afghanistan, she articulated her concern for Afghani women and girls.[8] This concern, however, was not limited to their protection. Drawing her speech to a close, Mrs. Bush argued, "The fight against terrorism is also a fight for the rights and dignity of women." Her statement reflected much wartime rhetoric, which typically blends calls for protecting women and children with appeals for liberating them from uncivilized domestic systems.

Religious leaders and representatives, who often invest both American warfare and the nation's regard for women and children with moral meaning, have played an important role in blurring the lines between calls for protection and projects of liberation. Analysis of two historical situations—nineteenth-century Indian wars and President Obama's drone policy—reveals how public religious figures have, perhaps unconsciously, obscured the difference between protection and liberation. Their discourse classifies Native American and Muslim women and children as innocents who desire liberation from their hostile, extremist, or terrorist male relations.[9]

Indian Wars: Civilian Causalities and Domestic Sensibilities

In November 1864, Colonel John Chivington led his Colorado militia troops to the edge of a Cheyenne and Arapaho encampment along Sand Creek in the southeastern part of the territory. In what became one of the most infamous attacks by American armed forces on an unsuspecting

Indian community, Chivington's men killed scores of women, children, and elderly members of Black Kettle's Cheyenne band.[10] In defense of the "battle," Chivington later testified that the attack punished Indians who resisted American authority and preyed upon innocent white people. He also suggested that his soldiers killed "but few" women and children.[11]

Some of Chivington's men disagreed. In a letter to his mother, militia captain Silas Soule offered gruesome details about the Sand Creek attack. "I was present at a Massacre of three hundred Indians mostly women and children. It was a horrible scene and I would not let my Company fire."[12] While soldiers under Soule's command held back, others inflicted brutal assaults on occupants of the Indian encampment. Soule, who emerged as one of Chivington's primary opponents in the Sand Creek investigations, wrote to his mother, "It looked too hard for me to see little children on their knees begging for their lives, to have their brains beat out like dogs."

The timing of Chivington's attack at Sand Creek mattered. It occurred toward the end of the American Civil War and after an 1863 Union Army order that reframed the way American military officials considered violence against civilians. To be sure, theorists of war had long debated how belligerents distinguished between their armed enemies, their enemies' supporters, and those members of an enemy's citizenry who played no part in conflicts.[13] In December 1862, just as the Union was about to initiate hard war against the Confederacy, President Lincoln commissioned a new code of war conduct.[14]

Franz Lieber, a German-American scholar and an appointee to Lincoln's committee, formulated a theory of warfare to address the ethical concerns raised by ongoing Union-Confederate engagements. As historian Harry Stout has observed, Lieber not only believed that soldiers were "moral beings" accountable to God, but he also had three sons fighting for the Union.[15] In April 1863, Lincoln signed Lieber's code into military law. While much of the document concerns enemy belligerents, it included a section on noncombatants. "The citizen or native of a hostile country is thus an enemy ... and as such is subjected to the hardships of war," the code affirms. Nevertheless, advances in "civilization" have made for "the distinction between the private individual belonging to a hostile country and the hostile country itself, with its men in arms."[16] As a result, Lieber's code demanded that the "unarmed citizen is to be spared in person, property, and honor as much as the exigencies of war will admit."[17]

While establishing the priority of protecting civilians, Lieber's code also included a clause about "military necessity." Securing the ends of war sometimes demanded targeting not only armed enemies but also "other persons whose destruction is incidentally unavoidable."[18] While Lieber renounced inflicting suffering for its own sake or to fulfill vengeful desires, the doctrine of military necessity gave Union commanders discretion to work around mandates for civilian protection.

Historians debate the effects of Lieber's code on Union engagements in the South as well as its impact in Indian country.[19] Conflicts between Americans and Indians were often brutal. Americans invoked Native Americans' racial and cultural differences, as well as their different warfare practices, to justify attacks that inadvertently resulted in women and children causalities. Even so, the commitment to civilian protection as detailed in Lieber's code reflected many Americans' concerns for protecting innocents caught up in war. Responses to Sand Creek revealed the strength of these convictions.

Within days of Chivington's attack, critics raised questions. Leaders of Christian organizations, as well as journalists for religious periodicals, called for a congressional investigation. While religious leaders were hardly the only citizens protesting Chivington's actions, they were singular in the way they theologized his offense. For example, when Colorado governor John Evans published a report claiming that Chivington's troops "indiscriminately slaughtered" every Cheyenne from "sucking babe to the old warrior," a Presbyterian paper out of New York reprinted it under the headline: "Indians Murdered By Our Troops: National Sins That Demand Punishment."[20]

The Chivington attack galvanized many religious leaders in the east. Over the next decades, Sand Creek came to symbolize American assaults on innocent Indian women and children. Quaker writer Gideon Frost, an avid voice in Indian affairs, argued that General Sherman's post-Civil War attacks on Indians were hardly different from Chivington's.[21] Catholic writers bemoaned an ongoing relationship with Indians modeled on Chivington, who "butchered" hundreds of Indians, "nearly all of them being women and children."[22] A writer for a Methodist paper compared an 1870 massacre of Piegan Indians to Chivington's attack.[23] To be sure, their opponents countered with stories of Indians attacking American women and children. Writers in the religious press acknowledged these attacks but typically attributed them to failed federal policies and brutal actions by overland emigrants.

This willingness to condemn US offenses while contextualizing
Indian ones reflected many Americans' sense that they, unlike Native
Americans, were civilized enough to refrain from killing innocent
bystanders.[24] Indeed, moral and immoral forms of warfare were considered markers of civilized and uncivilized societies respectively. So were
domestic ideals and gender norms. As historians and literary critics have
noted, Americans circulated many images of indigenous women, such
as the helpful Pocahontas, the savage mother, the promiscuous "squaw,"
and the domestic slave.[25] Stories of overworked Indian women married
to indolent men confirmed Americans' notions that native wives longed
for freedom from their savage husbands.[26] An 1852 article on Indians in
California affirmed that Indian women were "patient, laboring, and willing slaves" to Indian men, whose only responsibilities included hunting,
smoking, drinking, and killing white people.[27]

Missionaries to American Indians and their sponsors employed this
rhetoric of female degradation when they emphasized the domestic potential of converted Indian women. Jedidiah Morse, the foremost Christian
opponent of Cherokee removal in the late 1820s, argued that Indian
societies required conversion and civilization so that the Indian woman
could "rise into her high distinction and shine out in all her loveliness,
heaven's best gift to man."[28] Baptist missionaries celebrated Cherokee convert Catherine Brown's ongoing transition from uneducated heathen to a
"model of white Christian womanhood."[29] As historian Louise Michele
Newman has observed, white commentators articulated what they
believed was an egalitarian vision that included Indian women, although
this equality could only be realized "in the future" after Indian societies
changed and gender norms had been realigned.[30]

In the nineteenth century, writers in the religious press focused on
Indian women as they articulated concerns about noncombatants and
desires to transform Indian cultures. To be sure, some critics of violence
that failed to discriminate between Indian combatants and noncombatants emphasized other issues, such as the cost of ongoing military campaigns in the West or the damage such attacks did to efforts at treaty
making. Even so, religious leaders and writers declared that Chivington's
destruction of women and children failed to meet America's moral standards for warfare. This particular concern emerged in the midst of a
wider cultural conversation that imagined Indian women as "friendlies"
requiring rescue from the fathers and husbands who resisted American
expansion and held to uncivilized domestic arrangements.[31]

Drones in Afghanistan and Pakistan: Civilian Causalities and Domestic Sensibilities

Fourteen-year-old Faheem described the moment after a drone-fired missile slammed into the North Waziristan home he was visiting. "I felt my brain stopped working and my heart was on fire."[32] After stumbling out of the burning home, Faheem was rescued by neighbors who took him to the hospital. He suffered a skull fracture, as well as wounds and burns across his body. He lost his left eye. In coverage of the attack, American journalists differed, reporting anywhere from five to eleven civilian casualties.[33]

Reports about President Obama's reaction to the strike, which occurred just days after his January 2009 inauguration, also varied.[34] Journalist Bob Woodward claimed that Obama endorsed the action, even though it had not reached its intended "high-value target." Woodward said that Obama called the strike useful because "at least five Al Qaeda militants died."[35] On the other hand, political correspondent Daniel Klaidman wrote that Obama was "disturbed" and interrogated counterterrorism officials when he was informed that the strike not only missed its main target but also killed civilians, including two children.

These conflicting accounts reveal the tension at the heart of Obama's drone policy. Inheriting the War on Terror from his predecessor, the president faced immense pressure to cripple al-Qaeda while simultaneously ending American presence in Afghanistan and Iraq. Americans, as well as citizens around the globe, expected Obama to repair US relations with the wider Muslim world. Obama thus has been charged to make war on particular enemies in particularly difficult places while not only protecting the neighboring noncombatants from harm but also finding ways to befriend them.

Despite drone defenders' emphasis on the weapon's capacity for precision targeting and keeping American soldiers out of harm's way, Obama's expanded drone program has generated criticism from many corners. Perhaps no aspect of US drone policy has provoked more concern than civilian causalities. Many citizens, including religious leaders and writers in the religious press, invoke law of war principles as well as just war theory to argue that high numbers of civilian casualties demand that the drone program be radically altered if not ended altogether.

Agreed upon by a large portion of the international community, contemporary law of war includes principles related to declaring war as well as wartime conduct. One of these principles, necessity, requires that wartime actions must be directed at military targets and have the enemy's defeat as the primary goal. The law of war also provides for distinction, directing belligerents to differentiate between combatants and civilians. Finally, law of war addresses proportionality, mandating that any harm done to civilians not exceed the positive goal accomplished by a strategy or action.[36]

Like his predecessor, President Obama has invoked law of war principles in his discussion of the War on Terror generally and drones specifically. In 2013, the Department of Justice issued a white paper addressing questions about drone strikes targeting US citizens associated with al-Qaeda. While most of the paper considered due process, the writers also noted that drone strikes would be "conducted in a manner consistent with applicable law of war principles."[37] Anticipating the possibility that strikes might harm noncombatants, the writers stated, "It would not be consistent with [law of war] principles to continue an operation if anticipated civilian casualties would be excessive in relation to the anticipated military advantage."

While law of war principles have developed within the international community over the course of the twentieth century, they overlap with the centuries-old Christian tradition of just war theory. The fourth-century theologian Augustine articulated some of these principles, which the Dominican theologian Thomas Aquinas systematized in the thirteenth century. According to Aquinas, just wars are waged by rightful authorities and are fought with the goal of restoring peace. Christian theologians have continued to interpret just war tradition, eventually settling on two sets of principles. These include *jus ad bellum*, or criterion for going to war, and *jus in bello*, or measures for wartime conduct. Some *jus in bello* criteria—including necessity, distinction, and proportionality—eventually were accepted by the international community as part of the law of war.

In his public discussions of drones, President Obama has evoked not only law of war principles but also language from the just war tradition.[38] In a speech at the National Defense University in May 2013, Obama noted that all warfare involves moral questions about the potential for civilian casualties. Obama insisted that drone strikes could be undertaken only if there was "near-certainty that no civilians would be killed or injured." Despite this "highest standard" for strikes, Obama acknowledged civilian deaths due to American drone strikes in Pakistan and Yemen. These haunting losses, Obama argued, were necessary as the United States worked to reduce the civilian casualties that would result if terrorist networks operated without restriction. The use of drones in the War on Terror, Obama declared, could be considered part of a "just war—a war waged proportionally, in last resort, and in self-defense." Considering the requirements of *jus in bello*, Obama argued that drone use is proportional given the threat to other civilians if drones were not used to strike high-profile targets. Obama focused on necessity and proportionality in his speech, but he left the principle of distinction unmentioned.

Distinguishing civilians and combatants has been particularly difficult for those involved in the drone program. The January 2009 strike that injured Faheem is illustrative. In the days after the attack, the *Washington Post* reported that the strike targeted "suspected terrorist hideouts" and that at least ten insurgents had been killed.[39] Critics of the War on Terror and the drone program responded in earnest. *Harper's Magazine* writer Ken Silverstein suggested just months after the 2009 strike that the drone program's secrecy was being used "to hide abuses and high civilian casualties."[40]

The years 2009 through 2014 witnessed continued criticism of Obama's drone policy in major US news outlets. A 2010 *Atlantic* cover story noted the legal issues and secrecy concerns about drones but argued that civilian casualties constituted the drone's major drawback.[41] Several writers in secular outlets made moral arguments against the weapon's use. Writing in a 2011 issue of the *Atlantic*, Joshua Foust argued that "sloppiness and ignorance" allowed drone strikes to harm too many civilians and constituted a "substantial moral failing."[42] In 2013, Kenneth Roth of Human Rights Watch claimed that US drones harmed civilians in violation of the Geneva Convention.[43] Roth's piece emerged in a spring 2013 news cycle that featured bloody descriptions of children harmed by drones.[44]

Religious leaders and writers in the religious press have spoken particularly loudly against drone strikes, giving a theological cast to widespread criticism about civilian casualties. Some of these protests have emerged from pacifist traditions that object to US warfare in all its forms.[45] More frequently, these writers identify with the just war tradition and employ its principles and language to criticize the drone program. One example is a 2013 anti-drone video prepared by Christian and Jewish leaders.[46] The video, which was publicized by news outlets such as Alternet and CNN's Beliefnet, featured analysis of the Department of Justice white paper on drones. Franciscan friar Joseph Nangle argued, "[The Obama] administration is using just war theory to justify immoral conduct, the use of drones."[47] Other leaders in the video claimed that drones violated just war principles of necessity, proportionality, and distinction. A 2010 editorial in *Christian Century*, a mainline Protestant periodical, argued that drones' record of killing so many civilians disqualified them as weapons allowed in a just war.[48] The tradition, the editorialists argued, requires that belligerents consider losing their own soldiers rather than put so many enemy civilians in harm's way.

Several religious bodies, with varied theological and political alignments, have also issued statements about civilian casualties and Obama's drone program. In May 2013, the US Conference of Catholic Bishops sent letters to several government officials stating that drone use and the "high risk of civilian causalities" required reassessment of US policy.[49] Bishop Richard Pates of Des Moines followed up the letters with his own statement that the high number of civilian causalities, especially children, "makes it difficult to justify targeted killings under Catholic 'just war' theory."[50] Concerned about drone use in Pakistan as a form of "unlawful killing," leaders of the moderate Disciples of Christ issued a resolution condemning drones' ability to "kill innocent civilians."[51] The National Black Church Initiative, a coalition of fifteen African American denominations, condemned Obama's drone policy for killing "morally innocent" people who happen to be near an intended target.[52]

Even religious leaders and writers who have expressed support for the War on Terror have criticized Obama's drone policy for its failure to meet the distinction mandate. As Lutheran theologian and just war advocate Daniel Bell argued in a roundtable published in the evangelical monthly, *Christianity Today*, drones could be employed ethically if their use was both "discriminating and proportionate."[53] Matthew Schmitz wrote in the neoconservative magazine *First Things* that many Jews and Christians have voiced concern about noncombatants, even as they accept drone warfare in principle.[54] Whether generally supportive of Obama and the War on Terror or not, religious leaders and writers from across a wide denominational and political spectrum have invoked the language of just war theory to register their concern about civilian casualties.

As in other times of conflict, conversations about civilized forms of warfare have paralleled considerations of the enemy's domestic patterns. Since the beginning of the War on Terror, Americans may have certainly debated the terms of civilized warfare, but they have hardly questioned American domestic arrangements and gender norms. The women of Afghanistan require not only protection from war but also liberation from their husbands and religious leaders. Americans tend to see Afghan women's problems not as having a political or cultural origin, but a religious one. The women's identification with Islam connects them with a long history of Western "obsession with the plight of Muslim women."[55]

While American observers have expressed concerns over issues ranging from girls' education to women's healthcare in the Muslim world, they focus especially on practices of dress and veiling. The burqa, or full body and face veil required by the Taliban, has particularly occupied Americans' imaginations. As discussions of the burqa became part of the debate about the War on Terror, Americans slipped easily back and forth between designations of women's political identity as Afghans and their religious identity as Muslims. George W. Bush, in his 2001 press conference on the invasion of Afghanistan, expressed his concern for the country's "women of cover," for whom Americans have shown "friendship and support."[56]

First Lady Laura Bush also moved back and forth between political and religious markers when she delivered her November 2001 radio address.[57] Mrs. Bush enumerated the harsh realities women faced under the Taliban in Afghanistan. Mothers, she insisted, could not leave their homes accompanied, suffered beatings for laughing out loud, and lived with threats of their fingernails being pulled out if they dared to wear nail polish. While Mrs. Bush acknowledged that Muslims around the world decried Taliban treatment of women, she also compared women's status in Afghanistan to "brutality against women and children by the al-Qaida terrorist network," which extended around the globe. The struggle to free women, then, expanded beyond central Asia to any place that terrorists aligned with Islam suppressed them. "The fight against terrorism," Mrs. Bush insisted, "is also a fight for the rights and dignity of women."[58]

While other voices echoed Mrs. Bush's concern about the burqa, American religious commentators were not necessarily among them. In fact, the debate as it is has played out in US religious publications has been surprisingly nuanced on the question of Muslim women's dress. As religious studies scholar Stephen Prothero has noted, American Christians' reticence to judge reflects their own concerns about government interference with religious expression.[59] In a *Christianity Today* roundtable discussion on burqa and veiling bans in Europe, for instance, Yale Divinity

School's Joseph Cumming emphasized the need to show love to others and to listen to Muslim women's voices about their veiling choices.[60] At the same time, Cumming and two other contributors questioned whether Islam actually requires veiling. By questioning the Quranic interpretations of presumably male Muslim leaders, these American Christians expressed their concern about forced veiling and "invisible" women without criticizing the women themselves or Islam as a religion. Muslim men were the problem.

This concern about imposition by male religious leaders can be seen elsewhere in *Christianity Today*. In 2014, the magazine featured an American female fighter pilot who refused to follow US Army stipulations to wear an abaya, a kind of head and body covering, while off base in Saudi Arabia.[61] The report celebrated her refusal and focused on the unyielding demands Saudi men impose on not only Saudi women but also American women inside their borders. The writers referred to the "wrath of Saudi religious police" and stated that women who refused the abaya might be beaten with sticks or stoned. In this way, these writers connected Muslims who insist on veiling with their wider concern over Muslim women's freedom and choices.[62] As anthropologist of religion Saba Mahmood has observed, Westerners presume that religious agency requires independence and freedom. They conclude that many Muslim women share this conception of agency but are connected to men who deny them the possibility of expressing their agency.[63]

Reflecting these assumptions about Muslim women's desire to be free religious agents, Christian periodicals have highlighted occasions, both in the United States and abroad, when Muslim women have engaged in activities that Americans view as independent and free. To be sure, these examples come from more liberal Christian magazines, but the range of Muslim women's activity they highlight is telling. Since September 11, 2001, *Christian Century* has run articles on an American Muslim woman who started her own modeling agency and the number of American Muslims who support mixed-gender dances.[64] *Sojourners Magazine* ran a photo spread of Muslim women Olympians before the 2012 games in London and celebrated a new Pakistani animated television show, "Burka Avenger," which features a schoolteacher by day who at night dons a tight black burqa—along with black nail polish—to fight for women's education against Taliban-like enemies.[65] These visions of the Muslim female highlight devout women who value American notions of beauty, freedom, bodily expression, education, and independence.

These depictions of Muslim women, as both living under male constraints and desiring liberation and the freedom to live out American notions of womanhood, have a long history. As religious studies scholar Tracy Fessenden has noted, antebellum American writers imagined transformations in which they could "subtly pry ... despotic Muslims away from the unifying energies of Islamic faith, now abstracted from its social and human contexts in order to be better assimilated to the strand of Protestant liberalism it inspires."[66] Examples of Civil War-era writing on Native American women reveal a similar impulse. Imperial domesticity has a long tradition in American life and appears in especially amplified forms during wartime.

Parallel to presentations of Indian women as quintessentially "friendly" during decades of Indian war, the War on Terror has also occasioned rhetoric portraying Muslim women, in contrast to their husbands and male religious leaders, as "good" Muslims. Religious leaders and writers in the religious press generally assume that Muslim women and children are not connected to armed resistance against the United States. They take for granted that these women and children desire liberation from the familial and cultural bonds that ensnare them. If they weren't forced to veil, they wouldn't. If they were allowed to wear nail polish, they would.

Conclusion

Even as religious leaders and writers in the religious press have argued for protecting civilians in wartime, they have also articulated the claims about protecting and liberating foreign women at the heart of imperial domesticity. In the 1860s, proponents of imperial domesticity not only criticized Major Chivington's attack on Indian civilians but also depicted Indian women as slaves to men who resisted America's inevitable expansion as well as civilized society's domestic norms. This imperial domesticity, although somewhat changed, has persisted among religious leaders and commentators, including those concerned about Obama's drone policy. Christian and Jewish leaders, especially those committed to just war principles and otherwise supportive of some aspects of the War on Terror, have criticized drone attacks because of their deadly impact on civilians. At the same time, they voice their concerns that Muslim men deny women freedom and girls education. The Taliban, of course, is their prime example. But the anxiety extends to all Muslim women who veil for fear that this practice is imposed upon them.

At the very least, the sentiments at the heart of imperial domesticity have unconsciously shaped arguments for protecting civilians—who are usually women and children—from war's destruction. I would argue that, at times, these sentiments have also kept Americans from recognizing the kinds of damage that American attacks have done to civilians, even if their bodies have been spared. Americans often recommend the complete transformation of the things that these endangered women and children hold dear. Resistance to this transformation invites destruction. By linking the work of protection with visions of liberation, Americans can avoid reckoning with the violence women and children experience when the men, the communities, and the landscapes they love are deemed legitimate targets for death and destruction.[67]

I return, then, to Wendell Berry, whose poem requires us to reconsider actions that may result in destroyed lands, dismantled communities, or dead children. Berry challenges claims that violence liberates. Instead, he offers the disconcerting notion that violence secures American economic interests and the nation's comfortable level of material prosperity. Berry implies that violence justified as protective and liberating vulnerable others is better explained as shielding and sanctioning ourselves. In the last stanza, Berry establishes what he understands to be the reasons for persistent violence against foreign peoples, including the civilians among them:

> State briefly the ideas, ideals, or hopes,
> the energy sources, the kinds of security;
> for which you would kill a child.

The statement stuns. He inquires after the "energy sources" and the "kinds of security" that have driven American violence targeted at Indian "hostiles" and Muslim "extremists" that inevitably harms women and children. This violence does not save, Berry insists. It kills.

American ideals have often included a firm commitment to protecting civilians caught up in the horrors of war. As President Obama has affirmed, civilian deaths often haunt those who have made the choices that result in "collateral damage." At the same time, Americans have consistently, although perhaps not always consciously, assumed a domestic ideal for themselves and for others across the globe. Whether imagined as antebellum white, middle-class womanhood or the contemporary woman marked by her independence and smarts, Americans have perceived foreign women's situations through their own gendered visions. Foreign women need protection from belligerents as well as liberation from their husbands and cultures. Perhaps the "kind of security" we seek, despite our outrage at violence that harms civilians, is the assurance that our way of living—our vision of women's flourishing—is the right one.

Notes

1. Wendell Berry, "Questionnaire," in *Leavings: Poems* (Berkeley, CA: Counterpoint Press, 2010). Used by permission from Counterpoint Press.

2. "List of Children Killed," Global Drones Watch, January 20, 2013, http://drone-swatch.org/2013/01/20/list-of-children-killed-by-drone-strikes-in-pakistan-and-yemen/.

3. Omid Safi, "Boston Marathon, Terrorism, and President Obama," *What Would Muhammad Do* (blog), April 17, 2013, http://omidsafi.religionnews.com/2013/04/17/boston-marathon/.

4. For examples from the nineteenth century, see Joan Jacobs Brumberg, "Zenanas and Girlless Villages: The Ethnology of American Evangelical Women, 1870–1910," *The Journal of American History* 69, no. 2 (September 1, 1982): 349. For a more recent iteration of these concerns, see Kevin Lewis O'Neill, "Left Behind: Security, Salvation, and the Subject of Prevention," *Cultural Anthropology* 28, no. 2 (May 2013): 204–226.

5. Literature on Indian women will be reviewed below. On immigrant children, see Brian Gratton and Jon Moen, "Immigration, Culture, and Child Labor in the United States, 1880–1920," *Journal of Interdisciplinary History* 34, no. 3 (January 2004): 355–391.

6. Amy Kaplan, "Manifest Domesticity," *American Literature* 70, no. 3 (September 1998): 581–606. See also Karen Sánchez-Eppler, "Raising Empires Like Children: Race, Nation, and Religious Education," *American Literary History* 8, no. 3 (October 1, 1996): 399–425.

7. Kaplan, "Manifest Domesticity," 582–583.

8. "Radio Address by Mrs. Bush," http://www.presidency.ucsb.edu/ws/?pid=24992.

9. Saba Mahmood, *Politics of Piety: The Islamic Revival and the Feminist Subject* (Princeton, NJ: Princeton University Press, 2005), 5.

10. The number of victims was disputed for many years. According to the National Park Service, which administers the Sand Creek historical site and has worked closely with Cheyenne and Arapaho descendants, Chivington's troops killed approximately two hundred people.

11. Ari Kelman, *A Misplaced Massacre: Struggling over the Memory of Sand Creek* (Cambridge, MA: Harvard University Press, 2013), 13–15.

12. Silas Soule to his mother, December 18, 1864, Silas Soule Collection, Folder 14, Denver Public Library.

13. Richard Shelley Hartigan, "Introduction," in Francis Lieber, *Lieber's Code and the Law of War* (Chicago: Precedent, 1983), 19–20.

14. Harry S. Stout, *Upon the Altar of the Nation: A Moral History of the American Civil War* (New York: Viking, 2006), 191–192.

15. Ibid.

16. Hartigan, "Introduction," 19–20.

17. Ibid.

18. Ibid., 15.

19. On the Civil War, see John Fabian Witt, *Lincoln's Code: The Laws of War in American History* (New York: Free Press, 2012). On debate about warfare against Indians, see Robert Wooster, *The Military and United States Indian Policy 1865–1903* (Lincoln: University of Nebraska Press, 1995), 136–142, 214; Mark Grimsley, "'Rebels' and 'Redskins': U.S. Military Conduct Toward White Southerners and Native Americans in Comparative Perspective," in *Civilians in the Path of War* (Lincoln: University of Nebraska Press, 2002), 141, 154; and Tom Pessah, "Violent Representations: Hostile Indians and Civilized Wars in Nineteenth-Century USA," *Ethnic and Racial Studies* (2013): 1–19. Slotkin's argument that total war preceded the Civil War in American campaigns against Indians is also crucial. See Richard Slotkin, *The Fatal Environment: The Myth of the Frontier in the Age of Industrialization, 1800–1890* (New York: Atheneum, 1985), 304.

20. "Indians Murdered By Our Troops," *New York Observer and Chronicle*, August 3, 1865.

21. Gideon Frost, "The Indians and the Government," *Friends' Review*, December 14, 1867.

22. "The Indian War," *Morning Star and Catholic Messenger*, January 17, 1869.

23. *Zion's Herald*, March 10, 1870.

24. Pessah, "Violent Representations," 2.

25. Rayna Green, "The Pocahontas Perplex: The Image of Indian Women in American Culture," *Massachusetts Review* 16, no. 4 (October 1, 1975): 698–714; Margaret D. Jacobs, *White Mother to a Dark Race: Settler Colonialism, Maternalism, and the Removal of Indigenous Children in the American West and Australia, 1880–1940* (Lincoln: University of Nebraska Press, 2009); David D. Smits, "The 'Squaw Drudge': A Prime Index of Savagism," *Ethnohistory* 29, no. 4 (October 1, 1982): 281–306.

26. Smits, "The 'Squaw Drudge,'" 281.

27. "Scenes in California," *Gleason's Pictorial Drawing-Room Companion*, March 27, 1852.

28. Quoted in Thea Perdue, "Native Women in the Early Republic: Old World Perceptions, New World Realities," in *Native Americans and the Early*

Republic, edited by Frederick Hoxie, Ronald Hoffman, and Peter Albert (Charlottesville: University of Virginia Press, 1999), 121.

29. Theresa Strouth Gaul, "Introduction," in *Cherokee Sister: The Collected Writings of Catharine Brown, 1818–1823* (Lincoln: University of Nebraska Press, 2014), 46.

30. Louise Michele Newman, *White Women's Rights: The Racial Origins of Feminism in the United States* (New York: Oxford University Press, 1999), 20, 117.

31. See also Joshua David Bellin, "The 'Squaw's' Tale: Sympathy and Storytelling in Mary Eastman's *Dahcotah*," *Legacy* 17, no. 1 (January 1, 2000): 20.

32. International Human Rights and Conflict Resolution Clinic at Stanford Law School and Global Justice Clinic at NYU School of Law (IHR&CRC), "Living Under Drones: Death, Injury, and Trauma to Civilians From US Drone Practices in Pakistan," (2012): 70.

33. Ibid., 68.

34. Ibid., 73.

35. Ibid.

36. Ingrid Detter Delupis, *The Law of War* (New York: Cambridge University Press, 2000).

37. Department of Justice, *Lawfulness of a Lethal Operation Directed Against a U.S. Citizen Who Is a Senior Operational Leader of Al-Qa'ida or An Associated Force*, white paper, November 8, 2011.

38. "Obama's Speech on Drone Policy," May 23, 2013, http://www.nytimes.com/2013/05/24/us/politics/transcript-of-obamas-speech-on-drone-policy.html.

39. IHR&CRC, "Living Under Drones," 66–73.

40. Ken Silverstein, "Is Secrecy on Drone Attacks Hiding Civilian Casualties?," *Browsings* (blog), June 12, 2009, http://harpers.org/blog/2009/06/is-secrecy-on-drone-attacks-hiding-civilian-casulaties/.

41. Peter Bergen and Katherine Tiedemann, "The Drone Wars," *The Atlantic*, December 2010.

42. Joshua Foust, "Unaccountable Killing Machines: The True Cost of U.S. Drones," *The Atlantic*, December 30, 2011, http://www.theatlantic.com/international/archive/2011/12/unaccountable-killing-machines-the-true-cost-of-us-drones/250661/.

43. Kenneth Roth, "What Rules Should Govern US Drone Attacks?," *The New York Review of Books*, April 4, 2013.

44. Mirza Shahzad Akbar, "The Forgotten Victims of Obama's Drone War," *New York Times*, May 23, 2013.

45. See Jim Rice, "War Crimes and Misdemeanors," *Sojourners Magazine* 41, no. 8 (August 1, 2012): 23.

46. "What Religious Leaders Want to Tell Obama on Easter," YouTube video, 4:50, Brave New Foundation, March 27, 2013, http://www.youtube.com/watch?v=FkddrkzDg3I#t=67.

47. Ibid.

48. "Remote Control Warfare," *Christian Century* 127, no. 10 (May 18, 2010).

49. Adelaide Mena, "U.S. Bishops Ask Government to Reassess Drone Policy," Catholic News Agency, May 22, 2013, http://www.catholicnewsagency.com/news/us-bishops-ask-government-to-reassess-drone-policy/.

50. Joshua McElwee, "Key Bishop Questions U.S. Drone Warfare, Says Indiscriminate," *National Catholic Reporter*, June 13, 2013, http://ncronline.org/blogs/ncr-today/key-bishop-questions-us-drone-warfare-says-indiscriminate.

51. Christian Church (Disciples of Christ) in the United States and Canada, "GA-1331, Resolution Condemning Drone Warfare," 2013.

52. National Black Church Iniative, "NCBI Condemn's Obama's Drone Policy as Murderous and Evil," 19 February 2013.

53. Paul F. M. Zahl, Daniel M. Bell, and Brian Stiltner, "Just War vs. Technology: Is It Wrong for the U.S. to Use Unmanned Predator Drones to Kill People by Remote Control?," *Christianity Today* 55, no. 8 (August 1, 2011): 64–65.

54. Matthew Schmitz, "Jewish-Christian Consensus on Drones?," *First Things*, March 5, 2013.

55. Lila Abu-Lughod, "Do Muslim Women Really Need Saving?," *American Anthropologist* 104, no. 3 (September 2002): 783. See also Sunaina Maira, " 'Good' and 'Bad' Muslim Citizens: Feminists, Terrorists, and U.S. Orientalisms," *Feminist Studies* 35, no. 3 (Fall 2009): 631–656.

56. "President George W. Bush's Press Conference on 11 October 2001," http://www.whitehouse.gov. See also Christine McMorris, "Grappling with Islam: Bush and the Burqa," *Religion in the News* (Spring 2002): 14–15, 29.

57. "Radio Address by Mrs. Bush."

58. To be sure, some commentators have noted women's participation in terror campaigns, including suicide bombing.

59. Stephen Prothero, "A World Apart on the Muslim Veil," *USA Today*, August 2, 2010.

60. "The Village Green: Should Christians Support Laws That Ban Muslim Women from Wearing the Face Veil in Public?" *Christianity Today* 54, no. 11 (November 2010): 58–59.

61. Sheryl Henderson Blunt, "Out of Uniform: Flier Shuns Abaya," *Christianity Today*, March 11, 2002, http://www.christianitytoday.com/ct/2002/march11/17.21.html.

62. Scholars found that articles in *Christianity Today* after September 11, 2001, focused on violent tendencies within Islam. See Heather M. Gorman and A. Christian Van Gorder, "Portraits of Islam: *Christianity Today* in the Six Months after 9/11," *Perspectives in Religious Studies* 38, no. 3 (September 1, 2011): 314–315, 317, 324.

63. Mahmood, *Politics of Piety*, 5–17.

64. Omar Sacirbey, "Modeling Agency Helps Demure Muslims Keep It 'Underwraps,'" *The Christian Century*, January 31, 2013, http://www.christian-century.org/article/2013-01/modeling-agency-helps-demure-muslims-keep-it-underwraps; Omar Sacirbey, "Are Muslims Allowed to Dance? Depends Who You Ask," *The Christian Century*, August 30, 2012, http://www.christiancen-tury.org/article/2012-08/are-muslims-allowed-dance-depends-who-you-ask.

65. Cathleen Falsani, "Muslim Women Olympians: 'This Is Legacy,'" *Sojourners Magazine*, August 2, 2012; Richard S. Ehlich, "New Muslim Superhero? A Wonder Woman-like Education Warrior," *God's Politics* (blog), August 12, 2013, http://sojo.net/blogs/2013/08/12/new-muslim-superhero-wonder-woman-education-warrior.

66. Tracy Fessenden, *Culture and Redemption: Religion, the Secular, and American Literature* (Princeton, NJ: Princeton University Press, 2007), 101.

67. Newman, *White Women's Rights*, 8.

7

Crude Awakenings in the Age of Oil

Darren Dochuk

IN EARLY 2012, amid the dissonant warmth of one of the strangest springs in US history, Barack Obama journeyed to Oklahoma to jumpstart an "energy tour." The politician had work to do—win re-election—and seemed unfazed by the blistering temperatures and torrential storms that made March feel like July.

Of course there was no way he could ignore the surreal conditions; glaring signs were everywhere. In his native Chicago, locals decked out in Irish-green tank tops and flip-flops pub-crawled their way through the hottest St. Patrick's Day ever recorded, the third day of a history-making seven-day heat wave. Not far to the east, residents of Dexter, Michigan, spent St. Patrick's Day sweeping up damage from an F3 tornado. "It's like a war zone in here this morning," one resident sobbed, striking a heartrending contrast to the revelry seen on Chicago's streets. To the west, meanwhile, citizens of Minnesota and the Dakotas struggled to regulate their thermostats. Readings were off the charts: 81 degrees in Bismarck (41 above the norm), 94 degrees in parts of South Dakota. And in Rochester, Minnesota, the recorded *low* temperature for the day beat the existing record *high*, a baffling pattern that would be repeated many times over.[1]

But at a rally in Cushing, Oklahoma, Obama brushed over weather and talked energy instead. Flanked by steel pipes, he laid out his plans for America's future. First came a tribute to folks who drilled the nation's crude, then an appeal to their vote:

> America is producing more oil today than at any time in the last eight years. Over the last three years, I've directed my administration

to open up millions of acres for gas and oil exploration across 23 different states. We're opening up more than 75 percent of our potential oil resources offshore. We've quadrupled the number of operating rigs to a record high. We've added enough new oil pipelines to encircle the Earth and then some.[2]

Obama's statement of an "all-of-the-above energy strategy" came last. The plan was fourfold: "more jobs" for Americans; more "oil development and infrastructure," with government's help; more domestic production and "less dependency on foreign oil"; and more drive toward renewable energy and care of the environment, for the sake of "our kids." "We've got to have a vision for the future," he implored; "that's what America has always been about. That's how we have to think about energy . . . God bless you. God bless the United States of America."[3]

Obama's faithful cheered his sweeping promises for "more" (who wouldn't?), yet as policy the speech clanged with incongruities. Could Americans truly get more of everything with little cost? Would such an open-ended policy benefit the earth, or leave it vulnerable to an all-out assault by energy seekers of all kind? And would any of this actually reverse global warming, whose influence Obama's overheated listeners were sweating out? Republican and Democratic naysayers questioned the president's speech and pondered whether all of the above would result in none of the above results.[4]

To be fair, Obama's talk was boilerplate designed to rally troops, yet his speech also illustrates tentative thinking about energy as discordant as the times. When he won the Democratic primaries in 2008, he predicted that during his "administration[,] the rise of the oceans will begin to slow and the planet begin to heal." Yet in Cushing, amid evidences of rising waters and a wounded planet, he preferred to boast about "pipelines encircling the earth." Obama's broader presidential record further reveals uncertainty. The struggle over TransCanada's Keystone pipeline, for instance, inspired Obama's Oklahoma visit then generated controversy for most of his second term in office. He spoke for and against the enterprise, urged construction in some sections and delayed it in others, paused for environmental reassessment and infuriated activists (and Canadians) with his indecision. One can safely say that from early to late in his presidency, Obama remained trapped in the conundrums of energy politics.[5]

But it is too simple to highlight the disjointedness of Obama's agenda, for his conundrums were products of profoundly complex circumstances.

Defying neat partisan categories, irreducible to culture war binaries and red-blue divides, energy discourses are knotty, drawing into collision multiple ideals of economy and environment, community and the state, patriotism and America's global prospects. No simple matter of opposed self-interests, in other words, energy politics is totalizing and existential, even eschatological.

It has always been that way, especially with oil, the pivot around which Obama's—and everyone else's—energy politics spin. Since the dawn of their petrol age, Americans have viewed the black stuff as more than a source of illumination and fuel: it has defined their diet and daily suburban life, sent them to war, triggered hope about human potential and fed dreams of dystopia; it has allowed particular regions and economies within US borders to flourish, others to fall. Beyond dictating legislative wins and losses in Washington, it has also generated anxiety about America's place in this world and its people's prospects in the next. Considering oil's ultimate significance, it is fair to claim that energy politics has always been about more than a physical material and its basic technological applications, which is why it has proved to be so vexing for the politicians that seek to harness its power.[6]

In this vein, it is also fair to claim that oil has always carried religious weight. Scholars of religion have recently cast their gaze on land's extracted materials as sources of religious authority. In their renderings of coal and its importance to America's emerging industrial society, Richard Callahan, Kathryn Lofton, and Chad Seales suggest that this rudimentary carbon form did more than facilitate the construction of factories and fuel the massive equipment an industrialized state requires. Its power stemmed from its allegorical properties as well, and its ability to structure communities and notions of time and tie dreams of development on earth to the supernatural workings of the divine. They write:

> As a construct of industrial religion, coal powered progress itself, firing the imagination to visions of human potential and the salvations of modern civilization. At once substance and symbol, coal's power entwined matter and spirit in a particularly modern manner, congealing multiple meanings of progress into one enchanted material.[7]

Beyond its work in stimulating notions of the modern, coal also shaped structures of economy and the manner in which American citizens thought about and acted upon their financial concerns; coal was an ethic of work as well as of being, and an orienting force behind peoples' quests for democratic freedom, social and economic justice, and right governance.

In the twentieth century, oil performed these same tasks and assumed the same sacred clout, only at a rate that surpassed anything witnessed in the age of coal. Indeed, oil came to be seen by many Americans as the ultimate cause and justification of their nation's favorable standing in the world and before God. Inhabitants of America's oil patches simultaneously came to see it as essential to the expansion of churches and Christian democracy, the betterment of families and global humanity, and the basic building block of a strong, God-fearing nation state. No mere dark sludge from below the earth, the black stuff oozed promise of all tangible and imagined kind for a people who pursued divine blessing on a spectacular scale.[8]

Granted, oil's omnipotence did not result in Americans' unanimity of sacred vision or their shared political action. On the contrary, oil's very nature as the source of big dreams also made it a basis for perpetual dispute between citizens with different notions of God and good government. As a return glimpse at Obama's Cushing speech and a brief look at the history it opens up will affirm, America's struggles over pipelines and petroleum have always represented a clash of "carbon gospels"—competing notions of oil's special properties and potentials for humanity's advance, stemming from particularities of class, labor, and place, their renderings in sacred terms, and the disjunctive histories and visions of the future that frame their political possibilities. Obama's fourfold energy plan, introduced in Cushing, exposed Americans to at least four different carbon gospels, each of which pressed the president in the Keystone debate and rendered his subsequent policies complicated, and at times incongruent. Products of distinctive historical periods of religiously inflected political contestation—"crude awakenings," if you will—each of these gospels and their illustrious proponents deserve scrutiny, both for the way they reveal a rich and complex history of American religion and energy politics and for the way they help explain Obama's energy dilemma circa 2011 and the intensifying energy debates that animate our public discourse today.

First Crude Awakening (1900–1915): Muckraking the Petroleum Machine

At the heart of Obama's Cushing speech was a quest, illustrated by his simple promise of "more jobs," to help petroleum's underclass: land holders, oil patch workers, and average citizens in close proximity to drill sites and pipelines whose cries for access to the economic promises of oil and protection from overbearing oil companies have, since the first decade of the twentieth century, resounded with a familiar populist beat.

It is a cry that South Dakotans like John Harter and Bill Means issued while protesting Keystone late in the 2014 election campaign. A rancher and Republican, Harter was agitated by TransCanada's efforts to lay pipe over his terrain. Republican colleagues shared his angst yet hesitated to join his crusade. "It's lonely," he admitted when talking about his difficult stand, "kind of like being the Maytag repairman." "But now I've got a lot of friends standing with me—the Rosebud, Oglala, the Yankton" (Native Americans on his side of the divide). "To have land be threatened by eminent domain—I think the non-Indian community is beginning to feel the same way we do," Means, a Lakota activist and Harter's ally, observed at the time. "The farmers and ranchers, we call them the new Indians."[9]

As much as they were at odds with neighbors because of their vote against the pipeline, Means and Harter represented one of two widespread concerns about unfettered petro-capitalism. The other issue was jobs. In their evaluation of Keystone during the heated politics of 2014, most Americans favored the project because of its employment potential for "welders, mechanics, electricians, pipefitters, laborers, safety coordinators and heavy equipment operators," as well as service workers across the supply chain. Yet experts differed wildly in their predictions of a job boom, leaving Harter's pro-pipeline friends as uncertain about Keystone as he was. While TransCanada predicted a final tally of half a million jobs, skeptics, including Obama, cautioned that the number of permanent jobs would likely amount to one hundred.[10]

The bottom line is that these entwined land and labor concerns made oil patch locals of all political stripes a hesitant majority, convinced of only two things: oil companies could not be trusted to care for the land and labor pools they sought to tap, and local people deserved the fruits of the resource development that was disrupting their soil. In this rhetoric, they echoed a disquiet that has reverberated for over a century.

The first crude awakening in the early twentieth century created an attending gospel of protest against the petroleum machine. It was in the early 1900s that Americans came to terms with their energy revolution and its first victims. The victims were rank-and-file inhabitants of petroleum's earliest hubs, whose livelihoods were threatened by John D. Rockefeller's Standard Oil. A devout Baptist, Rockefeller was puritanical in his view of oil. Besides deeming his extraction of crude providential, he believed that his corporate ventures were themselves acts of redemption designed to rescue the oil business from chaos. As Ron Chernow writes, this Christian certainty gave Rockefeller a "courageous persistence" and "capacity to think in strategic terms, but also [a] messianic self-righteousness, and contempt for those shortsighted mortals who made the mistake of stand-ing in his way."[11]

The mortals saw him differently, of course, and clawed back with moral critique. Their champion was Ida Tarbell, a journalist who helped destroy the Standard Trust. What is less appreciated is the degree to which Tarbell's actions grew out of her wrestling with God and the ghosts of her youth. Born in 1857 in western Pennsylvania, raised by devout Methodists, Tarbell was truly a product of the oil field and its plebeian religion. As a child she attended Sunday school; as a teen she ventured with fellow Methodists one hour north to participate in the Chautauqua Movement. In her twenties, Tarbell gained journalistic know-how by editing *The Chautauquan*, the movement's paper. Even as she relocated from her hometown of Meadville to far-off cities, she guarded the faith of her parents, while supplementing it with new sci-entific thought. After attending a service at the American Chapel of Paris she wrote her brother to express some frustration with orthodox Christianity. "I am just home from church where I heard a senseless sermon on heaven ... If people who preached would only try to give a little more incentive to stay on earth and behave themselves for the sake of behaving themselves, instead of holding up heaven as a reward of merit, I'd have more hope for the church."[12]

Though assuming theological flexibility and harboring some doubt, Tarbell remained firm in her Christian moralism. As her career in muck-raking began to flourish, she found an outlet for her zeal. Oil had never left her imagination. When Tarbell was young, her father, beloved for his gentleness, had entered the oil business, but Rockefeller's monop-olizing killed his dream—and his generous outlook. In the cutthroat climate of Pennsylvania's oil patch, the Baptist titan's rule of capture easily trumped that of the compliant Methodist. The strains of this fam-ily history inspired Tarbell to research Standard Oil's dealings and learn of Rockefeller's every move. Tarbell carried her father's pain, and dis-dain for Rockefeller, with her; friends noted that Standard was a "strong thread weaving itself into the pattern" of her life. The rest of the story is well known. In 1903, Tarbell's first exposé of Standard appeared in *McClure's*; in 1904, she published the mammoth *History of the Standard Oil Company*, which identified Rockefeller as the man who symbolized "all that was wrong in national life." The Supreme Court's 1911 ruling, which dismantled Standard Oil, further solidified Tarbell's legacy as muckraker extraordinaire.[13]

But she also bequeathed to future generations of oil's rank and file a doctrine of pristine capitalism and Christian justice. When fighting Rockefeller, Tarbell stressed the innately pure qualities of the local oil patch in which she grew up. Hers was not a condemnation of petro-capitalism but a petition to clean it up. "Life ran swift and ruddy and joyous in these men," she writes glowingly of men like her father. "They looked forward with all the eagerness of the young who have just learned their powers, to the years of struggle. They would meet their own needs ... There was nothing they did not hope and dare." Tarbell's faith in oil's first generation mirrored her belief in the essential goodness of her church, and, more importantly, human ability to better society through smart application of biblical principles. "According to the Christian system as it is laid out in the Bible," she mused, "society should be a brotherhood of men—not a brotherhood of white men only, but of men of all colors." In the tenacious fellows of her father's ilk she saw evidence of this Christian comradeship, which, even if it was not as racially inclusive as she would have liked, still demonstrated the virtues of the Beatitudes:

> Hungering and thirsting after righteousness; merciful, pure in heart, meek in spirit, a peace-maker, willing even to be persecuted and reviled for righteousness' sake. This is the "whole" or perfect man in the Bible sense, and to produce him is its continuous concern.

To act on the essential teachings of the Bible, Tarbell asserted, was to strive "in solitude and silence to enter into a fuller understanding of the divine." In contrast to Rockefeller, in whom she saw the antithesis of scripture, small-producing oilmen like her father struck Tarbell as the last hope to recreate, perpetually, the "whole" and "perfect man in the Bible sense."[14]

This Bible-based viewpoint matched her conviction that petro-capitalism had to remain egalitarian if it were to thrive. "Free competition was her Eden," one chronicler offers, "and life outside it could not help but be sinful." She theologized oil's land and labor too. Shaped by her readings in Methodist theology and Christian socialism, she came to understand the struggle with Standard as one to protect the value of small-scale "production by individual laborers." She would write: "God gave man the land, but man has to use his hand and brain in its cultivation before he can feed and clothe and shelter himself. It is the partnership of the two—land and labor—which produces wealth." Because of big oil, she lamented, "labor had been made dependent on capital by capital's theft of the land which God gave to all." Though she could not imagine it at the time, her muckraking example and countering ethic of possessive individualism would endure among men and women like her parents for generations to come.[15]

Second Crude Awakening (1935–1950): Advancing a Civil Religion of Crude

Standard, of course, did not die at Tarbell's hand, nor did Rockefeller's utter dominance. Fractured into thirty-four companies, the largest being Jersey, New York, and California Standards (Exxon, Mobil, and Chevron), Rockefeller's corporate family benefited from enforced diversification. By 1935, it controlled the industry at rates similar to pre-1911 days, if through subtler means. And during the Depression, when booming fields in East Texas reignited oil's chaos, Standard's subsidiaries assumed even greater import as the counterweight to the deplorable conditions—excessive drilling, skyrocketing supplies, plummeting prices—that now plagued the petroleum business.

Into the fray, eager to partner with major oil companies in an effort to save the oil industry and offer it cohesion and shared vision, stepped the regulatory state. Although Franklin D. Roosevelt oversaw this expanding bureaucratic entity, it was left to a number of other voices to frame the New Deal government's handling of oil, carve out constructive relationships with large companies, and institute American petroleum's new order. These voices included Harold Ickes, Henry Luce, and William Eddy, all of whom used the contingencies of a second disruptive period in crude politics during the mid-twentieth century to craft a second carbon gospel, one that can be characterized as a "civil religion of crude." In accordance with this gospel, the federal government accepted the burden to invest in the management of the oil industry and to work with select oil corporations to coordinate expansion. This economic and political outlook was married to a religious hope—a notion epitomized in John D. Rockefeller Jr.'s, philanthropic work, which began to flourish at this time—that large-scale petroleum's beneficence could be channeled into liberal agencies such as the Federal Council of Churches and United Nations. Along with Rockefeller Jr., Ickes, Eddy, and Luce spoke for the aspirations of a whole cadre of elite visionaries, who believed that "big religion" (defined as ecumenical, internationalist, cosmopolitan) wedded to "big oil" (defined by integration, combination, and collective effort between state and company in foreign fields)—could guarantee the nation's global influence.

As Roosevelt's secretary of the interior, Ickes commanded the country's reserves. Seeking to clean up East Texas, Ickes spent the 1930s and early 1940s creating agencies with oil's leading CEOs in order to stabilize the business. Then, during war, he coordinated oil supplies for America's domestic and foreign demands. In biblical-laced language, he described his commission as something extraordinarily demanding, requiring a prophetic touch.

> I may as well confess at the outset that many times I have wished, with all of the fervency of prayer, for the spiritual power of a major prophet. There is no denying that there have been blue Mondays when I have wondered if our production and transportation of petroleum could possibly keep pace with the growing military and essential civilian needs. If it does, let me say right here ... that we will have been a witness to a miracle worthy of the saints.

Ickes's enemies, independent oilmen, saw his quest for order as collusion, a surreptitious ploy by the government and major oil companies to wipe them out. They readily identified him as "one of the more toxic of the New Dealers." Yet there was no denying the popular appeal of Ickes's vision for major oil and government's partnership: in this time of trial, marked by industry infighting and free-for-all drilling, oil needed managerial oversight, citizens the confidence that the nation's largest entities could work together.[16]

There was more to Ickes's vision than reaction, however. His conviction that Washington and major oil could work together for a collective good was also fueled by a deep belief that America's sense of exceptionalism and democratic promise could be affirmed by US petroleum's advance across the globe. His work on behalf of the Anglo-American Petroleum Agreement is one example of this ambition. Through this arrangement, proposed in 1944, Ickes hoped to see the British and American governments establish an international alliance with each other and with the Western world's largest oil companies in order to manage international petroleum supplies, demands, and drilling. An International Petroleum Commission was to oversee the entire operation, with Ickes implanted in a key role. However much Ickes promoted the initiative as a profound step forward for the international community, one that would expedite the spread of a fairer, more democratic capitalism, the agreement faced stiff opposition from smaller petroleum producers who feared the centralization and monopolization of oil governance. "Some of the industry are seeing ghosts where there are no ghosts," Ickes complained to Roosevelt. Roosevelt agreed, but in the name of expediency and fully aware that the agreement could not win, shifted his course. By January 1945, the initiative was dead.[17]

Luce and Eddy joined Ickes in the promotion of a civil religion of crude, but they were more successful at selling it. In 1941, Luce, the missionary-turned-publicist, used the pages of *Life* magazine to urge the United States to recognize its status as protector of the free world and "create the first great American Century." He tested his charge a month earlier while speaking to the American Petroleum Institute. There he praised oilmen as the vanguards of America's manifest destiny: "Having within you a dynamic spirit of freedom and enterprise, having within you a genius for cooperation and organization that doesn't stop at any frontier—I salute you."[18] For Luce, petroleum struck something unusual in the soul: a limitless power, which, when harnessed by God-fearing Americans, held the capacity to make the world godly and good.

Eddy, another missionary son, and an agent for the Office of Strategic Services, *acted* on this charge. At the time of Luce's call for an "American Century," Eddy was lecturing widely on "The Power of God and the Secular World," imploring laypeople to be the "shock-troops of the church" and transform each sector of the globe: "[We] who believe in Christendom [and] serve the only totalitarian King need to cover ourselves with tolerance, reverence, and charity, and then wherever we walk, we shall find ourselves on holy ground."[19] Three years later, as a consultant for California Standard (Aramco), he was surveying Arabia for crude. Five years later he was brokering a deal between Saudi's king and President Roosevelt. Eddy's assistance proved critical to triggering Saudi Arabia's age of oil (his uncanny ability to locate subsurface pools was key) and nudging the United States toward partnership with this emerging petroleum empire.

Eddy's subsequent career further testified to the potency of this liberal vision. An Arabist in his political sympathies, he continued to promote peace between Western and Saudi interests by way of mutual trust and shared fiscal ambition. In 1950, he addressed the Middle East Institute as a proud missionary son, advisor of Aramco, and advisor for the American Foreign Service and State Department. He was eager to share his knowledge of how oil extraction in Saudi Arabia was facilitating the spread of democratic aspirations and making possible different societies' participation in petroleum's promise. Two years later he delivered a similar message, only with more urgency. Fearful of a political sea change in the Middle East, Eddy wanted to make it clear that the work Aramco was doing in partnership with Washington and the Saudis was bearing the fruit of his (and Ickes and Luce's) vision. Besides listing off broader illustrations of corporate-government cooperation to prove his mission's progress, he also focused on the lived experiences of the oil rig as the signal example of oil's ecumenism.

> The oil industry is such that men have to work with their hands and in overalls. Arabs and Americans are working on the job, on machines, together. The result has been an unusual fraternization, unusual because difference in religion, language and background would seem to prevent it; but such fraternization has been the result of men working together.[20]

Eddy added that these roustabouts were working together only because generous government support and top-down guidance of the oil industry had made these mundane connections and their long-term advantages for all of humanity possible.

The religious fervor behind this message has abated, yet as witnessed in Barack Obama's Cushing speech, the remnants of this second crude awakening linger. Obama's appearance at Cushing in 2012 may not have produced a clear display of Ickes, Luce, and Eddy's civil religion of crude, but it did reverberate with this gospel's assumptions about the federal state's dominion over petroleum reserves and belief that this custodianship could be exercised with society's collective good in mind. The president's own efforts to stress his administration's fair handling of the Keystone pipeline and successes in drilling and producing and managing oil on behalf of the rank and file, revealed the enduring convictions of big oil's midcentury revival. So too Obama's decision to close proceedings with a nod to Judeo-Christian patriotism and a plea for God's special blessing.

Third Crude Awakening (1950–1975): The Wildcatter's Imperative

Barack Obama's message to Cushing advanced another gospel as well, one that had real traction on Oklahoma's terrain: wildcat Christianity. Promises to promote "domestic oil production," "end dependence on foreign oil," and ensure that the nation would no longer be "vulnerable to something that's happening on the other side of the world" were buzzwords meant to stir the loyalties of independent producers, who see it as their right and vocation—for God, country, and their children's future—to drill, drill, drill.

This fierce sense of independence has in some sense been present in petroleum politics since the very beginning: it was the very essence of the old oil town that Tarbell long celebrated. But as a political juggernaut it represented the outgrowth of a third crude awakening, which occurred largely in the American Southwest between the 1950s and the mid-1970s. Driven by their "rule of capture," which legitimized their personal access to resources and markets in the same way they approached God—on their terms—invigorated by the riskiest aspects of their chase, spurred on by new finds and evangelical fervor, Southwestern independent oilmen forged an ideology of wildcat Christianity.

What this ideology stood against was just as important as what it stood for. Forged at a time when Ickes and major oil companies were expanding into the Middle East and privileging global development, the wildcat imperative was defensive in nature. If left in Ickes's hands, independent oilers believed, America would lose control of its resource advantage, expose the country to foreign influences, and succumb to the threat of peak oil, the scenario M. King Hubbert outlined in the 1950s that predicted US production would crest by 1971 and then decline. If Washington did not honor and protect wildcatters' courage in discovering new domestic reserves, Hubbert's prophecy would come true—or so the Southwest's small producers believed.

Though driven by this sense of alienation, these producers also held beliefs that were substantive on their own. Theirs was an ethic that connected the priorities of a personal relationship with Jesus and personal reading of the Bible to a sense of spiritual empowerment and millennialist expectation, and a conviction that as truly free—spiritually, economically—individuals, they represented the antidote to the dehumanizing machinations of the secular, monopolistic age and the threat of atheistic communism. Their politics came to reflect their theology as they attached ideals of frontier discovery to laissez-faire labor and land-use and with accelerating intensity after World War II, a right-wing Republican agenda. Dwight Eisenhower's victory in 1952 marked the beginning of wildcat oilmen's political ascent; Ronald Reagan's in 1980, the zenith.[21]

Considering the radical nature of this third insurgence in the faith and politics of oil, it is no wonder that the prophets were many, their voices cacophonous. The range of wildcat proponents included oilmen, politicians, and preachers, whose theologizing of oil came in both measured and extreme tones. One of the earliest and measured champions was Robert Kerr. As Oklahoma's governor and senator in the 1940s and 1950s, Kerr labored to meet independent oil's needs and carried the mantle for the dispossessed, working all of his connections to give small producers the protections they desired.

Already independent oil's supreme arbiter in politics and business (he was a successful oilman), Kerr also became its spokesman on religion, and in these interlocking vocations he deftly combined petroleum's profane and divine imperatives. At one gathering of the Independent Petroleum Association he beseeched his brethren to assume their rightful duty as head of America's quest for freedom. "The golden age of America is not in decades past," he charged, but—with God's blessing—still ahead "in the development of her limitless resources, in the boundless courage of her people, in the hearts and souls of her sons and daughters." He also cautioned that theirs was a heavy responsibility, to guarantee America's security (by supplying its primary energy source) and protect its natural resources. Kerr advocated an ethic of stewardship that linked the wildcatter's providence to judicial use of earth's minerals. He offered this same message to fellow Southern Baptists and compelled them to embrace their role in the petro-fueled advances of their country. For modest working folks like himself, he offered, it was a matter of duty to "bear witness for the Master" by marching fellow citizens into the future, with grit under their fingernails and faces upturned "into the rising sun."[22]

Where Kerr revealed the hopeful side of wildcat Christianity, other preachers leaned to its sharper edge. By the 1970s, this edge was evident in independent oil's aggressive lobbying, which generated tax concessions in Washington. It was also apparent in the religious culture they generated. Premillennialism, the end-times theology that helped shape the born-again phenomenon of the 1970s, offered oil-patch Christians a special opportunity in that it lined up perfectly with peak-oil thinking. Among the most popular producers of this eschatology was John Walvoord. From his professorship at Dallas Theological Seminary, a school that served as a bastion of wildcat Christianity, Walvoord spoke to a national audience by way of his pen. His 1970s text *Armageddon: Oil and the Middle East Crisis* reached millions of readers. Blending hope that Middle Eastern turbulence was a sign of Christ's impending return with criticism of the US government for letting this chaos occur, Walvoord focused his end-times anger on environmentalists who had made America dependent on non-Christian others. He also outlined the wildcatter's ethic. Were Americans able to tap freely the bountiful oil pools in the Gulf Coast and Alaska, underneath Southwestern soil, and in the shale deposits of Colorado, he asserted, they would realize anew the natural (and biblical) order of things.[23]

Upon entering the White House, Ronald Reagan honored Walvoord's theology by naming James Watt, a premillennialist from the West, secretary of the interior. Watt saw to it that wildcat Christianity shaped policy. In the spirit of the Southwest's independent oilmen who had begun their fight by confronting an interior secretary of a different ilk, he promised to restore custodianship of the oil patch to the people who had long worked it as theirs.[24]

Fourth Crude Awakening (2000–Present): The Carbon-free Gospel

Try as he might, Watt did not manage to reverse the regulatory state. Quite the opposite, he helped trigger yet a fourth crude awakening, out of which emerged calls for more government rollback of the wildcat imperative. Begun during the 1970s oil crisis, this latest insurgence in the faith and politics of oil, led by avid environmentalists who promoted a carbon-free gospel, has not yet played out completely. That is why Obama was particularly eager in Cushing to package his "all-of-the-above" energy plan as healthy for the earth and its people. And it is why he was earnest in his effort to balance carbon fuel scenarios with alternatives: "What we're going to be doing as part of an all-of-the-above strategy is looking at how we can continually improve the utilization of renewable energy sources." "That means producing more biofuels. It means solar power. We want every source of American-made energy."[25]

Despite his sweeping promises, Obama failed to convince proponents of the carbon-free gospel. "It makes no sense at all," one detractor wrote of the president's Cushing earth-care rhetoric. "Drilling everywhere you can and then putting up a solar panel is like drinking six martinis and then topping them off with a VitaminWater—you're still drunk, you just have your day's full allotment of C and D." Obama is "still drunk on oil," another critic averred, running with the theme. "The worst speech ever," a third chimed in. A fourth response came with a simple question: imagine what "liberals would be saying if President Bush had given the speech?" What became obvious at Cushing is that the testiest of Obama's naysayers were his one-time champions: earth-care activists whose faith in reform was bolstered by Obama's stirring speech during the 2008 Democratic National Convention, but whose trust had been battered since.[26]

Among them several voices stood out, but none was more eloquent or earnest than Bill McKibben, the man responsible for the martini and VitaminWater quip. McKibben came reluctantly to his place at the head of the anti-Keystone crusade. The Harvard-trained, Vermont-based environmentalist made a name for himself in the 1990s and early 2000s as a spokesperson for the anti-carbon campaign group he founded, 350.org, and as author of some of the most popular jeremiads against global warming, none more heralded than *The End of Nature*, published in 1989. By 2010, his penmanship on behalf of these causes had vaulted him to international fame.[27]

McKibben did not rest on his laurels, however. In 2011, he shifted vocations from author-activist to straight-up activist. Inspired by a course on social movements that he was teaching at Middlebury College that spring, he imbibed the teachings of Gandhi and Martin Luther King Jr. and decided to enlist his small army of young activists in the fledgling anti-Keystone crusade. McKibben was convinced that the plan to process and move a million barrels a day of Alberta's tar sands to the Gulf of

Mexico was a game-changer, and possibly "game over for the climate." During 2011 and 2012, he led nonviolent protests in Washington, DC, for which he spent three days in prison. His July 2012 essay in *Rolling Stone*, "Global Warming's Terrifying New Math," tore through social media and led one pundit to name him "Nature's Prophet." In 2013, the prophet won the Gandhi Peace Award. In late September of that year, McKibben stepped up his rhetoric (promising "a call to arms" and an "invitation to change everything") and ambition by coordinating the People's Climate March, which drew over 300,000 to New York City.[28]

With each step forward, McKibben became more deliberate in reaching back, into the repositories of scripture and back-to-the-land spirituality. In a way, his current view of oil as the ultimate moral test for humanity mirrors that of his muckraking predecessor, Ida Tarbell, with whom he shares his Methodism and a theological eclecticism that blends love of the Bible with awe of nature's mysteries and a transcendent view of terrestrial things. Today, tucked away in a Vermont valley, he writes amid waterways and foliage of the kind that inspired Tarbell to write in her Allegheny village. Little wonder that he has found further inspiration for his prose in Wendell Berry, whose Christian gospel of sustainability and back-to-the-land communalism is tuned to good husbandry.

Still, McKibben's is a theology shaped by global exchange in a postindustrial age. The self-proclaimed "Methodist Sunday School teacher" has traveled the world, conversing with Buddhists, Greek Orthodox priests, and socialists, while resisting their labels and choosing to apply the best (in his mind) that they offer to his homespun faith. Through all of these channels, he has accessed an inner light that has inspired his moral aggression against the petro-state on one hand, and on the other, his first-desire to chase quietly "woods east and west," "words and gods and hopes and fears."[29]

His followers love him for it. Though an admirer of Job, McKibben has been bestowed the title of "New Noah" by one of 350.org's core constituencies: young evangelicals aligned with Sojourners. "Bill's been tapped to be the Noah to our faithless generation," one of them wrote to her peers; "it's his job to warn us that we have 'grieved the Lord in his heart' and that the flood waters will rise again if we don't get back to working within our 'original contract' and reverse climate change." Alongside McKibben, these evangelicals have borrowed ideas that resonate with Berry. They decry society's unreflective commitment to industrialism and modern technology, and the way (quoting a *Sojourners Magazine* essayist) that "humans serve the economy, not vice versa." "The proposed pipeline," this author asserts, is evidence that our modern, technocratic, "myth-spinning machine" is "strangling God's world."[30]

Evangelicalism's rising radicals have also acted out their convictions with McKibben by their side. Since 2012 they have initiated social media (and prayer) campaigns, lobbied public and corporate institutions to divest their portfolios of oil, pushed for heavier taxes on carbon emitters, and educated their churches and communities. They have marched. Oil-patch pentecostal and Baptist youth have journeyed to Washington to stand with McKibben, nuns, Mennonites, Quakers, ranchers, and indigenous communities in opposition to Keystone. In other isolated moments they have traveled to Nebraska and Texas to chain themselves to bulldozers, pray on pipes, and use faith to subvert oil's order. One evangelist for the carbon-free gospel states it simply: "Many people see the pipeline as a political or an economic issue, but I see it as a moral issue." Invoking Charles Finney, another proselyte promises a "power shift":

> If Christians and other people of faith . . . rise up and demand that our nation turn away from the planet-threatening actions that have fed global warming, it will launch an irresistible force for change. But such a faith-based uprising will take a "revival" movement every bit as significant as the Great Awakenings led by Finney. We need a faith of revival on behalf of the world as God intends, a planet where life not simply survives but thrives, a creation where God is at the center and delights in it.

McKibben would disagree with this zealous evangelical on only one point: the fires of revival, he would charge, are already burning bright.[31]

God and Black Gold's New Millennium

You might say that Barack Obama also sensed the heat. Unlike McKibben's straightforward charge, Obama's were manifold. Living with the legacy of several crude awakenings, encountering carbon gospels on multiple sides, his was a tough task that demanded a careful sorting out. This is why his all-of-the-above energy policy seemed to be a path of some convenience, and why his energy dilemma could very well be his successor's dilemma too.

But that is a misleading conclusion, because change is surely coming. Keystone's final decisions are impending; its destiny and the consequences for people on the plains will be decided soon, especially with pipeline-supporting Republicans taking control of the Senate in the 2014 midterm elections. According to several Washington insiders, Keystone was seen as "a big winner" at the polls, and one of the most heralded victories in GOP circles. In the wake of the election, Republican leaders promised to make the pipeline a priority, with the goal of sending the president a bill to authorize its completion and daring him to veto it. Some advocates were convinced that the chamber's new leadership would shift the balance of power in the oil-versus-environment contest that has raged since Obama's first election, with the former gaining an upper hand. Others predicted another bloody round, with the president vetoing any bill granting oil expansion free rein. "This president is not going to approve Keystone," Republican strategist Michael McKenna declared. "It's a religious item among environmentalists. He's just not going to approve it, and that's that."[32]

That bloody round played out in early March of 2015, when the president did what McKenna predicted he would do: veto a bill advanced by a majority of senators that approved completion of Keystone. "The president's veto of the bipartisan Keystone bill represents a victory for partisanship and for powerful special interests," bemoaned Senate majority leader Mitch McConnell. "The president's veto ... represents a defeat for jobs, infrastructure, and the middle class." In response to his Kentucky Republican foe, Obama explained that his action was motivated by a desire to protect his "authority to make the final decision on the project," not necessarily to nix the project altogether. Much to the ever-mounting frustration of his environmental supporters and pro-pipeline opponents, Obama admitted that his final decision on Keystone was still weeks, likely months, away with clear outcomes yet to be determined.[33]

Whether lost or won long term, Keystone is only the tip of mounting warfare between multiple parties, all of which hold deep convictions about the proper place of oil and energy in the new millennium. McKibben's carbon-free campaign may end up losing the Keystone fight—wildcatters may win—but his movement for reform is forcing many North Americans to a place of reckoning where carbon emissions, global warming, and earth care are concerned. The reckoning has already produced surprising results and more curious evidence of new directions. Even as the wildcatters' pipeline-friendly initiatives have raised the ire of

American liberals, in Alberta, home to the oil sands, it is "green 'salvationist' billionaires" (borrowing from a Canadian journalist) who seem
threatening to the order. Among the "salvationist billionaires" of whom
the angry Canadian speaks are the Rockefellers, whose foundation is leading a wider anti-tar sands campaign and divesting their oil holdings. The
Rockefellers abandoning petroleum? Such are the striking signs of revolution that would surprise Ida Tarbell and worry beyond measure the likes
of Walvoord and Watt.[34]

American historians, of course, should not be so surprised—change
is what we write about, so too, contingency and the fleetingness of tidy
analytical categories. Even a quick glance at these four turns in the life
of twentieth- and twenty-first-century oil should remind us of that. Here,
in the first place, are a host of characters and dynamics that do not necessarily line up with the conventions of religious and political history. The
spiritual calamity of oil in the early 1900s, 1930s, 1970s, and 2000s created flashes of insurgence that shattered familiar binaries (conservative
vs. liberal, sacred vs. secular, evangelical vs. non-evangelical) and bound
uncommon faith partners (along with the nonreligious) together behind
shared ethics and spirituality of place, capital, labor, and custodianship
over earth's most valued treasure. The degree to which these insurgen-
cies will further disrupt familiar narratives and categories and produce
religious and political realignments is a question yet to be answered (how
significant is it that oil-patch evangelical young people are locking arms
with nuns, ranchers, and indigenous communities to protest the resource
that made their hometowns prosper?).

What is striking, in the second place, is the way in which those locking
arms have made pipelines and the black stuff a transcendent ambition
and worry for many Americans. Scholars and pundits shortchange the
history of modern America when they do not calculate the deep structures
of meaning that those living in oil- (and gas-) rich zones ascribe to their
labor on and below the land and measure the lengths to which they will go
politically to protect their rights to these encounters. They also fall short
when not allowing for dense complexities in this relationship. No simple
conspiracy of interests—big oil vs. the people—oil has a way of eliciting
divergent imaginations (for Rockefeller it was industrial America's lifeblood; for Tarbell it also meant the devil's excrement) and notions of work
and family, patterns of time, and the nation's proper engagement with the
world. It is the ethical and ideological tussle within oil culture that has
prompted some of America's most profound political and religious turns.

Notes

1. See Paula Gardner, "Tornado Aftermath: Cleanup Begins in Dexter," *Ann Arbor News*, March 16, 2012, www.annarbor.com/news/dexter-tornado-damage-aftermath-schools/; Bill McKibben, *Oil and Honey: The Education of an Unlikely Activist* (New York: Times Books, 2014), 90–94.
2. "Remarks by the President on American-Made Energy," March 22, 2012, Cushing Pipe Yard, Cushing, Oklahoma, http://www.whitehouse.gov/the-press-office/2012/03/22/remarks-president-american-made-energy.
3. Ibid.
4. McKibben, *Oil and Honey*, 95.
5. Ibid., 89–92.
6. Brian C. Black, "Oil for Living; Petroleum and American Conspicuous Consumption," *Journal of American History* 99 (June 2012): 41.
7. Richard J. Callahan Jr., Kathryn Lofton, and Chad E. Seales, "Allegories of Progress: Industrial Religion in the United States," *Journal of the American Academy of Religion* 78 (March 2010): 7. See also Richard J. Callahan Jr., *Work and Faith in the Kentucky Coal Fields: Subject to Dust* (Bloomington: Indiana University Press, 2009).
8. On oil's religious influence in modern America, see Darren Dochuk, "Blessed by Oil, Cursed with Crude: God and Black Gold in the American Southwest," *Journal of American History* 99 (June 2012): 51–61.
9. Peter Moskowitz, "Plains Bedfellows," *Al Jazeera America*, October 31, 2014, http://projects.aljazeera.com/2014/pipeline-politics/south-dakota-pipeline.html.
10. Meghan McCarthy, · "Poll: Majority Support Keystone XL Pipeline," *The Morning Consult*, May 6, 2014, themorningconsult.com/2014/05/majority-support-keystone-xl-pipeline; Albert Huber and Peter Bowe, "The Keystone Pipeline Would Create Thousands of Jobs," *Forbes*, February 7, 2014, www.forbes.com/sites/realspin/2014/02/07/the-keystone-pipeline-would-create-thousands-of-jobs/; Tom Murse, "Number of Keystone XL Pipeline Jobs is a Matter of Dispute," uspolitics.about.com/od/energy/a/Are-Keystone-Pipeline-Jobs-Estimates-Just-Pipe-Dreams; Michael D. Shear and Jackie Calmes, "Obama Says He'll Evaluate Pipeline Project Depending on Pollution, *New York Times*, July 27, 2013.
11. Ron Chernow, *Titan: The Life of John D. Rockefeller Sr.* (New York: Vintage Books, 1998), 133.
12. Steve Weinberg, *Taking On the Trust: The Epic Battle of Ida Tarbell and John D. Rockefeller* (New York: W. W. Norton, 2008), 3, 59, 109, 139–140; Ida Tarbell, "My Religion," manuscript draft in "IMT: Autobiography" Folder, Box 53:4, Ida Tarbell Papers (ITP), Special Collections, Allegheny College, Meadville, Pennsylvania.

13. Weinberg, *Taking On The Trust*, 3, 207; Ida M. Tarbell, *The History of Standard Oil Company, Briefer Version*, edited by David M. Chalmers (New York: W. W. Norton, 1966), xiii.

14. Ibid., xvi. Tarbell, "My Religion," 6–7, 8, "IMT: Autobiography" Folder, Box 53:4, ITP.

15. Tarbell, *The History of Standard Oil Company*, xvi.

16. Harold L. Ickes, *Fightin' Oil* (New York: Alfred A. Knopf, 1943), 7, 71.

17. Daniel Yergin, *The Prize: The Epic Quest for Oil, Money and Power* (New York: Simon and Schuster, 1991), 403.

18. Henry Luce, "Address to Annual Meeting of the American Petroleum Institute," February 1941, Tulsa, Oklahoma, Folder 7, Box 2, Speech Series, Robert S. Kerr (RSK) Papers, Carl Albert Center, University of Oklahoma.

19. William Alfred Eddy, "The Power of God and the Secular World," Address to Woman's Auxiliary, Kansas City, October 9, 1940, Folder 8, Box 15, William Alfred Eddy Papers (WEP), Mudd Manuscript Library, Princeton University.

20. William A. Eddy, "How Arabs See the West Today," Address to Middle East Institute, December 19, 1950, Folder 16, Box 15, WEP; William A. Eddy, "The Impact of an American Private Company on a Middle East Community," Folder 19, Box 15, WEP.

21. For fuller analysis, see Darren Dochuk, "There Will Be Oil: Presidents, Wildcat Religion, and the Culture Wars of Pipeline Politics," in Brian Balogh and Bruce Schulman, eds., *Recasting Presidential History* (Ithaca, NY: Cornell University Press, 2015).

22. Robert Kerr, "Always Bearing Our Witness as Christian Citizens," May 20, 1949, Folder 7, Box 3, Speech Series, RSK; Robert Kerr, "America Unlimited," American Petroleum Institute, November 10, 1949, Folder 23, Box 3, Speeches Series, RSK. See also Robert Kerr, "Oil For American Defense," February 20, 1949, Folder 90, Box 2, Speeches Series, RSK.

23. John F. Walvoord, *Armageddon: Oil and the Middle East Crisis*, rev. ed. (Grand Rapids, MI: Zondervan, 1974), 46–47.

24. James Morton Turner, "'The Specter of Environmentalism': Wilderness, Environmental Politics, and the Evolution of the New Right," *Journal of American History* 96 (June 2009): 134; Dochuk, "There Will Be Oil," 171–172.

25. "Remarks by the President on American-Made Energy," March 22, 2012, Cushing Pipe Yard, Cushing, Oklahoma, http://www.whitehouse.gov/the-press-office/2012/03/22/remarks-president-american-made-energy.

26. McKibben, *Oil and Honey*, 95. See also www.climatesciencewatch.org/2012/03/23/still-drunk-on-oil-obama's-speech-in-cushing/.

27. "Foreign Policy's First Annual List of the 100 Top Global Thinkers," *Foreign Policy*, November 26, 2012; Anis Shivani, "Facing Cold, Hard Truths about Global Warming," *The Boston Globe*, May 30, 2010.

28. McKibben, *Oil and Honey*, 13–14.

29. Ibid., 71, 105.

30. Rosie Marie Berger, "Why Bill McKibben is the New Noah," *Sojourners Magazine*, August 8, 2012. Charles Redfern, "Why I'm Praying President Obama Will Reject Keystone XL," *Sojourners Magazine*, April 25, 2014.

31. Rosie Marie Berger, "For God So Loved the World," *Sojourners Magazine*, May 2013.

32. Laura Litvan, "Keystone Approval Sought by Republicans Daring Obama Veto," *Bloomberg Business*, November 5, 2014, http://www.bloomberg.com/news/articles/2014-11-05/keystone-approval-sought-by-republicans-daring-obama-veto.

33. Coral Davenport, "Senate Fails to Override Obama's Keystone Pipeline Veto, *New York Times*, March 4, 2015, http://www.nytimes.com/2015/03/05/us/senate-fails-to-override-obamas-keystone-pipeline-veto.html.

34. Peter Foster, "Peter Foster: Green Billionaires Undermining Canada," *Financial Post*, August 8, 2014, http://business.financialpost.com/2014/08/08/peter-foster-green-billionaires-undermining-canada/.

8

The Welfare of Faith

Alison Collis Greene

"THE QUESTION WE ask today is not whether our government is too big or too small, but whether it works—whether it helps families find jobs at a decent wage, care they can afford, a retirement that is dignified." Barack Obama's first inaugural address in 2009 seemed a repudiation of his predecessor, George W. Bush, who shrank domestic programs in favor of sharp tax cuts for wealthy Americans even as defense spending ballooned. "The nation cannot prosper long when it favors only the prosperous," Obama went on. "The success of our economy has always depended not just on the size of our gross domestic product, but on the reach of our prosperity, on the ability to extend opportunity to every willing heart—not out of charity, but because it is the surest route to our common good."[1]

Democrats celebrated Obama's "echoes of Jefferson, Lincoln, and Roosevelt," and many hoped most fervently that he would emulate the latter.[2] Liberals and church-state separation advocates expected the new president to fulfill his campaign promise to reform the controversial Bush-era Office of Faith-based and Community Initiatives and return to Roosevelt's emphasis on federal aid administered through public agencies. Many expressed disappointment when Obama simply renamed the organization the Office of Faith-based and Neighborhood Partnerships (OFBNP), appointed pentecostal minister Joshua DuBois to head it, and vaguely promised that it would make its programs more transparent and recruit a broader spectrum of religious agencies into cooperation with federal ones. Yet that office, headed since 2013 by church-state separation attorney Melissa Rogers, has also worked to advise the administration in negotiations with religious bodies over same-sex marriage and women's health coverage under the Affordable Care Act (ACA). Those battles, as well as the ongoing if largely unnoticed work of the OFBNP, have demonstrated the degree to which explicitly religious and proselytizing bodies have entwined their work ever more closely with that of the federal government in the decades since the New Deal.[3]

Seventy-six years before Obama entered the White House, Franklin Roosevelt took office during an even bleaker economic depression than that of 2008, and in the face of worldwide financial and political instability. He stood on the steps of the Capitol building and pronounced Americans' commitment to one another and the nation a "sacred obligation," and then concluded with a prayer that God bless and protect the nation and his administration's effort to preserve it.[4] Roosevelt populated his cabinet with more Catholics and Jews than any president before him; he cultivated a close relationship with the liberal Federal Council of Churches; and he spoke often of the New Deal's welfare and reform programs as an outgrowth of a century of Catholic, Jewish, and Protestant social activism.[5]

Yet Roosevelt separated the work of the expanded federal state from that of private and religious agencies whose efforts he—and many Americans—deemed "scattered, uneconomical, and unequal."[6] Harry Hopkins, head of Roosevelt's largest relief program, the Federal Emergency Relief Administration (FERA), announced in the summer of 1933 that his agency would work only through other public agencies, not through private and religious ones. In practice, FERA's work often took place with the cooperation of local churches, and organizations like Catholic Charities quickly learned how to reclassify their work as public. The New Deal's commitment to local administration of federal programs also guaranteed at least the indirect participation of religious leaders and churches that had long helped to distribute social services in tandem with public agencies. Nonetheless, Hopkins's largely successful effort to draw a line between church and state relief provided a blueprint for the administration's subsequent programs, from the Works Progress Administration to the Social Security Administration.[7]

Both Roosevelt and Obama rode into office on a wave of desperation and hope, on the promise that they would harness the power of the federal government to restore the nation to prosperity. When Obama shepherded the ACA through Congress, liberals celebrated his success in achieving one of Roosevelt's unmet goals.[8]

The comparisons ended there. When Roosevelt took office, Americans clamored for the federal government to intervene in the suffering they faced—and many churches led the way. From left to right, north, south east, and west, religious leaders celebrated the handoff of social welfare from church to state and heralded the New Deal as the realization of their own reform efforts and aspirations. Christian organizations gradually reclaimed a role in distributing aid, supported by federal funds. First, the federal government funneled post-World War II international relief funds through mainline and Catholic organizations. Many conservatives protested such church-state collaboration as an encroachment on religious liberty and warned that religious agencies that accepted federal funds would be held accountable to the government. Yet the trend continued into the 1950s. Church-state collaboration in social action increased again with Lyndon B. Johnson's Great Society programs of the 1960s, which favored cooperation with voluntary agencies over direct federal action. By this time, sectarian hospitals and social service agencies of all types found federal support irresistible, even as conservatives attacked the growing welfare state. Bill Clinton provided still more direct sectarian access to public welfare funds when he signed off on the Charitable Choice provision to the 1996 welfare reform law. By the time of Obama's inauguration, Christian organizations simultaneously controlled and denounced federal support for those in need.[9]

Franklin Roosevelt oversaw the creation of the federal welfare state; Barack Obama works to hold together what remains of it. Yet Obama's major domestic efforts, including the OFBNP and even the ACA, represent an extension of a privatized, associationalist state that resembles Herbert Hoover's vision of federally supported voluntarism almost as much as it does Franklin Roosevelt's vision of a coherent federal welfare state. This privatization preceded Obama's tenure, and his attempts to push it back—in the form of single-payer healthcare, for instance—have met with quick and vehement opposition. Furthermore, the increasing separation of federal funds from federal oversight and their administration through voluntary and religious bodies obscures the essential role of taxpayer dollars in maintaining private and religious social services. By the 1990s, Catholic Charities, Lutheran Social Ministries, and a majority of the nation's Christian child service agencies relied on public funds for more than half their income. Bush's faith-based initiatives extended an already established trend by allowing churches themselves, not just religious charities, to receive taxpayer dollars.[10] Those same churches and agencies denounce the welfare state for usurping their moral authority even as they depend on federal funds to extend it.[11]

Public arguments about the relative effectiveness of federal and volun-tary aid agencies build on two contradictory historical narratives, both of which take Roosevelt's New Deal as a turning point. Advocates of a priva-tized state, or of a shrunken state that turns over the functions of social welfare to voluntary agencies, stress the pre-New Deal power of charitable institutions to care for the needy. Most successfully put forward by his-torian Marvin Olasky, whose work helped to reshape the 1990s debate over welfare reform, this narrative describes a golden age of mutual concern and support among Americans that lasted from early America until the 1930s. Then, according to Olasky, the New Deal began to under-mine Americans' innate compassion by creating an impersonal and per-manent welfare state that rendered the poor helpless and dependent. In 2012, Franklin Graham, son of Billy Graham and head of Samaritan's Purse—an evangelical agency that has drawn heavily on federal funds for its international aid work—put the popular expression of this posi-tion most succinctly. In an interview with ABC's Christiane Amanpour, Graham explained, "A hundred years ago, the safety net, the social safety net in the country was provided by the church . . . But the government took that. And took it away from the church." What the churches lost, accord-ing to this narrative, was not just a public role in charity but also the moral authority to cultivate good citizens by tying aid to prescribed behaviors.[12]

Scholars and activists who defend the welfare state even as they seek to redress its inequities tell a different story, one in which churches play little part. Scholars of poverty and welfare, like Michael Katz and Theda Skocpol, demonstrate that, as Katz put it, "American public welfare has a very old history. Public funds have always relieved more people than private ones." From disaster relief to veterans' pensions to funds for moth-ers and orphans to municipal poor relief, state aid for people in need expanded dramatically in the nineteenth and early twentieth centuries, and religious agencies lost ground to charity organization societies that blended public and private aid. Yet both nonsectarian and public agen-cies built on the private agencies' work and their racialized and gendered notion that some poor people deserved help and some did not. The New Deal wove these inequities into a social safety net that disproportionately benefited white men even as it forced women and minorities to submit to insulting means tests—when it covered them at all. For many scholars and activists, the appropriate redress for the New Deal's injustices is not to dismantle or privatize welfare but to restructure it on a more equitable model.[13]

The divide between these two narratives is clear. Advocates of voluntarism point to churches' and private organizations' illustrious history of caring for those in need; advocates of a federal safety net point to the longstanding role of state and public agencies in individual welfare, even before the federal government intervened in the 1930s. Both camps base their arguments primarily on examples from the cities of the Northeast and the Midwest, however, where both private and public agencies proved most powerful. In short, both focus on the best version of their preferred model.

But what of the places where people relied almost entirely on a limited scope of voluntary, largely church-based aid right up to 1933? What kind of help did these groups offer, to whom, and under what conditions? Did either providers or recipients deem it to be enough? How did voluntary and religious agencies fund their work? How did they navigate the greatest economic crisis since the Civil War? And how did their work change in response to the New Deal?

Memphis, Tennessee, and the surrounding Delta regions of Mississippi and Arkansas provide one set of answers to these questions. Memphis and the Delta make for an interesting case study because the region lacked the state and municipal relief that historians of welfare have stressed as a predecessor to the New Deal, and because it boasted the private, primarily religious sources of aid that conservatives celebrate—and which proved inadequate in the best circumstances and disastrous in the worst. The Great Depression crippled the efforts of even the most robust public and private agencies across the nation. For instance, Lizabeth Cohen has examined the extensive public, ethnic, and religious safety nets that supported Chicago workers in the 1920s and shown how rapidly they collapsed with the onset of the Great Depression. Chicago workers demanded that the federal government step in, and they organized to ensure that they could help shape its efforts. Even in places like New York City, where both municipal and private relief expenditures soared during the Depression, the increased help could not match the need brought on by a national unemployment rate of 25 percent and widespread hunger and homelessness. Southern cities generally provided less public aid than their northern and Midwestern counterparts, and the rural South provided less still. Rather than rallying around their suffering community members when the Depression began, already weak southern aid structures folded, leaving people in need with nowhere to turn. Neither the New Deal's public antecedents nor its private alternatives could address the region's widespread suffering and starvation. Here, the necessity of federal intervention in the Great Depression is clear.[14]

Both Memphis and the Delta relied almost entirely on voluntary aid until the 1930s. While relief in the Delta proved patchwork and sparse, Memphis boasted a well-organized Community Fund, a nonsectarian central source of charity and social services whose member organizations were overwhelmingly religious. In 1930, Memphis was a city of 250,000, the nation's thirty-sixth largest. Memphis was majority white and over a third African American; much of the Delta was majority black. Thus, the region also provides some insight into the distinct forms of aid available to black and white southerners in a Jim Crow order. Significant populations of Catholics and Jews and strong Catholic and Jewish charities in the city further illuminate the distinct operations of Catholic, Jewish, and Protestant aid societies.[15]

The South's first serious foray into public aid came during the Civil War and in its aftermath in the form of state pensions for Confederate veterans. States also funded prisons and asylums, and many cities operated poorhouses for the indigent and elderly. The pensions—the South's only real form of relief—went only to white men. In 1898, after two devastating yellow fever epidemics, Memphis established a city hospital that included wards for both black and white patients. For a brief period in the 1920s, the city distributed privately donated milk to needy infants of both races. Between 1911 and 1930, most states established small Mothers' Aid funds. These funds, designed to provide pensions so that widowed or abandoned mothers could care for their children at home rather than institutionalizing them, supported only whites in Memphis and the Delta, reached only a few hundred families altogether, and provided a few dollars a month at best. Before the New Deal, that was the extent of public aid in the region.[16]

Private charities, most of them religious, accounted for 76 percent of per-capita expenditures on relief in Memphis in 1930, and for nearly 100 percent in the Delta. Those organizations made no pretense of serving all equally. Between the Civil War and the Great Depression, Protestant women's societies and home mission organizations built schools, hospitals, orphanages, and settlement houses to reach the city's needy whites, but they served only those they deemed deserving and appropriately deferent. Concerned that their members not be deemed a burden on the larger Protestant community, Memphis's Catholic and Jewish charities served their own communities first. But the Catholic House of the Good Shepherd cooperated with the city's juvenile court system to house both Catholic and non-Catholic troubled girls. The Jewish Neighborhood House fed poor children of all backgrounds. Black churches and fraternal orders provided the only source of support for most African Americans in need, and they established schools, medical facilities, and insurance programs in both city and countryside.[17]

Yet the need these various organizations sought to alleviate far outpaced the resources they could gather even before the Depression. For families that did not need the institutional help religious societies favored but instead faced chronic poverty and hunger, little assistance was available. Southern charities generally ascribed chronic poverty to individual shortcomings and deemed it the responsibility of extended families and churches to care for their own members. Only the Salvation Army offered a comprehensive soup kitchen, and that agency focused its efforts in Memphis on white men and boys. People in the countryside relied entirely on informal aid or—more frequently—went hungry, as state-level nutrition studies clearly demonstrate. But the constant requests for support from underfunded voluntary societies, and their stories of families helped (rather than those they missed), could easily leave the impression that anyone who truly needed help had only to ask.[18]

In 1923, several of the city's charitable organizations consolidated their fundraising efforts under the umbrella of the Memphis Community Fund, which vowed to reduce the pleas for help and increase the efficiency of aid. The Community Fund's member agencies primarily served whites, and still its resources proved inadequate. The fund met its minimal fundraising goals in its founding year and then failed to reach them again for a decade. Its organizers, who believed that poverty generally resulted from individual failures, lamented that they could not raise the funds even to help those few souls they deemed both needy and worthy of help.[19]

And then disaster struck. The 1929 stock market crash left most Memphians and Delta residents unfazed, their fortunes tied instead to the cotton and agricultural markets. But a record-setting drought in the spring and summer of 1930 parched the cotton in the fields as the prices for what was salvageable plummeted to a third of the previous year's rates. Food crops shriveled alongside the cotton, and farmers faced a long winter with neither food to store nor income for basic staples. Then, a wave of bank failures swept the region, and even those who had managed to put by a little money saw their savings disappear. With federal support, the Red Cross provided minimal emergency aid starting in December, often distributed through churches whose members so universally suffered that they could not aid one another without outside help. But the help was not enough, and reports soon emerged of people walking miles for food, their feet wrapped in sacks, and of "frantic women begging for medical aid for babies dying of malnutrition or the many forms of disease that attack the underfed and underclothed." Some of those people arrived only to find that their townships or county Red Cross chapters had run out of ration cards and refused to provide aid without them.[20]

The private aid organizations that had proudly proclaimed their success at caring for all who really needed help now faced three crises at once. First, the number of people seeking help skyrocketed. Second, the argument that many of the poor deserved their lot fell apart in the face of widespread environmental and economic crisis. And last, donations to charities and churches plummeted and any savings these organizations had often vanished in the same bank failures that crushed farmers and the middle class.

Voluntary agencies tried to help. In December of 1929, the Salvation Army—a member of the Community Fund—had served 1,700 meals; by December of 1930, that number ballooned to 6,500 meals; by April, 10,250 meals. Also a men's shelter, the Salvation Army drained its pool to make room for extra pallets on the pool floor.[21] But many agencies cut back. In 1931, the Community Fund pared its fundraising goals to a minimum, and it still brought in only $462,344 of its $609,553 goal—a 24 percent shortfall.[22] Many women's clubs, fraternal orders, and other quasi-religious private organizations suspended their work or disbanded.[23]

Churches fared still worse, often struggling just to keep their doors open. Between 1929 and 1932, national income dropped by more than 50 percent. Wage earners' income sank by 60 percent, salaried workers' by 40 percent. Because of the drought and the lost cotton crop, that loss came earlier to Memphis and the Delta. Until 1933, church giving held steady as a proportion of national income, but a 50 percent loss proved crippling at the very moment that demands on church resources escalated. More ominously, the churches cut benevolent spending first.[24] As the president of the cash-strapped Southern Baptist Convention put it in 1931, "We are putting off the Lord's cause while we try to settle with our other creditors."[25] When the money ran out, the churches turned their spending inward, not outward.

As they faced the suffering before them and their own inability to alleviate it, even conservative religious leaders joined social workers and hungry Americans to call for federal intervention. In January 1932,

Herbert Hoover's administration established the Reconstruction Finance Corporation (RFC), which Congress authorized to provide emergency loans to banks and corporations. In July, Congress expanded its powers to provide loans to states and municipalities for public works projects that would employ out-of-work citizens. States often disbursed those funds through private agencies like the Memphis Community Fund, cementing such agencies' support. Yet the measure did little to stem the Depression. Democrat Franklin Roosevelt trounced Hoover in the 1932 election, largely on the promise that he would use the power of the federal government to address the crisis. Even as many Protestants opposed Roosevelt's vow to end Prohibition, southern clergy enthusiastically supported the new president's first efforts to address the Depression.[26]

The barrage of legislation that Roosevelt signed in early 1933, in what would become known as the First Hundred Days, included a provision to create an agency that drew a clear line between federal and private relief: FERA. FERA replaced Hoover's RFC loans with grants to the states for relief projects. Headed by Iowan Harry Hopkins, FERA was the first program to put federal funds not only toward employment relief but also toward direct aid for the suffering, in whatever form city and state aid administrators saw fit. It was also the program that most directly engaged with the work once conducted by private aid organizations.[27]

In June 1933, Hopkins stipulated that as of July 1 only public agencies could administer FERA funds. With so much at stake both financially and politically, Hopkins wanted to avoid the problems and complaints that plagued Hoover's inadequate RFC. Yet he had to honor Roosevelt's commitment to maintain local control of aid. Public aid on the RFC's scale was such a novelty that many states—particularly in the South—lacked the infrastructure and experience to administer it, and many had simply subsidized private work rather than establishing new public programs. As Josephine Brown, a social worker and FERA field agent, explained, Hopkins's decision meant "the financing and administration of public benefits for persons in need was definitely established as being the responsibility of government and not of private citizens, however organized or however charitably disposed."[28] Leaders of private and religious agencies often simply transitioned to public positions, while other private agencies—like Catholic Charities in Chicago—gained public certification. Hopkins's decree nonetheless established a clear public-private boundary both for FERA and for subsequent New Deal programs.[29]

Government aid quickly outpaced that of all private agencies, because it could leverage a vastly larger pool of resources. Across the nation, but especially in places like Memphis and the Delta that had offered little aid to the poor, New Deal spending made previous private contributions look like pocket change. At the peak of private giving, in 1931, Memphians raised $.88 in aid per person, $.75, or 85 percent of it, private. By 1934, the New Deal in full swing, Memphians received $7.21 per capita in aid for direct relief and work relief. Private contributions that year amounted to only $.13 per capita—1.6 percent of the total. By comparison, the average aid per person in the nation's 116 major urban areas increased from $2.36 per person, 29 percent ($.45) of it private, in 1931 to $16.51 per person in 1934, with only 1.8 percent ($.15) provided by private sources. Nationally, and even more so in Memphis, this was a striking reversal. In just five years, as federal dollars provided the work and food Memphians so desperately needed, private aid dropped from nearly three-quarters of relief spending in the city to less than 2 percent. The shift from private to public responsibility for the needy could hardly have been more dramatic.[30]

The swing from private to public aid was easier to track in the city, but it was even more pronounced in the countryside, where fewer resources of either kind were available. In the Delta, neither public nor private charity was organized enough to provide accurate reports before 1933. By the end of July 1933, FERA had made grants to every state and the District of Columbia. Between January 1933 and December 1935, eleven states—including Arkansas, Mississippi, Tennessee, and most of the South—received more than 90 percent of their total work relief funds from the federal government.[31]

Because it was the only New Deal agency to provide direct aid to the needy, FERA proved particularly important to religious leaders. People had finally begun to receive the help that they so desperately needed and that the churches and civic organizations had proven unable to provide. Now those people began to turn to the state rather than to local religious groups for both material aid and personal guidance. Some clergy celebrated the transition and asked for more. A white Arkansas Sunday School superintendent wrote to the nonexistent "Welfare Society" in Washington, DC, to ask for help with a pair of tough local children. "If you have a place for such lads, to have them reformed," wrote the superintendent, "the community would be much pleased." He was almost certainly disappointed to receive a quick response from Eleanor Roosevelt's secretary reporting that the federal government could do nothing to address the matter, which instead "would come under the jurisdiction of local authorities."[32]

This emphasis on local distribution of federal aid secured the support of white southerners who distrusted the federal government's commitment to the region's Jim Crow capitalist economy, but ministers concerned with social and racial justice denounced FERA's unequal implementation. Local relief administrators often represented the economic elite, and they structured the new system to humiliate those who sought help and to deny them when possible. Southern capitalism depended on a dual wage system that kept African American workers poor, and local administration guaranteed the perpetuation of that system. One Mississippi minister wrote to Roosevelt to "call attention to the Southern negro who has not had a square deal of the many projects since the depression."[33]

Yet black religious leaders also applauded signs that the Roosevelt administration cared more for African Americans' safety and well-being in the South than had previous administrations. In 1934, Harold Ickes, Roosevelt's secretary of the interior and head of the Public Works Administration, created an "Interdepartmental Group Concerned with Special Problems of Negroes" to push for inclusion of African Americans in the major New Deal programs. Though the group had little power, its existence seemed a hopeful step. The overall standard of living for black workers who kept their jobs also increased slightly as their employers found a way to cheat the government and stopped working so hard to cheat their workers.[34]

Although its separation of public and private relief work proved more durable, FERA was itself a temporary measure, intended only to meet the immediate physical needs of people devastated by the Depression. The program expired in 1935, replaced in part by two programs at the heart of Franklin Roosevelt's Second New Deal: the Works Progress Administration and the Social Security Act. Perhaps because these two programs created permanent structures that overlapped with work that churches had once done, in September 1935 Roosevelt's administration sent a letter to the nation's clergy asking for feedback on them. He received more than 12,000 replies within two months, a full 84 percent of which proved generally favorable in tone, particularly toward the Social Security Act, which made provisions for the elderly, the orphaned, and the disabled.[35]

"Above all else, as I see it, is your Social Security Program," wrote the editor of the South's major white Methodist journal. "For the first time in our history we have a National Administration that is seeking to realize practically all the objectives of the 'Social Creeds' of the Churches—Catholic, Protestant, Jewish."[36] For religious leaders like this one, the welfare state represented a religious achievement rather than an encroachment on the churches' work. Indeed, it freed the churches to focus on supplementary care or return to a focus on evangelism.

But a few clergy expressed concerns that would grow more widespread by the late 1930s, particularly among conservative and evangelically oriented white Protestants. Although Social Security excluded domestic and agricultural workers, and thus most southern African Americans, some whites nonetheless complained—inaccurately—of the "high cost to the white population" of Social Security because "one-half of the citizenry pays a very small part of the taxes."[37] Others feared their loss of power over white community members as well. One Mississippi Presbyterian and self-proclaimed "southern Democrat" worried that the state had severed the church's hold on community members who now had someplace else to find help. "Where they once had community contacts for cooperation and sympathy they now look to the Government for all," he declared.[38] It is possible that federal aid made it easier for some poor families to disconnect from middle-class churches where they felt out of place. Now, they had options other than local paternalism, and clergy already inclined to question the New Deal expressed both alarm and outrage.

Although dissent grew in Memphis, the Delta, and across the South during the late 1930s, Roosevelt's programs remained popular in the region and its churches for decades. Black and white workers proved loyal to the president they credited with pulling them out of the Depression, as did much of the region's middle class. Some southern whites defected from the Democratic Party because they believed that the New Deal threatened white supremacy in the region. But the South's Republican turn lay in the future. With the memory of private relief's utter collapse in a moment of crisis still fresh, southerners in the 1930s and 1940s embraced the nascent welfare state.[39]

Soon American religious institutions began to take roles not only complementary to the welfare state but also integral to it—and funded by it. After World War II and increasingly as the Cold War dragged on, both secular and religious nonprofits worked as subsidiaries of the federal government to provide overseas relief, education, and aid. As the domestic welfare state expanded under both Republican and Democratic presidents from the 1940s to the 1960s, federal officials increasingly relied on private subsidiaries, including religious organizations, to administer new programs. Lyndon

Johnson's War on Poverty sped this transition, as its most important provisions for health and child welfare were often administered through subsidies to religious hospitals and church-based child care providers.[40]

As conservative critics of the welfare state rose to power in the 1980s and 1990s, they pushed both elimination and privatization of services. By the 1980s, the National Association of Evangelicals and other conservative organizations that had once spurned government support now embraced tax credits for private child care, fought for public vouchers to parochial schools, and relied heavily on federal support for international missionary and relief work.[41] But it was Democrat Bill Clinton who signed the Personal Responsibility and Work Opportunity Reconciliation Act into law in 1996, and with it Charitable Choice, a provision that ensured that religious providers received equal consideration in competition for federal funds and removed stipulations that those providers qualify for tax-exempt status.[42]

His successor George W. Bush established the more famous White House Office of Faith-based and Community Initiatives, which allowed churches themselves, and not just religious charities, to receive federal funds. Obama promised more transparency about the disbursement of federal funds to proselytizing bodies in his continuation of the faith-based initiatives effort. Yet even as he has shifted emphasis from such programs, the funding for them remains robust. As the welfare state has shrunk, it has also made an increasing proportion of its remaining funds available to explicitly religious providers.[43]

Indeed, many religious organizations rely so heavily on federal dollars today that they would likely fold without them. More than eighty years since the New Deal first established a federal safety net, it is difficult to imagine the United States without such basic protections for its citizens. Many conservatives and libertarians call for just that, however, recalling an American past that never existed, in which unfettered capitalism ensured a robust economy and the deserving poor received what they needed from generous private and religious charities. Those very charities have become so deeply entwined in the federal government in the post-World War II decades that in dismantling the welfare state they risk dismantling themselves. In short, religious and private agencies grow fat on federal dollars that allow them to extend their moral and political authority with little oversight. In a deceptive sleight-of-hand and a bald-faced denial of history, anti-government Christian conservatives like Franklin Graham demand an end to the very federal programs that they—and many far more vulnerable Americans—rely on to survive.

Notes

1. "Transcript, Barack Obama's Inaugural Address," New York Times, January 20, 2009.

2. George Packer, "Let Us Now Set Aside Childish Things," The New Yorker, January 20, 2009. On Bush spending priorities from both a conservative and a liberal perspective, see Veronique de Rugy, "Spending Under President George W. Bush," working paper 09-04, March 2009, Mercatus Center, George Mason University; John Cassidy, "Reagan, Bush, and Obama: We Are All Still Keynesians," The New Yorker, June 4, 2012, http://www.newyorker.com/news/john-cassidy/ reagan-bush-and-obama-we-are-all-still-keynesians.

3. "Obama Wants to Expand Role of Religious Groups," New York Times, July 2, 2008; "White House Faith Office to Expand," New York Times, February 9, 2009; "Despite a Decade of Controversy, the 'Faith-Based Initiative' Endures," New York Times, July 31, 2009; "White House Picks Church-State Lawyer Melissa Rogers to Head Faith Office," Washington Post, March 13, 2013.

4. "Text of New President's Address at Inauguration," Washington Post, March 5, 1933.

5. Gary Scott Smith, Faith and the Presidency from George Washington to George W. Bush (New York: Oxford University Press, 2006), 191–220; Alison Collis Greene, "The End of 'The Protestant Era'?," Church History 80, no. 3 (September 2011): 600–610.

6. "Text of New President's Address at Inauguration."

7. Josephine Chapin Brown, Public Relief, 1929–1939 (New York: Octagon Books, 1971), 172–190; Michael B. Katz, In the Shadow of the Poorhouse: A Social History of Welfare in America, 2nd ed. (New York: Basic Books, 1996 [1986]), 224–231; Dorothy M. Brown and Elizabeth McKeown, The Poor Belong to Us: Catholic Charities and American Welfare (Cambridge, MA: Harvard University Press, 1997), 163–173.

8. Nicolaus Mills, "Roosevelt and the Affordable Care Act," Huffington Post, July 16, 2013, http://www.huffingtonpost.com/nicolaus-mills/roosevelt-and-the-afforda_b_3600103.html; Al Carroll, "Franklin Roosevelt and the New Deal Compared to Obamacare," Daily Kos, May 27, 2014, http://www.dailykos.com/story/2014/05/27/1298267/-Franklin-Roosevelt-and-the-New-Deal-Compared-to-Obamacare.

9. Alison Collis Greene, "'A Divine Revelation?': Southern Churches Respond to the New Deal," in Andrew Preston et al., Religion and American Politics (Philadelphia: University of Pennsylvania Press, 2015); John P. Bartkowski and Helen A. Regis, Charitable Choices: Religion, Race, and Poverty in the Post-Welfare Era (New York: New York University Press, 2003), 1–6; Axel R. Schäfer, Piety and Public Funding: Evangelicals and the State in Modern America (Philadelphia: University of Pennsylvania Press, 2012), 1–20, 194–214. I rely most heavily on Schäfer's examples and argument, focused primarily on conservatives, as I describe transitions in public funding of religious agencies from the 1940s to the present.

10. Axel R. Schäfer, "The Cold War State and the Resurgence of Evangelicalism: A Study of the Public Funding of Religion Since 1945," *Radical History Review* 99 (Fall 2007): 33, 42.

11. See, for instance, recent comments by Joni Ernst: O. Kay Henderson, "Ernst carries concealed weapon '90 percent of the time,'" Radio Iowa, August 20, 2013, http://www.radioiowa.com/2013/08/20/ernst-carries-concealed-weapon-9 o-percent-of-the-time-audio/.

12. Marvin Olasky, *The Tragedy of American Compassion* (Washington, DC: Regnery, 1992); Franklin Graham, "This Week's Transcript: God and Government," ABC News, http://abcnews.go.com/ThisWeek/week-transcript-god-government/story?id=13446238#.TySHQ-NSSso. I have written briefly about Graham's comments before. See Greene, "Let's Remember History, When Religious Institutions Welcomed Government Support," The Table, *Religion and Politics*, June 4, 2012, http://religionandpolitics.org/2012/06/04/lets-remember-history-when-religious-institutions-welcomed-government-support/.

13. Katz, *In the Shadow of the Poorhouse*, xiv; Theda Skocpol, *Protecting Soldiers and Mothers: The Political Origins of Social Policy in the United States* (Cambridge: Belknap Press, 1992). This body of scholarship is enormous and varied. See also Michele Landis Dauber, *The Sympathetic State: Disaster Relief and the Origins of the American Welfare State* (Chicago: University of Chicago Press, 2012); Ange-Marie Hancock, *The Politics of Disgust: The Public Identity of the Welfare Queen* (New York: New York University Press, 2004); Linda Gordon, *Pitied But Not Entitled: Single Mothers and the History of Welfare, 1890–1935* (New York: Free Press, 1994).

14. Lizabeth Cohen, *Making a New Deal: Industrial Workers in Chicago, 1919–1939* (New York: Cambridge University Press, 1990), 1–9, 213–289; David M. Kennedy, *Freedom from Fear: The American People in Depression and War* (New York: Oxford University Press, 1999), 88. For a Southern comparison, see Elna Green, *This Business of Relief: Confronting Poverty in a Southern City, 1740–1940* (Athens: University of Georgia Press, 2003).

15. Bureau of the Census, *Census of the United States, 1930*; Bureau of the Census, *Census of Religious Bodies: 1926, Part I* (Washington, DC: Government Printing Office, 1930), 466–467, 580–582, 632–634.

16. Elna Green, ed., *Before the New Deal: Social Welfare in the South, 1830–1930* (Athens: University of Georgia Press, 1999), ix–xviii; Jennifer Ann Trost, *Gateway to Justice: The Juvenile Court and Progressive Child Welfare in Memphis* (Athens: University of Georgia Press, 2006), 65; Skocpol, *Protecting Soldiers and Mothers*, 102–151; *Directory: Social Welfare Agencies* (Memphis: Council of Social Agencies of Memphis and Shelby County, 1941), 9–11, 14–15; US Department of Labor, Children's Bureau, *Mothers' Aid, 1931*, Bureau Publication 220 (Washington, DC: Government Printing Office, 1933), 1, 7–9,

14, 17, 26; Charles O. Lee, *1931 Annual Report, Memphis Community Fund,* Memphis-Charities-Community Fund Clippings File, Memphis-Community Chest Clippings File, Memphis Public Library (MPL), 10; Skocpol, *Protecting Soldiers and Mothers,* 424–479.

17. Enid Baird, *Public and Private Aid in Urban Areas, 1929–1938* (Washington, DC: Social Security Board, 1942), 115; Trost, *Gateway to Justice,* 64–67, 136–138; "All Creeds Meet at Welfare School," *Memphis Commercial-Appeal,* July 9, 1932; *Open Your Heart: Memphis Cares for Her Own,* Memphis Community Fund, 1928, back page, MPL.

18. *Twelfth Annual Appeal of the Memphis Community Fund,* 1933, 12; *1931 Annual Report, Memphis Community Fund,* 2. On nutrition, see "A Nutrition Investigation of Negro Tenants in the Yazoo Mississippi Delta," *Bulletin* no. 254, Mississippi Agricultural Experiment Station, A & M College, Starkville, Mississippi, 1928.

19. *1940 Annual Report, Memphis Community Fund, with Historical Supplement, Memphis, Tennessee,* Mayor Watkins Overton Papers, MPL; *Open Your Heart,* Memphis Community Fund, 1928, back page, MPL.

20. "Hunger-1931," *The Nation,* February 11, 1931, 151–152; *Statistical Abstract of the United States, 1941* (Washington, DC: Government Printing Office, 1942), 741; Nan Elizabeth Woodruff, *As Rare As Rain: Federal Relief in the Great Southern Drought of 1930–31* (Urbana: University of Illinois Press, 1985), 30–36, 50–52; "$962,000 Is Obtained for Drought Relief," *New York Times,* January 22, 1931, 3.

21. *Twelfth Annual Appeal of the Memphis Community Fund,* 1933, 12; *1931 Annual Report, Memphis Community Fund,* 2; "Boys, Old Men—All Poor and Hungry, Swarm to Salvation Army for Shelter," *Memphis Press-Scimitar,* February 9, 1933.

22. *1931 Annual Report,* Memphis Community Fund, 4, 9.

23. Marsha Wedell, *Elite Women and the Reform Impulse in Memphis, 1875–1915* (Knoxville: University of Tennessee Press, 1991), 106–107; David Beito, *From Mutual Aid to the Welfare State: Fraternal Societies and Social Services, 1890–1967* (Chapel Hill: University of North Carolina Press, 2000), 1–16, 181–221; Benson Y. Landis and George Edmund Haynes, *Cotton-Growing Communities Study no. 2: Case Studies of 10 Rural Communities and 10 Plantations in Arkansas* (New York: Federal Council of Churches, 1935), 9, 21.

24. Rosemary D. Marcuss and Richard E. Kane, "U.S. National Income and Product Statistics: Born of the Great Depression and World War II," *Survey of Current Business* (February 2007): 32–46; "Bowing Out 1931," *New Orleans Christian Advocate,* January 7, 1932, 4; Samuel C. Kincheloe, *Research Memorandum on Religion in the Depression* (New York: Social Science Research Council, 1937), 17, 23, 28.

25. "Our Present Denominational Situation," *(Arkansas) Baptist Advance*, August 7, 1930, 1, 9.
26. Corrington Gill, "Unemployment Relief," *American Economic Review* 25, no. 1 (March 1935): 176–185; Kennedy, *Freedom from Fear*, 84–85; "Fund Shakeup Nears; R.F.C. Drops Support," *Memphis Commercial Appeal*, June 26, 1933.
27. Brown, *Public Relief*, 184–190; Kennedy, *Freedom from Fear*, 131–159.
28. Brown, *Public Relief*, 172–190 (quotation on 190).
29. Brown and McKeown, *The Poor Belong to Us*, 164–166.
30. Baird, *Public and Private Aid*, 86–151.
31. *Final Statistical Report of the FERA*, 102–104; Brown, *Public Relief*, 205.
32. J. F. Dodd, School Director, Supt. of Sunday School, Alpena Pass, Arkansas, to Welfare Society, Washington, DC, October 9, 1934, Box 264, Correspondence with Government Departments, Eleanor Roosevelt Papers, Franklin D. Roosevelt Presidential Library and Archives, Hyde Park, NY [FDR Library]; Secretary to Mrs. Roosevelt to J. F. Dodd, October 12, 1934, Box 264, Eleanor Roosevelt Papers, FDR Library.
33. I. C. Franklin, Port Gibson, Mississippi, to Franklin D. Roosevelt, October 16, 1935, Folder: Mississippi, Box 30, President's Personal File 21A-Church Matters, [Clergy Letters], FDR Library.
34. John B. Kirby, *Black Americans in the Roosevelt Era: Liberalism and Race* (Knoxville: University of Tennessee Press, 1980), 24. See also Ira Katznelson, *Fear Itself: The New Deal and the Origins of Our Time* (New York: Liveright, 2013); Harvard Sitkoff, *A New Deal for Blacks: The Emergence of Civil Rights as a National Issue: The Depression Decade* (New York: Oxford University Press, 2009 [1978]).
35. For more detail about these results, see Greene, "A Divine Revelation?" For more detail on the Roosevelt administration's motivation in sending out the letter, and the controversy it provoked, see Matthew Avery Sutton, "Was FDR the Antichrist? The Birth of Fundamentalist Antiliberalism in a Global Age," *Journal of American History* 98, no. 4 (January 2012): 1052–1074.
36. John S. Chadwick, ed., *Christian Advocate*, Nashville, October 3, 1935, Authors and educators folder, Box 35, Clergy letters (CL), FDR Library.
37. Henry G. Hawkins, Vicksburg District, MECS, September 30, 1935, Mississippi Folder, Box 16, CL; George D. Booth, First Presbyterian, Natchez, Missisippi, September 30, 1935, Mississippi Folder, Box 16, CL.
38. Rev. R. L. Phelps, Synod of Mississippi, PCUSA, September 30, 1935, Church officials folder, Box 35, CL.
39. On the South and the New Deal, see Katznelson, *Fear Itself*; Glenda Elizabeth Gilmore, *Defying Dixie: The Radical Roots of Civil Rights, 1919–1950* (New York: W. W. Norton, 2008); Roger Biles, *The South and the New Deal* (Lexington: University Press of Kentucky, 1994).

40. Schäfer, *Piety and Public Funding*, 1–59, 123–162; Peter Dobkin Hall, "Historical Perspectives on Religion, Government, and Social Welfare in America," in Andrew Walsh, ed., *Can Charitable Choice Work? Covering Religion's Impact on Urban Affairs and Social Services* (Hartford, CT: Pew Charitable Trusts, 2001), http://www.trincoll.edu/depts/csrpl/Charitable%20Choice%20book/hall.pdf.

41. Schäfer, "The Cold War State and the Resurgence of Evangelicalism," 28–34.

42. Bartkowski and Regis, *Charitable Choices*, 1–59.

43. Ibid.; Schäfer, *Piety and Public Funding*, 210–214.

9

Latino/a Religious Communities and Immigration in Modern America

Arlene Sánchez-Walsh

BARACK OBAMA WAS twice elected with the overwhelming support of Latinos/as.[1] One reason for that support was Obama's promise to make comprehensive immigration reform a priority. But immigration reform appears to be dead, despite the best efforts of religious communities. Conservative evangelicals, progressive Christians, and the Roman Catholic Church—historically, the most fervent and consistent supporter of immigrants' rights—all lobbied feverishly. Even the Dream Act, which offered much more limited reforms, has gone nowhere. Obama's immigration policy has been reduced to a limited executive action that is far from likely to survive legislative and judicial challenges.[2]

How could an administration that seemed so promising for Latinos/as fail them so thoroughly? How could one of Latinos/as' critical priorities be put off until his second term and—amid the congressional intransigence and the fervent opposition of the Tea Party—allowed to die? What made President Obama think he could pass any legislation through a Republican Congress?

Perhaps a more intriguing question is why Latinos/as supported President Obama at all. After his failed legislative battles over immigration, his continued support for deportations (400,000 a year since 2008), and the more than $18 billion allocated for the militarization of the border—more border agents, drones, and stations—why did Latinos/as support Obama even more strongly in 2012 than in 2008?[3] Moreover, why did representatives of key religious groups who support Obama's immigration reform efforts not support Obama?

Latino/a Catholics, mainline Protestants and evangelicals, and Latter-day Saints (LDS) all had vested interests in passing immigration reform. Religious activists attempted to create alternative representations of Latino/a immigrants by stressing stories of hard-working people and how they are similar to earlier waves of immigrants. They also focused on the sanctity of the family in an attempt to win over conservatives. Activists interweaved their impassioned pleas to treat Latino/a immigrants humanely and with dignity. But these groups failed to appreciate that the dominant white culture—the backbone of today's GOP—has its own immigrant narrative, rooted in rhetoric about the rule of law and "undesirables." This mythology, rooted firmly in what historian Eric McDaniel calls "Christian nationalism," and what others view as civil religion, has been used to preserve a sense of American difference and to diminish the historic role of Latino/a immigrants in building the nation. Latinos/as have never been viewed as "American" enough. The struggle between these competing narratives is centuries old.

IN 1848, MEXICO lost half its land mass and more than seventy-five thousand of its citizens to American annexation. Crossing the border became illegal in 1929.[4] Throughout the twentieth century, mass deportations occurred frequently, often when economic pressures dictated that precious resources of local, state, and federal governments should only be used to support "Americans," a not-so-subtle code for "whites." During the 1930s, nearly half a million Mexican and American citizens were sent back to Mexico. The next wave occurred under Operation "Wetback" in the 1950s, when more than one million people were deported. Today's deportations, similarly, began in earnest with the economic downturn of 2008. Indeed, deportation is the most significant way that the federal government regulates immigration. Deportation allows even the most sympathetic political leaders to claim that they are merely adhering to the rule of law.[5] Coupled with the militarization of the border, deportation reinforces the dominant historical narrative.

After 1848, the Texas and Arizona Rangers were authorized to police Mexicans who remained in the United States. Immigration laws have allowed limited numbers of Mexicans into the United States to work, but have criminalized other forms of immigration.[6]

Historian David Manuel Hernández notes that the regulation and criminalization of immigration were based on well-worn fears of Mexican immigrants as disease carriers, criminals, political subversives, and national security threats—existential threats to weak US economies. From 1917 to the 1930s, during what historian Natalia Molina calls a period of "medicalized nativism," Mexicans (who were not subject to racial exclusion acts or the quota system) were subjected to medical detention and quarantines, which helped control immigration during the upheaval of the Mexican Revolution (1919–1920).[7]

These narratives of contagion and criminality fueled the recent ugly clashes in Murrieta, California, and elsewhere, in which anti-immigrant protesters blocked buses transporting detainees to a local Border Patrol station. Some protesters carried signs alleging that the women and children in those buses were carrying diseases or harboring gang members. While anti-immigration activists stressed the rule of law, religious activists decided that it was again time, amid an upsurge in xenophobia, to push for immigration reform.

At Murrieta, anti-immigrant mobs successfully turned back a bus full of women and children—most, if not all, escaping ultra-violent countries. These protests were catalyzed by rumors that more "illegals" were on their way. There were more children to be dropped off, children of a criminal class, possibly carrying exotic contagious diseases, and perhaps working in tandem with an elaborate syndicate of drug cartels and the Mexican prison gang La Eme. Those buses never came.[8]

What the Murrieta action and the subsequent gatherings unleashed was a pent-up fear and anger that this sleepy, industrious exurb was about to be invaded. Residents' feelings of safety and serenity, rooted in a romanticized vision of suburbia, were under imagined siege. The voices of Latino/a religious communities crying out for decency, mercy, and family became lost in the alarmist rhetoric expertly deployed by anti-immigrant Tea Party groups and their sympathizers.

Probably no other internal debate about immigration demonstrates these clashes more clearly than the tensions that arose when the LDS church, Latino/a LDS members, and immigration activists clashed over the support of the "Utah Compact." The LDS church supported the compact as a "responsible approach to the urgent challenge of immigration reform."[9] Specifically, the church was against forced family separation, which was not in keeping with its moral teachings. But while the

LDS leadership supported reform, they also sought to remain politically neutral. Dieter Uchtdorf, a leader in the church hierarchy, said: "As a church, we do not tell anyone how to vote. We are totally politically neutral, but we stand up for the values we have. We supported the Utah Compact with its values and principles; we have done this publicly and in writing, so everyone knows that. We hope that our view of these important matters for our communities will, at least, be considered by those who have to make the final decisions."[10] Despite the church's desire not to wade into the political waters of immigration reform, LDS support for the compact caused at least a portion of the church to rebel against such support as politically troubling and theologically treacherous.

In a 2011 article in the *Backgrounder*, LDS member and former foreign service officer Ronald Mortensen took the LDS hierarchy to task for supporting the compact and a proposed state law in Utah, which Mortensen said was an amnesty bill. He quoted the church's twelfth Article of Faith, which pledges that LDS members will be subjects to "Kings, Presidents, rulers, and magistrates in obeying, honoring and sustaining the law."[11] Mortensen lamented the loss of an America that, he imagined, had existed not long ago.[12] Once, LDS leaders had "openly taught that the founding fathers were guided by the hand of God, that the U.S. Constitution was divinely inspired & that the U.S. was a chosen land for the restoration of Christ's true church." What had changed? Mortensen speculated the answer lay in the changing demographics of the church: out of the thirteen million Mormons worldwide, nearly one-third (four million) are Spanish speakers.[13]

Particularly appalling to Mortensen and some LDS members was the reality that the church baptized "illegal aliens," accepted temple recommends (membership cards for temple entrance) for them, and allowed them to serve in important church positions. Mortensen lays blame on the church's refusal to acknowledge that they even had a position on immigration reform. "Mormons are left to try and discern what this change means for the gospel as they have known it." The church was instrumental in getting former US senator Robert Bennett to insert an exemption for the LDS church to be allowed to use "illegal aliens" to be ministers and volunteer for missions work. Mortensen argues that the LDS's call for compassion for the undocumented has shifted the narrative. Social justice had trumped the rule of law, demonstrating "how far the LDS church has moved from its American roots." Instead, they were trying to placate their large Latino/a constituency. "As the church found it more difficult to gain converts among American citizens, LDS officials increasingly focused the church's mission activities on the "illegal immigrant."[14]

Mortenson's article offered a lament for the loss of the law, the loss of an imagined America, and the loss of the church—a church whose demographics are changing so rapidly that its continued growth depends on its Latin American missionaries and immigrant converts.

Similar battles played out on the state level. In June 2011, Alabama legislators passed HB 56 making it illegal to rent to, hire, or transport suspected undocumented persons. It also required schools to turn in children who were suspected of being undocumented and allowed law enforcement to detain people who were reasonably suspected of being undocumented. Immediately, the Roman Catholic Church and mainline Protestants called on citizens to treat people humanely. Catholic Charities stepped in to provide services to immigrants, and United Methodists followed suit. Both groups actively lobbied against the implementation of the bill.[15] Latino/a evangelical pastors, on the other hand, had difficulty mobilizing their own fight against HB 56.

Two groups that did make very public and pronounced efforts to pass immigration reform were the National Latino Evangelical Coalition (NLEC), headed by Nazarene pastor Gabriel Salguero, and the National Hispanic Christian Leadership Conference (NHCLC), led by Assemblies of God pastor Samuel Rodriguez. Both organizations attempted to tap into what they assumed would be productive avenues to lobby Congress for immigration reform. Both badly misjudged the influence of the Tea Party on the Republican Party's agenda. Neither group had the benefit of viewing the immigration debate in a historical context where reform only becomes broadly acceptable if it sheds the image of the law-breaking illegal. Latinos/as have not secured reforms and rights without some hint that those who did not support those reforms would pay politically by being voted out of office.

United Methodist bishop William Willimon joined the Episcopal and Catholic bishops and sued Alabama governor Robert Bentley, stating that HB 56 impeded religious freedom by forbidding churches to offer help to strangers and administer sacraments. Willimon claimed that the implementation of the law would affect the more than 338,000 undocumented members of their respective denominations.[16] Mainline Protestants like the United Methodists have long focused on social justice issues. Their consistent support of social justice for Latino/a immigrants has not translated to more Latinos/as joining their ranks, an irony that has likely not gone unnoticed.

Evangelicals, on the other hand, were not roused to action, spurring NHCLC leader Rodriguez to travel to Alabama to mobilize Spanish-speaking pastors. Rodriguez noted: "The pastors are failing, within the evangelical movement, in contextualizing the message to their members to call elected officials at the local and federal level and encourage an immigration reform that is not amnesty, but it's not Alabama either."[17] Some white and Latino/a evangelical clergy lobbied hard, but the GOP was not going to side with them over their fervent anti-immigration constituency.

McDaniel notes that there are three traditional categories that help produce opinions about immigration: economic, symbolic, and cultural. Historically, Latino/a immigrants have been viewed as threats to all these categories. Rhetoric about "stealing American jobs" and fear that Latinos/as will fail to assimilate at rates similar to other, more acceptable (European) immigrants are all part of the historic pattern. To white evangelicals, steeped in American civil religion, Latino/a immigrants are also a religious threat. These evangelicals fear the loss of an imagined America, founded by white evangelicals with God's help, its people united in one common faith and one common purpose. For McDaniel, there is a "fear that immigrants will neither recognize nor fulfill the standards of behavior accepted by those in the host country. Believing that outsiders will violate the meaning of what it means to be American leads to animus toward policies like bilingual education."[18] Why did evangelical elites, both white and Latino, seek to lobby GOP leadership as well as the Obama administration in favor of immigration reform? Aside from their legitimate and sincere belief in the cause, these same leaders can count, and their demographic futures depend on Latinos/as. But then why did their lobbying efforts fail?

The Latino/a evangelical elites who created NHCLC inflated their political influence and overstated their ability to deliver votes. The very loose ecclesiology that binds Latino/a evangelicals together makes it difficult to organize voters effectively. Latino/a evangelicals have no central organization, and if they are bound together at all, it is around individual issues and personalities. The NHCLC believed that the same "glue" that binds Latino/a ethnic identity and thereby helped create a reliable voting block for Democrats would come together under their banner. It is unclear whether Latino/a evangelical identity works this way outside of its religious context.

Research shows that church attendance and what is heard at church both matter. Latino/a evangelicals go to church often, but they do not hear about immigration; they hear sermons about the importance of voting, abortion, and LGBT issues. Latino/a evangelicals have a higher proportion of anti-immigrant attitudes than Latino/a Catholics and main-line Protestants. Thirty-five percent of Latino/a evangelicals believe that immigration threatens society. Among that group, 54 percent are US born.[19] Part of what may be happening here is a phenomenon I noted in analyzing Latino/a pentecostal religious identities and what social scientists have found in looking at how "Protestantism animates a decoupling of ethnic/religious identity."[20] Latino/a Protestants, for a host of reasons, tend to move more rapidly toward assimilation. Viewing other Latinos/as as undocumented and themselves as Americans is one of many ways that Latino/a evangelicals "decouple" from being Latino and identify with white evangelicalism's political agenda. Mobilizing Latino/a evangelicals to engage in immigration reform should begin in churches. Since it currently does not, it is no surprise that Alabama's pastors were not stirred to action.

The Roman Catholic Church is the most consistent supporter of immigrants' rights and the most vocal religious group in support of immigration reform, as well as a vocal opponent of harsh anti-immigrant bills in Arizona, Alabama, and a half dozen other states. The reasons for this are rooted in Catholic social teaching, the activism of the Catholic Church on behalf of Latinos/as, and the role that Catholic Charities plays in serving displaced people such as refugees and detained immigrants. Fully one-third of US Catholics are Latinos/as, and if current demographic projections are correct, they will be the majority by mid-century. Clearly the Catholic Church has an interest in maintaining good relations with their majority constituency. This is perhaps made more urgent by the aging of the white Catholic population, who tend to vote more like white evangelicals or Mormons than like Latino/a Catholics or evangelicals. It may be, as political scientists Lyman Kellstadt and James L. Guth have written, that Latino/a Catholics fill in the "gap" left by deserting white Roman Catholics, who have been reliable Democratic voters for decades.[21]

Catholic opinion on immigration reform certainly is not monolithic. Conservative publications such as *First Things, Crisis,* and *The Wanderer* all capture the anti-immigration reform views and focus on how Latino/a immigrants do not assimilate like past Catholic immigrants, are a drain on the government coffers, and demonstrate how Catholic bishops have become dupes for the Obama administration.[22] A quick perusal of the progressive *National Catholic Reporter* over the last few years finds that many Catholics, from grassroots parishioners to the US Conference of Catholic Bishops (USCCB), are involved in immigration debates. There are lots of stories about parishes in transition: formerly all-white Old European immigrant parishes making the uneasy transition to majority Latino/a. These transitions created some problems, but overall, the *Reporter* stresses the successes. One story concerned the suburban Illinois town of Woodstock, which had zero ethnic diversity throughout the 1950s and the 1960s. The parish recently started having Spanish-language masses to accommodate the growing Latino/a population. The article's author, rather than take a wistful approach to the loss of his boyhood home, sounds grateful for the diversity of the church:

> This is the new St. Mary Catholic Church. And although no doubt there are cultural and racial tensions below the surface in this attractive exurb of Chicago, it's clear that the old ways of thinking and of living are rapidly passing away to make room for a more robustly diverse population in which whites and blacks and Latinos and Asians and others all can learn from one another.[23]

Other transitions did not go so well, as the *New York Times* reveals in a series about Highway 35, a Midwest corridor that Latino/a immigrants take from Texas to Minnesota, following a migratory trail of harvests. The tensions at a once all-white parish in Tulsa, Oklahoma, led some older whites to leave rather than see "their" parish change. The parish is now over 90 percent Latino/a. The *Times* series makes the case that people may have been worn down by the issue; they are tired of it and have resigned themselves to immigrants being here to stay. As proof, the reporters cite the fact that in 2011 state legislatures passed more laws extending rights to immigrants without legal status than laws adding restrictions.[24]

What these stories suggest is that, at the grassroots level, Catholics act to implement church teachings regarding the treatment of undocumented persons. It does not always happen, and there are failures, but the *National Catholic Reporter* promotes the idea that the church is a welcoming and open place for immigrants. A recent story focused on the work of a laywoman in a parish in Texas She spoke eloquently about how proud she was to be a Catholic as she helped with the unaccompanied minors. This kind of grassroots effort by Catholics brought a whole new humanizing dimension to the immigration debate in the summer of 2014. For this woman, this is what Catholics do, because it is what Jesus would do.[25] Local settings showing practical results that are consistent with Catholic social teachings can make immigration a winning issue. This personal touch—stories of women singing to young, scared children in an attempt to assuage their fears—make the Catholic Church look compassionate. In some sense, it may be on this personal level of helping the stranger and the "alien" that religious sensibilities can be most readily felt.

The USCCB and other concerned Catholic clerical organizations were nearly uniformly in favor of immigration reform and lobbied extensively for it. Through websites such as "justice for immigrants," the Catholic Church did and continues to lobby politicians, particularly Catholics.[26] Perhaps it is no surprise that the most prominent Catholic politicians in Congress, Speaker John Boehner and Representative Paul Ryan, have done little to further the cause of reform out of fear of the Tea Party, which has demonstrated that it can oust GOP office holders if that is what adherence to ideological purity demands. Indeed, lobbying by Roman Catholic bishops and evangelical leaders failed to carry the day not because the GOP wants to divorce itself from these religious constituencies but because these constituencies are reliable votes that do not require immediate mollification on such an unpopular issue.

Journalist Jacob Lupfer diagnosed the failure of immigration reform and why, even with conservative evangelical support, leaders like Joel Hunter and Rick Warren were incapable of moving the House GOP to action. He argued that immigration reform is simply not a "salient" issue for white evangelicals. White evangelicals are mostly walled off from immigrants in a kind of religious gerrymandering: they find themselves in suburban churches, not in neighborhoods populated by immigrants. For them, immigration reform takes a back seat to any number of culture war issues. The two Latino evangelical lobbying groups that advocated for immigration reform for years may have been unsuccessful because while the GOP claimed to be fighting for the Latino/a vote it had little practical reason to do so.[27]

The calculus looks something like this. White Catholics, Mormons, and evangelicals—animated by a host of cultural and economic issues—will, for the foreseeable future, be the bedrock of the GOP. Ethnic Catholics,

African Americans, Latinos/as, and the catchall category of "other" will continue to support Democrats. Many, if not all, of these religious groups did not grasp the Tea Party's animus toward immigrants. In fact, this sentiment, along with the desire to limit or eliminate federal government programs, is the lifeblood of many Tea Party groups.

Religious groups hoping appeals to faith, family, and fairness would move politicians to vote for immigration reform did not anticipate the Tea Party's immense influence on the GOP. They did not succeed in breaking the intractable hold that an imagined America has on segments of the white population. Tea Party followers see their idealized American Dream under attack, particularly with reference to immigration, they seemed resigned to the country's ongoing demographic changes. Tea Partiers feared that immigration reform would further undermine the values and ideals that they espoused and would challenge their efforts to transform American politics.

The GOP base, Mormons, conservative white Catholics, and white evangelicals fear that immigrants will change their country and make it unrecognizable. Forecasting past the Obama administration into the future of immigration reform, one can see the potential candidacy of Jeb Bush as a possible way to break the stalemate. It may be a matter of time, especially if Bush becomes the nominee, for him to be opposed from the right on immigration.

But will Jeb Bush and his family be subjected to the same scrutiny that Obama has been? Will there be a website dedicated to questioning Bush's "Americanness" simply because he married a Mexican woman and speaks Spanish? Will Bush's conversion to Catholicism spur the same kinds of questions about loyalty that John F. Kennedy faced in his 1960 campaign? As the privileged son of a political dynasty, Bush may not be subjected to those indignities. One doubts that Bush or any GOP candidate will be subjected to the same kinds of questions regarding their place of birth and suspicions about whether they will "sell out" the country will probably be nil. In an age when the Tea Party commands the allegiance of one of the two viable political parties, there may be no level of loyalty that Jeb Bush, or Mario Rubio or Ted Cruz can attain in a political climate so polarized that questions about the President's birthplace and religion are still fodder for Tea Party websites and blogs. For the Tea Party, the America they long for has already disappeared.

Notes

1. In 2008, Latinos/as voted 67 percent for Obama and 31 percent for McCain. In 2012, Latinos/as voted 71 percent for Obama and 27 percent for Romney. Mark Hugo Lopez and Paul Taylor, "Latino Voters in the 2012 Election," Pew Research Center's Hispanic Trends Project, November 7, 2012, http://www. Pewhispanic.org/2012/11/07/latino-voters-in-the-2012-election/.

2. With new GOP majorities in both Congress and Senate, it is unclear whether President Obama's executive action will survive what will undoubtedly be efforts to de-fund his immigration initiatives and/or tie them up in legal challenges until the end of his term.

3. Christie Thompson, "Billions Proposed for New Border Security. Where Would the Money Go?," *ProPublica*, April 26, 2013, http://www.propublica.org/article/billions-proposed-for-new-border-security.-where-would-the-money-go.

4. Gustavo Cano and Alexander Delano, *The Mexican Government and Organized Mexican Immigrants in the United States: A Historical Analysis of Political Transnationalism 1848–2005*, Working Paper 148, Vol. 148 (Washington, DC: Mexico North Research Network, 2007).

5. Jaqueline Hagen, "Social Effects of Mass Deportations, 2000–2010," *Ethnic and Racial Studies* 34, no. 8 (August 2011): 1374–1391.

6. Mexicans have a unique immigration history because of the contiguous border with the United States and because they have been part of a foundational immigration base from Latin America. However, in terms of how Latino/a immigrants of other nationalities have been treated, there are many similarities. A complicated series of economic and political factors created very different circumstances for Puerto Ricans, who share similar colonial roots with Mexicans. After 1917, they found themselves made US citizens, as did the Mexicans in New Mexico after 1848. For Puerto Ricans, being US citizens meant that they could move from Puerto Rico to the continental United States freely. Puerto Rican "immigration" then has not been hampered by the specter of illegality, though it has been spurred by the perpetual economic instability of the island and the frustrated political desires of its inhabitants, who can be full-fledged US citizens if they move to the United States or US colonial subjects if they stay on the island. Cuban immigrants, have been considered refugees fleeing communist Cuba from the 1960s until the "Mariel Boatlift" of 1980, when the narrative began to mirror a much more familiar one. Cuban "refugees" are now unwanted immigrants, detained as criminals and treated as people fleeing Castro's jails, bringing with them all kinds of contagious diseases. The latest waves of Latin American immigration occurred during the 1970s and 1980s, when Central American immigrants, fleeing war-torn countries like El Salvador, Honduras, and Guatemala, established themselves as the newest group of Latino/a immigrants to be viewed as undesirable, as a strain on government resources, and as unassimilable.

7. David Manuel Hernandez, "Pursuant to Deportation: Latinos and Immigrant Detention," *Latino Studies* 6 (2008): 35–634; Natalia Molina, *Fit To Be Citizens? Public Health and Race in Los Angeles 1879–1939* (Berkeley: University of California Press, 2006), 58.

8. M. Hansen and K. Linthicum, "Murrieta Protesters Turn Back Border Patrol Detainees," *Los Angeles Times*, n.d., //www.latimes.com/local/la-me-murrieta-immigrants-20140702-story.html.

9. "Mormon Newsroom—Church Supports Principles of Utah Compact on Immigration," December 5, 2014, http://www.mormonnewsroom.org/article/church-supports-principles-of-utah-compact-on-immigration.

10. The Church of Jesus Christ of Latter-day Saints, "President Uchtdorf Represents the Church in White House Meeting—Church News and Events," March 18, 2013, https://www.lds.org/church/news/president-uchtdorf-represents-the-church-in-white-house-meeting?lang=eng.

11. R. Mortenson, "The Mormon Church and Illegal Immigration," *Backgrounder* (April 2011), https://heartland.org/sites/default/files/lds-and-immigration.pdf. Unless otherwise noted, all quotes in this section are from this article.

12. I am using Benedict Anderson's concept of "imagined communities" to play off the often-used trope that in the not-too-distant American past immigration was not an issue and, by extension, the supposed homogeneity of the American people led to a more prosperous, peaceful, and moral nation. Philosophers call this the "golden-age" fallacy. Promoters of this imagined America, like Anderson's case study of Southeast Asia, don't actually live in such communities. Instead, they create these communities based on mutual affinities. For my purposes then, the "imagined America" is a fictive community created to bind together "law-abiding Americans" and "law-abiding immigrants" in order to exclude "illegal aliens." The result is the historic exclusion of Latino immigrants, who are cast as a law-breaking, disease-carrying, criminally subversive class.

13. Mortensen, "The Mormon Church and Illegal Immigration."

14. Ibid.

15. Iulia Filip, "Bishops Say Alabama's High Immigration Law Would Criminalize Religious Sacraments," *Courthouse News*, August 4, 2011, http://www.courthousenews.com/2011/08/04/38714.htm.

16. Joel Rosenblatt, "Alabama Churches Sue to Block State Immigration Law Enforcement," *BusinessWeek: Undefined*, August 1, 2011, http://www.businessweek.com/news/2011-08-01/alabama-churches-sue-to-block-state-immigration-law-enforcement.html.

17. Gustavo Valdes, "Latino Evangelicals Challenge Alabama Brethren on Immigration," *CNN Belief Blog*, November 13, 2011, http://religion.blogs.cnn.com/2011/11/13/latino-evangelicals-challenge-alabama-brethren-on-immigration/.

18. Eric Leon McDaniel, Irfan Nooruddin, and Allyson Faith Shortle, "Divine Boundaries: How Religion Shapes Citizens' Attitudes Toward Immigrants," *American Politics Research* 39, no. 1 (January 1, 2011): 205–233.

19. Adrian Pantoja, "Republicans Should Look for a New Playbook to Win Latino Evangelicals," *Latino Decisions*, May 5, 2014, http://www.latinodecisions.com/blog/2014/05/05/republicans-should-look-new-playbook-to-win-latino-evangelicals/.

20. Jonathan Calvillo and Stanley Bailey, "Latino Religious Affiliation and Ethnic Identity," *Journal for the Scientific Study of Religion* 54, no. 1 (2015): 57–78.

21. L. A. Kellstedt and J. L. Guth, "Catholic Partisanship and the Presidential Vote in 2012: Testing Alternative Theories," *The Forum* 11, no. 4 (2013): 623–640.

22. For some examples from the conservative Catholic press see Christopher Manion, "The Catholic Bishops and Immigration Reform," *Crisis Magazine*, May 14, 2013, http://www.crisismagazine.com/2013/the-catholic-bishops-and-immigration-reform; William Chip, "Of Bishops and Business," *First Things*, May 12, 2014, http://www.firstthings.com/web-exclusives/2014/05/the-folly-of-comprehensive-immigration-reform; Dexter Duggan, "Show GOP Honchos the Exit Door ... Republican Leaders Give Obama What He Wants For Amnesty," *The Wanderer*, March 10, 2015, http://thewandererpress.com/frontpage/show-gop-honchos-the-exit-door-republican-leaders-give-obama-what-he-wants-for-amnesty/.

23. Bill Tammeus, "Diverse Future a Blessing for Illinois Hometown," *National Catholic Reporter*, July 9, 2014, http://ncronline.org/blogs/small-c-catholic/diverse-future-blessing-illinois-hometown.

24. Damien Cave, "The Way North," *New York Times*, May 17, 2014, http://www.nytimes.com/interactive/2014/us/the-way-north.html#p/35.

25. Megan Sweas, "Ministering to Unaccompanied Immigrant Children," *Global Sisters Report*, June 19, 2014, http://globalsistersreport.org/news/migration/ministering-unaccompanied-immigrant-children-5051.

26. http://www.justiceforimmigrants.org/index.shtml

27. Jacob Lupfer, "Even Conservative Evangelical Support Couldn't Save Immigration Reform," *The Daily Beast*, July 6, 2014, http://www.thedailybeast.com/articles/2014/07/06/even-conservative-evangelical-support-couldn-t-save-immigration-reform.html.

10

Teaching About Religion in Red-state America

Mark A. Chancey

"THESE BOOKS MAKE Moses the original founding father and credit him for virtually every distinctive feature of American government." So argued Kathleen Wellman, a history professor at Southern Methodist University when she appeared before the Texas State Board of Education (SBOE) on September 16, 2014. Wellman hoped to dissuade that body from approving social studies textbooks she regarded as historically inaccurate. Some texts were so flawed, she lamented, that students might even end up "believing that Moses was the first American."[1] Despite her protests, those of other scholars, and the efforts of watchdog groups (such as Texas Freedom Network, with which the present author is affiliated), many of the books endorsed two months later by the SBOE affirmed the importance of Mosaic influence on American law.[2]

If Moses was startlingly prominent in proposed US history and government textbooks, it was because in order to be approved by the SBOE, the books had to cover topics identified in the curricular standards the board created in 2009–2010. Those controversial standards characterized Moses as an individual "whose principles of laws and government institutions informed the American founding documents." They portrayed the Ten Commandments as a predecessor to the Declaration of Independence and the Constitution and identified "biblical law" as one of the "major intellectual, philosophical, political, and religious traditions that informed the American founding." The standards went so far as to elevate "the Judeo-Christian legal tradition" to the status of the starting

point for the American institution of "democratic-republican government."[3] For the standards' supporters, this portrayal of Moses and biblical
law exemplified a rightly enhanced treatment of religion in general and
the Bible in particular; for some critics, it fit into a larger pattern of bias
toward Christianity over other traditions.[4]

Texas has famously long been the site of school board battles. The
state was home to the late activists Mel and Norma Gabler, who pioneered
the strategy of reviewing textbooks line by line for errors and bias and
whose work continues today through the Educational Research Analysts.[5]
Historically, however, most controversies over social studies in Texas and
elsewhere have focused not on representations of religion per se but on
issues related to multiculturalism, feminism, and political ideology.[6]
These latter issues, to be sure, have figured prominently in the latest
round of Texas's social studies wars, but the inclusion of religion alongside them marks a relatively new development.[7]

In Texas, curricular wars are fought in an explicitly partisan arena.
Texas is one of only a few states in which SBOE members achieve their
positions through partisan elections.[8] Debates over what to teach in public schools thus pit Democrats against Republicans. They also often put
competing factions within a party at odds, such as Tea Party Republicans
against more moderate members of the GOP. Republican domination of
the Texas SBOE means that the party has often succeeded in shaping many
aspects of the state's curriculum to fit its members' views and values.

The political implications of this state of affairs are particularly significant when it comes to social studies because of the subject matter's
traditional association with the tasks of fostering the knowledge, skills,
and virtues needed for responsible citizenship.[9] The Texas standards fore-
ground this civic component with an oft-repeated directive: "The content . . .
enables students to understand the importance of patriotism, function in
a free enterprise society, and appreciate the basic democratic values of our
state and nation."[10] Viewed in this light, the standards' references to religion function as Texas's official statement of the minimal knowledge that
students—and by implication, citizens—should have about the subject.

This chapter explores how Texas's 2010 standards reflect attempts to
teach students to understand religion through a lens colored with red-state
sensibilities. It focuses on the standards' portrayal of Christianity's impact
on the founding of the United States, their consideration of the so-called
world religions, and their treatment of Islam in particular. A look back at

Texas's earlier social studies guidelines provides historical perspective on just how unusual its new standards are.

Religion in the 2010 Social Studies Standards

The Texas SBOE revises standards for every subject roughly once per decade. Although it solicits input from committees of teachers and citizens, a small number of board-appointed subject-area experts, and the general public, the board itself retains final authority to define the standards through majority vote. The current standards are known collectively as Texas Essential Knowledge and Skills or simply TEKS. The starting point for the 2010 TEKS was an earlier version drafted in the mid-1990s under Governor George W. Bush and implemented in 1998. The 1998 TEKS frequently referenced religion, and so in this general respect, the 2010 TEKS follow the lead of their predecessors.[11] Several 2010 standards, in fact, preserve language from 1998 about the roles of "various racial, ethnic, and religious groups" in American history and society.[12]

What was markedly different in 2010 was the visible influence of a particular theopolitical ideology, Christian Americanism.[13] Proponents of this ideology believe that the United States was established to be a distinctively Christian nation, with its founding documents, form of government, and legal system shaped primarily (though not exclusively) by biblical principles and Judeo-Christian beliefs (with the term "Judeo-Christian" seemingly equated at times with positions held by socially and theologically conservative Christians). Furthermore, they regard it as a patriotic and religious duty to preserve American's Christian identity. The influence of Christian Americanists within the Texas GOP is indicated by the inclusion of materials in its 2010 platform such as its "Traditional Principles in Education" plank: "We support school subjects with emphasis on Judeo-Christian principles (including the Ten Commandments) upon which America was founded and which form the basis of America's legal, political and economic systems."[14]

Seven of the board's ten Republican members in 2009–2010 openly and diligently worked to promote Christian Americanist ideology through the TEKS, picking up the necessary additional votes from the other three Republicans and occasionally from Democrats.[15] Members of this bloc, including board chair Gail Lowe, regularly referred to Christian Americanist views as indisputable historical facts in board meetings, public speeches, and comments to journalists. Bloc members appointed amateur historians (Christian Right celebrities David Barton and the late Peter Marshall) famous for advocating such arguments to the handful of experts assigned to recommend changes to the standards, as well as an academic perceived as sympathetic, Daniel Dreisbach of American University.[16]

The blatant nature of the bloc's Christian Americanist sensibilities and agenda is illustrated by an incident that occurred at the end of the TEKS process. At the May 21, 2010, SBOE meeting, board member Cynthia Dunbar (now a law professor at Liberty University) delivered the opening prayer:

> I believe no one can read the history of our country without realizing that the Good Book and the spirit of the Savior have from the beginning been our guiding geniuses. Whether we look to the first charter of Virginia, or the charter of New England or the Charter of Massachusetts Bay, or the Fundamental Orders of Connecticut, the same objective is present: a Christian land governed by Christian principles. I believe the entire Bill of Rights came into being because of the knowledge our forefathers had of the Bible and their belief in it . . . I like to believe we are living today in the spirit of the Christian religion.

Given the tense and contentious atmosphere of the board, which had been battling for months over this interpretation of history, Dunbar's invocation struck many as a galling act of political showmanship.[17]

The discovery of the source of Dunbar's prayer added a strong dose of irony to the situation. Rather than offering a prayer she composed herself, Dunbar read one written decades earlier by none other than Chief Justice Earl Warren. It was Warren who had presided over the landmark 1960s Supreme Court decisions prohibiting school-sponsored Bible reading and prayer. Dunbar's re-use of his comments about "a Christian land governed by Christian principles" seemed designed to signal to church-state separationists that even one of their greatest heroes had, in fact, sided with her own camp. In contrast to Dunbar, however, Warren had offered the prayer not in his official capacity at a governmental function but as personal sentiments at a private event, the 1954 prayer breakfast of the International Council for Christian Leadership. Despite those sentiments, he still ruled against school prayer and Bible reading less than a decade later.[18]

Dunbar's prayer may have been a symbolic statement, but the Christian Americanist bloc's overall accomplishments were concrete. They inserted a strong dose of Christianity into the American history and government TEKS, adding references to religious revivals, conservative icon Phyllis Schlafly, the Moral Majority, evangelist Billy Graham, and the "meaning and historical significance" of the national motto "In God We Trust."[19] The most significant change they made was in regard to religious influences on early American political thought. Moses was not the only new addition; the board also inserted Thomas Aquinas and John Calvin into a standard formerly devoted to Enlightenment philosophers.[20] To draw attention to the Christian identities and religious hopes of some early colonists, they added "religious [reasons]" to a standard on the "political, economic . . . and social reasons for the establishment of the 13 English colonies" as well as an additional reference to the Mayflower Compact.[21] They also introduced the names of individuals celebrated as paragons of piety in Christian Americanist historiography, such as Henry Blackstone, Thomas Hooker, George Mason, Charles Pinckney, Benjamin Rush, John Witherspoon, and John Jay.[22]

One of the board's most controversial acts was its creation of a new high-school standard requiring students to "examine the reasons the Founding Fathers protected religious freedom in America and guaranteed its free exercise by saying that 'Congress shall make no law respecting an establishment of religion, or prohibiting the free exercise thereof,' and compare and contrast this to the phrase, 'separation of church and state.'"[23] Though the standard's wording is somewhat ambiguous, its supporters clearly intended it to reflect the Christian Americanist claim that the Founders did not envision a separation of church and state that extended beyond the eschewal of a national church (an idea also ensconced in the 2010 state GOP platform).[24]

The standard thus seemed intended not to foster serious discussion of the diverse ways in which the First Amendment has been interpreted from its inception but to preclude consideration of separationist positions of the sorts traditionally associated with Thomas Jefferson and James Madison. For their part, Democrats introduced an unsuccessful amendment suggesting that students study the reasons the Founders "protected religious freedom in America by barring government from promoting or disfavoring any particular religion over all others." This proposal, too, oversimplified a complicated history by ignoring such factors as the First Amendment's original inapplicability to the states.[25]

The SBOE also elevated the TEKS' attention to other religious traditions, though not to the same degree as Christianity.[26] In response to concerted efforts by members of the Texas Sikh community, the board acknowledged Sikhism as a major world religion, listing it with Buddhism, Christianity, Confucianism, Hinduism, Islam, and Judaism in an older world history standard, and with animism, Buddhism, Christianity, Hinduism, Islam, and Judaism in a new geography standard.[27] It also further diversified a sixth-grade list of religious holidays and added two new standards emphasizing interaction between different religious communities in different parts of the globe.[28] Even with such revisions, the standards gave relatively little explicit consideration to religions originating in Asia. Judaism did not fare much better, despite references to the Holocaust, the nation of Israel, Jewish holidays, the origins of monotheism, and, of course, America's purported biblical roots.[29]

Islam, however, received several new TEKS, perhaps an unsurprising development in light of all that has occurred since the attacks of September 11, 2001. The 2010 standards categorize the "development of Islamic caliphates" as one of the "important turning points in world history" and cite "the political, economic, and social impact of Islam on Europe, Asia, and Africa."[30] They also direct students to "explain how Islam influences law and government in the Muslim world."[31]

Chronologically, however, Islam seems to fade away after references to the early Ottoman Empire, not to reappear until discussions of contemporary conflicts.[32] Several standards directly or indirectly associate the religion with terrorism, the most explicit of which links "radical Islamic fundamentalism" to "Palestinian terrorism," "the growth of al Qaeda," and 9/11. Indeed, with the exception of one generic usage, every reference in the TEKS to terrorism arguably relates in some way to Islam, a point that prompted strong criticism from the American Civil Liberties Union of Texas.[33] A standard that attributes sole responsibility for "ongoing conflict" involving modern Israel to "Arab rejection" of that nation does not technically refer to Islam but bears obvious conceptual kinship to the standards on terrorism and fundamentalism; it is also the only place in the TEKS where the word "Arab" occurs.[34] Given the absence of references to other aspects of modern Islam, the overall impression such TEKS give is that the most salient features of contemporary Islam are terrorism, conflict, and hostility to Israel—linkages also reflected in the 2010 state Republican Platform.[35] The board rejected a motion by two Democrats to add a reference to "other acts of terrorism prior to September 11, 2001, not related to

Islam, including the U.S. Cavalry against American Indians, the Texas Rangers against Mexican Americans, and for decades by the Ku Klux Klan and other white supremacist groups right here in our own country."[36]

One Islam-related amendment was withdrawn in the face of heated opposition. At the May 20, 2010, meeting, Democrat Lawrence Allen, an African American Muslim, moved to add the name "Barack Obama" to a standard mentioning "the first black president." His Republican counterpart, David Bradley, a board member not known for sympathy toward Islam, proposed to modify further that standard by referring to the president as "Barack Hussein Obama," thus giving him "the honor and privilege of his full name." Bradley's amendment seemed to allude to concerns in some conservative sectors that Obama's name marks him as a "foreigner," perhaps one not even legitimately eligible to be president, and a Muslim. Some interpreted Bradley's facial expression at the time as a smirk. "To start throwing out a name so it sounds derogatory and you're grinning and making fun, it's really quite upsetting," Democrat Helen Berlanga chastised. "It's the first time that a black person has been elected president and you're somehow making it sound almost humiliating." After a lengthy discussion among board members, Bradley retracted the motion "to put an end to the whining," he explained, and the name remained simply "Barack Obama."[37]

Overall, the TEKS provide only the most general guidance for studying traditions other than Christianity. The high-school world history standard listing them broadly recommends that pupils study the "historical origins, central ideas, and spread of major religious and philosophical traditions."[38] In contrast, references to events and personages important to Christianity are woven throughout the TEKS. That religion fares best in one especially crucial regard: it is the only tradition for which the standards acknowledge internal diversity, explicitly referencing Roman Catholicism, Eastern Orthodoxy, and Protestantism.[39] One might easily conclude from the TEKS' vague wording that the other religions are all monolithic.

Religion in Past Texas Social Studies Guidelines

Course standards (that is, standardized and required student learning objectives) are a relatively recent educational innovation, but states have long issued course guidelines of varying degrees of detail and levels of authority.[40] In Texas, the first such recommendations for social studies—at the time a new blend of what had formerly been taught simply as history, civics, and geography—appeared in the 1920s. In 1926 and 1929, the State Department of Education published two editions of a bulletin titled *Texas High Schools: The Teaching of History and Other Social Subjects*.[41] Those bulletins' suggestions reflected so great a Western bias that the rest of the world typically appears only in relation to its engagement with Europe and North America. Both publications regularly referred to religious events and figures, especially in the premodern period, but in ways that usually privileged Christianity.

Yet these bulletins' level of detail surpassed that of most subsequent state documents, a fact that allows us to get a good sense of how Texas taught about religion at the birth of social studies as a field. The 1926 booklet, for example, indicated that students should learn about matters such as the "birth of Christ," the Edict of Milan, the Council of Nicaea, the Papacy, the Crusades, and the Protestant Reformation. Of the other traditions, Islam by far received the most attention, primarily because of European and Arab contacts and conflicts in the Middle Ages. The guidelines encouraged teachers to instruct students about Mohammad, the growth of Islam, "the importance of checking [the] advance" of Islam at the Battle of Tours, and the "civilizing influence of Islam." The book recommended coverage of the biblical period but largely neglected Jewish history after the destruction of the temple in 70 CE, an approach typical of traditional Christian supersessionism. Its limited coverage of Asia and Africa almost ignored religious dimensions of cultures there. Of the major traditions other than Judaism, Christianity, and Islam, only Buddhism was mentioned by name—and that in a list of terms related to European colonialism.[42]

In contrast to its prominent place in the suggestions for Western history classes, religion was mostly absent in descriptions of American history and civics classes. Issues of religious liberty appeared primarily in a 1926 nod to "religious toleration in the colonies" and a 1929 reference to Thomas Jefferson's promotion of "religious freedom," the latter a detail that might suggest sympathy for separationist sensibilities.[43] After coverage of the earliest decades of American history, religion largely disappeared from the bulletins' recommendations. They provided no evidence of the sort of Christian Americanist narrative that would undergird some of the 2010 TEKS.

The state published several pertinent guidelines in the next two decades. In 1937, the Department of Education issued its first *Standards and Activities of the Division of Supervision*, a bulletin it regularly updated until the mid-1940s.[44] The different versions of this document are help-ful for charting the approval of different types and names of social courses (world geography, for example, which first appeared in 1943), but they included little detail about the intended contents of those courses.[45] Instead, *Teaching Social Studies in Junior and Senior High Schools of Texas*, which appeared in 1938, became the authoritative guide. Its references to "church" as a primary social unit clearly indicated an assumption of shared Christian identity, but its recommendations for history, both American and Western, largely overlooked religion as a sphere of culture worthy of consideration.[46]

In light of religion's generally small role in early twentieth-century guidelines, its prominence in the 1957 publication *Social Studies in Texas Schools: A Tentative Curriculum Guide Grades One through Twelve* is strik-ing. Issued in the midst of the Cold War in the face of the threat of god-less communism, this book placed religion, albeit vaguely defined, at the very center of American history and public life. In doing so, it reflected the national tenor of heightened religiosity characteristic of the era of Eisenhower, who famously proclaimed that "our form of government has no sense unless it is founded in a deeply felt religious faith, and I don't care what it is."[47] In a similar vein, the 1957 Texas guide identified the notions that "our country was founded by people of religious faith" and "faith in God and faith in man are basic to our democratic way of life" as core principles for young students. Yet it was also intentional in expos-ing students to religious diversity, perhaps in recognition of America's broader involvement in the world. Fourth graders learning about "the peoples of the world in their communities," it advised, should be taught about the "cultures of the peoples of different national, racial or religious heritages." High schoolers in world history were expected to study the "world's great religions" and to recognize that "man expresses his faith through many religions."[48]

Texas documents from the 1960s and 1970s were comparatively mini-malist in approach. What meager guidelines they contained rarely men-tioned religion explicitly, although their more general references to the study of various cultures implicitly included it. The specific references to religion that did appear were typically in the context of world history, not American history. The 1961 standards bulletin, for example, pointed to "contributions of the Moslem, Byzantine, and European cultures of the late Middle Ages" and "how philosophical, political and religious beliefs of people are influenced by their experiences."[49]

The 1980s were a key turning point for Texas public education, mark-ing the beginning of the state's shift toward mandatory and standard-ized course objectives. In terms of both content and format, the origins of what would later be called the TEKS are clearly visible in the decade's educational documents. Nonetheless, specific course requirements still remained general in scope and short on detail, demonstrating much less preoccupation with specific figures, incidents, and documents than the 2010 TEKS. Religion continued to figure more prominently in expecta-tions for world religion courses than for US history and to focus more sharply on the Abrahamic traditions than on those originating outside the Middle East. Most of the religion-related objectives in a 1981 publication on geography, for example, focused on the encounter between the Roman Catholic Church, Byzantine Empire, and "Moslem World," although one directive mentioned "the effects of religions on the landscapes of India."[50] Standards from 1984 and 1988 occasionally included religion as a category of identity alongside race, ethnicity, and nationality, although those latter categories received the lion's share of attention.[51] They contained no hint of the Christian Americanist historical narrative presupposed by some members of the twenty-first-century SBOE. For example, a standard on "the foundation of the United States system of government" traced its philosophical origins more broadly to "the Ancient World" and "Western Europe," with no specific mention of Moses or the Bible.[52] The general world history class continued to recognize the importance of Christianity, Islam, and Judaism, while not even mentioning Asian religions by name, although standards for the (short-lived) course "World Area Studies," which allowed students to focus on specific geographical regions, did cite religion as an area of culture meriting study.[53]

Texas thoroughly revised all of its K–12 standards and renamed them as the TEKS in the mid-1990s, with the first version going into effect in the fall of 1998.[54] Christian conservatives on the SBOE at the time opposed the new TEKS, but their primary complaint was that they were vague and insufficiently rigorous, not that they mishandled presentations of reli-gion.[55] The 1998 social studies standards reflected the lingering influ-ence of earlier versions but included far more specific details, personal names, and supporting examples. In comparison to the guidelines from the 1980s, they even more regularly included religion alongside categories of race and ethnicity.[56] New standards focused specifically on religious freedom, religious holidays, and religious diversity throughout American history.[57] A few introduced themes that would be amplified in 2010. One, for example, noted "how religion contributed to the growth of representative government in the American colonies," while another attributed the sources of important legal concepts such as "equality before the law" to "Greco-Roman and Judeo-Christian ideals."[58] World history standards grouped a diverse range of religious traditions together for the first time, specifying that students should "compare the historical origins, central ideas, and the spread of major religious and philosophical traditions including Buddhism, Christianity, Confucianism, Hinduism, Islam, and Judaism."[59] Overall, the 1998 standards took more notice of religion than previous versions, perhaps reflecting conversations in educational and scholarly circles in the 1980s and 1990s about the importance of incorporating its study in the public school curriculum.[60] Their generalizing tone contrasts starkly with the pointed specificity, particularly regarding Islam and America's Christian heritage, that characterizes the 2010 TEKS that supplanted them.

Making History in a New Way

How does this historical review illuminate Texas's 2010 standards and the intersection of religion and politics they represent? It shows just how much a departure from previous state practice the 2010 TEKS make. In past standards and guidelines, Western and world history courses, not American history or civics, were the usual venue for study about religion. Texas guidelines traditionally favored the Abrahamic traditions over others and Christianity most of all, a pattern the 2010 standards continue. Of the other traditions, Islam has usually been the most visible in course guidelines because of the long history of Western relations with the Arab world. Most of the previous guidelines' attention to Islam, however, focused on those past encounters rather than present geopolitical circumstances. In contrast, the 2010 TEKS devote significant attention to modern Islam, but almost entirely in conjunction with terrorism and Middle Eastern conflicts. It seems reasonable to say that this lopsided focus on Islam and violence, inserted into the TEKS over the objection of Democratic members, reflects anxieties about the religion widely held in GOP circles.[61] To some degree, those anxieties will now be formally incorporated into the public school curriculum of one of the most populous states in the Union.

This look backward at how earlier guidelines treated religion in American history shows that they mostly ignored it, especially after the early period. Religion's low profile in state recommendations is thus not a result of the secularization of public schools that accelerated in the 1960s following the Supreme Court decisions on prayer and Bible reading; it was the norm for the entire twentieth century. The only noteworthy exception to this pattern was the 1957 bulletin issued during the Cold War at a time of unusually heightened public religiosity. The education of many older Texans was no doubt greatly shaped by that bulletin, which explains the fervor with which some members of the public hold to the notion that at one time public schools not only promoted religious practices but also conflated national and religious identity in their presentation of history. In Texas, the state did indeed urge teachers to do the latter—but only in one anomalous bulletin. By the 1970s, the integration of religion into American history classes appears to have been just as minimal as it had been in the 1940s, at least as far as one can tell from state documents. As for the more specific claim that the Founding Fathers established the United States to be a distinctively Christian nation with laws and a form of government based on the Bible—an idea that greatly influenced the formation of the 2010 TEKS—this notion is simply absent from all Texas guidelines from the previous one hundred years. The Republican majority in the 2010 SBOE succeeded in introducing into the curriculum elements of the larger Christian Americanist historical narrative that had never before appeared in official state guidelines.

The 2010 TEKS thus mark a high point for attention to religion in Texas social studies. They emphasize American religion in general and American Christianity in particular more than any earlier guidelines have done, and even their limited treatment of other traditions in some ways surpasses the consideration given to non-Christian faiths in the past. Shaped largely by Republicans on the SBOE, their specific content reflects the political *Zeitgeist* of the early twenty-first century in many red-state, Bible-Belt contexts: they emphasize the importance of Christianity for understanding American identity and reflect unease with Islam, suggesting that it is the dangerous "other."

Yet when the SBOE voted in November 2014 to approve textbooks covering these TEKS, observers commented that the books in question were qualitatively a mixed bag.[62] In summing up the results of the months-long textbook consideration process, Texas Freedom Network (TFN) claimed that publishers had largely pledged to remove what TFN described as "inflammatory content stereotyping Muslims." Those same publishers, however, had also often retained "passages that suggest Moses influenced the writing of the Constitution and that the roots of democracy can be found in the Old Testament."[63] The final word on what those textbooks actually contain cannot be pronounced until they appear in print, a development months away at the time of this writing.

One thing that is clear, however, is that whatever appears in those textbooks will almost certainly appear in editions used in other states as well. While the exact content for a given textbook varies across the states, publishers try to recycle as much material between different editions as possible to minimize production costs. Because of the sheer size of the Texas textbook market, publishers often prioritize that state's curricular requirements when developing their products, and content developed for the Lone Star State seeps into books used elsewhere.[64] In this way, red-state understandings of Moses and Mohammad—the first interpreted as a national inspiration, the second as a national threat—may well find their way into schools in red and blue states alike.

Notes

1. Terrence Stutz, "New Social Studies Textbooks Draw Fire from All Sides during Public Hearing," *Dallas Morning News* Education Blog, September 16, 2014, http://educationblog.dallasnews.com/2014/09/new-social-studies-textbooks-draw-fire-from-all-sides-during-public-hearing.html/. Wellman's comments were included in the video of the meeting posted by the Texas Education Agency (TEA): http://www.texasadmin.com/tea.shtml.

2. Associated Press, "Texas Approves Disputed History Texts for Schools," *New York Times*, November 22, 2014, http://www.nytimes.com/2014/11/23/us/texas-approves-disputed-history-texts-for-schools.html?_r=0.

3. I have written several studies on public school Bible courses for Texas Freedom Network (see www.tfn.org/biblecourses) and joined its board of directors in 2014. Texas's 2010 social studies standards are found in the Texas Administrative Code, Title 19, Part II, chapter 113, accessible at http://ritter.tea.state.tx.us/rules/tac/chapter113/index.html; the quotations are drawn from §113.44(c)(1)(C), 113.44(c)(20)(B), 113.44(c)(1)(B), and 113.44(c)(20)(A).

4. Details on the creation and early reception of the standards are available in Keith A. Erekson, ed., *Politics and the History Curriculum: The Struggle over Standards in Texas and the Nation* (New York: Palgrave Macmillan, 2012), and in Mark A. Chancey, "Rewriting History for a Christian America: Religion and the Texas Social Studies Controversy of 2009–2010," *Journal of Religion* 94, no. 3 (July 2014): 325–353.

5. http://www.textbookreviews.org.

6. James R. Durham, *Secular Darkness: Religious Right Involvement in Texas Public Education, 1963–1989* (New York: Peter Lang, 1995); Jonathan Zimmerman, *Whose America? Culture Wars in the Public Schools* (Cambridge, MA: Harvard University Press, 2005); Joan DelFattore, *What Johnny Shouldn't Read: Textbook Censorship in America* (New Haven, CT: Yale University Press, 1992), 138–166.

7. Erekson, *Politics and the History Curriculum.*

8. Texas Freedom Network, *The State of the Religious Right 2008: The State Board of Education* (Austin: Texas Freedom Network Education Fund, 2008), 15, available at www.tfn.org.

9. For a concise, insightful consideration of the history of social studies, see Loretta Sullivan Lobes, "Surveying State Standards: National History Education Network's 1997 Report on State Social Studies Standards," *History Teacher* 31, no. 2 (February 1998): 221–234.

10. For the quote, see §113.41(b)(5), 113.42(b)(7), 113.43(b)(5), and elsewhere.

11. J. Kelton Williams and Christie L. Maloyed, "Much Ado about Texas: Civics in the Social Studies Curriculum," *History Teacher* 47, no. 1 (November 2013): 25–40.

12. E.g., §113.20(b)(23).

13. Chancey, "Rewriting History for a Christian America"; Justine Esta Ellis, "Constructing a Protestant Nation: Religion, Politics, and the Texas Public School Curriculum," *Postscripts* 7, no. 1 (2011): 27–58.

14. *2010 State Republican Party Platform*, 21, available at the *Texas Tribune* website, http://static.texastribune.org/media/documents/FINAL_2010_STATE_REPUBLICAN_PARTY_PLATFORM.pdf.

15. TEA documents and SBOE minutes allow identification of the advocates of particular changes to the TEKS.

16. For examples of Christian Americanist statements from SBOE members, see Chancey, "Rewriting History for a Christian America." On Barton and Marshall, see Randall J. Stephens and Karl W. Giberson, *The Anointed: Evangelical Truth in a Secular Age* (Cambridge, MA: Harvard University Press, 2011), 74–78 and 83–91, and John Fea, *Was America Founded as a Christian Nation?* (Louisville, KY: Westminster John Knox, 2011).

17. Brian Thevenot, "SBOE Conservative Dunbar Reads a Liberal's Prayer," *Texas Tribune*, May 21, 2010, http://www.texastribune.org/2010/05/21/sboe-conservative-dunbar-read-a-liberals-prayer/, with an accompanying recording.

18. "Breakfast in Washington," *Time* 63, no. 7 (February 1954): 51.

19. §113.20(b)(1)(A), 113.41(c)(10)(E), 113.41(c)(24)(B), and 113.41(c)(26)(E).

20. §113.42(c)(20)(C).

21. §113.20(b)(2)(B), 113.20 (b)(1)(C); cf. 113.20(b)(3)(B) and 113.20(b)(15)(A), retained from 1998.

22. §113.42(c)(20)(C), 113.16(b)(3)(B), 113.41(c)(1)(C), and 113.44(c)(a)(D). On Christian Right historiography, see Chancey, "Rewriting History for a Christian America," and Kate Carté Engel, "The Founding Fathers in Modern America," in this volume.

23. §113.44(c)(7)(G).

24. *2010 State Republican Party Platform*, 15.

25. Terrence Stutz, "Texas Education Board Rejects In-Depth Study of First Amendment," *Dallas Morning News*, March 12, 2010, http://www.dallasnews.com/news/education/headlines/20100311-Texas-education-board-rejects-in-depth-985.ece.

26. My discussion of the presentation of world religions in the TEKS is greatly indebted to David Brockman, *More Balanced Than the Standards: A Review of the Presentation of Religion in Proposed Textbooks for High School World History in Texas* (Austin: Texas Freedom Network Education Fund, 2014), available at www.tfn.org/TextbookReview. On religious influences on American government, see Emile Lester, *A Triumph of Ideology over Ideas: A Review of Proposed Textbooks for High School U.S. Government in Texas* (Austin: Texas Freedom Network Education Fund, 2014) at the same site.

27. Brian Thevenot, "State Board of Education Takes Up Multiculturalism," *Texas Tribune*, January 13, 2010, http://www.texastribune.org/2010/01/13/state-board-of-education-takes-up-multiculturalism/; §113.42(c)(23)(A), 113.43(c)(17)(B); cf. also 113.42(c)(1)(B).

28. §113.18(b)(19)(B), 113.42(c)(4)(E–F).

29. §113.41(c)(7)(D), 113.42(c)(12)(C), 113.42(c)(22)(D), 113.42(c)(13)(F). 113.18(b)(19)(B), 113.42(c)(3)(B), and 113.42(c)(23)(A).

30. §113.42(c)(1)(C), 113.42(c)(4)(D); cf. also 113.42(c)(4)(G) and 113.42(c)(4)(K).

31. §113.42(c)(4)(D).

32. On the Ottomans, see §113.42(c)(1)(D) and 113.42(c)(7)(D).

33. §113.42(c)(14), 113.42(c)(14)(A–B); cf. 113.41(c)(2)(D), 113.41(c)(11)(A), and 113.43(c)(18)(B); Fred Knack, ed., *The Texas State Board of Education: A Case of Abuse of Power* (Austin: American Civil Liberties Union of Texas, 2010), 16, available at www.aclutex.org.

34. §113.42(c)(4)(F).

35. *2010 State Republican Party Platform*, 21, 22.

36. Report of the State Board of Education Committee of the Full Board, March 10, 2010, 11. Unfortunately, this document is no longer available at the TEA website (www.tea.state.tx.us).

37. §113.41(c)(2)(D); Report of the State Board of Education Committee of the Full Board, May 20, 2010, http://www.tfn.org/site/DocServer/cofb_05_20_10_1__GM.pdf; a video of the exchange is available through the link for item 11 at http://www.texasadmin.com/cgi-bin/agenda.cgi?location=tea&savefile=TEA_FB052010. On Bradley, see Lisa Falkenberg, "It's Culture, Not an Effort to Convert," *Houston*

Chronicle, October 28, 2008, http://www.chron.com/news/falkenberg/article/It-s-culture-not-an-effort-to-convert-1589090.php. On Obama as a Muslim, see Pew Research Religion and Public Life Project, "Growing Number of Americans Say Obama is a Muslim," August 18, 2010, http://www.pewforum.org/2010/08/18/growing-number-of-americans-say-obama-is-a-muslim/, and Rebecca Goetz, "Barack Hussein Obama: The First Muslim President," in this volume.

38. §113.42(c)(23)(a); cf. 113.43(c)(17)(B).

39. §113.42(c)(4)(B), 113.42(c)(4)(G).

40. On the history of Texas's social studies curriculum, see also J. Kelton Williams, "God's Country: Religion and the Evolution of the Social Studies Curriculum in Texas," *American Education History Journal* 37, no. 2 (2010): 437–454.

41. *Texas High Schools: The Teaching of History and Other Social Subjects,* Bulletin 208 (Austin: State Department of Education, 1926), and *Texas High Schools: The Teaching of History and other Social Subjects,* Bulletin 260 (Austin: State Department of Education, 1929).

42. *Texas High Schools* (1926), unnumbered pages.

43. *Texas High Schools* (1926),unnumbered page; *Texas High Schools* (1929), 76.

44. *Standards and Activities of the Division of Supervision 1936–1937,* Bulletin 372, Austin: State Department of Education, 1937).

45. *Standards and Activities of the Division of Supervision State Department of Education 1943–1944,* Bulletin 438 (Austin: State Department of Education, 1944), 16.

46. *Teaching Social Studies in Junior and Senior High Schools of Texas,* Bulletin 392 (Austin: Texas State Department of Education, 1938); for examples of references to religion in the guidelines for history, see 79, 133, and 178.

47. Andrew Preston, *Sword of the Spirit, Shield of Faith: Religion in American War and Diplomacy* (New York: Alfred A. Knopf, 2012), 440–441; on the Eisenhower quote, see Gary Scott Smith, *Faith and the Presidency from George Washington to George W. Bush* (Oxford: Oxford University Press, 2006), 254.

48. Texas State Teachers Association Committee on Improving Educational Services, *Social Studies in Texas Schools: A Tentative Curriculum Guide Grades One Through Twelve* (Austin: Texas Education Agency, 1957), quotes from 10, 52, 64–65.

49. *Principles and Standards for Accrediting Elementary and Secondary Schools and Description of Approved Courses Grades 7–12,* Bulletin 615 (Austin: Texas Education Agency, 1961), 244, 252–253. For the 1970s, see *Principles and Standards for Accrediting Elementary and Secondary Schools and List of Approved Courses—Grades 7–12,* Bulletin 560 (Austin: Texas Education Agency, 1970), and *Framework for the Social Studies Kindergarten—Grade 12* (Austin: Texas Education Agency, 1970).

50. *Geographic Skills in the Social Studies Grades 7–12* (Austin: Texas Education Agency, 1981), 35–43.

51. *State Board of Education Rules for Curriculum: Principles, Standards, and Procedures for Accreditation of School Districts* (Austin: State Board of Education, 1984), 147.

52. *State Board of Education Rules for Curriculum* (1984), 64, 145–146; cf. *State Board of Education Rules for Curriculum* (Austin: Texas Education Agency, 1988), 85–86.

53. *State Board of Education Rules for Curriculum* (1984), 144, 147; cf. *State Board of Education Rules for Curriculum* (1988), 193–195, 198–199.

54. The 1998 TEKS are available at the TEA website: http://ritter.tea.state.tx.us/rules/tac/ch113.html.

55. Terrence Stutz, "Curriculum Rewrite Wins Tentative OK," *Dallas Morning News*, July 11, 1997, 1A; Paul Burka, "The Disloyal Opposition," *Texas Monthly* 26, no. 12 (December 1998): 116–117, 141–144; Williams and Maloyed, "Much Ado about Texas."

56. E.g., §113.6(a)(1), 113.6(b)(4.20), 113.7(a)(1), 113.7(b)(5.23), and 113.24(b)(8.24).

57. §113.24(b)(8.26), 113.7(b)(5.21)(B), 113.22(b)6.19(B), 113.24(b)(8.24); 113.7(b)(5.23), and 113.32(c)(21).

58. §113.24(b)(8.23)(C), 113.33(c)(18)(B).

59. §113.33(c)(19)(A).

60. See, for example, the numerous references in Paul Boyer, "In Search of the Fourth 'R': The Treatment of Religion in American History Textbooks and Survey Courses," in Bruce Kuklick and D. G. Hart, eds., *Religious Advocacy and American History* (Grand Rapids: Wm. B. Eerdmans, 1997), 112–136.

61. See, for example, Pew Research Center for the People and the Press, "Continuing Divide in Views of Islam and Violence," March 9, 2011, http://www.people-press.org/2011/03/09/continuing-divide-in-views-of-islam-and-violence/.

62. See, for example, Rick Jervis, "Controversial Texas Textbooks Headed to Classrooms," *USA Today*, November 17, 2014, http://www.usatoday.com/story/news/nation/2014/11/17/texas-textbook-inaccuracies/19175311/.

63. Kathy Miller, "The Textbook Vote Is In—Here's What We Accomplished," *TFN Insider*, November 21, 2014, http://tfninsider.org/2014/11/21/the-textbook-vote-is-in-heres-what-we-accomplished/.

64. DelFattore, *What Johnny Shouldn't Read*; Diane Ravitch, *The Language Police: How Pressure Groups Restrict What Students Learn* (New York: Knopf, 2003).

II

America's World Mission in the Age of Obama

Andrew Preston

FOR OVER A century, for better or worse, religion has provided much of the ideological glue holding US foreign policy together. It has played a large role in infusing Americans with a sense of global mission, prioritizing their foreign-policy goals, and identifying their allies and adversaries around the world. It has been a key instrument in mobilizing political will and grassroots support for national-security objectives. It has also provided one of the main tools to forge national unity and a shared sense of purpose during times of war. Religion has rarely determined US foreign policy, but it has helped shaped the contours of America's role in the world.

The sources of the religious influence on US foreign relations have been both top-down and bottom-up. At the top, political elites have used religion to inform their own decisions, mobilize opinion, and justify policies. From the bottom, religious Americans who don't necessarily wield political power or policymaking authority have relentlessly pressured lawmakers and policymakers to pursue certain foreign-policy goals; they have also used indirect means, such as shaping opinion and mobilizing action on foreign-policy issues in local communities and through small media outlets. Religious Americans care about the welfare and political status of their co-religionists abroad and thus have an inherently transnational perspective. In a highly religious country such as the United States, religion has provided common ground for elites and non-elites through a widely shared moral vocabulary and set of values.

Has all this changed in the age of Obama? Both of these influences, top-down and bottom-up, were destabilized after Barack Obama entered the White House in 2009. At the top, old uncertainties have become more complicated. From what we know of it, Barack Obama's own personal and Christian faith is devout but unusually subtle and complex, and it does not easily convert into political capital or a foreign-policy vision. Aside (perhaps) from his two secretaries of state, Hillary Clinton and John Kerry, no member of Obama's national-security team is identifiably religious in the sense that religion is a major aspect of their politics or public agenda. Perhaps unsurprisingly, then, religion has featured in Obama's conduct of foreign policy episodically and, in his second term, infrequently. Moreover, from the bottom up, three contemporary phenomena—religious diversity, the growth of secularism, and the controversial nature of religion in politics—are challenging the once-sacred hold religion had on the American worldview. None are new, but they have all intensified over the last decade, and more Americans are aware of their salience to public life. Most important, these bottom-up shifts have coincided, and probably reinforced, the uncertainties at the top. As a result, we have likely reached an important threshold: the historical foundations underlying the religious influence on American war and diplomacy have begun to creak, perhaps even to the point of toppling.

Religion featured consistently in the nation's foreign policy between the Revolutionary War and 1898, but it was not until the Spanish-American War, the conquest of the Philippines, and World War I that religious ideologies played a key, sometimes predominant, role. Not coincidentally, these were America's first major wars that were truly foreign. They were not justified in the name of self-defense, national security, or the protection of US sovereignty, as in 1812; they were not propelled by territorial expansion, as in 1846; and they were fought either partly or entirely outside the Western Hemisphere. Once separated from the North American continent, where the imperatives of defense and territorial expansion were obvious (although still contested and controversial), US foreign policy needed strong and compelling ideological justification to pursue national objectives that were often ephemeral and tangential to the nation's actual security needs.

Few aspects of American political culture were as ideally suited to the task as religion. With a few exceptions during the secular high modernist period in the middle of the Cold War,[1] presidents from William McKinley to George W. Bush found a ready source of support in the values, customs, and communities of American religion. Of course, religion was not exactly absent before 1898, but McKinley, Theodore Roosevelt, and Woodrow Wilson embedded it in the conduct of US foreign relations with unprecedented formality and consistency. Later, Franklin Roosevelt, Harry Truman, and Dwight Eisenhower significantly deepened and extended the role of religion in American foreign policy. Moreover, from the bottom up, the 1890s marked the intensification of faith-based activism on foreign relations (as on domestic issues, such as temperance) among religious Americans. Previously confined mainly to Protestant missionaries, the late nineteenth century witnessed a surge of activity from a wider range of Protestants, clergy and laity alike, in addition to Catholics and Jews. This continued into the twentieth century.

Among elites, the period between 1961 and 1980 marked a secular exception to America's otherwise pious twentieth century. This was the era when modernization theory moved from academic fashion to the inner circles of policymaking, and when intellectuals proclaimed the death of God and predicted the end of religion. From John F. Kennedy to Jimmy Carter, presidents and their advisers deliberately sidelined religion from foreign policymaking and sought to downplay its rhetorical and symbolic importance. Whereas Franklin Roosevelt had deployed religion as a powerful political weapon against Nazism, and Truman and Eisenhower had invited religious leaders and activists into the forging of containment, Kennedy and Carter publicly argued that there was no place for religion in their administrations. Lyndon B. Johnson, Richard Nixon, and Gerald Ford often paid political lip service to religion's place in American public life, but they did little to encourage its role in foreign policy. Indeed, Nixon and his key foreign-policy adviser, Henry Kissinger, worked hard to ensure that religious interests did not disrupt their carefully calibrated policies of détente with the Soviet Union and the opening to China. Among the high-modernist presidents from 1961 to 1980, then, only Nixon spent much effort genuflecting to American religion, but he did so almost entirely for domestic political advantage and marginalized religion even on major foreign-policy issues of domestic political importance, such as the fate of Jews in the Soviet Union.

However, as presidents in the 1960s and 1970s (especially Nixon and Carter) discovered to their cost, the era also witnessed a surge of religious activism. The rise of what came to be known as either the Religious Right or, more narrowly, the Christian Right catalyzed the emergence of a broad-based political movement of religious conservatives. They prioritized issues such as pornography, gay rights, and abortion (from the late 1970s onward), but they also paid close attention to foreign affairs. In the 1980s, antiabortion protests brought Protestant evangelicals and Roman Catholics together and broke down a long tradition of mutual hostility. But decades before abortion became a salient national issue, evangelicals and Catholics had found common ground over their shared hatred of communism. This strand of visceral anti-communism continued through the 1960s and into the 1970s, even after the last embers of McCarthyism had gone cold and many other Americans, horrified by the nation's misadventure in Indochina and enticed by the peaceful promise of détente with the Soviet Union and Nixon's trip to Beijing, stopped perceiving international communism as a menace to the American way of life. In fact, large numbers of Catholics and evangelicals actively opposed the détente-driven foreign policies of Nixon, Ford, and Carter. The fate of Soviet Jewry, as well as other sensitive issues that had little to do with religion per se, such as the Panama Canal Treaties, spurred the political activism of Christian conservatives. The ties that bound religious conservatives together on these issues were a belief in American virtue and strength and a hatred of communism (particularly with regard to the Soviet Union).

After a deliberate hiatus under Carter, religion once again became a central feature of US foreign policy under Ronald Reagan. Along with other creedal aspects of American political culture, religion represented the antithesis to communism. The imagery of a faithful America challenging a godless Soviet Union for the hearts and minds of people worldwide featured prominently in Reagan's rhetoric, most notably but not solely in his "evil empire" speech to the National Association of Evangelicals in 1983. But Reagan significantly altered the terms of the religious influence on foreign relations. Presidents from Theodore Roosevelt to Eisenhower had portrayed religion not only as an ideal that could lead the way against America's enemies but also as a unifying force that could bind all Americans together. Only atheism and irreligion could undermine America from within, and even this domestic threat was assumed to be foreign in origin, usually the work of Bolshevists, anarchists, and other leftist radicals from abroad. Reagan differed from his predecessors in that he used religion as a weapon against foreign enemies but did not use it as a binding force domestically. Quite the opposite, in fact: in Reagan's hands, religion—conflated with Protestant evangelicals and conservative

Catholics and Jews—became a litmus test to determine who was genuinely American (and, eventually, loyally Republican). In Reagan's account, secular Americans, now hostile rather than indifferent to religion and growing in numbers and stature, were corroding the nation's Judeo-Christian heritage. By championing the celebration of that heritage in public places, including government venues and public schools, Reagan drove a wedge between Americans even as he used religion to separate communists from the "free world."

The end of the Cold War brought further changes in the symbolic and substantive use of religion in foreign policy. Yet the religious influence did not disappear, or even particularly wane. Indeed, after a brief lull under George H. W. Bush and Bill Clinton—both paid lip service to religious values but mostly ignored them in foreign policymaking—the top-down religious influence reached its apogee under George W. Bush, who invoked religion in the name of America's global mission with unusual force. Indeed, Bush combined overt (usually Christian) religious imagery and rhetoric with an unabashed American nationalism in a manner unseen for decades, even during the Reagan era.[2]

Bottom-up pressures also increased dramatically in the George W. Bush era, beginning in the 1990s and then, not coincidentally, peaking after the turn of the century. Bush's support for faith-based communities, including the unprecedented granting of official cooperation and extension of federal monies, certainly eased the re-entry of popular religion into policymaking circles. But faith-based activism over America's role in world affairs had already begun in earnest before Bush reached the White House. This groundswell of religious pressure was epitomized by the International Religious Freedom Act of 1998 (IRFA), which compelled a reluctant State Department to monitor religious freedom globally, much as it was already monitoring the status of human rights around the world; each country was to receive a score on how well it maintained its citizens' right to the freedom of worship. Violators could then be exposed, by members of Congress if not the State Department, and possibly subjected to economic or diplomatic sanctions. IRFA also mandated the appointment of an ambassador-at-large, whose portfolio would deal solely with religious liberty. Madeleine Albright, the secretary of state who had to implement the terms of IRFA, was personally and morally sympathetic to the aims of religious activists but worried they would interfere with the normal sensitivities of delicate diplomacy. "Those eager to promote religious liberty must also recognize that there is a right and a wrong way to go about it," she admonished after leaving office. "Lasting change is more likely to come through persuasion than by making blunt demands."[3]

Yet blunt demands carried the day, at first haltingly under Clinton and then resoundingly under his successor. Bush seemed to be a throwback to the style of Reagan, Eisenhower, and Truman, and in many ways he was. But there were also key differences. The foreign enemy this time wasn't Catholicism, as it had been for many American Protestants until the middle of the twentieth century, and it wasn't secularism, statism, or materialism, as it had been when irreligious Nazi Germany and the atheistic Soviet Union were America's enemies. The enemy this time was a phenomenon swiftly dubbed "Islamism," and it presented Bush with a difficult task. When Catholicism helped define the enemy, represented by *ancien regime* France, Mexico in the 1840s, or Spain in the 1890s, Americans were for the most part robustly Protestant—at least, in terms of national political culture—and weren't at all reluctant to portray their struggle as one of the true faith against a supposedly dangerous and authoritarian heresy. When the paganism and atheism of Nazi Germany and the Soviet Union provided a foil, Americans had become more tolerantly Judeo-Christian, and America's mission was redefined as one of religion versus irreligion, of godly liberty against aggressive and godless statism. Still, with few secularists at home to protest and few dissenting from the negative portrayal of fascists and communists, the use of religion remained straightforward and unproblematic. Islam, however, presented Bush with an altogether different challenge. Protestant exceptionalism was no longer acceptable, but in an age of pluralistic diversity, both domestically and globally, the Judeo-Christian triumphalism of the sort deployed by Truman and Eisenhower was also inappropriate and counterproductive. And in a struggle with Islamism, Bush couldn't lead the forces of religion against the forces of irreligion, as Reagan had done.

Bush's solution was as subtle as it was difficult: he would highlight the post-9/11 world as one of a struggle between America's tolerant, pluralistic religion and specific strains of Islam's extremist, fundamentalist faith. This would serve two purposes: define the struggle's moral terms and prevent Americans from seeking vengeance against Muslims, including Muslims living in the United States. "These acts of violence against innocents violate the fundamental tenets of the Islamic faith. And it's important for my fellow Americans to understand that," Bush declared a few days after the September 11 attacks. "The face of terror is not the true faith of Islam. That's not what Islam is all about. Islam is peace. These terrorists don't represent peace. They represent evil and war."⁴ Neither George W. Bush nor the nation he led always lived up to these words. But a doctrine of fighting the ideology of Islamism but not the religion of Islam quickly crystallized within the post-9/11 American worldview and has helped define US foreign policy ever since.

In several ways, Barack Obama inaugurated an era of transition in US foreign policy. Some of this was intended: he sought to differentiate his policy from that of his predecessors, particularly George W. Bush but also Clinton, in the sheer frequency and scale of America's military interventions in the world, especially in the Middle East. In his first term, Obama announced that his foreign policy would pivot from the Middle East to eastern Asia and the western Pacific, where the rise of China was threatening to upset regional security.⁵ But he also pointedly reminded Americans that the immense power they wielded had limits and toned down the exceptionalist rhetoric that had prevailed under Bush and Reagan, and to a lesser extent Clinton. Carter had tried to do much the same in the 1970s, but even his foreign policy, with its crusade for human rights, was more idealistic than Obama's. If Obama had a true predecessor in his stewardship of America in the world, it was actually the arch-realists Richard Nixon and George H. W. Bush.⁶

Where would religious values and idealism fit within such a realist framework? Carter, himself a religious man, had solved that problem by drawing on his reading of Southern Baptist doctrine and rigorously separating church from state and religion from politics. And it would have been relatively straightforward for Obama to do the same: though he too is a devout Christian, Obama has never been widely known for his piety, and few Americans could have expected a president of uncertain religious pedigree, from the Democratic Party no less, to mix religion and politics willingly and openly. In diplomatic circles, where hard-headed realism reigns and compromise is a virtue, expectations for a religious revival in foreign affairs were low. Even Bill Clinton, who unabashedly mixed religion with politics on the domestic front, kept faith to one side when conducting foreign policy.

Yet at first, Obama acted differently. Presidents often signal national-security priorities through speeches. International relations is shaped by symbols and abstract notions like credibility, and US foreign policy is driven by a single individual, the president. Thus it is normal for a presidential set piece rather than congressional legislation to unveil a major objective for the US in the world or effect a sudden shift in the geopolitical landscape. In international relations, rhetoric shapes reality. In this sense, the rhetorical choices a president makes before a global audience, in terms of theme, tone, language, and setting, are absolutely critical.[7] They are also reliable indicators of an administration's goals, as well as methods of achieving such goals. And by these criteria, Obama was—initially at least—a president who clearly had a place for religion in his foreign policy.

Obama's application of religion to world affairs could be conventional, and squarely within the tradition established by his predecessors. On a 2009 trip to China, for instance, he gently admonished an audience in Shanghai that respect for religious liberty was one of the foundations for a healthy democracy—and, by extension, for a society that would be at peace with its neighbors as well as with itself. The United States had its own problems, he acknowledged, but whatever strides American society had made were due to a respect for basic human rights that included religious liberty. "These freedoms of expression and worship," he told the Chinese, "we believe are universal rights. They should be available to all people, including ethnic and religious minorities, whether they are in the United States, China, or any nation." Given the trouble the People's Republic was having with religious dissenters, be they Muslim Uighurs in Xinjiang province or Roman Catholics and members of Falun Gong in the burgeoning cities back east, it was bracing criticism, however softly delivered. "Indeed," Obama continued, "it is that respect for universal rights that guides America's openness to other countries, our respect for different cultures, our commitment to international law, and our faith in the future."[8]

Religious liberty also provided a familiar centerpiece for what was— and probably still is, despite its obvious lack of success—Obama's most important foreign-policy initiative: his address to Cairo University in June 2009.[9] Grandly entitled "A New Beginning," the speech was Obama's attempt to usher in a total change in America's troubled relationship with the Arab Middle East. Doing so would fulfill two campaign pledges: to restart US-Middle East relations and to do so via an unprecedented address to the Muslim world by a US president. America's path out of the Middle East, Obama had decided, would begin from Cairo.

It was an exceedingly ambitious and difficult undertaking, yet instead of treading cautiously the Obama administration used the months leading up to the speech to draw attention to it and heighten expectations. And while not everyone agreed with its content or believed the United

States would actually follow through on its leader's stirring words, the Cairo speech was widely hailed as a momentous event. Obama acknowledged American mistakes in the region, such as the Iraq War, but he also declared that the United States was a model of democratic religious pluralism, possible only because the nation protected religious freedom—enjoyed by American Muslims as well as Christians, Jews, and others—which in turn created a tolerant society. To a region riven with endless interfaith conflicts, Obama offered American religious politics as a potential framework for peace and stability. Only by tolerating religious differences, he warned, could the Middle East escape its cycle of sectarian conflict. In fact, according to Obama (echoing Franklin Roosevelt), the entire basis for peace and freedom rested on the protection of religious liberty. In the carefully crafted speech, Obama used the word "freedom" five times; four of those instances specifically referred to religious freedom as the cornerstone of all freedoms. As Obama argued, "freedom in America is indivisible from the freedom to practice one's religion. That is why there is a mosque in every State in our Union and over 1,200 mosques within our borders." But Americans didn't have a monopoly on religious freedom. Islam, too, "has a proud tradition of tolerance," either in historical terms (Obama cited Moorish rule in early modern Spain) or in more recent periods: "I saw it first-hand as a child in Indonesia, where devout Christians worshiped freely in an overwhelmingly Muslim country. That is the spirit we need today." Obama wanted his audience to appreciate that he was not espousing lofty ideals but a practical plan for modern societies and polities. "People in every country should be free to choose and live their faith based upon the persuasion of the mind and the heart and the soul," he declared. Tolerance of other faiths was "essential for religion to thrive," but even more importantly, "freedom of religion is central to the ability of peoples to live together."[10]

Given his repeated emphasis on religious pluralism, as well as the tenor and objectives of his own foreign policy, it is unsurprising that Obama continued to invoke George W. Bush's formula that Islamism was the problem, not Islam itself. In Cairo, he acknowledged "civilization's debt to Islam."[11] A month later, he said that "Al Qaida and its affiliates have defiled a great religion of peace and justice and ruthlessly murdered men, women, and children of all nationalities and faiths. Indeed, above all, they have murdered Muslims."[12] Two years after that, he revealed that America's conflict was with violent religious extremism, not a religion itself. While "Al Qaida seeks a religious war with the West," he declared on a visit to London, Americans and Britons must remember that they "are not and will never be at war with Islam. Our fight is focused on defeating Al Qaida and its extremist allies."[13] Later, on the tenth anniversary of 9/11, he vowed that the United States "will never wage war against Islam."[14]

The Cairo speech, reinforced by Obama's subsequent pronouncements on interfaith dialogue and especially his outreach to Islam, spurred the national-security bureaucracy in Washington into action. Between 2009 and 2013, the State Department created several internal centers to explore the potential religion had for furthering both US interests and international security. For example, Obama not only kept Bush's office for faith-based initiatives, he and his secretaries of state gave the department an international component by creating the Office of Faith-based Community Initiatives; planning for this new office commenced under Hillary Clinton and was implemented by her successor, John Kerry. Under Clinton, the State Department also inaugurated other religion-focused groups, such as the Global Engagement Directorate, the Religion and Foreign Policy Working Group, the Religious Engagement Report, and the Interfaith Working Group. Under Judd Birdsall's energetic leadership, the forum on Religion and Global Affairs (also housed in the State Department) highlighted issues of faith as a diplomatic priority.[15]

Still, Obama was no Reagan; his deployment of religion in the service of US foreign policy was much more subtle. That could be attributed to the fact that Reagan was a conservative Republican and Obama a liberal Democrat, but Obama wasn't even akin to fellow Democrats like Harry Truman or Franklin Roosevelt. This partly stemmed from the president's own complicated religious history and his intellectualized approach to religious faith. Partly it stemmed from the controversy this complicated religious baggage had brought, as when Obama's association with Reverend Jeremiah Wright of Trinity United Church of Christ in Chicago exploded into the nation's headlines during the 2008 Democratic primaries. And partly it stemmed from the simple fact that, in the age of Reagan, deploying religion in a politically effective manner was easy for conservative Republicans and enormously difficult for liberal Democrats. But whatever the reason, when it came to foreign policy, Obama's use of religion was marked by a deep and uneasy ambivalence.[16]

The fact that Obama approached "religion in the world" from a more oblique angle than had been customary for US presidents was clear from another of his major foreign-policy speeches. When he traveled to Oslo to accept the 2009 Nobel Peace Prize, Obama unveiled a thoughtful, albeit more complicated, version of a faith-based foreign policy. Given that he had only been on the job a few months and at that point had no achievements under his belt as president, receiving the prize was itself an awkward moment. But instead of attempting to avoid controversy with anodyne, boilerplate rhetoric about a general goal of world peace, Obama decided to embed his foreign policy within the tradition of Christian realism. A doctrine which emphasized morality but tempered it with a recognition of inherent human fallibility, Christian realism was ideally suited to Obama's worldview. As a realist, Obama acknowledged the limits of power, including America's, while simultaneously justifying the use of force under certain circumstances. Mahatma Gandhi and Martin Luther King Jr., he argued, would have had no answer to the power of Nazi Germany or the terror of al-Qaeda. Sometimes peace comes through strength. But Obama was also a Christian, a deliberate and reflective one at that, and not simply some amoral realist in the mold of Henry Kissinger. Thus realism could only be a properly guiding principle if it was infused with morality. In Oslo, Obama said that while he believed in peace, he also believed in "the notions of just war and the imperatives of a just peace"— both of which would often require the use of force.[17]

As commentators at the time observed, Obama drew inspiration for his Oslo remarks more from the neo-orthodox Protestant theologian and public intellectual Reinhold Niebuhr than from Gandhi, King, or history's other notable peace crusaders. In the *Weekly Standard*, Matthew Continetti aptly dubbed Obama's worldview the "Good Niebuhr Policy," while *The New Yorker*'s George Packer noted that the "spirit of Niebuhr presided over the Nobel address."[18] Obama himself acknowledged his intellectual debt to Niebuhr and did little to discourage comparisons between his foreign policy and a programmatic philosophy shaped by Christian realism. Niebuhr is "one of my favorite philosophers," Obama told *New York Times* columnist David Brooks in 2007. When pressed by Brooks to elaborate, Obama did not invoke Niebuhr's activism on behalf of social justice or support for civil rights and organized labor. Instead, Obama pointed to Niebuhr's "compelling idea that there's serious evil in the world, and hardship and pain. And we should be humble and modest in our belief we can eliminate those things. But we shouldn't use that as an excuse for cynicism and inaction."[19]

Niebuhr aside, left-liberal religious commentators have been dismayed at the similarities between the foreign policies of George W. Bush and Barack Obama. Most problematic has been Obama's inability, or unwillingness, to halt America's part in the cycle of violence that grips the Middle East. Religious liberals, in other words, wanted from Obama more Cairo and less Oslo. Art Laffin of the *National Catholic Reporter* accused Obama of requesting $59 billion in additional funds for the wars in Afghanistan and Iraq (which Congress duly granted), even while "the poor get poorer, more social services are cut, and our environment becomes more endangered." Laffin rested his case on a kind of moral equivalence between the United States, with its quest for access to natural resources and reliance on secret, extra-judicial drone warfare, and its terrorist enemies: "if we are to be faithful followers of Jesus, we must reject, without exception, all forms of violence, whether it is U.S. bombing and occupation, or al-Qaeda and Taliban sponsored violence."[20] Four years later, the *Christian Century* sharply criticized Obama for asking Congress for authorization to halt the Islamic State in Syria and Iraq with military force. "The notion that the United States can shape its desired political outcome by air power (or ground troops) is misguided," intoned the magazine's editors in an August 2014 piece. Rather than further military intervention, "the United States should adopt a modest goal in Iraq: do no harm."[21]

As reflected in frequent criticism leveled by outlets such as the *National Catholic Reporter* and the *Christian Century*, there was widespread outrage among liberals at the continuance of America's wars in the Middle East. But among conservatives, criticism of "the long war" was less pronounced. Indeed, on foreign affairs, liberals and conservatives often switched roles. Jim Wallis of Sojourners, probably the nation's most prominent leftist evangelical and an early champion of Obama, criticized the 2009 troop surge in Afghanistan as "a mistake" that took both countries in "the wrong direction," while Tony Perkins of the deeply conservative Family Research Council, usually a bitter critic, offered Obama a rare endorsement by calling the surge "an act of gutsy leadership."[22]

Yet Obama certainly had a large number of critics on the right, who charged that he didn't take the protection and promotion of religious liberty around the world seriously enough. The president, said *Christianity Today*, was too passive in the face of "religicide"—the deliberate destruction of ancient Christian communities—in the Middle East.[23] When a coalition of battle-hardened extremists under the banner of the Islamic State conquered much of northern Syria and Iraq in 2014, persecuting ancient Christian communities along the way, Senator Rob Portman, an Ohio Republican, called on the president to intervene to protect religious liberty in the region. If Obama didn't act, Portman vowed to introduce a bipartisan Senate resolution calling on him to do so. "We are a country founded by people that were fleeing persecution," Portman told Fox News. The resolution "is an effort to light a fire under the State Department to get them to do more to protect these religious minorities, including Christians, and to do so urgently before we lose more lives and have this additional purging." The United States, Portman declared, "must stand up for religious freedom not only at home, but also in regions of the world experiencing turmoil like the Middle East." Portman's resolution would demonstrate that even if the president remained inactive, the American people "will not tolerate targeted violence against Christians in Iraq and that those persecuting Christians must be stopped."[24]

Obama's most prominent critic on religious freedom has undoubtedly been Thomas Farr, whom Bill Clinton appointed in 1999 as the first director of the State Department's Office of International Religious Freedom. After retiring in 2003, Farr became the widely respected director of the Religious Freedom Project at Georgetown University's Berkley Center for Religion, Peace, and World Affairs. There Farr promoted the role of religion, specifically the protection of the freedom of religion as an internationally recognized human right, as a central component of US foreign policy.[25] With international security constantly destabilized by religious violence, he argued, religious freedom was not simply a worthy goal in itself but a national-security imperative. When Obama moved slowly in implementing the religious-liberty objectives he had expressed at Cairo, Farr was unsparing in his criticism.[26] The main problem, as Farr and others saw it, was Obama's inattention to the role religion could and should play in US foreign policy, epitomized by his failure to nominate an ambassador for international religious freedom until the summer of 2010. When he did, he named Suzan Johnson Cook as his choice—"a pastor," groused Christianity Today, "long on religion but short on international human rights" or diplomatic experience.[27] Cook's tenure in the State Department was an unhappy one, and when she left after two years, the post remained vacant for nearly a year before Obama nominated Rabbi David Saperstein.

Still, others with experience on religious issues at the State Department, such as Judd Birdsall, have highlighted the quiet but steady success in Obama's construction of "an unprecedented diplomatic foundation and building a bureaucratic framework for a collaborative, holistic, and far-sighted religious freedom agenda." Under Birdsall and others, such as Shaun Casey, the State Department has launched endeavors aimed at quiet religious diplomacy and interfaith bridge-building rather than grand gestures that would garner headlines but achieve little substantive progress.[28]

With Obama nearing the end of his presidency, what does the future hold? Whither the religious influence on American war and diplomacy? The substantive divisions between seasoned observers like Farr and Birdsall hint at an obvious ambivalence in Obama's use of religion when formulating and implementing American national-security policy. But since at least the days of McKinley, nearly all presidents have harbored such ambivalence—even those, such as Franklin Roosevelt and Dwight Eisenhower, whose wielding of faith in the service of foreign affairs was consistently robust. In previous eras, presidents who harbored doubts about religion's place in foreign policy and international security, such as John F. Kennedy, Richard Nixon, and Jimmy Carter, were followed by holy warriors like Ronald Reagan and George W. Bush. So the individual faith of a particular commander in chief is not necessarily determinative, or even indicative, of future trends.

Yet as far as religion's place in US foreign policy is concerned, Obama's presidency does mark a crossroads, primarily due to changes that are emergingfrom the bottom-up. The fragmentation of American public life has been particularly acute when it comes to religious faith, which in turn has blunted religion's political appeal to many political elites. Moreover, the nation's religious identity is changing in far-reaching ways, either due to the pluralism wrought by the immigration of people holding religions other than Christianity and Judaism, or to the emergence of a much larger segment of Americans who are agnostic, atheistic, or secular. Whether or not observers have exaggerated the new religious pluralism, it is important that people accept that the United States is (and should be) diverse.[29] In this new era of religious pluralism, in which skeptics and atheists are a large minority in their own right, religious rhetoric will likely not have the easy, consensual appeal it once held. This is not to say that the religious influence in American war and diplomacy is disappearing. But it is changing in ways that are historically profound.

Notes

1. See Odd Arne Westad, *The Global Cold War: Third World Interventions and the Making of Our Times* (Cambridge: Cambridge University Press, 2005).

2. On religion and the George W. Bush presidency, see Gary Scott Smith, *Faith and the Presidency: From George Washington to George W. Bush* (New York: Oxford University Press, 2006), 365–414, and Kevin M. Kruse, "Compassionate Conservatism: Religion in the Age of George W. Bush," in *The Presidency of George W. Bush: A First Historical Assessment*, edited by Julian E. Zelizer (Princeton, NJ: Princeton University Press, 2010), 227–251.

3. Madeleine Albright, *The Mighty and the Almighty: Reflections on America, God, and World Affairs* (New York: HarperCollins, 2006), 97.

4. George W. Bush, "Remarks at the Islamic Center of Washington," September 17, 2001, *Public Papers of the Presidents: George W. Bush, 2001*, Book II (Washington, DC: Government Printing Office, 2002), 1121.

5. Barack Obama, "Remarks to the Parliament in Canberra, Australia," November 17, 2011, http://www.presidency.ucsb.edu/ws/index.php?pid=97064&st=&st1=.

6. On the foreign-policy principles and ideologies of the Obama administration, see James Mann, *The Obamians: The Struggle Inside the White House to Redefine American Power* (New York: Penguin, 2012).

7. On the power of ephemeral concepts like credibility, see Robert J. McMahon, "Credibility and World Power: Exploring the Psychological Dimension in Postwar American Diplomacy," *Diplomatic History* 15 (1991): 455–472.

8. Obama, "Remarks at a Town Hall Meeting and a Question-and-Answer Session in Shanghai," November 16, 2009, http://www.presidency.ucsb.edu/ws/index.php?pid=86909&st=these+freedoms+of+expression&st1=.

9. The best analysis of the speech's origins, drafting, and delivery, as well as the subsequent execution of its promises, is Judson Brent Birdsall, "A Great Leap Faithward: Barack Obama and Rise of Religious Engagement in American Diplomacy" (PhD dissertation, Cambridge University, 2015), esp. chapter 3.

10. Obama, "Remarks in Cairo," June 4, 2009, http://www.presidency.ucsb.edu/ws/index.php?pid=86221&st=&st1=.

11. Ibid.

12. Obama, "Remarks at a Graduation Ceremony at the New Economic School in Moscow, Russia," July 7, 2009, http://www.presidency.ucsb.edu/ws/index.php?pid=86379&st=religion+of+peace&st1=.

13. Obama, "Remarks to the Parliament in London, England," May 25, 2011, http://www.presidency.ucsb.edu/ws/index.php?pid=90446&st=islam&st1=.

14. Obama, "Remarks at 'A Concert for Hope' Commemorating the 10th Anniversary of the September 11 Terrorist Attacks," September 11, 2011, http://www.presidency.ucsb.edu/ws/index.php?pid=96677&st=islam&st1=.

15. On these initiatives, see Douglas M. Johnston, *Religion, Terror, and Error: U.S. Foreign Policy and the Challenge of Spiritual Engagement* (Westport, CT: Praeger 2011), 90–92; Mara Willard, "Shaun Casey Talks About Leading the State Department's Faith-Based Office," *Religion & Politics*, March 4, 2014,

http://religionandpolitics.org/2014/03/04/shaun-casey-talks-about-leading-the-state-departments-faith-based-office/#sthash.RFdZSw8n.dpuf; and, most comprehensively, Birdsall, *Great Leap Faithward*, chapter 4.

16. On Obama's unique personal religious history, which has made for a complicated approach to the place of religion in politics and a mixed record of success in deploying faith in the service of his political goals, see James L. Guth, "Obama, Religious Politics, and the Culture Wars," in *Transforming America: Barack Obama in the White House*, edited by Steven E. Schier (Lanham, MD: Rowman & Littlefield, 2011), 77–100.

17. Obama, "Remarks on Accepting the Nobel Peace Prize in Oslo," December 10, 2009, http://www.presidency.ucsb.edu/ws/index.php?pid=86978&st=gandhi &st1=.

18. Matthew Continetti, "A Good Niebuhr Policy," *Weekly Standard*, July 13, 2009; George Packer, "Peace and War," *The New Yorker*, December 21, 2009.

19. David Brooks, "Obama, Gospel and Verse," *New York Times*, April 26, 2007. For more on Obama and Niebuhr, see James T. Kloppenberg, *Reading Obama: Dreams, Hope, and the American Political Tradition* (Princeton, NJ: Princeton University Press, 2011), 16–17, 22, 26, 119–121, 142–143, 215, 243–244, 250, 260.

20. Art Laffin, "Secret Wars and the Gospel of Nonviolence," *National Catholic Reporter*, August 2, 2010, http://ncronline.org/news/peace-justice/secret-w ars-and-gospel-nonviolence.

21. From the editors, "Back in Iraq," *Christian Century*, August 19, 2014, http://www.christiancentury.org/article/2014-08/back-iraq.

22. Perkins went further: he hoped Congress and Obama would pay for the surge by cutting spending on social programs at home. Both Wallis and Perkins quoted in Tobin Grant, "Who Backs Obama's Afghanistan Strategy?," *Christianity Today*, December 4, 2009, http://www.christianitytoday.com/ct/2009/decemberweb-o nly/148-51.0.html.

23. Dale Gavlak, "'Religicide' in Iraq," *Christianity Today*, February 16, 2011, http://www.christianitytoday.com/ct/2011/february/religicide.html.

24. Sandy Fitzgerald, "Sen. Rob Portman: Obama Must Protect Christians in Iraq," *Newsmax*, July 30, 2014, http://www.newsmax.com/Newsfront/ Iraq-Christians-Persecution-SenRob-Portman/2014/07/30/id/585796/.

25. Thomas F. Farr, *World of Faith and Freedom: Why International Religious Freedom is Vital to American National Security* (New York: Oxford University Press, 2005); Thomas F. Farr, "Diplomacy in an Age of Faith," *Foreign Affairs* 87 (March/April 2008): 110–124; Jennifer A. Marshall and Thomas F. Farr, "Public Diplomacy in an Age of Faith," in *Toward a New Public Diplomacy: Redirecting U.S. Foreign Policy*, edited by Philip Seib (New York: Palgrave Macmillan, 2009), 195–216.

26. See, for example, Thomas F. Farr, "Our Failed Religious Freedom Policy," *First Things*, November 2013.

27. "Who Fights for Religious Freedom? Obama's Ambassador Position Still Vacant," *Christianity Today*, January 18, 2011, http://www.christianitytoday.com/gleanings/2011/january/who-fights-for-religious-freedom-obamas-ambassador.html.

28. Judd Birdsall, "Obama and the Drama over International Religious Freedom Policy: An Insider's Perspective," *The Review of Faith & International Affairs* 10 (Fall 2012): 33–41.

29. On the exaggeration of just how pluralistic the American religious landscape is, see the chapter by Kevin Schultz in this volume.

III

Religion

12

Between Hope and Despair

OBAMA AND EVANGELICAL POLITICS

Steven P. Miller

AS BARACK OBAMA won and took office, accounts of demise shared space with dreams of rebirth. As is so often the case in American politics, religious language provided the metaphors for secular transitions. The rising "Joshua Generation" of black leaders and young evangelicals was within sight of the Promised Land. A "New New Deal" beckoned, as Obama asked the nation "to set aside childish things." A liberal publication ended its "The FundamentaList" column, while an Obama-backing minister called the 2008 election "an act of divine intervention." As much as any issue, the prospect of a "post-Religious Right America" was at the forefront of the hopes surrounding 2008.[1] In the long and varied history of evangelical Christianity in American life, this development was in certain respects a reversion to the mean. Gauged by the curve of American politics within Obama's adult lifetime, though, "change" was an appropriate word.

This chapter explores the significance of the Obama phenomenon—both his rise to power and his tenure in office—for the place of evangelicalism in recent American politics. The Obama years marked the waning of a period of special evangelical influence that commenced with the 1976 election of Jimmy Carter, whose candid born-again Christianity powered his outsider campaign. In 2000, political insider George W. Bush voiced a similar evangelical faith but proffered a different ideological vision. During the years between those two elections, evangelicalism—here defined broadly as the public expression of born-again Christianity—had merged with the Christian Right in the minds of many Americans. The

Christian Right became the most noted and analyzed expression of religious politics in a nation that was, in many other respects, growing more secular. (Partly because of the Christian Right's prominence, politicized evangelicalism remained a disproportionately, if by no means exclusively, white phenomenon during these years. Hence, this chapter primarily considers white evangelical actors.)

The 2008 presidential election upset the familiar narrative of evangelical politics. That year, progressive evangelicals helped to elect Obama and thus challenged the Christian Right's monopoly on the political meaning of born-again Christianity. The hope of one was the despair of the other. Soon, though, the rise of the Tea Party, followed by stark midterm losses for the Democrats, suggested a return to the status quo ante. Yet a false start did not a correction make. Even the Christian Right at its most partisan could not vote Obama out of office in 2012. In a notable shift from America's previous forty years, evangelical politics stopped functioning as a proxy for religious politics in general. Some evangelicals on the left learned to welcome the loss of status, while many on the right were determined to reverse it. Evangelicalism was not about to leave the public stage, of course. Yet the Obama era signaled its decline as a privileged political force.

From Bush to Obama

The political fortunes of Barack Obama rose alongside those of a resurgent evangelical left (the term commonly used to describe politically progressive evangelicals as a group). The broadly unpopular presidency of George W. Bush presented an opportunity for each. The junior senator from Illinois was hardly cut from evangelical central casting. However, he knew that outreach to evangelicals was critical to bridging the widely proclaimed "God Gap." As a fresh voice with little political baggage, Obama was in a position to say things that progressive evangelicals wanted to hear.

In 2005 and 2006, signs of a newly prominent evangelical progressivism were everywhere, from the opinion pages and bestseller lists of the *New York Times* to protests against President Bush's commencement address at the presumably friendly Calvin College. Jim Wallis, leader of the evangelical left flagship Sojourners, became a national celebrity. What journalists saw as an "evangelical crackup" was from another perspective the surfacing of differences that dated back to the 1970s, if not well before. Many on the evangelical left remained ambivalent about main-stream politics. As economic progressives and moral traditionalists, they were uncomfortable fits for the reigning two-party system. Yet the apparent political captivity of born-again Christianity to the Bush White House inspired a pragmatism born of frustration. This sentiment dovetailed nicely with the Democratic establishment's own desperation. In the aftermath of Bush's narrow reelection victory in 2004, Democratic leaders reached out to those evangelical power brokers who would grant them an audience, echoing the moves of Bill Clinton a decade earlier. These overtures, combined with Bush's growing unpopularity, gave the evangelical left rare political leverage.[2]

Obama had anticipated the Democratic Party's new evangelical strategy. He entered the national stage with a memorable keynote address at the 2004 Democratic National Convention. One of the most-quoted lines from his speech featured a brief but unmistakable flourish of evangelical parlance. "We worship an awesome God in the blue states," Obama declared in an effort to blur the shades of the culture wars, "and we don't like federal agents poking around our libraries in the red states." Many Americans knew the phrase "awesome God" as an allusion to the swaying chorus of a ubiquitous praise and worship song: "Our God is an Awesome God." Future Obama staffer Joshua DuBois recalled hearing the speech that way.[3]

One of the few political advantages that Obama's eclectic religious background provided him was the chance to fashion his own story, sans an obvious template. Obama was not the typical Democratic voice for faith in public life. He was not a white Southern moderate like Bill Clinton, an African American minister-activist like Jesse Jackson, or an urban Catholic like Mario Cuomo. In the world of presidential politics, there were no precedents for a Hawaiian whose background, more Pacific than Atlantic, merged Middle America with the post-colonial diaspora and the American racial binary. Yet Obama was able to craft an eloquent and appealing story about his spiritual and political coming of age. Spiritually, it was a tale of how a biracial product of a nominally Christian, if not at all observant, upbringing found identity, community, and meaning within the confines of Jeremiah Wright's largely African American Trinity Church in Chicago. Politically, it was the story of how an instinctively secular community activist, inspired by the witness of the Civil Rights Movement, came to see how faith offered something vital to the project of transforming neighborhoods. Obama's spiritual and political awakenings thus went hand in hand.

For an ambitious public figure, Obama was uncommonly candid about his lack of orthodoxy. His belatedly noticed 2004 interview with *Chicago Sun-Times* journalist Cathleen Falsani rested comfortably within her subsequent book profiling such spiritual and humanist wanderers as Bono and Melissa Etheridge. Obama was the voice of the candidate as Christian seeker. His multicultural childhood gave him a "suspicion of dogma," as well as distaste for "language that implies I've got a monopoly on the truth, or that my faith is automatically transferable to others." By this Obama meant not just shrill fundamentalism but also familiar Christian doctrine. "I find it hard to believe that my God would consign four-fifths of the world to hell," he told Falsani during their coffeehouse conversation.[4]

Despite Obama's appeal to common sense when describing his personal faith, his strengths as a communicator lay less in empathy than in narrative. The question ultimately became whether or not people bought his story. The public had plenty of opportunities to decide. Obama's "spiritual journey," excerpted from *The Audacity of Hope*, made the cover of *Time* in 2006, and his "religious biography" was *Newsweek*'s lead article two year later, by which time he had secured the Democratic nomination.[5]

The Obama faith story momentarily aligned with the trajectory of evangelical politics. Clearly, Obama saw this convergence as critical to his presidential ambitions. It had not been necessary for his ascendance up to that point, however. Ironically, Obama was the first successful presidential candidate since John F. Kennedy whose background gave him the option of operating wholly outside an evangelical framework. Yet Kennedy had felt obligated to assuage the fears of Southern white Protestants. Likewise, Obama made a conscious decision to engage evangelicals.

A key moment came when Obama spoke at a 2006 gathering of Call to Renewal, an activism campaign associated with the evangelical left. Obama framed his keynote address both as a strategic proposition to secular progressives and a challenge to evangelical progressives to step up their game. In the speech, he delivered shout-outs to several evangelical friends (Rick Warren, T. D. Jakes, Tony Campolo, and host Jim Wallis), as well as to a range of historical icons extending well beyond the expected Martin Luther King Jr. Obama also chided liberals, including himself, because "if we don't reach out to evangelical Christians and other religious Americans and tell them what we stand for, then the Jerry Falwells and Pat Robertsons and Alan Keyeses will continue to hold sway." The speech was not mere pandering. Obama's conventional liberalism was on full display, as he did not shy away from referring to his "pro-choice position." Just as boldly, he asked the faithful to adjust to a more pluralistic America. "Democracy demands that the religiously motivated translate their concerns into universal, rather than religion-specific, values," he declared. "It requires that their proposals be subject to argument, and amenable to reason." The speech rivaled Obama's 2004 convention address in terms of notoriety. It drew praise in evangelical left circles and liberal media forums. Jim Wallis likened the speech to Kennedy's olive branch to Southern Baptists. But Obama had achieved much more than a rapprochement. The "Obamagelicals" phenomenon was born.[6]

The storyline of a new direction for evangelical politics was a critical part of the Obama campaign narrative—more important, arguably, than the actual tally of evangelical votes the candidate received. Obama had obvious appeal to the evangelical left. More striking were those moderate evangelicals who, despite their ideological inclinations toward the GOP, came over to the most left-leaning presidential nominee in a generation. Obama made a point of reaching out to prominent evangelicals who were not customarily associated with the Christian Right. Several such figures, including popular devotional author Max Lucado and *Christianity Today* editor David Neff, were among the forty Christian leaders with whom candidate Obama met in June for an off-the-record conversation. *Christianity Today* described Obama campaign staffer and faith outreach coordinator Joshua DuBois as "the man behind the push to reach out to evangelicals." DuBois later drove the recruitment of celebrity pastor and author Rick Warren to give the invocation at the first inauguration.[7]

Amid an overwhelming sentiment that George W. Bush had damaged the evangelical brand, such gestures mattered. Irenic evangelical leaders like Richard Cizik of the National Association of Evangelicals (NAE), Orlando megachurch pastor Joel Hunter, and even Houston Methodist pastor Kirbyjon Caldwell (a confidant of President Bush) supported Obama the candidate, but not the urban liberal wing of the Democratic Party from which he hailed. A certain amount of opportunism surely factored into their friendliness, but their support did come with risks. Hunter, for example, was still recovering from a failed attempt to assume leadership of the Christian Coalition. He had planned to steer the well-known Christian Right group away from the familiar terrain of social conservatism and toward issues like creation care. Obama sought out Hunter after the pastor praised the candidate's "A More Perfect Union" speech, delivered in response to the controversy surrounding past sermons by Jeremiah Wright, Obama's pastor and erstwhile mentor. The flap threatened to do deep damage to Obama's religious image, and he made a point of not squandering the goodwill of Hunter and other unexpected allies. The Obama team gave weekly updates to the NAE during the 2008 campaign. Obama "understands evangelicals better than any Democrat since [Jimmy] Carter," gushed evangelical left veteran Ron Sider in *Christianity Today*.[8]

The boldness of Obama's evangelical strategy—namely, his unabashed attempt to drive a wedge between evangelicalism's center and right—tempted contemporaries to exaggerate both its breadth and depth. While Obama made inroads among moderate evangelicals and Catholics, the God Gap endured. Obama's substantive gains came elsewhere, especially among Latino voters, who were the main reason why Obama won a majority of the Catholic vote. White evangelical voters as a whole remained a reliable GOP bloc. Yet the reaction of the Christian Right's old and new guards to Obama suggested that they were on the defensive.[9]

The attractiveness of Obama caused no small amount of heartburn among Christian Right leaders. Religion mattered in 2008, but not in the manner to which those leaders had grown accustomed. Scholar Walter Russell Mead saw the election year as an indication of evangelicalism's "slow (and ongoing) shift from insurgent to insider, with all of the moderating effects that transition implies." Many evangelical insiders saw matters quite differently. Popular author Philip Yancey suggested that evangelicals should roll with their setbacks and then rebuild. "Some evangelicals are wringing their hands over their loss of access to the corridors of power," Yancey wrote. "Maybe it's time for us, too, to work from the bottom up." In fact, only a few influential evangelical conservatives were willing to accept Obama's extended hand. A more vocal group, epitomized by Christian Right warhorse James Dobson, stressed the connection between Obama's unorthodox faith and his liberal politics. Responding to the Call to Renewal speech two years after the fact, Dobson attacked candidate Obama for "deliberately distorting the traditional understanding of the Bible to fit his own world view, his own confused theology." Still, there was hope that younger leaders would heed Yancey's advice. Yet for every Rick Warren who was willing to pray at Obama's inauguration, there was at least one Franklin Graham who openly questioned the president's Christianity. During candidate Obama's private talk with Christian leaders, he and Graham had a back and forth about their differing views on salvation. As President Obama's popularity began to dip, the heir to the Billy Graham ministry went public with his concerns. In 2010, Franklin Graham told *Newsweek* that Muslims worldwide thought of the president "as one of their own."[10]

Evangelical Influence in the Age of Obama

In spite of Obama's electoral triumph in 2008, the Beltway conventional wisdom still held that the most authentic grassroots political trends come from the right.[11] The rise of the Tea Party movement seemed to prove this assumption true. In the end, though, it did not alter the perception that the Christian Right was tattered, or at least not its old self—a diagnosis the 2012 election confirmed. Less noted was the evangelical left's return to marginality.

The Jeremiah Wright controversy portended choppy waters for Obama's image once he took office. The evolving public response to Obama's faith story presented a paradox. The chapter-form transparency of his faith only made it the subject of wilder and wilder speculation. Here was a politician who had delivered what amounted to sermons at venues such as a 2008 African Methodist Episcopal Church gathering in Saint Louis, but whose religiosity simply was not taken at face value by millions of Americans. Obama talked a lot about his faith before and after January 2009. Still, by the time he entered the White House, he might well have concluded that he simply could not win when it came to doing so. Scarred by the Jeremiah Wright flap, the Obamas chose not to identify with a particular Washington, DC, church.[12]

Ultimately, President Obama was not able to control the politics of the story he had written so eloquently. In the hands of others, that story might have been one of, say, a revived mainline Protestantism, reflecting Obama's longtime association with the United Church of Christ. Decades of evangelical talk had truncated the national religious conversation, however. Besides "evangelical" itself, other available words for situating Obama's faith included "black" and, among elements of the right, "Muslim." Just after the 2008 election, journalist and Obama supporter Steve Waldman posted the full text of Obama's 2004 interview with Cathleen Falsani. Over a period of years, the reader comments pivoted sharply from affirming Obama to castigating him. For earlier commenters, Obama was a "beautiful enigma" who, to quote another supporter, "has a moral, not a fundamentalist, approach to integrating his religion into [h]is politics." As right-wingers discovered the transcript, he became, by 2010, the "Terrorist-in-Chief," the "Prince of Kenya," or simply "the devil incarnate." Amid the barrage of attacks and spam, one commenter joked about not being able to "tell the difference between 'Obama is part of Satan's army' and 'Easy payday loans!'" These online comments did not indicate a larger political turn, of course, but rather a shift in energy, as anger outshouted hope. Belief in the Muslim libel—the claim, explored further by Rebecca Goetz (Chapter 5 in this volume), that Obama was a stealth subscriber to the childhood faith of his absentee father—stood at 12 percent before Obama took office and would only grow from there.[13]

The midterm election cycle saw a momentary return of the thesis that evangelicalism was a political nemesis for Democrats. To be sure, the Tea Party promised something new on the right. As scholars David Campbell and Robert Putnam quickly demonstrated, however, the overlap between the Tea Party and the Christian Right was substantial, despite talk of the former's libertarian proclivities. A case in point was talk show host Glenn Beck's giant "Restoring Honor" rally on the Capitol Mall, which sparked understandable controversy because of its apparent appropriation of the 1963 March on Washington, also held on August 28. The revival-like gathering suggested what an ecumenical Christian Right politics might look like. Beck himself was a convert to Mormonism, and his rally featured an intentionally interfaith and multicultural mishmash of civil religion updated for post-Civil Rights Movement conservatism. "Look forward, look West, look to the heavens, look to God and make your choice," Beck told the crowd. The rallying cry of religious liberty, which grew louder during the 2012 election season, provided additional ecumenical glue. Because the Tea Party was cast as a novel phenomenon, the assumption that the Christian Right was declining remained largely unchallenged. At best, 2010 was a half-way rebirth for the Christian Right.[14]

The status of the evangelical left in national politics was even less certain. Echoing the history of its counterpart on the right, the evangelical left's profile had peaked with an election. Still, it was not merely a media construct. Like other progressive activists, evangelical leftists pushed Obama on economic matters, criticizing the president's willingness to compromise with Republicans on tax cuts. At the same time, what historian Brantley Gasaway has called "the agony of abortion" did not go away. Abortion was a major reason why the editors of a scholarly volume about evangelical social activism doubted that progressive evangelicals and the

Democratic Party would ever form a permanent union. In other areas, though, there were signs of a general convergence between the evangelical left and mainstream liberalism. For the Christian Right, something along these lines had happened regarding fiscal policy, as low taxes became part of the family values mantra. For the evangelical left, the trend surfaced in a surprising area: same-sex marriage.[15]

As Obama came out for gay marriage in 2012, several evangelical left bellwethers did likewise. That same year, Brian McLaren, a pioneering critic of the megachurch-Christian Right nexus, further riled his many evangelical detractors by presiding over a marriage commitment ceremony involving his gay son. McLaren and Richard Cizik (who had been ousted from his position with the NAE after voicing support for gay civil unions) later joined the advisory board of the newly formed Evangelicals for Marriage Equality. Meanwhile, Jim Wallis drew national attention for reversing his position on same-sex marriage. The same-sex marriage debate increasingly showed signs of better resembling past arguments about the acceptability of segregation than ongoing conflicts over abortion. At the very least, discussions of sexual orientation had entered new territory. Exodus International, the perennially controversial "reparative therapy" organization, closed in dramatic fashion in 2013, offering a public apology for "the pain and hurt" its work had caused. Within conservative Protestant congregational life, another possible analogy was with divorce, a divisive issue well into the 1970s that dissipated soon thereafter. As had been true with civil rights, secular society was ahead of the church on gay rights. Thus, church polity matters concerning membership and hiring usually remained unresolved. Moderate evangelical organizations like World Vision, along with a host of Protestant denominations, congregations, and schools, still had to work through the issue. Politically, though, something had changed. Many, perhaps most, on the evangelical left now accepted gay rights as a civil rights issue. After the 2012 election, Obama's inaugural committee again tapped a megachurch pastor with a history of opposition to gay rights to pray at the ceremony. Unlike Rick Warren, though, Louie Giglio (whom Obama had praised for his work on human trafficking) quickly withdrew from the program.[16]

The 2012 election offered a new explanation for the travails of the Christian Right: demographic transition. Declining numbers, rather than threats from the evangelical left, were what truly hindered evangelical conservatives. Several reports funded by the Pew Charitable Trusts highlighted the implausibility of lingering assumptions that evangelicalism

represented a majority—silent, moral, or otherwise. Religiously unaffiliated Americans—whom, as Matthew Hedstrom elucidates in Chapter 15,
scholars and pundits labeled the "nones"—now comprised a proportion
of the population (one-fifth) in line with conventional measurements of
American evangelicals. In fact, Pew noted, Protestant Christians as a
whole were no longer a majority of the American population. Pew also
documented the increasing influence of Latinos (a decidedly Democratic
voting group) across the religious spectrum, especially within the broader
Charismatic-evangelical milieu. Even there, though, Latino movement
toward evangelicalism showed signs of slowing among young adults.[17]

Such outside pressure had the effect of intensifying partisanship
within the core of the Christian Right. Even though most GOP frontrun-
ners in 2012 were not evangelicals in the commonly understood sense of
being conservative Protestants, they largely came wired to talk as if they
were. Rick Santorum, an ultraconservative Catholic, was a case in point.
So, in his own fashion, was the eventual nominee, Mitt Romney, whose
Mormonism was at least as exotic as Obama's religious background.
According to a May 2012 poll, a higher percentage of Americans knew that
Romney was a Mormon than identified Obama as a Christian. However,
Romney's main problem with evangelical voters was not his affiliation but
his record as a social moderate. Romney ultimately embraced a version
of George W. Bush's 2004 strategy. The assumption was that the evangelical electorate remained a slumbering giant. Ralph Reed, the most visible Christian Right leader during his run with Christian Coalition in the
1990s, returned to prominence by seeking to turn religious freedom into
a grassroots galvanizer. Another group highlighted Romney's pledge to
"not take God out of the public square." The base angle made some sense.
Four years after the Bush-era nadir, white evangelicals were as Republican
as ever, if not more so.[18]

On the ropes, Christian Right activists felt little need to restrain
their partisan preferences. Southern Baptist leader Richard Land openly
backed Romney, breaking with his previous policy of avoiding specific
endorsements. Franklin Graham apologized to Obama for questioning
his faith, but clarified that he still wanted the president tossed from office.
Graham also stated he was not going to hold Romney to a similar standard. "There are great theological differences between what he believes
and what I believe, but that's OK," Graham said of Romney. "We have
common moral ground with people of the Mormon faith." To the surprise of observers who had lionized Franklin Graham's father as someone

who stood above the culture wars, the ninety-three-year-old Billy Graham lent his voice to an advertisement urging Christians to vote along Biblical lines, citing heterosexual marriage, "the sanctity of life," and religious freedom. It ran in the swing state of Ohio in late October. Similar versions of Billy Graham's non-endorsement endorsement (which echoed his approach to previous Republican nominees) appeared nationally. White evangelicals turned out in great numbers for Romney, but Obama still won comfortably.[19]

As usual, the political winds were easier to detect than actual policy changes were to effect. Indeed, the precise parameters of an evangelical policy agenda—that is, what distinguished it from existing party options—had never been clear. Likewise, the extent to which progressive evangelical support for Obama would influence his policies remained uncertain. Joshua DuBois was an important test case. As a young African American evangelical, DuBois was a prototype for Obama's coalition. The pentecostal pastor directed the White House Office of Faith-based and Neighborhood Partnerships during the first Obama administration. Obama's decision to retain the controversial office, which George W. Bush had created under a slightly different name, was an acknowledgement that faith-based initiatives were not just a species of the right. The revamped office actually had a broader mandate than the Bush-era one, although it kept a much lower public profile. As an administration official, DuBois was best known for his pastoral work with Obama, namely the devotionals that he emailed to the president each morning. DuBois did his best to try to maintain the cooperative ethos of 2008, connecting Obama with open-minded evangelicals and highlighting the president's church attendance and periodic phone prayers with a range of Christian leaders. He successfully encouraged Obama to see the aging Billy Graham during a 2010 visit to North Carolina. Such outreach yielded few political benefits other than putting on the spot prominent Christians (including the younger Graham) who doubted the president's piety.[20]

While Obama's faith-based office received little fanfare in an era of recession-induced pessimism about civil society, it came replete with political trapdoors. DuBois was keenly aware of the touchy politics of his position, despite the fact that he operated with wide latitude. Support for faith-based institutions was one area where Obama had not posited a wholesale break with the Bush administration, save for a campaign pledge to repeal Bush's executive order allowing religious charities that accept federal funding to make religion-based hires. Before Obama took office,

Jim Wallis said of Obama that charitable choice—the policy of allowing faith-based organizations to receive relatively unrestricted public funds— "is him, this is who he is." The matter was hardly so simple, of course.[21]

There were signs from the start that the issue of religious liberty might exacerbate the historic tension within American liberalism between individual rights and group protections. The former priority reflects liberalism's philosophical origins, while the latter reflects its electoral evolution. Obama's preferred approach to this dilemma, voiced in his Call to Renewal speech, echoed and likely drew from political philosopher John Rawls's concept of "overlapping consensus." Religion-based policy prescriptions must be translated into secular terms—that is, they must be universalized—and then subjected to democratic scrutiny. Following this logic, policies promoting access to contraceptives (a clear stumbling block for a vocal minority of religious organizations, whether the topic was sex education or individual health insurance policies) should be treated as just that—policy concerns—with appropriate weight given to the popularity and health benefits of requiring insurance policies to cover contraceptives. Yet many Obama backers saw access to birth control as a right (rather than just a worthy policy), while others saw religious liberty as a similarly unassailable first principle (subject to majoritarian interference only in extreme cases). DuBois leaned strongly toward the latter perspective, but was outgunned on the question of whether religious organizations should receive a blanket exemption from the Affordable Care Act's contraceptives mandate. Like most evangelical progressives, though, he did not see religious liberty as a make-or-break matter. Within progressive circles overall, as he well knew, critics of Obama's faith-based policies had the rhetorical upper hand. DuBois took note of liberal journalist Sarah Posner's use of the phrase "faith-based failure" to describe his agency. Posner and others blasted Obama for not keeping his pledge to end the hiring policy exemption.[22]

Obama's take on religious liberty translated better in the international arena. There, the issue often concerned not special privileges but mere survival, and there, religious NGOs generally prioritized economic development over social agendas. In 2014, the State Department created an Office of Faith-based Community Initiatives, headed by seminarian Shaun Casey, who had overseen Obama's outreach to evangelicals during the 2008 campaign (playing a more behind-the-scenes role than Joshua DuBois). Academics and critics on the left immediately worried that the administration would privilege some expressions of religion over others.

On the issue of immigration, though, something like an overlapping consensus seemed to be evident everywhere other than in the Republican-led House of Representatives.[23] During his first six years in office, then, Obama proved to be a consistent social liberal who operated within the faith-based framework that he inherited.

The Decline Narrative Reaches Evangelicals

Nearly four decades removed from Jimmy Carter's election in 1976—the climax of what George Gallup Jr. hailed as the "Year of the Evangelical"— the perpetual relevance of evangelicalism no longer was taken for granted. Among the chattering classes, all signs suddenly pointed toward decline. Markers ranged from the sale of the iconic Crystal Cathedral megachurch to the increasing number of Americans who considered themselves "spiritual but not religious." Even the relative growth of pentecostal groups (which, in 1976, likely would have been included in the evangelical camp) did not detract from the new conventional wisdom. From within came calls for reflection and restraint. "It hasn't been a good year for evangelicals," wrote journalist John Dickerson at the close of 2012. A self-described evangelical, Dickerson embraced what he saw as his faith's momentary irrelevance. "Weakness is a potent purifier." This was both a theological point and a strategic one. "The understanding that the evangelical vote is a kingmaking vote," declared Shaun Casey, "I think, is now dead." Ralph Reed scrambled to make sure that the GOP did not "round up" evangelicals and other social conservatives, never mind that countless Republican officeholders still fit both categories.[24]

Despite continued talk of a "new evangelical social engagement," few now dared to imagine that the evangelical left would ever become the Democratic Party's version of the Christian Right. "The 'nones' are to the Democratic Party what evangelicals are to Republicans," opined one journalist. Even as the evangelical template lingered, the story was often less about the evolution of evangelicalism than about the changing political climate.[25]

Within the limited but protean vocabulary of American politics, change is ever a creature of the moment. The Obama presidency promised a new twist on the old, old story of American faith and politics. In Obama's first inaugural address, he spoke of "a nation of Christians and Muslims, Jews and Hindus, and non-believers."[26] Religion—so often defined in evangelical terms—had a special place in the pantheon of

American worldviews, but not an exclusive one. Yet many of the issues that powered the Christian Right and mobilized its discontents have not run their course. Abortion, especially, will remain salient, and might become more so if *Roe v. Wade* does not survive. Many voters in the center and on the left still view conservative Christian activism as a threat to American democracy. These postures are now entering their second generation, and they are easy to spot. Obama offered to change the subject. He was better equipped than any president before him to grasp American pluralism in all its fullness. If his story is America's story, though, then its next turn is no more certain than the latest election cycle or Supreme Court decision.

Notes

1. David Remnick, "The Joshua Generation," *The New Yorker*, November 17, 2008; Tony Dokoupil, "Faith Beyond His Father's," *Newsweek*, January 26, 2009; *Time* cover, November 24, 2008, http://content.time.com/time/covers/0,16641,20081124,00.html; "President Barack Obama's Inaugural Address," January 20, 2009, http://www.whitehouse.gov/blog/inaugural-address; Sarah Posner, "The FundamentaList No. 86," *The American Prospect*, June 24, 2009, http://prospect.org/article/fundamentalist-no-86; Marvin A. McMickle, "When the Walls Came Tumbling Down," in *The Audacity of Faith: Christian Leaders Reflect on the Election of Barack Obama*, edited by Marvin McMickle (Valley Forge, PA: Judson Press, 2009); Jim Wallis, *The Great Awakening: Reviving Faith and Politics in a Post-Religious Right America* (New York: HarperCollins, 2008).
2. Charles Marsh, "Wayward Christian Soldiers," *New York Times*, January 20, 2006; "Discover Author Jim Wallis," http://www.harpercollins.com/cr-101138/jim-wallis; Collin Hansen, "Bush Visit to Calvin College Exposes Divisions," *Christianity Today*, May 20, 2005, http://www.christianitytoday.com/ct/2005/mayweb-only/53.0b.html; David D. Kirkpatrick, "The Evangelical Crackup," *New York Times*, October 28, 2007; Steven P. Miller, *The Age of Evangelicalism: America's Born-again Years* (New York: Oxford University Press, 2014), 152–153; David R. Swartz, *Moral Minority: The Evangelical Left in an Age of Conservatism* (Philadelphia: University of Pennsylvania Press, 2012).
3. "Transcript: Illinois Senator Candidate Barack Obama," July 27, 2004, http://www.washingtonpost.com/wp-dyn/articles/A19751-2004Jul27.html; Joshua DuBois, *The President's Devotional: The Daily Readings That Inspired President Obama* (New York: HarperLuxe, 2013), no page numbers.
4. Cathleen Falsani, *The God Factor: Inside the Spiritual Lives of Public People* (New York: Farrar, Straus, and Grioux, 2006); Steven Waldman, "Obama's Fascinating Interview with Cathleen Falsani," blog post, November 11, 2008,

http://www.beliefnet.com/columnists/stevenwaldman/2008/11/obamas-interview-with-cathleen.html#.

5. Barack Obama, "My Spiritual Journey," *Time*, October 23, 2006, 52–60; Lisa Miller et al., "Finding His Faith," *Newsweek*, July 21, 2008, 26–32.

6. "Obama's 2006 Sojourners/Call to Renewal Address on Faith and Politics," *God's Politics* (blog), February 21, 2012, http://sojo.net/blogs/2012/02/21/transcript-obamas-2006-sojournerscall-renewal-address-faith-and-politics; Biff Rocha and Jeffrey L. Morrow, "Dancing on the Wall: An Analysis of Barack Obama's 'Call to Renewal' Keynote Address," in *What Democrats Talk About When They Talk About God: Religious Communication in Democratic Party Politics*, edited by David Weiss (Lanham, MD: Lexington, 2010), 130; Miller, *Age of Evangelicalism*, 155–156; Ronald Eric Matthews Jr. and Michele A. Gilbert, *Obamagelicals: How the Right Turned Left* (Newcastle upon Tyne, UK: Cambridge Scholars, 2010).

7. John W. Kennedy, "Preach and Reach," *Christianity Today*, October 2008, 27–30; Stephen Mansfield, *The Faith of Barack Obama*, rev. large print ed. (Detroit and other cities: Gale, 2011), 166.

8. Kennedy, "Preach and Reach"; Mansfield, 152–156.

9. Corwin E. Smidt et al., *The Disappearing God Gap? Religion in the 2008 Presidential Election* (New York: Oxford University Press, 2010), 152–153; Gaston Espinosa, ed., *Religion, Race, and Barack Obama's New Democratic Pluralism* (New York: Routledge, 2013).

10. Walter Russell Mead, "Born Again: America's Evangelicals Are Growing More Moderate—and More Powerful," *The Atlantic*, March 1, 2008, http://www.the-atlantic.com/magazine/archive/2008/03/born-again/306634/; Philip Yancey, "Working From the Bottom Up," in *Audacity of Faith*, 54; Kennedy, "Preach and Reach," 28–29. Miller et al., "Finding His Faith"; " 'Muhammad Only Leads to the Grave,' " *Newsweek*, May 17, 2010.

11. For a similar critique, see Josh Marshall, "Wired," Talking Points Memo, February 19, 2009, http://talkingpointsmemo.com/edblog/wired.

12. Valerie C. Cooper and Corwin E. Smidt, "African Americans, Religion, and the 2008 Election Cycle," in *Religion, Race, and Barack Obama's New Democratic Pluralism* (New York: Routledge, 2013), 196; Jonathan Alter, *The Promise: President Obama, Year One* (New York: Simon and Schuster, 2010), 301.

13. Waldman, "Obama's Fascinating Interview with Cathleen Falsani"; Miller et al., "Finding His Faith"; Pew Research Center, "Growing Number of Americans Say Obama is a Muslim," August 18, 2010, http://www.pewforum.org/2010/08/18/growing-number-of-americans-say-obama-is-a-muslim/.

14. David E. Campbell and Robert D. Putnam, "God and Caesar in America," *Foreign Affairs* 91, no. 2 (March/April 2012); "D.C. Rallies Illuminate Racial Divide," *Tell Me More*, transcript, August 30, 2010, http://www.npr.org/templates/story/story.php?storyId=129530565; Jo Becker, "An Evangelical is Back from Exile, Lifting Romney," *New York Times*, September 23, 2012.

15. "Jim Wallis and Evangelical Left Hit Obama on Tax Cut Extension," Institute on Religion and Democracy press release, December 10, 2010; "Obama No Longer Evangelical Left Messiah?," *Targeted News Service*, February 22, 2010; Brantley W. Gasaway, *Progressive Evangelicals and the Pursuit of Social Justice* (Chapel Hill: University of North Carolina Press, 2014), 128; Brian Steensland and Philip Goff, "Introduction: The New Evangelical Social Engagement," in *The New Evangelical Social Engagement*, edited by Steensland and Goff (New York: Oxford University Press, 2014).

16. "Trevor McLaren and Owen Ryan," *New York Times*, September 23, 2012, http://www.nytimes.com/2012/09/23/fashion/weddings/trevor-mclaren-owen-ryan-weddings.html; Jim Hinch, "Evangelicals Are Changing Their Minds on Gay Marriage," *Politico*, June 7. 2014, http://www.politico.com/magazine/story/2014/07/evangelicals-gay-marriage-108608.html#.VACogmMXNWx; Jaweed Kaleem, "Jim Wallis Talks Faith's Role In Politics, Gay Marriage and Immigration," *Huffington Post*, April 5, 2013, http://www.huffingtonpost.com/2013/04/05/jim-wallis-faith-politics-immigration_n_3024458.html; Evangelicals for Marriage Equality website, http://www.evangelicals4equality.com/advisory-board/; John Turner, "Religion and the Victory of Same-Sex Marriage," *Patheos*, April 11, 2013, http://www.patheos.com/blogs/anxious-bench/2013/04/religion-and-the-victory-of-same-sex-marriage/; Randall Balmer, "When Evangelicals Change with the Culture," *Christian Century*, August 15, 2013, http://www.christiancentury.org/blogs/archive/2013-08/when-evangelicals-change-culture; Sarah Pulliam Bailey, "World Vision's Rich Stearns: 'A Bad Decision, but We Did It with the Right Motivations," *Religion News Service*, March 27, 2014, http://www.religionnews.com/2014/03/27/qa-world-vision-president-rich-stearns-sponsors-staff-lost-sex-marriage-announcements/; Verne Schirch and Lisa Schirch, "News Analysis: Peacebuilding in a Divided Pacifist Church," *The Mennonite*, August 1, 2014, http://www.themennonite.org/issues/17-8/articles/NEWS_ANALYSIS_Peacebuilding_in_a_divided_pacifist_church; Sarah Posner, "Unpacking the Giglio Imbroglio," *Religion Dispatches*, January 11, 2013, http://religiondispatches.org/unpacking-the-giglio-imbroglio/.

17. Miller, *Age of Evangelicalism*, 162; Pew Research Center, "The Shifting Religious Identity of Latinos in the United States," May 7, 2014, http://www.pewforum.org/2014/05/07/the-shifting-religious-identity-of-latinos-in-the-united-states/.

18. John-Charles Duffy, "What Happened to Romney's 'Evangelical Problem'?," *Religion & Politics*, July 9, 2012, http://religionandpolitics.org/2012/07/09/what-happened-to-romneys-evangelical-problem/; "Obama's Religion a Mystery to Many; Romney Dominating Evangelical Vote: Poll," *International Business Times News*, May 10, 2012; Janet Hook, "Romney Supporters Make Push for Evangelical Voters," *Wall Street Journal*, October 23, 2012; "Evangelical Voters: Lift Every Voice," *The Economist*, May 5, 2012.

19. David Gibson, "Richard Land, Top Southern Baptist Official, Endorses Romney," *Religion News Service*, October 31, 2012, http://www.huffington-post.com/2012/10/31/richard-land-endorses-mitt-romney_n_2047812.html; Adelle M. Banks, "Franklin Graham Apologizes for Doubting Obama's Faith," *Christian Century* (RNS), March 21, 2013; Peter Nicholas, "Sunday Sermons Promote Turnout," *Wall Street Journal*, November 5, 2012; Robin Abcarian, "Billy Graham Takes Full-page Ad in Ohio Newspaper to Back Romney," *Los Angeles Times*, October 21, 2012, http://articles.latimes.com/2012/oct/21/news/la-billy-graham- takes-ohio-newspaper-ad-backing-romney-20121021; Jonathan Merritt, "Election 2012 Marks the End of Evangelical Dominance in Politics," *The Atlantic*, November 13, 2012, http://www.theatlantic.com/politics/archive/2012/11/election-2012-marks-the-end-of-evangelical-dominance-in-politics/265139/.

20. Alex Altman, "Obama's Pastor-in-Chief," *Time*, February 6, 2009, http://content.time.com/time/nation/article/0,8599,1877501,00.html; DuBois, *President's Devotional*; George E. Condon Jr., "Joshua DuBois: The Man Who Helps Obama Pray," *National Journal*, April 2, 2011.

21. DuBois, *The President's Devotional*; Peter Wallsten, "Keeping Faith, Courting Conservatives: Obama's Willingness to Continue Bush Approach to Religious Charities Aims to Woo Evangelicals but Vexes Liberals," *Wall Street Journal*, February 4, 2010; "Obama and the Religious Right," *Church & State*, January 2009, 9.

22. James T. Kloppenberg, *Reading Obama: Dreams, Hope, and the American Political Tradition* (Princeton, NJ: Princeton University Press, 2011), 144–145 passim; DuBois, *The President's Devotional*; Sarah Posner, "A Faith-based Opportunity for Obama," *Salon*, May 1, 2013, http://www.religiondispatches.org/dispatches/sarahposner/6823/a_faith_based_opportunity_for_obama/.

23. Leslie Larson, "The Obamas Show Their Spiritual Side at the National Prayer Breakfast," *New York Daily News*, February 6, 2014, http://www.nydailynews.com/news/politics/president-obama-national-prayer-breakfast-article-1.1604182; Sarah Pulliam Bailey, "Obama, Evangelicals Meet on Religious Concerns," *Christian Century* (RNS), November 15, 2001; Mara Willard, "Shaun Casey Talks about Leading the State Department's Faith-based Office," *Religion & Politics*, March 4, 2014, http://religionandpolitics.org/2014/03/04/shaun-casey-talks-about-leading-the-state-departments-faith-based-office/; "Engaging Religion at the Department of State," *The Immanent Frame* (blog), July 30, 2013, http://blogs.ssrc.org/tif/2013/07/30/engaging-religion-at-the-department-of-state/; Jordan Miriam, "Evangelicals Leaders Urge Immigration Shakeup," *Wall Street Journal*, November 14, 2012.

24. Jim Hinch, "Where Are the People?," *The American Scholar*, Winter 2014, http://theamericanscholar.org/where-are-the-people/#.U9qcSWPQqsN; Steven Barrie-Anthony, "'Spiritual but Not Religious': A Rising, Misunderstood Voting Bloc," *The Atlantic*, January 14, 2014, http://www.

theatlantic.com/politics/archive/2014/01/spiritual-but-not-religious-a-rising-misunderstood-voting-bloc/283000/; David Roozen, "Negative Numbers: The Decline Narrative Reaches Evangelicals," *Christian Century*, December 3, 2013, http://www.christiancentury.org/article/2013-11/negative-numbers; John S. Dickerson, "The Decline of Evangelical America," *New York Times*, December 16, 2012; Merritt, "Election 2012 Marks the End of Evangelical Dominance in Politics"; Ralph Reed, "Round Up the Usual Social Conservative Suspects," *Wall Street Journal*, November 26, 2012.

25. Brian Steensland and Philip Goff, eds., *New Evangelical Social Engagement* (New York: Oxford University Press, 2014); Jeff Kunerth, "'Nones,' Evangelicals Played Similar Roles in Election 2012," *McClatchy-Tribune Business News*, November 14, 2012.

26. "President Barack Obama's Inaugural Address," January 20, 2009, http://www.whitehouse.gov/blog/inaugural-address.

13

Secrets and the Making
of Mormon Moments

J. Spencer Fluhman

IN THE 2012 presidential election, both the Obama and Romney campaigns fastidiously avoided mention of Mr. Romney's religion. Though ducked by both sides, religion nevertheless spilled out, hot, everywhere. The Obama campaign fumed when Romney, in a nod to Protestant evangelicals, told Sean Hannity in February 2012 that Mr. Obama wanted to make America "a less Christian nation." (Asked about the statement, Romney said he wasn't familiar with what he had said, but that "I stand by what I said, whatever it was."[1]) Tellingly, even with such non-statements about faith in the air, neither candidate could quite take Mormonism head-on. Those official evasions of Mormonism stood in tension, of course, with a wave of media obsession that conjured a "Mormon moment" that filled periodicals and twenty-four-hour news programs with ostensibly informational profiles of the Church of Jesus Christ of Latter-day Saints (LDS) and its members.

Is there a relationship between those ubiquitous media "discoveries" of Mormonism and the fact that modern politicos scrupulously avoid discussing it? This chapter offers a historical explanation for those discoveries and silences by linking Mormonism's political implications with Americans' profound ambivalence over religion and the public sphere. More narrowly, it contends that the specific form that American engagement with Mormonism has long taken—that of the exposé—encourages reflection within the study of religion and politics about the meanings of religious secrecy. What can we say about the repeated keeping and disclosing of Mormon secrets? Put more crassly, what does it mean that

American political culture has long demanded that Mr. Romney account for his underwear? The incessant American exposé of Mormonism results in part from cultural developments quite apart from the controversial faith, but also from its own persistent secrets, both real and imagined. Journalists in 2012 were thrust into the basic paradox of this history: is Mormonism an exotic creation with strange rituals and secretive patriarchs, or is it the quintessentially American religion, a patriotic if bland church extolling large families and capitalist achievement?

In part, it is Mormonism's blurring of traditional religious categories that has marked it for such continuing political controversy: Americans have viewed it as both Christian and not quite Christian, both as a religion and somehow more or less than one. I offer secrecy as a key factor in the distance that many Americans perceive between Mormonism and normative Christianity. Mormonism's secrets have thus helped constitute it as a classificatory problem for Americans and scholars alike, but, at the same time, its secrets have helped make a distinctive Mormon people possible. Accordingly, I'll trace American readings of Mormon secrecy over the past century and a half alongside episodes of the Latter-day Saints' management of their mysteries to illuminate how central the tradition has been for negotiations of American religious authenticity and hence for religion's political framing. In other words, since secrecy points us to a kind of intentional silence, it points us unavoidably to power.[2] Seen in this light, the consequential effects of Mormon secrecy give us more than additional details to round out the religion's historical portrait.[3] Rather, they provide us with the gritty mechanics of power itself: how it is constituted, contested, and remade.[4] The keeping and exposing of Mormon secrets form a kind of political ritual that punctuates the repeated "Mormon moments" in American history. Their repetition and regularity tell us something about both Mormonism and its changing political contexts. And since Mormonism's stubborn concealment impulses in some ways run right into the teeth of our scholarly and democratic projects, they necessarily beg important questions of both American politics and those of us who study them.

The Origins of Mormon Secrecy

Many religious traditions acknowledge some kind of hidden knowledge. Just as sacred space can enclose secrets and mark membership in a Pueblo kiva or for Muslims in Mecca, so it has been with Mormon temples' spatial restrictions.[5] But especially during periods of social or political strain, religious secrets often arouse suspicions. This was true of earliest Christianity, after all. The *disciplina arcani* kept the faith's mysteries not only from the heathen but even from those receiving their first instructions in the faith. Based on Jesus's instructions in Matthew 7:6, the "discipline of the secret" guarded Christian practices and doctrines amid a skeptical pagan populace but also marked them as potentially subversive.[6] In the American context, nonbelievers warned against similar dangers related to secrecy with the nineteenth-century Mormons and Catholics, with black sects such as the Moorish Science Temple and the Nation of Islam in the twentieth century, with the Church of Scientology after World War II, and with Muslims after September 11, 2001. Legally, the absence of a constitutional definition for religion has helped check the development of any formal right to religious privacy, though privacy itself developed a strong legal framework in the twentieth century. As a result, religious free exercise and privacy rights sometimes meet but are not overlapping concepts—a still forming "legal frontier," in the words of Michael Barkun.[7]

Mormonism may seem to be an especially secretive faith, but it did not emerge that way. There is some irony, in fact, with this essay's attention to secrecy given that the first Latter-day Saints would likely have chosen *revelation* to summarize their faith. The early Mormon mix of ecstatic religious experience and miracle show helped create the concealment tradition. The founder's "golden plates" were hidden from most eyes, after all, and so the mystery of the Book of Mormon's printed text was understood as nothing less than a founding miracle or as evidence of boldfaced fraud, depending on one's perspective. (As one scholar has written, a "secret may look quite different depending on whether it is real or imagined, or whether one has it, wants it, or fears it."[8]) Similarly, early LDS missionaries dabbled in a kind of miracle performance for potential converts, but it quickly became clear that to do so amounted to an evangelistic gamble since some public healings, for instance, worked and others did not. Observability and feats of spiritual power made for unpredictable partners in the founding of a new religion. Signs would only follow faith, they learned—the Saints would enjoy the ancient powers privately, away from the hostile gaze of critics.

LDS texts helped forge a tradition of secrecy as well. The new scriptures often trafficked in the promise of more: hidden pasts still to be revealed, divine mysteries yet to be made known. Mormons thus tore the covers off the Bible and lived in a state of "canonical expectancy."[9] But hiddenness played other roles in Mormon texts, too, as history and scripture bled together in the first Mormon moments. As violence came to define the early Mormon/non-Mormon interactions, Mormons edited their revelations. To conceal what had been revealed, Joseph Smith himself sometimes substituted code names and words in the 1835 published compilation of his revelations.[10] Mormons understood this use of codes as politically expedient but not without scriptural warrant and religious significance. Just as Jesus's parables simultaneously explained and obscured truths from the unprepared or insincere, they could safeguard their pearls from the hostile "gentile" swine.

This historical, almost accidental presence of secrecy in Mormon texts mirrored the tradition itself as it entered a generative second stage in 1840s Illinois. With Mormon daring and creativity on the rise, anti-Mormonism surged accordingly. Facing foes within and outside the church, Smith elaborated on the faith by putting secrecy at its administrative and sacramental core. Secrecy thus did important cultural work in the founder's autobiographical crescendo: it enhanced loyalty among the loyal, guarded the more radical theological and theocratic possibilities, and marked "them" and "us" in new and powerful ways. Mormons had been multiplying governing conferences and councils for a decade, but Smith's Illinois additions lurched in secretive directions. One secret council, the "Council of Fifty," blurred politics and religion in such a way as to haunt American perceptions of Mormonism to this day. The council was charged with orchestrating Smith's 1844 run for the US presidency and, in the likely scenario it would falter, scout a new Western settlement for the church.[11] When word of the council and its plans began to leak out, critics charged that Mormonism was more a political empire-in-the-making than a church. That these secret plans occurred in a particular American moment, with its particularly violent politics, in view of a particular American West, was lost on both Mormons and their antagonists. Both groups came to see the secrets as essential to Mormonism.

Smith's other secret council, the "Quorum of the Anointed," was linked to still other secrets. Polygamy and the rituals of the rising Mormon temple proved most explosive, and Smith's anointed quorum formed an inner circle of those initiated into the new mysteries.[12] In retrospect, Smith's innovations seem to fit well in their historical moment. They are comprehensible given other contemporaneous new religious movements protesting evangelical concepts of family, for instance. Despite the obvious differences in detail, the radical Mormon marriage doctrine is analogous to Shaker or Oneida sexual experimentation.[13] Secondly, Smith's innovations are comprehensible given the pervasive institutionalization of hermetic practices in the United States. Freemasonry offered Smith a ritual vocabulary, and his initiation into an Illinois lodge just days before his closest confidants experienced his reformatted temple rites is surely not coincidental. He even safeguarded his rites' secrecy with violent, Masonic-style penalty vows. It is telling that early Mormons themselves were not scandalized by these historical connections. The Masons among the Latter-day Saints celebrated them, in fact, with tenuous readings of sacred and secular history that cast their religion as the reconciler of Freemasonry's weakened, but still redeemable, transmission of ancient wisdom.[14]

But for most Mormons, the new rituals' historical dimensions were beside the point. Because the rituals did more than cultural work, they fixed secrecy not on the edges but at the core of their religion as they understood it.[15] The new rites did important theological and soteriological work, too, and can only be summarized here. Smith's complicated notion of "sealing," by which he meant the linking of families to God in relationships that would persist for eternity, was literally embodied in the ceremonies. Mormons understood that they were forging holy bonds—like "welding iron to iron"—that would transcend time, space, and the grave.[16] Through this robust but hidden sacramentalism, Mormons redefined Christianity, family, sexuality, time, and human bodies themselves. Indeed, where Mormon conceptions of space and time had earlier worked on the axis of a holy city and a millenarian countdown, the 1840s innovations set the project on a new footing. As historian Stephen Taysom has argued, the temple had earlier functioned as the *axis mundi* for the millennial city, but now the Saints' own bodies formed the holy of holies within Mormon sacred edifices.[17] Appropriately, Mormons both donned ceremonial clothing for the rites and wore special underclothing thereafter. The underclothing thus both marked and obscured the new relationships. Modern Mormon ideas about the family, inscribed on their hearts' fleshy tablets and on Utah bumper stickers featuring slogans like "families are forever," have their foundations in those Illinois secrets. And the secrets were in part made valuable by their inaccessibility: one could not be *casually* Mormon and obtain the exalting knowledge.[18] Thus, Mormons could scarcely jettison their secret things without pulling the foundations out from under some substantial ritual and theological structures.

It is not surprising, then, that ex-Mormons have long known exactly how to leave or where to strike: the secrets are just waiting to be exposed. The secrets have thus functioned as a lever for Mormon identity, marking passageways both into and out of the religion's beating heart. When some early Mormons pulled back from these innovations, they published a prospectus for an aptly named *Expositor* newspaper, which promised to tell the tales—the secret plural marriages, the secret councils, all of it. The loyalists' 1844 overreaction in destroying the dissident press was only an overreaction from a political standpoint. Seen from the vantage of the secrets' still-forming meanings, the press ransacking, however politically naïve or misguided, can be read as a profoundly *religious* form of conservative social action. In their own minds, the faithful were protecting God's truth from desecration. When Brigham Young added what came to be known popularly as a "vengeance oath" to the temple liturgy's covenantal obligations in 1845, after the founder's murder, he admitted what most Americans would not: sometimes religion is about vengeance. Good American religions are not supposed to be about such things. By adding the promise to pray for "God to avenge the blood of the prophets upon [the] nation," Young vividly affirmed what scholars tell introductory religious studies students: rituals make evident a group's moods, its priorities.[19] Strained to their breaking point by violence and circumstances spiraling beyond their control, Latter-day Saints practiced their pain in ritualized, thunderous whispers.[20]

Renegade Mormons ensured that the temple rites were among the nation's worst-kept secrets. John C. Bennett was so entrenched in the LDS hierarchy's top echelons that his 1842 *History of the Saints, or an Exposé of Joe Smith and Mormonism* threatened to do real harm to the secrets, but he overreached, as was his wont, and his creative flourishes subverted his influence once Mormons exposed his excesses. Catherine Lewis regretted her conversion to Mormonism and wrote of her unhappy stay in the Mormon capital in 1848. She included what portions of the temple ceremonies she could remember, but added some fantastic flourishes of her own. Increase and Maria Van Dusen knew of Young's reformulated ceremony and offered their exposé in several editions beginning in 1849. Like Bennett and Lewis, they mixed accurate description with breathless embellishment, but even their title beat a path to the vengeance oath: *Startling Disclosures of the Great Mormon Conspiracy Against the Liberties of this Country*. And the founder's own brother, William Smith, remonstrated against the admission of the Saints' 1849 proposed state of Deseret, arguing that his Rocky Mountain cousins had compromised their national loyalty with Young's ritual addition. (William Smith's Midwest Mormons would eventually construct a temple, too, but one shorn of both high ritual and secrecy.)[21]

With ex-Mormons supplying the data, Americans constructed layered arguments about Mormon un-Americanness. Whether esteeming Mormonism as a fake religion, a foreign one, or a merely false one, notions of secrecy figured prominently in the antagonistic polemics. The early critiques charged that Mormonism was not a religion but a scam. With confidence men and painted ladies seemingly on every corner, American vigilance against religious impostors was historically apropos.[22] In similar fashion, theocracy and polygamy functioned as both means and ends in formulations of Mormon foreignness. American concerns over Mormon and Roman Catholic hierarchies provoked a democracy bent on shining righteous light on the minority faiths' secrets. No less a scholar than David Brion Davis was struck by the correspondences between anti-Mormon, anti-Catholic, and anti-Masonic rhetoric more than a half century ago: each genre sought enhanced controls of the subgroup in the name of combatting un-American concentrations of power. Each unpopular minority was thought to maintain those concentrations through secrecy and coercion, which, as David Chidester has argued, have long functioned as the chief markers of religious inauthenticity in the Western religious classification project.[23] Indeed, the anti-Mormon versions of the American captivity narrative tradition echoed the early century "convent tales." Dangerously hidden from view, American femininity risked spoilage at the hands of Catholic hierarchs and Mormon patriarchs—sometimes imagined as almost interchangeable threats.[24]

By the Civil War era, Mormons and their observers were dug in over the secrets. The secrets, in fact, could stand in for and summarize the underlying contest over religion itself. With every disclosure, one can almost feel critics sneering: you call *that* sacred? Mormons shook a fist back: is *nothing* holy in America? Mormons prize their pioneer-era temples for their rough-hewn beauty and the sunbaked powers of will that called them up from the desert floor. But, given the history narrated here, their similarities of form speak an altogether different sermon: they are, after all, each castles. As citadels of the secrets, they call up defiance, entrench-ment, and resistance. Mormons quickly understood their relationship to the "gentile" East and to the federal government as one of colonization, and the temples seemed to mark a symbolic line in the Great Basin sand. They seem to echo with Brigham Young's own anguish and anger at hear-ing that the US Army was on its way to invade Utah in 1857. Preaching less than two months after learning of the invasion and by his own account "too angry ... to preach," he warned against further incursion into the Saints' Rocky Mountain refuge: "God Almighty being my helper, they cannot come here."[25]

Secrets and the Making of Modern Mormonism

Subsequent Mormon moments have followed the basic revelatory recipe with stunning regularity. What emerges from the cycle of secret keep-ing and exposé is a cultural script, an American political ritual, that has continued unabated to our time.[26] Memorable rehearsals of this political theater coincided with polygamy's slow demise. As the 1880s' antipolyg-amy crusade wreaked havoc throughout Mormondom, the LDS hierarchy made gradual accommodations to put off the seemingly inevitable. They curtailed the strident public calls for resistance, largely shut down the plural marrying (at least those that could be easily confirmed), and even stopped preaching the scandalous doctrine (at least in public). Privately, they fumed. With more than 1,300 Mormons imprisoned, more disen-franchised, and church property in federal hands, still they hoped for a workable middle way. Only when backchannel communications warned that their temples, too, would be seized did the great accommodation come. The US secretary of the interior sent word in August of 1890 that he would not abide the earlier gentlemen's agreement sparing the tem-ples. LDS president Wilford Woodruff's polygamy "Manifesto" ending the practice came just days later. Even polygamy, which Mormons had sworn could not be given up without wrecking everything, turned out to be expendable when compared with the maintenance of the sacred places and the holy secrets they guarded. For their part, federal officials had hap-pened onto a powerful lever of political and cultural coercion for the unre-pentant Saints.

It should come as no surprise that the Latter-day Saints met the challenges of the post-polygamy period with new secrets. Some church leaders maintained a program of secret post-Manifesto polygamy, some three hundred secret sealings at least, in expectation of Christ's vindicating return or, short of that, a more congenial Supreme Court.[27] But quiet resistance went hand in hand with public integration strategies, including the Mormon choir's near victory at the world choral competition in 1893 and Utah's election of a church apostle, Reed Smoot, to the US Senate. The hearings over the apostle's election offered the concealment/exposé drama on a grand stage. The hearings became less an inquiry into Smoot's fitness for office and more an exploration of Mormonism's acceptability as an American religion. For example, before the committee came a disillusioned former botany and history professor at Brigham Young Academy in Utah. He rehearsed the temple vengeance oath for the gathered senators to judge: had Senator Smoot compromised his national loyalty?[28] Church president Joseph F. Smith, nephew of the founding prophet, also took the stand to answer for the church and sparked one of the more memorable moments of cat and mouse in Senate hearing history. One senator pressed: "Suppose you should receive a divine revelation . . . commanding your people to-morrow to do something forbidden by the law of the land. Which would it be their duty to obey?" The politically savvy church president fired back: "They would be at liberty to obey just which they pleased. There is absolutely no compulsion."[29] Both sides had learned the script and knew their lines.

As it turned out, the furor over the Smoot hearings died a slow death. The National Reform Association (NRA) had helped lead the antipolygamy crusade, though its main goal was a constitutional amendment declaring the nation an explicitly Christian one. But even after the great polygamy accommodations of 1890 and 1904, NRA leaders clung to their belief that Mormonism threatened the nation. By the nineteen-teens, they had their key ex-Mormon: the politically connected and articulate son of one the most powerful nineteenth-century LDS hierarchs. Frank Cannon supplied the secrets and the arguments this time, and he and other NRA polemicists energetically crossed blades with the Mormons' bright young apostle, James E. Talmage. Talmage was among the first Mormons to receive a doctorate, had earned an academic reputation as a geologist and university president, and had become the faith's gentleman theologian.

By the time his sparring with the NRA came to a head, Talmage was a veteran of the battles over the secrets. In 1912, he had published his seminal *House of the Lord*, which offered the most complete descriptions of Mormon temple worship to date. The book had been prompted by a scandal. The previous year, antagonists had threatened to publish surreptitiously taken photos of the Salt Lake Temple interior unless LDS leaders provided a hefty ransom. Talmage suggested preemptive publication of temple images and was tasked with writing the accompanying account of the rituals. Not only did this mark an important moment in Mormons' determination to manage their public image, it solidified Talmage as the visible face of the church's sophisticating apologetics. When the NRA pit bulls warned that Mormons were sneaking their dubious theology through a cultural back door by means of their moral rectitude, sobriety, and famous choir, Talmage set theology up front with weekly tidbits in national papers. The back and forth came to a climax in 1919, when Talmage audaciously showed up at the third NRA world conference in Pittsburg. He was eventually allowed to speak for five minutes amid a hail of hisses, but the speaker following him suggested he be stripped to reveal his temple undergarments bearing the marks of his "treasonous" oaths. The crowd hemmed him in for an hour before he could slip away.[30]

Mormon Secrets in the Era of the Romneys

The Great Depression and World War II changed the game for Mormons in America. Depression-era church welfare measures won praise from conservatives, and positive depictions in national publications finally outnumbered negative ones for the first time in LDS history.[31] The war laid the groundwork for a global expansion that had begun almost as soon as the church was born but was not fully realized until after 1950. In the 1950s, the Mormons' image enjoyed a brief day in the sun, when its institutional efficiency, clean living, and family values seemed in lock step with the American mainstream. In such a setting, an auto industry titan like Mormon George Romney could mount a presidential campaign that came reasonably close to succeeding. Importantly, many took his Mormonism as a political asset.[32]

But Mormon success would create its own problems. In the United States, numbers swelled such that Protestant evangelicals took note, especially when it became clear that Mormons were sheep-stealing from their churches. The LDS church announced its growth and confidence in dramatic fashion with the 1974 dedication of its temple just north of the nation's capital. Situated rather conspicuously on the Maryland Beltway, the temple mimicked the Salt Lake Temple, but with a shiny, modern, and (some said) gaudy update that struck many as an unmistakably conscious assertion of power and presence. Cold War-era Mormons had swung hard to the political right after vacillating between the national parties in the early twentieth century. But surging conservatism did Mormons no favors at the time with the evangelicals, who responded with an invigorated "counter cult" movement that targeted Latter-day Saints in particular.

The most visible ex-Mormons in this moment were Ed Decker and Dave Hunt, whose book/movie combo *The God Makers* became a touchstone for evangelical resistance to Mormonism. The film, complete with spooky music and wonky animated segments, was condemned by the Anti-Defamation League and the National Conference of Christians and Jews, but its effects were substantial. It disturbed evangelical audiences across the nation for years. The film builds, predictably, to reenactments of the LDS temple rites. Over the eerie audio effects track, a voice introduces viewers to the secrets: "What you are seeing is an authentic, first-hand, first-time ever on film reenactment of secret Mormon temple ceremonies."[33]

George's son Mitt came of political age in this era of evangelical anti-Mormonism. By the time Mormons were basking in the glow of the so-called Mormon Olympics in 2002 and taking on the swagger of a suitable American faith, the younger Romney had emerged as the visible symbol of the ostensible newfound acceptability. The 2008 election cycle cured that. Romney's first run and the LDS church's involvement in California's 2008 marriage equality initiative sparked a backlash. Several outlets agreed that HBO's decision to portray the LDS temple ceremony in a 2009 "Big Love" episode had something to do with the church's California political activism from the year before. The episode actually provided some nuance for the rite, however, with Jean Tripplehorn's character, Barb, voicing the comfort that many Mormons associate with temple worship. But the particular selections from the ceremony formed a conspicuous poke in the eye, since they exposed the most private of the rite's sacred language.[34]

During this most recent Mormon moment, in 2012, the political ritual played out in new media and on seemingly ever grander platforms, but it remained a recognizable performance still. In one of the more memorable enactments of the routine, a journalist, following clips of ex-Mormons reenacting the by-then-discontinued temple penalty oaths, asks for an explanation from an LDS apostle. After being reminded of their discontinuance, the interviewer pressed. Wouldn't Mr. Romney have taken these vows in the past, before the changes? "That sounds Masonic, sir," the interviewer continued. "It sounds Masonic." The skepticism in the interviewer's voice rings familiar: you people used to call *that* holy? The frustration on the apostle's face is familiar, too: is *nothing* sacred anymore?[35] Not long thereafter, right on cue, in this recent moment's appropriate media format, and just days before the election, progressive blogger Andrew Sullivan posted footage of the entire LDS temple endowment ceremony, secretly filmed by an ex-Mormon. The film's subtitle brings us full circle, to that worst kept secret of the 1840s: "Never-Before-Seen Videos of Secret Mormon Temple Rituals."[36]

Secrets. Sacred. Ritual. Exposé. These words form a narrative trajectory for American religious history. A generation ago, the narratives of US religious history were crafted as tales of pluralism, democratization, and laicization—a rowdy but still lovable marketplace of individuals making independent spiritual choices. The history recounted here adds to a generational chorus of dissent from those depictions. Hardly a master narrative, it looks more like a contest over power, spaces, bodies, and the stories themselves, of the sacred as a placeholder for identity and politics. On the one hand, this account is a story of the Americanization of Mormonism, of the ways modern political and social worlds have chipped away at its secrets. One by one, the vengeance oath, the penalty oaths, starkly sectarian references, and some of the more severely gendered language were revised out of the ceremony. But Mormons could scarcely let go all the secrets without risking dreaded assimilation.[37]

But at the same time, it must be noted that the fruits of these Mormon moments are a decidedly mixed lot. If I've waxed nostalgic at all for the bearded, defiant communitarians of the nineteenth century, let me here restate the obvious: silences and secrets oppress and marginalize as well as unite and fortify; they can mystify and reinforce power as easily as pull it down.[38] The real secret is that everyone has blood on his or her hands. The keeping and telling of secrets, then, pushes scholars and commentators onto unstable ground. How should one study or narrate what partisans either want to keep hidden as an article of faith or want to expose as an act of democratic righteousness? These rituals of disclosure and concealment, after all, both patrol and punish, generate and liberate, build and destroy. What do we do with secrecy's evidential "torment," as Hugh Urban put it? For him, the secrets represent nothing less than "the dilemma of all ethnography," the very "crisis of representation" writ small.[39] And if I've made a case that one simply cannot comprehend the place of Mormonism in America without wrestling with the weighty silences shot through its stories, let me wonder aloud about the inverse: can we hope to comprehend American religious or political history without understanding its management of secrets and silences? Can we understand Romney's nods to evangelicals or evasions of Mormon distinctiveness without wrestling with this history? Scholars, journalists, and political commentators, it seems to me, might profitably seek that space between taboo and fetish with regard to secrets. Ideally, we steer clear of both the zealotry of determined secret keeping and the zealous compulsion to expose. At the very least, we must position ourselves so as to better explain what is at stake in the keeping and exposing, across time and in the present.

Notes

1. Aamer Madhani, "Obama Campaign: We Won't Talk About Romney's Mormonism," *USA Today*, May 20, 2012, http://content.usatoday.com/communities/theoval/post/2012/05/obama-campaign-we-wont-talk-about-romneys-mormonism/1 -.UUtpt1uaThM.

2. "Silence itself . . . is less the absolute limit of discourse . . . than an element that functions alongside the things said, with them and in relation to them." Michel Foucault, *The History of Sexuality, Vol. 1: An Introduction*, translated by Robert Hurley (New York: Random House, 1978), 27.

3. Hugh B. Urban writes that "much of the literature on secrecy remains disappointingly vague, universalistic, and divorced from social and political context." Urban, "Fair Game: Secrecy, Security, and the Church of Scientology in Cold War America," *Journal of the American Academy of Religion* 74, no. 2 (2006): 360.

4. For Elias Canetti, "secrecy lies at the very core of power." Canetti, *Crowds and Power* (New York: Viking Press, 1962), 290.

5. The relationship between religion and secrecy across time and space is, as one scholar put it, "manifold, complex, and at times contradictory." "Editor's Introduction: Religion and Secrecy," *Journal of the American Academy of Religion* 74, no. 2 (2006): 273. Paul Johnson writes, "In its broad sense secrecy is not rare but is rather constitutive of social relations in general . . . religion as a general category universally entails secrecy." Johnson, "Secretism and the Apotheosis of Duvalier," *Journal of the American Academy of Religion* 74, no. 2 (2006): 421. Jonathan Malesic adds, "Kantian philosophy and revealed religion stand at odds over secrecy's normative status: philosophy condemns secrecy and religion approves of it." Malesic, "A Secret Both Sinister and Salvific: Secrecy and Normativity in Light of Kierkegaard's *Fear and Trembling*," *Journal of the American Academy of Religion* 74, no. 2 (2006): 446.

6. Guy G. Stroumsa, *Hidden Wisdom: Esoteric Traditions and the Roots of Christian Mysticism*, 2nd ed., rev. and enl. (Leiden: Brill, 2005), 29–32.

7. Michael Barkun, "Religion and Secrecy After September 11," *Journal of the American Academy of Religion* 74, no. 2 (2006): 276–278. See also Maria Dakake, "Hiding in Plain Sight," *Journal of the American Academy of Religion* 74, no. 2 (2006): 324–25; Urban, "Fair Game."

8. Barkun, "Religion and Secrecy After September 11," 276.

9. David F. Holland, *Sacred Borders: Continuing Revelation and Canonical Restraint in Early America* (New York: Oxford University Press, 2011), 141–157.

10. David J. Whittaker, "Substituted Names in the Published Revelations of Joseph Smith," *BYU Studies* 23, no. 1 (1983): 103–112.

11. Smith's concealment program was inscribed in the very pen strokes of the council's minutes. In one entry, a scribe recorded deliberations with key words written backwards in something of a makeshift (but quite crackable) code:

> Joseph asked, can this council keep what I say, not make it public, all held up their hands. [several lines left blank] ... Copy the Constitution of the U S [several lines blank] hands of a select committee. No laws can be enacted but what every man can be protected. Grant their petition, go ahead concerning the Indians and Southern States &c. Send 25 men by/the yrenip/ through to Santa Fee/Atnas Eef/ &c, and if ~~Houston~~/Notsuaoh/will embrace the gospel [several lines left blank] can amend the constitution and make it the voice of Jehovah and shame the U[nited] S[tates].

Smith hoped to create a Mormon republic on Sam Houston's western flank. The plan never materialized, due in no small part to the US annexation of Texas the following year. Scott H. Faulring, ed. *An American Prophet's Record: The Diaries and Journals of Joseph Smith* (Salt Lake City: Signature Books, 1989), 458; Michael S. Van Wagenen, *The Texas Republic and the Mormon Kingdom of God* (College Station: Texas A&M University Press, 2002).

12. Devery S. Anderson and Gary J. Bergera, eds., *Joseph Smith's Quorum of the Anointed, 1842–45: A Documentary History* (Salt Lake City: Signature Books, 2005).

13. Lawrence Foster, *Religion and Sexuality: The Shakers, the Mormons, and the Oneida Community* (Urbana: University of Illinois Press, 1984).

14. Michael W. Homer, *Joseph's Temples: The Dynamic Relationship Between Freemasonry and Mormonism* (Salt Lake City: University of Utah Press, 2014).

15. Kathleen Flake, "'Not to be Riten': The Mormon Temple Rite as Oral Canon," *Journal of Ritual Studies* 9, no. 2 (Summer 1995): 1–21.

16. Joseph Smith Jr., July 23, 1843, discourse, in *The Words of Joseph Smith: The Contemporary Accounts of the Nauvoo Discourses of the Prophet Joseph*, edited by Andrew F. Ehat and Lyndon W. Cook (Provo: Religious Studies Center,

Brigham Young University, 1980), 234. The phrase "welding iron to iron" was added when the sermon was prepared for publication but did not appear in the original transcription. Joseph Smith Jr., *History of the Church of Jesus Christ of Latter-day Saints*, edited by B. H. Roberts (Salt Lake City: Deseret Book Co., 1967 [reprint]), 517. On sealing, see Samuel M. Brown, *In Heaven as It Is On Earth: Joseph Smith and the Early Mormon Conquest of Death* (New York: Oxford University Press, 2011), 145–247.

17. Stephen C. Taysom, *Shakers, Mormons, and Religious Worlds: Conflicting Visions, Contested Boundaries* (Bloomington: Indiana University Press, 2011), 51–99.

18. Barkun, "Religion and Secrecy," 277.

19. Kathleen Flake, *The Politics of American Religious Identity: The Seating of Senator Reed Smoot, Mormon Apostle* (Chapel Hill: University of North Carolina Press, 2004), 142–143.

20. David J. Buerger, *The Mysteries of Godliness: A History of Mormon Temple Worship* (Salt Lake City: Signature Books, 2002); Devery S. Anderson, ed., *The Development of LDS Temple Worship, 1846–2000: A Documentary History* (Salt Lake City: Signature Books, 2011).

21. John C. Bennett, *The History of the Saints, or, An Exposé of Joe Smith and Mormonism* (Boston: Leland and Whiting, 1842); Catherine Lewis, *Narrative of Some of the Proceedings of the Mormons; Giving an Account of Their Iniquities, with Particulars Concerning the Training of the Indians by Them, Description of the Mode of Endowment, Plurality of Wives, &c., &c.* (Lynn, MA: printed by author, 1848); Increase M. Van Dusen and Maria Van Dusen, *Startling Disclosures of the Great Mormon Conspiracy Against the Liberties of This Country: Being the Celebrated "Endowment," as It Was Acted by Upwards of Twelve Thousand Men and Women in Secret, in the Nauvoo Temple, in 1846, and Said to Have Been Revealed from God. By I. M'gee Van Dusen and Maria His Wife, Who Were Initiated into These Dreadful Mysteries* (New York: printed by authors, 1849); William Smith and Isaac Sheen, *Deseret: Remonstrance of William Smith et al., of Covington, Kentucky, Against the Admission of Deseret into the Union* (Washington, DC: Wm. M. Belt, 1850).

22. For American anti-Mormonism, see J. Spencer Fluhman, *"A Peculiar People": Anti-Mormonism and the Making of Religion in Nineteenth-Century America* (Chapel Hill: University of North Carolina Press, 2012).

23. David Chidester, *Authentic Fakes: Religion and American Popular Culture* (Berkeley: University of California Press, 2005), 193.

24. Terryl L. Givens, *The Viper on the Hearth: Mormons, Myths, and the Construction of Heresy* (New York: Oxford University Press, 1997), 97–120.

25. Brigham Young, "The United States' Administration and Utah Army," in *Journal of Discourses Delivered by President Brigham Young, His Two Counsellors [sic], the Twelve Apostles, and Others*, 26 vols. (Liverpool: F. D. and S. W. Richards, 1854–1886), 5:226.

26. Hugh Urban writes that "secrecy is often a dynamic process that involves a spiraling feedback loop of concealment, espionage, and counter-espionage, as esoteric groups strive to conceal themselves, government forces attempt to penetrate them by clandestine means, and persecuted groups in turn develop ever more elaborate tactics of dissimulation." Urban, "Fair Game," 359.

27. B. Carmon Hardy, *Solemn Covenant: The Mormon Polygamous Passage* (Urbana: University of Illinois Press, 1992).

28. Flake, *Politics of American Religious Identity*, 140–143.

29. Michael H. Paulos, ed., *The Mormon Church on Trial: Transcripts of the Reed Smoot Hearings* (Salt Lake City: Signature Books, 2007), 103.

30. Bradley Kime, "Exhibiting Theology: James E. Talmage and Mormon Public Relations, 1915–20," *Journal of Mormon History* 40, no. 1 (Winter 2014): 208–238.

31. Jan Shipps, *Sojourner in the Promised Land: Forty Years Among the Mormons* (Urbana: University of Illinois Press, 2000), 51–89.

32. J. B. Haws, *The Mormon Image in the American Mind: Fifty Years of Public Perception* (New York: Oxford University Press, 2013), 12–46.

33. Ibid., 106–30.

34. Matthew B. Bowman, "The Temple and Big Love: Mormonism and American Culture," *Patheos*, June 22, 2009, http://www.patheos.com/Resources/Additional-Resources/The-Temple-and-Big-Love-06222009.html.

35. http://youtu.be/XNHM7I1WJIk (accessed March 28, 2013).

36. Andrew Sullivan, "When Christianism Bites Back," *The Dish: Biased and Balanced* (blog), October 29, 2012, http://dish.andrewsullivan.com/2012/10/29/when-christianism-bites-back/.

37. As empathetic an observer as Noah Feldman granted that Mormon "soft-secrecy" still dominates Mormon culture, but he may underestimate its theological and ritual centrality. Feldman, "What Is It about Mormonism?" *New York Times*, January 6, 2008, http://www.nytimes.com/2008/01/06/magazine/06mormonism-t.html?_r=2&pagewanted=print&.

38. Dakake, "Hidden in Plain Sight," 336. For Foucault, "silence and secrecy are a shelter for power, anchoring its prohibitions; but they also loosen its hold and provide for areas of tolerance." Foucault, *History of Sexuality*, 101. As evidence of the mixed legacy of the various Mormon moments, this most recent one provided the impetus for the most explicit Mormon acknowledgement and regret for institutional racism to date—the result of a BYU faculty member's paternalistic attempt to fill the vacuum of institutional silence since the 1978 extension of LDS priesthood to black men in a *Washington Post* interview. (For black Mormons, this official acknowledgement was woefully late, still too tepid, and yet entirely appreciated.) My framework in this essay pulls attention away from the racialized priesthood restriction and toward the fact that despite being members of the church, black Mormons, men and women, were kept from the temple and its rituals, troubling the assertion of their

pre-1978 "membership." See "Church Statement Regarding 'Washington Post' Article on Race and the Church," Church of Jesus Christ of Latter-day Saints "Newsroom," *LDS.org*, February 29, 2012, http://www.mormonnewsroom.org/article/racial-remarks-in-washington-post-article.

39. Hugh B. Urban, "The Torment of Secrecy: Ethical and Epistemological Problems in the Study of Esoteric Traditions," *History of Religions* 37, no. 3 (February 1998): 210.

14

Preparing for Doomsday

Matthew Avery Sutton

ON SEPTEMBER 26, 2011, a heckler at a Democratic fundraiser in Los Angeles interrupted a speech by Barack Obama. The president, the heckler harangued, was none other than the Antichrist. While this protest represented little more than the fantasies of one delusional critic, the idea of seeing American political leaders as representative of the Antichrist has a much deeper history. This heckler was tapping into the convictions of millions of Americans who believe that the end is near. Whether fretting about millennium bugs; obsessing over zombies; counting down to the Mayan apocalypse; predicting that the ice caps will melt and coastal cities will flood; tracking the spread of global pandemics; or stocking basements with guns, gold, and dehydrated food, Americans—especially since the birth of the atomic age—have been consumed by apocalyptic nightmares. Substantial numbers of people believe that the universe is rapidly moving toward its close.

The dominant religious tradition in the United States, Protestant Christianity, has played a substantial role in shaping Americans' apocalyptic sensibilities. Millions of Christians expect Jesus to make a violent and dramatic return to earth in the very near future. A 2010 Pew poll revealed that 41 percent of all Americans (well over one hundred million people) and 58 percent of white evangelicals believe that Jesus is "definitely" or "probably" going to return by 2050. According to the 2014 *Bible in American Life* report, of the 50 percent of Americans who had read the Bible at all in the previous year, over one-third claimed that they did so "to learn about the future." The men and women who responded to these polls saw the Bible as a guidebook that reveals in fairly specific detail how history will end. While they may have little to no understanding of the complex theology undergirding their opinions, they illustrate how thoroughly Christian apocalyptic ideas have saturated modern American culture.[1]

For some Christians, the conviction that Jesus is coming back does little more than assure them of a glorious eternal destiny. But for others, apocalypticism functions in more powerful ways. It provides a clear worldview and an explicit framework through which to understand their place in history as well as the trajectory of their nation and world. The conviction that time is running out has fostered among some Christians an absolute morality; a passion to right the world's wrongs; a hopeful longing for the end of time; a profound sense of urgency; and a refusal to compromise, negotiate, or mediate. They believe that judgment is coming and justice will be served; God will soon right all wrongs. For these believers, anything is possible and everything has purpose. Governments, they are sure, will topple; businesses will collapse; and the centers of power will fail. Such beliefs have impacted the modern world, shaping everything from politics to education to popular culture to national defense.[2]

Many religious traditions have fostered apocalypticism. Islam has bred various apocalyptic movements; Catholicism has provided the theological context for doomsday thinking; and countless small nontraditional religious groups have preached apocalypse. But in the United States, Protestant apocalypticism has exercised the greatest influence. To examine the sway of apocalypticism on the recent American past, this chapter analyzes the beliefs and convictions of three very different individuals—David Koresh, Harold Camping, and Billy Graham—each of whom led doomsday movements of various sizes. Each of these individuals, like millions of other Americans, drew inspiration from the Bible and treated it as a guide for understanding the future. Nevertheless, the futures that each of them saw, as well as their personal roles in bringing that future to fruition, differed dramatically. While most Americans may want to separate the violent prophecies of Koresh, the date-setting urgency of Camping, and the mainstream evangelicalism of Graham, the work of these prophets of apocalypse has far more in common than most men and women realize. Small variances of theology led to very different outcomes.

This chapter argues that the ideas of Koresh, Camping, and Graham all emerged from the same long river of American Protestant apocalypticism and that together they demonstrate the continuing power and appeal of doomsday beliefs in modern US history. The sacred text has offered those anxious about the world's problems secret knowledge of ages past, present, and to come. Apocalypticism has fostered among adherents a powerful sense of purpose and personal identity; it has helped them interpret the challenges around them; and it has provided them with a triumphant vision of the future. It has offered them the promise of transformation and redemption in a world that seems to lack both. It has also served as a call to battle rather than as a justification for withdrawal. God has given believers much to do and very little time in which to do it. Positive that Jesus is coming soon, they have preached revival and engaged directly and aggressively with their culture.

For the first couple of centuries after Christ's death, most Christians believed that Jesus would soon return to orchestrate a violent apocalypse, vanquish evil, and establish a millennium of peace and prosperity. In the wake of the Christianization of the Roman Empire, however, Augustine insisted that the faithful should interpret many of the Bible's prophecies more metaphorically than literally. "As Christianity triumphed," historian Paul Boyer summarized, "its millennialist strand faded."[3]

Apocalypticism ebbed and flowed over the next one thousand years. It occasionally emerged in marginal, dissenting groups, and it helped inspire some of the Crusades. Near the time of the Protestant Reformation, radical Christians breathed new life into the apocalyptic views of the early church. They believed that the book of Revelation laid out a literal history of the past, present, and future, a history in which faithful readers could place the major events of the previous fifteen hundred years. The turmoil caused by the Reformers' attack on the Catholic Church and the Catholic reaction indicated to these readers that the return of Christ had to be near.

Apocalypticists in North America debated how best to understand the Bible's prophetic books. Eventually, two primary schools of interpretation emerged. Influenced by various ideas popularized and debated in Europe, the representatives of one school took a "historicist" position, which held that the fulfillment of prophecy had unfolded over time and was continuing to unfold. Others developed a more radical "futurist" position, which argued that the book of Revelation described what was to come in the "last days" immediately before the return of Christ. Christians also debated the relationship of the return of Christ to the prophesied millennium, a future period of peace, prosperity, and bliss. The majority of nineteenth-century American millennialists hoped to help establish the kingdom of God on earth and believed that the return of Christ would

mark the conclusion of the millennium. Thus they identified as "postmil-
lennialists" based on their conviction that the second coming of Christ
would occur after the millennium. Others, however, identified as "premillennialists." They believed that the world would come to a violent end at
the battle of Armageddon. Only after this apocalyptic cataclysm would
Jesus establish the millennium.[4]

In the nineteenth and twentieth centuries, some millennialist Christians also developed a theory of the "Rapture." Proponents
described the Rapture as a dramatic experience in which all living
Christians will mysteriously vanish from the earth and the dead will
rise to heaven. Many of those Christians who expected the Rapture to
occur near the end of the age believed that it would immediately precede
a short period of time called the tribulation, a horrific period in which
evil would envelop the globe. They expect the battle of Armageddon, the
second coming, and the destruction of the earth as we know it to follow
the tribulation. But others believed that the Rapture would occur slightly
later in the prophetic scheme. They anticipated a "mid-tribulation" or
"post-trib" Rapture.

Although the theological divides between the historicist and the futurist positions, the premillennial and postmillennial positions, and the
pre-tribulation and post-tribulation rapture might seem to be the stuff of
navel-gazing theologians, the differences on these issues have led to profound outcomes in the modern United States. Theology matters. The stories of David Koresh, Harold Camping, and Billy Graham illustrate how
important apocalyptic theology has been in recent American history, as
well as how small differences lead to very different results.

David Koresh was born in 1959 in Houston, Texas. His mother raised
him in the Seventh-day Adventist tradition, but in the early 1980s he left
the church to join the Branch Davidians, a small splinter group. He eventually became the Davidians' leader. The roots of the Branch Davidian
movement ran deep, dating back to the work of William Miller, perhaps
the most famous doomsday prophet in American history. A farmer and
Baptist who grew enamored with biblical prophecy, Miller drew on historicist interpretations of the book of Revelation, believing that the events
described in it had slowly unfolded since the first century. Eventually he
determined that Jesus would return in 1843. When Jesus did not return
as expected in 1843, the Millerites developed a new calculation and
date: October 22, 1844. Journalists dubbed Jesus's failure to appear yet
again the "Great Disappointment."[5]

Rather than admit defeat, some of Miller's followers, under the leadership of Ellen G. White, built a new movement and denomination, the Seventh-day Adventists. Although early Adventists claimed that the Bible was their only authority, they believed that White served as a prophet, selected by God to help shape, reform, and purify the church. Until Christ returned, they expected God to choose spokespeople on earth to deliver and affirm his messages.[6]

In the late 1920s and early 1930s, a group of Adventists broke away from the main church. Calling themselves "Davidian Seventh-day Adventists," they emphasized the significance of the Old Testament's Davidic kingdom. Their leader, Victor Houteff, taught that in the last days, God would raise up an earthly leader, a type of King David, to establish an earthly kingdom of God. As they awaited this leader, Davidian Adventists preached that judgment was soon to come. They expected to face horrific persecution and go through an intense tribulation that would ultimately lead to the premillennial—but post-tribulation—return of Christ. They preached that at Jesus's return he would cleanse the earth of all impurities in a bloody apocalypse.

Houteff died in 1955, and after years of tumult, a young leader named Vernon Howell took the reins of the movement. He believed that God had given him, like Ellen G. White, prophetic visions and revelations, which he shared with the community. He also believed that he was the new King David, the leader God had chosen to preside over the holy remnant of true believers as the world careened toward Armageddon. This conviction led Howell to change his name to David Koresh, an amalgamation of "David" for the Old Testament king and "Koresh," the Hebrew form of "Cyrus," an Old Testament figure God had used to help protect his people and execute his judgment on evil.

Koresh proved to be a confident and compelling leader for the Branch Davidians. Like many apocalypticists before him, he preached that the tribulation was imminent and that all people would soon face the judgment of God. Since God had chosen the Davidians to be his sole representatives on earth during the tribulation, Koresh explained, they were sure to face the forces of evil. To prepare for the inevitable confrontation, Branch Davidians began stockpiling guns and various other weapons. Koresh also warned his followers that the forces of evil would likely take form as agents of the American government. Like many other premillennialists, Adventists—both in the mainstream movement and in splinter groups including the Branch Davidians—believed that when the tribulation begins, the US government will likely be on the wrong side. The kingdoms of this earth will be duped by Satan and will serve as his tools to persecute the faithful.

Almost completely oblivious to Koresh's theology and beliefs, agents from the Bureau of Alcohol, Tobacco, Firearms, and Explosives (ATF) attempted to storm Koresh's Waco compound on February 28, 1993. They believed that Koresh had violated federal weapons laws and that he was sexually abusing children. The ATF badly bungled the raid. The result was a confrontation with an armed and prepared group of Davidians. A bloody ninety-minute gun battle ensued, which left four ATF agents dead and at least twenty wounded. Koresh was shot twice in the confrontation. The battle ended with a cease-fire followed by a fifty-one-day standoff. To the Davidians, the government's actions seemed to mark the beginning of the end. The US government, in turning against them, was fulfilling prophecy. The tribulation had begun, and it would last until Jesus's return.[7]

The ATF and then the FBI had from the beginning refused to take Koresh's apocalyptic views seriously. Shortly after the raid began, Koresh called 911 begging for help and for the government to call off the raid. Dispatchers put him through to the local sheriff, with whom he had a relationship. Koresh tried to explain how the raid had fulfilled Branch Davidian prophecy, but the sheriff cut him off. Law enforcement authorities expressed little interest in listening to or trying to understand Koresh's worldview. But "this is life and death," Koresh responded, "theology ... is life and death." Despite Koresh's efforts to explain himself, he understood that negotiation with agents who refused to engage with him on a theological level was impossible. "We come from two different worlds, you know what I mean?," he told one agent. But he still tried over the course of the siege to explain his apocalyptic theology to the government.[8]

As the standoff continued, Koresh maintained that he had received new revelations from God. He claimed that he was the "Lamb of God" and that it was his job to open the "seven seals" from the book of Revelation, which would herald the apocalypse. Then citing Revelation 22, he claimed that he had come "to give unto every man the knowledge of the seven seals." He believed that if only he could convey the message of the seven seals to the public, people would realize that he spoke for God. Rather than see the world end in a bloody apocalypse, he held out hope that the wicked would repent and turn from their ways. If they did, God might spare the earth. "We believe," he preached to a negotiator, "that America is a great nation and that it, like Assyria and Nineva of old, can hear the message of Jonah and it can have a chance to say hey, you know, this, this—what this guy's teaching out of the book is straight out of the Bible, it's in harmony, it's perfect. Maybe there's a misunderstanding here."[9]

Over the course of the siege, Koresh made clear that he was not going to relent. "You got to do the truth no matter what they do to you," he insisted. Nor was the government going to back down. Nevertheless, FBI agents had no sense of the powerful apocalypticism that undergirded Koresh's worldview. "From the very beginning," Congressional investigators later wrote, "negotiators failed to take seriously the point of view of the Davidians." On April 19, the FBI attacked the compound with tear gas, hoping to drive the Davidians out. Within a few hours, horrific fires had started that soon consumed the complex and killed many of those inside. The standoff ended with the deaths of more than eighty Davidians, including many children.[10]

Koresh's apocalyptic views emerged from within a long tradition of millennial thought. Like millions of Christians before him, he believed in the imminent second coming of Christ. Yet his understanding of a very minor issue within premillennial theology, the tribulation, distinguished his movement from most others. He saw in the Bible evidence that the faithful would live through the tribulation and that during that time God wanted the small remnant of saints to battle physically the forces of the Antichrist. When the ATF launched a heavily armed raid against the Branch Davidian compound, this minor point of theology produced truly cataclysmic results. The US government attacked the Davidians' community with overwhelming firepower, naïvely and inadvertently playing directly into the Davidians' apocalyptic expectations. The results were tragic. As Koresh had explained, theology was indeed life and death.

While one group of Christians anticipating the coming apocalypse died in an awful inferno, another faded into obscurity. On May 21, 2011, thousands of Christians living around the globe expected to be raptured to heaven. As they prepared to leave this world, millions of Americans followed the story via newspapers, the Internet, and television. Some pitied the faithful while others playfully mocked them with rapture parties, apocalyptic playlists, and humorous tweets. Some more creative observers even inflated blow-up dolls with helium and released them to the heavens. At the center of the rapture drama was Harold Camping, an elderly radio preacher from Oakland, California. Much like William Miller, his apocalyptic pronouncements combined with his media savvy helped make the failed rapture one of the most intriguing apocalyptic non-events of the new millennium.

Camping was born in Southern California in 1921. In 1958 he and a couple of friends formed an evangelistic radio ministry, which they called Family Radio. As the ministry grew, Camping sold his construction business and went to work full time for Family Radio. Throughout his ministry, Camping taught a traditional Calvinist message of individual salvation through the grace of God. The ministry grew to such extent that by the early 2000s, Family Radio owned 140 radio stations in the United States and translated Camping's broadcasts into dozens of foreign languages. The ministry distributed Camping's Open Forum show internationally via shortwave, and fans could also follow the show live through the Family Radio website.

In 1992, the Family Radio rapture controversy began. That year Camping announced to his worldwide audience that after a lifetime of intense study he had decoded secret numerical messages hidden throughout his King James Bible. His conclusions were based on traditional premillennial beliefs in a post-tribulation rapture combined with his own innovative and unique brand of numerology. "The big question," he asked, "is: Has God also hidden within the pages of the Bible the secrets of the timing of His return at the end of the world?" The big answer: yes. Camping knew when Jesus was coming back.[11]

To publicize his findings, Camping self-published *1994?*, a long and complicated book that covered Camping's theology, the calculations that led him to the date of Christ's return, and the ramifications of those calculations. To determine the date of the second coming, Camping started with the creation of Adam, which he traced to 11,013 BCE. From there he charted the dates of various other important Old Testament events and then subtracted them from one another in a variety of combinations. What he found was that certain numbers regularly repeated themselves. Based on the sums he derived from his equations, he determined that a few numbers had particular significance. The number 13,000, he concluded, was especially important. He believed that it held the key to unlocking the timing of Jesus's return. Beginning with Adam's creation and moving forward exactly 13,000 years led him to the year 1988. He determined that this date marked the start of the tribulation. The second coming, he continued, should occur six years after the start of the tribulation, or in 1994. Furthermore, Camping determined that it was likely to occur between September 15 and September 27.

Camping could not be any more specific since Jesus had warned that no person could determine the day or the hour of his return—just, apparently, the week. Near the end of the tribulation, on September 6, 1994, Camping expected the rapture to occur, and shortly after that, God would judge the world. However, he noted that there was the slight possibility that his calculations were wrong and that the second coming might come twenty-three years after 1988, or in 2011, since both the numbers six and twenty-three had biblical significance. Despite his confidence in the imminent second coming, he instructed followers not to plan for the rapture but to live "as if Christ's return is still a hundred years away."[12]

Camping's understanding of the tribulation differed in significant ways from that of Koresh and others. For Camping, the tribulation was more of a theological crisis than a political one. Gross immorality, not the actions of totalitarian government groups, marked the end of time. He believed that the signs of the tribulation included such things as divorce, birth control, the increasing practice of women serving as church leaders, growing numbers of same-sex relationships, and sexual promiscuity. "The plague of AIDS," he further explained, "demonstrates in no uncertain terms that eternal damnation is coming." Nevertheless, Camping felt no need to arm himself against gays, divorcees, or female pastors. While Koresh had been practicing a kind of sexual libertinism while stockpiling weapons in his Waco compound, Camping was damning mainstream American ideas of sex and gender as evidence that God would soon destroy the earth.[13]

Camping and Koresh did agree, however, that American Christianity had become apostate. Camping insisted that he alone understood the truth of the end times and that in these days of approaching Armageddon, the major churches and denominations had all fallen into hopeless heresy. "There is no time left to trust your pastor or your church," Camping explained at the end of his book. "You must trust only the Bible."[14]

The 1994 date came and went; Camping was not raptured. While his movement faded from the public consciousness, it did not dissipate. Camping continued preaching his unique brand of apocalypticism and tribulation-era conservative social values over the Family Radio network. In 2005 he published another book, *Time Has An End: A Biblical History of the World, 11,013 B.C.–A.D. 2011*. In it he claimed that Christ had come in 1994 "to begin the completion of the evangelization of His true people" rather than to rapture them to heaven. The rapture, he now believed, would happen on May 21, 2011, with the final judgment to follow on October 21. Once again, however, Camping did not urge despair or drastic action—just radical evangelism. "At Family Radio," he explained, "we make decisions as if the end could be quite far away.... We are the first ones to understand that we are not infallible in our conclusions."[15]

The new book made clear that in the intervening years, Camping's anti-denominationalism and anti-institutionalism had become even more strident—he argued in the starkest terms yet that all organized Christianity was now apostate. "God," he wrote, "has abandoned each and every local congregation so that the true believers in Christ, if they have not already been driven out, are commanded to come out.... This is the time when the Gospel is no longer under the care of the local congregations but is being sent into the world by individuals who are not under any church authority but who are definitely under the authority of the Bible."[16]

Camping's views and book initially received little attention outside of Family Radio circles. But on New Year's Day 2010, the *San Francisco Chronicle*, Camping's hometown paper, ran one of the first substantial stories outlining the minister's predictions for 2011. The paper even took a stab at explaining the calculations behind the date.[17]

Inspired by Camping, some of the radio preacher's followers found new and creative ways to get the message out. A young army veteran bought advertising space on ten bus benches in her community to announce the rapture date. Others parked RVs at malls around the country with the message: "Have you heard the awesome news? The end of the world is almost here. The Bible guarantees it. It begins on May 21, 2011." Rapture billboards also began appearing in a handful of American cities. By May, believers had printed over one hundred million pamphlets in sixty-one languages and raised 5,500 billboards in the United States and abroad. The costs to followers were substantial. Despite Camping's warnings that his calculations were not infallible, some had even budgeted all of their money to last only until May 21, 2011.[18]

But the rapture did not happen. In the aftermath of yet another great disappointment, Camping acknowledged that he had had a "tough" weekend and that he had been partially mistaken. He had expected the rapture to be physical; instead, he now claimed, a spiritual judgment had occurred. He also reiterated his commitment to October 21, 2011, as the date that the world would end. When the apocalypse once again failed to materialize, Camping apologized. He also vowed to continue studying the Bible to work out the correct numbers. Camping believed that he would eventually get the math—and the rapture date—right. He died in 2013. As historian Jay Rubenstein wryly noted at the conclusion of the Camping debacle, "Hope for doomsday springs eternal." Indeed, Camping served as a symbol of Americans' enduring fascination with the second coming.[19]

Unlike David Koresh and Harold Camping, Billy Graham has been revered by millions of Americans as one of the greatest religious leaders in this nation's history. In fact, most Americans would probably find it troubling to mention his name in the same context as Camping and especially Koresh. Yet Graham has also made a strident apocalypticism a core part of his ministry. However, he has managed to preach his doomsday message in a way that attracts rather than repels a mainstream American audience.

Born in 1918 in Charlotte, North Carolina, Graham converted as a teenager to fundamentalist Christianity, through which he encountered a powerful, adaptable, and increasingly influential form of futurist, premillennial, pre-tribulation theology. In the mid-1940s, he embarked on a career as an evangelist and began preaching apocalypse. Just two days after Harry S. Truman announced that the Soviet Union had built an atomic weapon, Graham warned a Southern California audience: "I think that we are living at a time in world history when God is giving us a desperate choice, a choice of either revival or judgment. . . . Time is desperately short!" With that revival, his career was launched.[20]

Over the course of Graham's long ministry, he never doubted that the time was nigh. Graham's invocation of the coming apocalypse served to instill in followers a belief that time counted and that it mattered how they spent their lives. In the wake of the world wars, the Great Depression, and the hydrogen bomb, an ancient doctrine "had become the great hope of the church in the middle of the twentieth century."[21]

As Graham's influence grew, he began putting his apocalyptic ideas into books. In 1965, Graham published *World Aflame*, a powerful, apocalyptic diagnosis of the era that tied together the many themes of his work up to that point. "The salvation of society . . . will come about by the powers and forces released by the apocalyptic return of Jesus Christ." The book illustrated Graham's positions on the great social and political issues of the day. Like Camping, Graham believed that certain signs would mark the nearness of the end times. "Today," he wrote, "it would seem that those signs are indeed converging for the first time since Christ ascended into heaven." They included hydrogen bombs, the population explosion, increasing crime, sexual perversion, same-sex relations, immorality, dependence on pills and alcohol, political turmoil, feminism, turmoil over the Civil Rights Movement, and the battle against communism. Graham's work illustrates how evangelicals in the 1960s understood the dramatic changes afoot as well as how premillennialism continued to shape the ways in which the faithful apprehended the world in which they lived.[22]

Throughout the 1970s and 1980s, Graham returned to his apocalyptic message over and over again. During every major evangelistic crusade, he preached on the imminent second coming of Jesus. In 1983 he published *Approaching Hoofbeats: The Four Horsemen of the Apocalypse*, a commentary on the book of Revelation that explained its relevance to the current generation. Then in the early 1990s, Graham decided to once again put his doomsday ideas into print. While Koresh was building a small community in Waco and Camping was crunching numbers from the Bible, Graham offered millions of Americans watching the collapse of the Soviet Union, the war in the Persian Gulf, and the growing economic recession a new guide for understanding the times. In 1992 he published *Storm Warning*, an updated version of *Approaching Hoofbeats*. "From many points of view," he wrote, "the world seems to be entering a time of peace and calm. But no one should run up the all-clear flags just yet. There is still cause for alarm; there are storms on the horizon."[23]

In this book Graham blamed many of the problems of the United States on the legacy of the 1960s. But he believed it was not too late to repent. Like Koresh, he hoped that if enough people turned to God, God might withhold his judgment. "We must not feel that we are to sit back and do nothing to fight evil just because some day the four horsemen will come with full and final force upon the earth." Graham continually called unbelievers to faith while he reminded the faithful that they had an obligation to do all that they could before time ran out.[24]

As Graham nears the end of his life, he has not ceased from preaching apocalypse. In 2010, the elderly evangelist updated and reiterated his premillennial convictions in a new edition of *Storm Warning*. "Now at ninety-one years old," Graham explained to readers, "I believe the storm clouds are darker than they have ever been. . . . Benevolent hands reach down from heaven to offer us the most hopeful warning and remedy: 'Prepare to meet your God.' . . . The signs of His imminent return have never been greater than now." Graham's signs included the 9/11 attacks, the global economic recession, the ever-growing power of the state, the environmental crisis, the influence of godless popular culture on American society, secular school curriculum, and the rise of multiculturalism.[25]

Graham's work illustrates how evangelical premillennialists have masterfully linked the major issues of every generation to their reading of the coming apocalypse with the goal of transforming their culture in ways that have been much more attractive than the theologies of Koresh and Camping. In some ways, Graham's theology was more about ideas of the future rather than religious day-to-day religious practices. But there were real ramifications to his theology. The conviction that we are living in the last days shaped his followers' views of the economy, politics, global events, and much more. While the signs of the apocalypse have changed over time, they have never stopped appearing. Discerning their meaning has given Graham's followers a powerful sense of urgency, a confidence that they alone understand the world in which they are living, and a hope for a future in which they will reign supreme. They also know that their critics will soon face the wrath of the Almighty and the torments of hell.

Despite all that Graham's premillennial apocalypticism has in common with Koresh and Camping, he differs from them in a few significant ways. First, and most importantly, he does not believe that the faithful will experience the tribulation. Graham's reading of the prophetic books of the Bible convinced him that true Christians will be raptured off the earth before the tribulation and before the battle of Armageddon. Graham's pre-tribulation theology also means that his followers, unlike those of Koresh and Camping, do not need to abandon their churches. They will be raptured out of them. Graham believes that God has used him to bring revival to the nation and the world; he is not explicitly condemning other religious leaders nor calling people out of their fellowships. In fact, one of Graham's goals has been to strengthen the established churches of many denominations. That Graham has been willing to work with various other religious leaders made him far less threatening to most Americans than Koresh or Camping.

Graham's faith in a premillennial, pre-tribulation rapture has another significant ramification. His followers, unlike the Branch Davidians, do not need to stockpile arms to prepare for a coming inferno. They are going to escape the apocalypse unscathed. Jesus is slated to return with an army of heavenly saints for the battle of Armageddon. It is not the responsibility of Christians on earth to fight. God will arm his own soldiers.

Finally, unlike Camping, Graham knows better than to set dates. While he has kept the imminent second coming at the center of his ministry, he has never given a specific time for Christians to expect the rapture. For Graham, the rapture is always coming; it is always imminent. His followers maintain a perpetual state of anticipation and urgency. If Jesus is not around this corner, he is around the next one.

While Koresh and Camping condemned the institutional church, Graham built bridges between denominations. While Koresh and Camping criticized the American state, Graham befriended politicians of both political parties. While Koresh became the target of the government, Graham provided presidents Ronald Reagan and George W. Bush with an apocalyptic rhetoric that they used to explain their foreign policy to the American people. In this way, Graham may have actually been more dangerous than his doomsaying counterparts. He helped justify American intervention abroad, legitimizing untold death and destruction (although he certainly believed the causes were just).

In sum, the work of these three prophets of doom gives life to the polling data that indicate that millions of Americans believe the time is nigh. It also helps explain why one heckler at an Obama fundraiser can make national news by using the word "Antichrist." Why Americans in particular are so obsessed with the imminent end of the world is not entirely clear. Nevertheless, the United States has produced creative and innovative religious leaders who have drawn on the deep tradition of Christian apocalypticism in order to get their message out. Sometimes, like David Koresh, their work threatens the nation. Sometimes, like Harold Camping, their work provides belittling amusement. And sometimes, like Billy Graham, their work can shape national and international politics and penetrate the White House.[26] Regardless, the stories of all three reveal that apocalypticism has been essential for understanding recent American history.

Notes

1. Pew Research Center, "Jesus Christ's Return to Earth," July 14, 2010, http://www.pewresearch.org/daily-number/jesus-christs-return-to-earth/; http://www.raac.iupui.edu/files/2713/9413/8354/Bible_in_American_Life_Report_March_6_2014.pdf.

2. For an excellent overview of millennialism, see Richard Landes, "Millennialism and the Dynamics of Apocalyptic Time," in *Expecting the End: Millennialism in Social and Historical Context*, edited by G. C. Newport and Crawford Gribben (Waco, TX: Baylor University Press, 2006), 1–23. I expand on these issues in the particular case of fundamentalism in Matthew Avery Sutton, *American Apocalypse: A History of Modern Evangelicalism* (Cambridge, MA: Harvard/Belknap, 2014).

3. Paul Boyer, *When Time Shall Be No More* (Cambridge, MA: Harvard/Belknap, 1992), 48.

4. On the varying versions of premillennialism see Timothy P. Weber, "Dispensational and Historic Premillennialism as Popular Millennialist Movements," in *A Case for Historic Premillennialism: An Alternative to "Left Behind" Eschatology*, edited by Craig Blomberg and Sung Wook Chung (Grand Rapids, MI: Baker Academic, 2009).

5. On the history and theology of Koresh and the Branch Davidians, see Kenneth G. C. Newport, *The Branch Davidians of Waco: The History and Beliefs of an Apocalyptic Sect* (Oxford: Oxford University Press, 2006). See also Eugene V. Gallagher, "'Theology Is Life and Death': David Koresh on Violence, Persecution, and the Millennium," in *Millennialism, Persecution, and Violence: Historical Cases*, edited by Catherine Wessinger (Syracuse, NY: Syracuse University Press, 2000), 82–100; James R. Lewis, *From the Ashes: Making Sense of Waco* (Lanham, MD: Rowman and Littlefield Publishers, Inc., 1994); Catherine Wessinger, *How the Millennium Comes Violently: From Jonestown to Heaven's Gate* (New York: Seven Bridges Press, 2000); Malcolm Gladwell, "Sacred and Profane," *New Yorker*, March 31, 2014.

6. On Ellen G. White and the rise of the Seventh-day Adventists, see Ronald L. Numbers, *Prophetess of Health: A Study of Ellen G. White* (New York: Harper and Row, 1976).

7. On the Waco siege, see US House of Representatives, *Investigation into the Activities of Federal Law Enforcement Agencies Toward the Branch Davidians: Thirteenth Report* (Washington, DC: Government Printing Office, 1996); John C. Danforth, *Final Report to the Deputy Attorney General: Concerning the 1993 Confrontation at the Mt. Carmel Complex Waco, Texas* (Washington, DC: Department of Justice, 2000).

8. US Department of the Treasury, Bureau of Alcohol, Tobacco, and Firearms *911 Tape #1AA* (2/28/93), 6–7, https://digital.library.txstate.edu/bitstream/handle/10877/1914/463.pdf?sequence=1; "Waco FBI Transcripts Tapes 01-003," February 28, 1993, Federal Bureau of Investigation, FBI Record: The Vault (www.vault.fbi.gov), 49; see also "Waco FBI Transcripts Tapes 01-003," February 28, 1993, Federal Bureau of Investigation, FBI Record: The Vault (www.vault.fbi.gov), 32–33.

9. "Waco FBI Transcripts Tapes 01-003," February 28, 1993, Federal Bureau of Investigation, FBI Record: The Vault (www.vault.fbi.gov), 17; "Waco FBI Transcripts Tapes 01-003," March 1, 1993, Federal Bureau of Investigation, FBI Record: The Vault (www.vault.fbi.gov), 23.

10. US House of Representatives, *Investigation into the Activities of Federal Law Enforcement Agencies Toward the Branch Davidians: Thirteenth Report* (Washington, DC: Government Printing Office, 1996), 60–61; "Waco FBI Transcripts Tapes 01-003," February 28, 1993, Federal Bureau of Investigation, FBI Record: The Vault (www.vault.fbi.gov), 50.

11. Harold Camping, *1994?* (New York: Vantage Press, 1992), xvi.

12. Ibid., xviii.
13. Ibid., 213.
14. Ibid., 534.
15. Harold Camping, *Time Has an End: A Biblical History of the World, 11,013 B.C.–A.D. 2011* (New York: Vantage Press, 2005), xv, xxii.
16. Ibid., xvii.
17. Justin Berton, "Biblical Scholar's Date for Rapture: May 21, 2011," *San Francisco Chronicle*, January 1, 2010.
18. Mark Barna, "The End Is Not Just Nigh, It's in May 2011," *Colorado Springs Gazette*, July 26, 2010; Jessica Ravitz, "Road Trip to the End of the World," CNN, March 23, 2011, http://www.cnn.com/2011/LIVING/03/06/judgment.day.caravan/; Bob Smietana, "Nashville Billboards Claim Jesus Will Return May 21, 2011," *Tennessean*, December 1, 2010; Scott James, "From Oakland to the World, Words of Warning: Time's Up," *New York Times*, May 20, 2011; Ashley Parker, "Make My Bed? But You Say the World's Ending," *New York Times*, May 20, 2011.
19. Jay Rubenstein, "Apocalypse Deferred," *Los Angeles Times*, November 6, 2011.
20. *Revival in Our Time: The Story of the Billy Graham Evangelistic Campaigns* (Wheaton, IL: Van Kampen Press, 1950), 70, 73.
21. Billy Graham, *Christ is Coming* (Minneapolis: Billy Graham Evangelistic Association, 1955).
22. Billy Graham, *World Aflame* (New York: Doubleday and Company, 1965), xiii, 203, 216.
23. Billy Graham, *Storm Warning* (Dallas: Word Publishing, 1992), 7.
24. Ibid., 170–171.
25. Billy Graham, *Storm Warning*, rev. ed. (Nashville: Thomas Nelson, 2010), 3, 130.
26. On Graham's influence, see Steven P. Miller, *Billy Graham and the Rise of the Republican South* (Philadelphia: University of Pennsylvania Press, 2011); and Grant Wacker, *America's Pastor: Billy Graham and the Shaping of a Nation* (Cambridge, MA: Belknap/Harvard, 2014).

15

Rise of the Nones

by Matthew S. Hedstrom

"WHAT HAPPENED TO Judeo-Christian America?," asked religion scholar Diana Butler Bass in a *Washington Post* online essay in January 2014.[1] The question was not a lament, just a sincere inquiry rooted in a basic but far-reaching observation. Bass's question arose from the simple fact that the religious demographics of the United States, and the religious sensibilities of many Americans, have undergone profound shifts in the last two decades. Increased religious diversity and, even more significantly, a marked rise in religious disaffiliation, especially among the young, are transforming longstanding realities of American religious life, and therefore American politics. The era when coalitions of Protestants, Catholics, and Jews more or less fully described the arena we call "religion and politics" is over.

Religious disaffiliation is a matter of grave concern to those committed to traditional religious life (and perhaps a cause to rejoice for those less favorably disposed toward religion). But its consequences reach far beyond religion itself into social, cultural, and even political realms. Al Gore, for example, received 61 percent of the unaffiliated vote as the Democratic candidate for president in 2000, a share that increased to 67 percent for John Kerry in 2004 and 75 percent for Barack Obama in 2008.[2] While these numbers do not necessarily reflect a shift of new voters to the Democratic Party, they do indicate a shift in the makeup of the Democratic Party base. President Obama recognized the changing demographics of the nation in his 2009 inaugural address, when he described the United States as "a nation of Christians and Muslims, Jews and Hindus, and non-believers."[3] Though inartfully phrased, since many of those without formal religious ties are nevertheless "believers" of one kind or another, Obama's statement garnered headlines.[4] Never before had a president so publicly acknowledged, and embraced, nonreligious Americans.

So what *did* happen to Judeo-Christian America? And what is taking its place? What light can history shed on these developments? This chapter explores these questions through three historical shifts: in the changing religious and political alignments of recent decades, including the arrival of religious "nones" and the language of "spirituality" on the American political scene; the intellectual and theological history of religious liberalism in the nineteenth century; and the way global encounters with diversity transformed that Protestant liberalism into the broader, more inclusive religious cosmopolitanism in the twentieth century. As Barack Obama looked out from the Capitol steps on a cold January midday in 2009 to deliver his first remarks as president, the throng assembled before him represented a nation transformed by this history.

Religion and Politics in the Age of Obama: A New Restructuring

Judeo-Christianity, it must be said, had a good run. The term "Judeo-Christian" itself dates from the late nineteenth century and acquired its current meaning in the 1930s.[5] Originally coined to describe the common ancient heritage of Jews and Christians, the term was redeployed in the 1930s by leaders of the ecumenical and interfaith movements to indicate the joint contributions of Catholics, Jews, and Protestants to American democracy. It was, in this way, a term of social and political inclusion, meant to signal liberal opposition to discrimination at home and fascism abroad. As historian Kevin Schultz notes, the ideological pressures and realignments of the Second World War and the Cold War soon to follow "brought almost all Americans into the fold of civic Judeo-Christianity."[6] Obviously, Americans as individuals did not join a new amalgam religion called Judeo-Christianity. Rather, the public discourse of American religion, what some scholars have called America's "civil religion," employed biblical rhetoric and a broad if vague monotheism as a basis for thinking and talking about common values and national purpose.

To speak in these terms about shared language and values is not in any way to diminish the very real and often fierce battles about religion and politics that occurred with regularity in the decades after the Second World War. Far from it. Evangelicals fought with liberals; Protestants fought with Catholics—we think most notably in this regard about the great consternation among many prominent American Protestants over the election of John F. Kennedy, a Roman Catholic, to the presidency in 1960—and Jews fought, with newfound success, against dominant Christianity in schools and other venues of public life. Nevertheless, the reigning paradigm of Judeo-Christianity meant that the terms of these debates were at least clearly circumscribed. Diana Bass, in her *Washington Post* essay, notes the various phases that American civil religion has gone through over the course of four centuries. "The stern God of Puritan Calvinism," she writes, eventually gave way to "the revolutionary God of Deist Providence; the activist God of Protestant Benevolence; the sword-wielding God of the Civil War; the earnest God of Progress; [and finally] the tolerant God of Judeo-Christian America." Under the terms of the Judeo-Christian framework, Bass writes, shared monotheism; biblical language; and imagery of sacrifice, redemption, and exodus provided the common tropes and idioms of national political discourse.

Bass labels the God of Judeo-Christian America "tolerant," and certainly this late twentieth-century version of American civil religion was more tolerant than, say, the "stern God of Puritan Calvinism." Congregationalists were not hanging Quakers in New England town squares in 1955. But the Protestant-Catholic-Jewish "tri-faith" arrangement, for all its very real and significant moves toward inclusion and equality, always had a lead partner. For the first four decades of Judeo-Christianity's reign, from the 1930s through roughly 1976, it was ecumenical Protestants who ran the show. As historian David Hollinger has noted, if one looked at nearly any large and powerful institution of American public life in the mid-twentieth century, including government, major corporations, media, and universities, one could be quite sure that a white mainline Protestant was in charge.[7] These establishment Protestants, based in the historic denominations and the ecumenical National Council of Churches, politically and socially marginalized conservative evangelical and fundamentalist Protestants—a point we need to understand well if we want to appreciate the energy with which evangelicals built parallel media and political operations from at least the 1940s onward. Catholics and Jews, too, faced discrimination in housing, politics, business, university admissions, and many aspects of everyday social life.

Through dynamics that historian Darren Dochuk and others have analyzed, the tables began to turn by the mid-1970s, and for roughly the next three decades, from about 1976 to 2004, evangelical Protestants had the upper hand, both in national electoral politics and in the rhetorical framing of Judeo-Christianity. What had been a term of ecumenical and interfaith inclusion in the 1930s became, increasingly, a weapon in a new kind of culture war, deployed especially to critique the social revolutions of the 1960s. Secularists, communists, gays and lesbians, feminists, counterculturalists—these were the forces arrayed against America's Judeo-Christian values and heritage. By the 1980s, the term "Judeo-Christian" was more likely to pass the lips of conservative evangelists like Pat Roberston or Jerry Falwell than those of a mainline preacher, and by the 1990s the term had come to signify most especially the revisionist historical agenda of "Christian America" advocates like David Barton. No longer a term of inclusion, Judeo-Christianity in this final phase of its reign functioned as little more than a smoke screen to obscure a much more narrow, and decidedly evangelical, conception of national identity.

The era of Judeo-Christianity, with liberals in the lead through the 1970s and conservatives through the early 2000s, came to an end in the first decade of the new millennium. We might, for convenience sake, date the end to 2004. In that year, George W. Bush narrowly won re-election, and his margin, according to many observers, came through galvanizing evangelicals, especially around opposition to gay marriage. A decade on, this win seems more and more like the last hurrah for such tactics. The watershed year of 2004 also witnessed an unknown state senator from Illinois, Barack Obama, deliver an electrifying speech at the Democratic National Convention and win election to the US Senate. In his 2004 convention speech, Obama famously spoke of the values shared between conservative "red states" and liberal "blue states." "We worship an awesome God in the blue states," he proclaimed, borrowing a line from a popular evangelical praise song.[8] Though Obama failed to bring many evangelical voters to the Kerry campaign (or his own four years later) with this inclusive gesture, that failure was of less consequence than it appeared at the time. Just beyond his gaze, a demographic stampede was beginning to rumble among those leaving organized religion.

A quarter century ago, sociologist Robert Wuthnow famously wrote of a restructuring of American religion, a shift from denominationalism to broad liberal and conservative coalitions. It seems we are witnessing early in the twenty-first century yet another restructuring, away from the Judeo-Christian era during which liberals and conservatives vied for dominance, and toward a new paradigm in which the major fault line runs between "religion" and "spirituality." This paradigm of "spiritual but not religious," it has become increasingly clear, is key to unlocking the history and significance of our new national religious and political alignments.

The turn away from religion and toward spirituality has been underway for decades now, even centuries. We can follow a rather straight line, in fact, all the way back to the transcendentalist revolt against New England Unitarianism in the 1830s, and before that to the eighteenth-century Enlightenment in Europe and America. But this trend began to accelerate remarkably in the 1990s and reached a critical mass only in the new century. Some basic polling data reveal the magnitude of the transformation underway. On the one hand, the percentage of Americans who identify as Christian has dropped from 95 percent in 1960 to 82 percent in 1999 to 72 percent today. Some of this is due to the changes to immigration laws in the 1960s, which facilitated the arrival of more Muslims, Buddhists, Hindus, Sikhs, and others. But these "new religious Americans" account for only about 3 percent of the national population. Over roughly the same period of time—from 1950 to the present—the ratio of Jews, the largest non-Christian religious group in the United States, has actually fallen, from around 4 percent to less than 2 percent today.[9] In other words, the percentage of Christians in the United States is collapsing without a concurrent rise in religious non-Christians.

On the other hand, as the percentage of Christians has plummeted, the percentage who claim no religious affiliation has skyrocketed. Around 7 percent in 1970, the religiously unaffiliated remained below 10 percent through the early 1990s, at which point their number began to rise steadily.[10] The best accounting today shows that roughly 20 percent of the population is now unaffiliated, including one in three of those under age thirty. Much of this growth has been very recent. Between 2007 and 2012 alone the unaffiliated grew 4.3 percent, from 15.3 to 19.6 percent of the total population. This growth is nearly equal to the 4.7 percent of Americans that come from all non-Christian religions combined. In other words, all the Jews, Muslims, Buddhists, Hindus, Jains, Sikhs, Zoroastrians, and everyone else totaled together—every religiously identifying non-Christian in the entire country—roughly equal in number those who dropped out of Christianity in just the five years from 2007 to 2012.

What the data reveal, then, is that these two phenomena, the decline of Christianity and the rise of the unaffiliated, are two sides of the same demographic coin. The newly unaffiliated almost entirely consist of former Christians—former white Catholic and Protestant Christians, to be more precise.[11] These religious nones, as they are sometimes called, have been easy to caricature, and we have no shortage of critics who have taken their potshots, from Christopher Lasch in the 1970s to Robert Bellah in the 1980s to the *New York Times* columnist Ross Douthat more recently.[12] While theology has certainly informed each of these critiques, for the most part these and other critics of contemporary spirituality have lamented the alleged social and political ills of religious disaffiliation. In Lasch's terms, these critics fear a "culture of narcissism," an ethos of individualism run amok that will lead to the withering of social engagement, political activism, and willingness to sacrifice for the common good.

These fears are understandable, but all available evidence indicates they are misguided, at least when it comes to the recent and ongoing exodus from organized Christianity. What recent polling data indicate is that rather than an apolitical act of social withdrawal—rather than an act of narcissism—dropping out of organized religion, for the white former Christians who constitute the new nones, has typically been precisely an act of politics. The category of the nones—those who respond "no religion" or "none of the above" when asked by pollsters to state their religious affiliation—is first and foremost a political rather than a religious or theological category. Religious disaffiliation has profound consequences for religion, to be sure, including for theology, but the impetus behind the exodus from religion is in fact largely political.

The journalist Peter Beinart, in a recent essay on "The End of American Exceptionalism," made this case well. Minor changes in family and work patterns, he observes—upper-middle-class families having fewer kids, for example, and having them later—account for a modest share of the uptick in disaffiliation. But the heart of the story is political. "In the mid-20th century," Beinart writes, "liberals were almost as likely to attend church as conservatives. But starting in the 1970s, when the Religious Right began agitating against abortion, feminism, and gay rights, liberals began to identify organized Christianity with conservative politics. In recent years, the Religious Right's opposition to gay marriage has proved particularly alienating to Millennials." Recent survey data from sociologists Michael Hout, Claude Fischer, and Robert Putnam back this up.[13] The "religiously unaffiliated," Beinart goes on, "are disproportionately liberal, pro-gay marriage, and critical of churches for meddling too much in politics." Many young Americans, he concludes, "have begun voting against the GOP on Sundays by declining to attend church."[14] Beinart's emphasis on politics rather than religion itself here is noteworthy, and again borne out by the data. In 2012, just 3 percent of Americans reported that they did not believe in God, a number that rose only slightly from 2.1 percent in 1990.[15] Americans are not, by and large, leaving church because of a rejection of God or even Christianity; they are leaving as an act of political protest against the alliance between churches and the Republican Party on social issues. As the sociologist Philip Rieff observed prophetically in the late 1980s, "faith must always fail when it goes political."[16]

While this politicizing of Christianity has been terrible for churches, as evidenced by the exodus from the pews, it portends good times ahead for the Democratic Party. Again the data tell a compelling story. "White evangelicals vote roughly 3 to 1 Republican," reports the religion scholar Mark Silk, "while the 'nones' vote roughly 3 to 1 Democratic." These numbers, when considered alongside the clear generational divide in religious affiliation, signal a potentially large-scale realignment to come. White evangelicals, mainline Protestants, and Catholics, who tend to skew Republican, account for 69 percent of those sixty-five and older, yet only 25 percent of voters under thirty. The unaffiliated, on the other hand, who lean Democratic, claim only 11 percent of seniors but fully one-third of those under thirty. In addition, we must note that African Americans and Latinos are not fleeing organized religion, yet remain loyal Democratic voters. In the 2012 election, "25 percent of all Obama voters identified as 'unaffiliated,' while only 7 percent of Mitt Romney's voters" were nones, a disparity that is all the more remarkable considering how significant black and Hispanic voters were to Obama.[17] If present trends continue, the nones may well become the foundation of an enduring Democratic majority.

This is about as far as survey data will take us in understanding the restructuring of religion and politics that we are witnessing in the age of Obama. To probe more deeply, we need to begin to think historically, especially about the elusive but essential category of "spirituality." Spirituality, after all—as a word, as an idea, as a set of practices—is what now occupies the cultural and political space vacated by religion in the lives of so many Americans. Diana Bass contends, in fact, that Obama has presided over a shift from "civil religion" to "civil spirituality," and whether we accept this phrasing or not, certainly most religiously unaffiliated Americans choose to describe themselves with some variant of the now familiar formulation "spiritual but not religious." If we want to understand the tectonic shifts underway in religion and politics, we need to explore the history of the nones. And if we want to understand the history of the nones, we need to investigate the deep history of spirituality in America.

Transient and Permanent in Nineteenth-century American Religion

Spirituality is a concept that might seem to have no history. Contemporary Americans who employ the term, after all, most frequently do so to contrast the eternal, timeless truths of deepest reality with the particular forms the various religions have assumed over the centuries. Another common, related framing is that spirituality refers to a pure, divine essence, while religion refers to the human creations—the churches, doctrines, and rituals—designed to preserve, transmit, and some might say "tame" that essence.[18] When the nones of the Obama coalition leave organized religion because of its political entanglements but still pray regularly and affirm faith in God, they often rest their case on this basic distinction. Not only can they be spiritual without religion, they might even be more spiritually pure for having left religion behind.

Though cast as a retreat from the corruptions of history, this notion of spirituality has in fact a very specific history. The spiritual but not religious of today are inheritors of a theological legacy rooted in the liberal Protestantism of the eighteenth and nineteenth centuries. Thomas Jefferson, toward the end of his life, famously predicted in a letter to Dr. Benjamin Waterhouse, "There is not a young man now living in the United States who will not die an Unitarian."[19] This forecast reflected not only Jefferson's personal religious convictions but also his aspirations for the new nation. Alongside his fellow Enlightenment rationalists, Jefferson held a profound faith in reason and its myriad applications for human betterment, and particularly, in this case, in the form of disciplined inquiry just then emerging as the science of history. Through his reading of history, particularly *An History of the Corruptions of Christianity* (1782) by his friend, the Unitarian Joseph Priestly, Jefferson determined that the essential message of Jesus had been lost in the dogmas of the church. Jefferson applied this Enlightenment logic when he crafted his redacted version of the Gospels over the course of a couple evenings in the White House in the late winter of 1804. Just as he and his fellow Founders had established for the nation a form of government rooted in reason, now the new republic needed a suitable form of religion, one Jefferson aimed to uncover through his quest for the historical Jesus.

Jefferson's proudest political accomplishments, the writing of the Declaration of Independence and the Virginia Statute for Religious Freedom, represent these twin projects of political and religious liberation. He followed his political ontology from the Declaration—"all men are endowed by their Creator with certain inalienable rights"—with a similar assertion in the arena of faith, declaring three years later, in the 1779 Preamble to the Statute for Religious Freedom that "Almighty God hath created the mind free." Political freedom and religious freedom were collaborative projects, each rooted in God's universal plan for humanity. As Jefferson, steeped in this republican ideology (and the ever-present anti-Catholicism of his culture), wrote in his letter to Dr. Waterhouse, "I rejoice that in this blessed country of free inquiry and belief, which has surrendered its creed and conscience to neither kings nor priests, the genuine doctrine of one only God is reviving."[20] In a generation, America would fulfill its republican destiny, and released from inherited tyranny and superstition, its citizens would live as truly free persons. We would be a nation of yeoman Unitarians.

The history of religious liberalism in the United States since Jefferson reveals both its protean nature and its wide-ranging influence. The liberal strain of American Protestantism, as it developed after Jefferson's prognostication of 1822, grew to encompass a romantic and mystical element, most powerfully articulated by transcendentalists such as Ralph Waldo Emerson and Theodore Parker. From these streams of rationalism and romanticism flowed a broad cultural current of religious liberalism—or, more precisely, a variety of religious liberalisms—that came to include not just Unitarians and transcendentalists but a surprisingly wide array of Americans. Quakers, Spiritualists, and late nineteenth- and twentieth-century "spiritual but not religious" seekers of various stripes stand most obviously in the tradition. Even more, the course of mainline Protestantism and Reform Judaism over the last century and a half, and the engagement of Protestant, Catholic, and Jewish Americans with forms of Hinduism and Buddhism at various historical moments, cannot be understood without accounting for the shaping influence of this liberal religious culture.

The contributions of the transcendentalists Emerson and Parker bear further consideration. More than any other Americans of the nineteenth century, and perhaps more than any Americans of any century, Emerson and Parker gave voice to the spiritual impulse that animates today's religious nones. The religious legacy of Emerson and Parker, one might say, gives modern Americans permission to abandon their churches with clean consciences. Emerson, of course, was famous as the nineteenth-century prophet of self-reliance, a message he preached to great effect, and great scandal, to the Harvard Divinity School graduating class of 1838. Truth, he told the young graduates, ready to embark on preaching careers, "cannot be received at second hand. Truly speaking, it is not instruction, but provocation, that I can receive from another soul."[21] Therefore, he continued, "Let me admonish you ... to go alone; to refuse the good models, even those which are sacred in the imagination of men, and dare to love God without mediator or veil. ... The imitator dooms himself to hopeless mediocrity."[22] Though Emerson was scorned at Harvard for such blasphemous words, he soon found a wide American audience in print and on the lecture circuit. In one of his most widely cited essays, "Self Reliance" from 1841, he articulated the same ideas in a more secular voice. "Whoso would be a man must be a nonconformist," he argued. "Nothing is at last sacred but the integrity of your own mind. ... No law can be sacred to me but that of my nature."[23]

Emerson's friend and fellow transcendentalist Theodore Parker brought the matter back to religion in his most famous sermon, "A Discourse of the Transient and Permanent in Christianity," preached as an ordination sermon in Boston in 1841. Parker began with the simple observation that many in his day fretted over the fate of the Church, even though Christ had assured his followers, "Heaven and earth shall pass away: but my word shall not pass away" (Luke 21:33).[24] Parker used this promise from Jesus to assure his congregation that the essence of religion, the Word, was eternal and unchanging, even if the outer forms, including rituals and doctrines, might change. "While true religion is always the same thing," he preached, "in each century and every land, in each man that feels it, the Christianity of the Pulpit ... has never been the same thing in any two centuries or lands, except only in name."[25] Parker then famously divided Christianity into two elements, the transient and the permanent. "The one is the thought, the folly, the uncertain wisdom, the theological notions, the impiety of man," he proclaimed, while "the other, [is] the eternal truth of God."[26] Though preaching nearly two decades before the publication of Darwin's theory of evolution, Parker presented an evolutionary model of religious change, observing that religious rites and doctrines changed to suit changing historical circumstances. "In our calculating nation ... we have retained but two of the rites so numerous in the early Christian church," he noted, referring to the Protestant sacraments of baptism and the Lord's Supper, "and even these we have attenuated to the last degree, leaving them little more than a spectre of the ancient form."[27] Yet he saw that even this was but a phase in the continual change and adaptation of religious life. "Another age may continue or forsake both," he went on, "may revive old forms, or invent new ones to suit the altered circumstances of the times, and yet be Christians quite as good as we, or our fathers of the dark ages."[28]

One could track the course of these religious ideas from the era of Emerson and Parker down to the present, both in the high discourse of academic liberal theology and in the vernacular of popular religion. The American pragmatist philosopher and psychologist William James would serve, in this history, as the most significant intermediary between the transcendentalists and twentieth-century religious liberalism. In his magisterial Gifford Lectures, published in 1902 as *The Varieties of Religious Experience*, James assimilated the distinction between outer form and inner essence, and the evolutionary model of religious change, and adapted it to the scientific and psychological language of his day. James gave scientific and philosophical legitimacy to what we now call spirituality and presented it in a form that was readily available for a host of popularizers to come.

Spirituality and the Politics of Diversity in the Twentieth Century

The intellectual and theological revolt of religious liberalism against orthodoxy spread through popular media, especially books, all the while abetted by the increasing pervasiveness of consumerist values.[29] Americans trained to pick and choose consumer goods became adept pickers and choosers of religious goods as well. But another twentieth-century dynamic has also significantly influenced the flight from religion in the early twenty-first century: the religious quandary presented by religious others. A hallmark of religious liberalism since the days of the transcendentalists has been spiritual cosmopolitanism—a *religious* interest in *religious* others—a phenomenon nearly ubiquitous today, from Jews doing yoga to Presbyterians reading the Dalai Lama and much more. Historian David Hollinger employs the term "demographic diversification" to describe the processes by which nineteenth- and twentieth-century Americans became increasingly cosmopolitan as they accommodated their faith to a changing world. We might expand the term to include diversified awareness as well as diversified demographics.[30]

This process certainly resulted in many individual and corporate instances of what might properly be called secularization, but also in the new forms of religious faith and practice captured by the term "spirituality." The Society for Ethical Culture, for example, founded in 1876, offered what scholar Emily Mace calls a "post Jewish religion of 'deed rather than creed,'" a nontheistic religion devoted to community life and social activism.[31] More generally, myriad Americans across the twentieth century began to turn to nature, the arts, and social and humanitarian activism as arenas to pursue meaning and transcendence beyond religious parochialism. The emerging cosmopolitan orientations of the twentieth century, whether religious or spiritual, arose from the liberal accommodation to modernity and the ambition to speak in a universal spiritual idiom.

Sociologist Christian Smith, in his 2009 study of young adults, found that majorities agreed with the propositions "Many religions may be true"; "It is okay to pick and choose religious beliefs without having to accept teachings of faith as a whole"; and "It is okay to practice religions besides [one's] own." According to Smith, these modern developments correspond to the very institutional decline signified by the "rise of the nones." Echoing fellow sociologist Jay Demerath, Smith observes, "Liberal Protestantism's organizational decline has been accompanied by and is in part arguably the consequence of the fact that liberal Protestantism has won a decisive, larger cultural victory."[32]

A look back, to a period of perhaps the most consequential and challenging encounters of American religious liberalism with religious others, reveals the dynamics at play in the emerging cosmopolitan sensibilities. The early decades of the twentieth century were pivotal in the history of religious cosmopolitanism in America. While intellectuals embraced new anthropological and philosophical understandings of race stemming from the scholarship of Franz Boas and Horace Kallen, leaders in the churches worked to disentangle missionary work from Western cultural and racial imperialism, a project that resulted in the landmark 1932 report *Re-Thinking Missions*.[33] Significantly, colonial subjects themselves pressed these religious and theological shifts on Americans liberals as part of their own nationalist ambitions.

The most compelling example in this regard is that of Mahatma Gandhi. Gandhi was, of course, the Indian lawyer and anticolonial activist who led the nationalist struggle that eventually resulted in the end of British rule in his native country. His political struggle, and especially his use of nonviolent resistance based on his philosophy of *satyagraha*, or "truth force," made him a hero to millions around the world, including many African Americans and liberal and left-leaning whites in the United States. But Gandhi, to some, was more than a political hero. His political and religious example inspired these Americans to revere him in a way that can only be called a canonization. Gandhi became, in their eyes, a liberal Protestant saint. The canonization of Gandhi challenged American religious liberals to decouple their Christianity from its hegemonic Western identity—to find, once again, its permanent spiritual essence amid the corruptions of history. More than any other figure in the twentieth century, Gandhi—or, more precisely, the idea of Gandhi—demanded of American liberal Protestants a radical rethinking of the relationship of Christianity to the Western racial and economic order. Though an admirer of Christ, he was a fierce critic of Christianity, or at least Western Christendom. For this reason, the liberal Protestant canonization of Gandhi—a canonization that happened not only because of Gandhi's politics but also because of his perceived spiritual virtues—had far-reaching consequences. After Gandhi, Christian exclusivism proved much more difficult for liberal-minded Americans.

Many Americans, black and white, religious and nonreligious, played roles in bringing Gandhi's witness to the United States. John Haynes Holmes, the Unitarian minister of New York's Community Church, and Richard Gregg, an influential pacifist and political theorist, were perhaps Gandhi's earliest and most ardent devotees in the United States, each writing and speaking about Gandhi in the 1910s and 1920s. The African American preacher and mystic Howard Thurman made a celebrated pilgrimage to see Gandhi in India in the 1930s, as did the educator Benjamin Mays; each helped bring Gandhism to the black freedom struggle in the United States. But the figure who did the most to make Gandhi a saint in the eyes of ordinary Americans was E. Stanley Jones, a Methodist missionary to India for most of the first half of the twentieth century and author of the bestselling *Christ of the Indian Road* (1925). Jones, more than any other of Gandhi's many admirers in the United States, did the hard theological work of making sense of Gandhi for the mainstream North American Protestant audience. In Jones's presentation of Gandhi we see perhaps the best example of the process by which the liberalism of the nineteenth century was transformed into the cosmopolitanism of the twentieth.

How Jones, as the most famous missionary and one of the most admired men in the United States, framed Gandhi carried significant weight and entered a religious and political climate ripe for radical recalibration. He was an acquaintance and supporter of Gandhi for decades, and was scheduled to meet with the Mahatma on the day he was assassinated. Jones penned *Mahatma Gandhi: An Interpretation* in 1948 as a tribute to a fallen hero. In this work he presented Gandhi as a bridge between East and West, noting, "Through his methods and spirit they were in large measure reconciled."[34] Since the nineteenth century, liberal Protestants had sought to frame religious experience in human universal terms, and Jones presented Gandhi in just this way. "In spite of his constant protests against the Christian faith as represented in the missionary movement in India," Jones wrote, "he was more Christianized than most Christians." According to Jones, Gandhi "draws together people of varying viewpoints and makes them feel they have a common center. The Hindus pay their tribute to a Hindu who was deeply Christianized, and the Christians pay their tribute to a man, Christian in spirit, who was a Hindu."[35]

In some ways the veneration of Gandhi is so thoroughly established in our times that it can be hard to remember how radical this universalizing project was, and the degree of intellectual and theological contortionism required. "We must not try to claim him when he himself would probably repudiate that claim," Jones conceded.[36] "He was fundamentally a Hindu. The roots of his spiritual life were not in Christ; they were in the Bhagavad-Gita."[37] But Jones, who knew and loved Gandhi, was unable to let this be the last word, especially in the wake of Gandhi's assassination. So, Jones uprooted Gandhi, made him into a man of spirit and the eternal rather than a man of time and place. He became, in other words, a liberal Protestant. The phrases Jones uses to bridge this gap are remarkable. "He was a Hindu by allegiance and a Christian by affinity," Jones claimed.[38] Even more strongly, when commenting on Gandhi's death, Jones wrote: "Orthodox Hinduism took over his body and burned it according to Hindu orthodoxy, but the ideas and concepts he represented seemed strangely Christian. And yet again it would not be orthodox Christianity. The Mahatma was a natural Christian rather than an orthodox one."[39]

This distinction between a "natural" Christian and an "orthodox" one reveals the manner in which Gandhi, as defined by Jones, embodied the very essence of liberal Protestantism. The term "natural" in this period certainly carried racial and colonial overtones, as it was often used to mark those who were not "civilized." Yet in Christian theology "natural" also signaled forms of religion rooted in reason and experience rather than revelation, and therefore potentially available to all. As a "natural" Christian, then, Gandhi transcended the constraints of orthodoxy, and in Jones's estimation reached a higher plane of faith that was pure, spiritual, unbounded, and universal. Jones discussed at length, as one might expect, Gandhi's teaching of nonviolence and the manner in which, through fasting and labor—through the power of his life and example—he embodied the principles he taught. His life, in this manner, was his greatest witness. "One of the most Christlike men in history," Jones concluded, "was not called a Christian at all." Yet despite the labels, through the power of his life and personality, "the man who fought Christian civilization, so-called, furthered the real thing. God uses many instruments, and he has used Mahatma Gandhi to help Christianize unchristian Christianity."[40] For this reason, Gandhi's death, Jones remarked, was "the greatest tragedy since the Son of God died on a cross."[41]

Conservative mainline and evangelical Protestants excoriated Jones for embracing a Hindu as both a political and religious inspiration. A prominent Baptist preacher, for example, circulated widely a pamphlet describing Jones's admiration of Gandhi. "This Is What E. Stanley Jones Believes," was the pamphlet's title, and it bore the additional tag line, "If You Believe the Lord Jesus Christ is the Savior of the World and Not Mahatma Gandhi, Read This."[42] But Jones was not to be deterred. He prepared his own circular called "Are We Too Proud to Learn from a Hindu?," which favorably cited Gandhi's political critiques of the "so-called Christian nations." Jones also regularly spoke from his experiences in India about the need for a more equitable economic order in the United States. Even more controversially, he condemned American Jim Crow through comparisons to the Indian caste system.

Since the 1920s, Jones had written of his desire to disentangle the message of Jesus from its Western cultural manifestations. "Are We Too Proud to Learn from a Hindu?" asked Jones of his fellow liberal Protestants. This question, and the many questions that lay behind and within it—questions about the truth claims of Christianity, about white and Western supremacy, about capitalism and imperialism—heralded the arrival of an emerging transformation in American religious and political life. As religious liberals pursued these questions in the tumultuous decades of the 1950s and 1960s, they forged alliances with African Americans, secular leftists, and others that facilitated the demise of Jim Crow, protested the war in Vietnam, and advanced human rights, feminist agendas, and global economic development. As these political projects unfolded at home and abroad, the encounters and questions that ensued also fostered increasingly cosmopolitan modes of spiritual life.

As Emerson and Parker did in the nineteenth century, the cult of Gandhi in the twentieth—and the broad move toward increasing spiritual cosmopolitanism it represents—laid the groundwork for the religious and political shifts now underway. Leaving organized religion is a viable religious option for young Americans today because they affirm, with their liberal religious predecessors, that truth is not exclusive to any one faith tradition, and certainly not to be found in religion's creeds or rituals.

Yet, as the examples of nineteenth-century transcendentalism and twentieth-century cosmopolitanism make clear, the American revolt against Christian exclusivism, and indeed against organized (and politicized) Christianity, does not arise from a widespread revolt against belief itself. Though atheists cheered when Obama embraced them in his 2009 inaugural address, we are not witnessing the transformation of the United States into a North American Sweden. Not only will large numbers of Americans remain affiliated with traditional organized religion for the foreseeable future, those who do abandon traditional religion are not typically abandoning religion itself, broadly understood. If anything, the religious nones aim to give religion an even wider berth, to liberate it from its political shackles. The German sociologist Max Weber argued at the dawn of the twentieth century that Western modernity was in the thralls of a thoroughgoing "disenchantment," a de-spiritualization of culture and consciousness brought about by science and bureaucratic rationality. Yet the rise of the nones, as a revolt against politicized Christianity, signals nothing more clearly than a massive generational shift toward re-enchantment. Political Christianity has lost its spark; where that spark may now be found is the great question of American religious life in the twenty-first century.

Notes

1. Diana Butler Bass, "The Obama Doctrine: American Civic Spirituality," Faithstreet, an online publication of *The Washington Post*, January 24, 2014.

2. Pew Forum on Religion and Public Life, *"Nones" on the Rise*, October 9, 2012, 66, http://www.pewforum.org/2012/10/09/nones-on-the-rise/.

3. For the full text, see http://www.whitehouse.gov/blog/inaugural-address.

4. See, for example, "Obama Acknowledges 'Non-Believers,'" *USA Today*, January 20, 2009.

5. Mark Silk, "Notes on the Judeo-Christian Tradition in America," *American Quarterly* 36, no. 1 (Spring 1984): 65–85.

6. Kevin Schultz, *Tri-Faith America: How Catholics and Jews Held Postwar America to its Protestant Promise* (New York: Oxford University Press, 2011), 63.

7. David Hollinger, "After Cloven Tongues of Fire: Ecumenical Protestantism and the Modern American Encounter with Diversity," *Journal of American History* 98, no. 1 (June 1, 2011): 23.

8. "Transcript: Illinois Senate Candidate Barack Obama," *Washington Post*, July 27, 2004. The song "Awesome God," by Rich Mullins, which first appeared on the album *Winds of Heaven, Stuff of Earth* (Reunion Records, 1988), has been covered by many artists since and has become a staple of contemporary evangelical worship.

9. Pew Forum, "U.S. Religious Landscape Survey," February 22, 2008, 10; Bass, "The Obama Doctrine: American Civic Spirituality."

10. Pew Forum, *"Nones" on the Rise*.

11. Mark Silk, "White Christians Turning into Nones," *Spiritual Politics* (blog), February 13, 2014.

12. Christopher Lasch, *The Culture of Narcissism: American Life in an Age of Diminishing Expectations* (New York: W. W. Norton, 1979); Robert Bellah et al., *Habits of the Heart: Individualism and Commitment in American Life* (Berkeley: University of California Press, 1985); Ross Douthat, *Bad Religion: How We Became a Nation of Heretics* (New York: Free Press, 2012).

13. Michael Hout and Claude S. Fischer, "Why More Americans Have No Religious Preference: Politics and Generations," *American Sociological Review* 67, no. 2 (April 1, 2002): 165–190; Robert D. Putnam and David E. Campbell, *American Grace: How Religion Divides and Unites Us* (New York: Simon and Schuster, 2010).

14. Peter Beinart, "The End of American Exceptionalism," *The Atlantic Monthly*, February 3, 2014.

15. Michael Hout, Claude S. Fischer, and Mark A. Chaves, "More Americans Have No Religious Preference: Key Finding from the 2012 General Social Survey," press release summary, March 7, 2013.

16. Philip Rieff, "New Preface, 1987," to *The Triumph of the Therapeutic: Uses of Faith After Freud* (Chicago: University of Chicago Press, 1978 [1966]), x.

17. Bass, "The Obama Doctrine: American Civic Spirituality."

18. See Leigh Eric Schmidt, "The Making of Modern 'Mysticism,'" *Journal of the American Academy of Religion* 71, no. 2: 273–302.

19. Thomas Jefferson to Dr. Benjamin Waterhouse, June 26, 1822. The Thomas Jefferson Papers Series 1. General Correspondence. 1651-1827. Library of Congress.

20. Thomas Jefferson to Dr. Benjamin Waterhouse, June 26, 1822. The Thomas Jefferson Papers Series 1. General Correspondence. 1651-1827. Library of Congress.

21. Ralph Waldo Emerson, "An Address" (Harvard Divinity School Address), delivered July 15, 1838, quoted from *The Selected Writings of Ralph Waldo Emerson*, edited by Brooks Atkinson (New York: Modern Library, 1992), 66.

22. Emerson, "An Address," 75.

23. Ralph Waldo Emerson, "Self-Reliance," in *Selected Writings of Ralph Waldo Emerson*, edited by William H. Gilman (New York: Signet Classics, 2003), 269–270.

24. Theodore Parker, "A Discourse of the Transient and Permanent in Christianity," delivered May 19, 1841, quoted from *Electronic Texts in American Studies*, Paper 14, Digital Commons, University of Nebraska-Lincoln, 136.

25. Ibid., 139.

26. Ibid., 140.

27. Ibid., 141.

28. Ibid.

29. See Matthew S. Hedstrom, *The Rise of Liberal Religion: Book Culture and American Spirituality in the Twentieth Century* (New York: Oxford University Press, 2013).

30. David Hollinger, "The Accommodation of Protestant Christianity with the Enlightenment: An Old Drama Still Being Enacted," in *After Cloven Tongues of Fire: Protestant Liberalism in Modern America* (Princeton, NJ: Princeton University Press, 2013), 6.

31. Emily Mace, "The 'Nones' Are Here ... And Have Been for over 100 Years," *Religion Dispatches*, January 13, 2015.

32. Christian Smith, *Souls in Transition: The Religious Lives of Emerging Adults* (New York: Oxford University Press, 2009), 287.

33. William Ernest Hocking and the Laymen's Foreign Missions Inquiry Commission of Appraisal, *Re-thinking Missions: A Laymen's Inquiry After One Hundred Years* (New York: Harper and Brothers, 1932).

34. E. Stanley Jones, *Mahatma Gandhi: An Interpretation* (New York: Abingdon-Cokesbury Press, 1948), 21.

35. Ibid., 28.

36. Ibid., 56.
37. Ibid., 28.
38. Ibid., 56.
39. Ibid., 59.
40. Ibid., 77.
41. Ibid., 11.
42. *Wealthy Street Baptist Temple News*, Vol. 14, No 31, Box 4, Folder 9, ESJ Papers, Asbury Theological Seminary.

16

The Blessings of American Pluralism and Those Who Rail Against It

Kevin M. Schultz

WHEN, ON AUGUST 6, 2009, the US Senate voted to confirm Sonia Sotomayor's nomination to fill David Souter's seat on the Supreme Court, hardly anyone thought it worthwhile to mention her faith. Reporters talked a great deal about the fact that she was the first Latino ever nominated to the court, and that she seemed to be the living embodiment of whatever was left of the American Dream, having raised herself up from an impoverished childhood in a housing project in the Bronx to rack up an unbelievably distinguished career in the world of law. Even those who opposed her nomination (thirty-one of the forty Senate Republicans, for instance) didn't bother to mention her faith, choosing instead to criticize her for being an "activist judge" who would inevitably toe the liberal line. But hardly anyone pointed out that she would become the sixth Catholic then sitting on the bench, not only giving Catholics a supermajority on the country's highest court but—and perhaps more strikingly—taking the spot of the last remaining Protestant. Once she was sworn in, all the non-Catholics were Jews. Of the predominance of Catholics, the bombastic and militantly watchful Catholic conservative Bill Donohue commented: "Barely a peep was made." And of the fact that, for the first time in American history, not a single Protestant sat among the constituents of one of the three branches of the federal government, hardly anyone seemed to notice.[1]

Among the many transformations experienced in the age of Obama, surely one of the most vital has to be the almost casual way in which the country has come to accept religious pluralism. Religious discrimination is down in America even as it has risen sharply throughout the world.[2] The US Equal Employment Opportunity Commission (EEOC) reported a sharp rise in claims after the attacks of 9/11 before noting a gentle decline since 2009. In addition, a large percentage of the EEOC's claims were found to lack merit, suggesting more fear than bona fide abuse.[3] And perhaps the most compelling evidence of the lack of interfaith strife comes from the fact that the loudest claims of religious discrimination during the first decades of the twenty-first century have come not from some persecuted minority but from the largest, most powerful religious groups in the country, including evangelical Protestants who historically have dominated the moral life of the nation and that group with the supermajority on the Supreme Court, American Catholics. And what have been their complaints? Not that they themselves have been prevented from worshiping as they see fit, nor that they have been persecuted for believing what they believe. Instead, they complain that, in America's quest to honor its minority faiths, the country has curtailed the rights of large groups to impose their beliefs on others. No Catholic, for instance, was ever forced to practice contraception under President Obama's Affordable Care Act, but some Catholic employers were asked to contribute to the contraceptive efforts of their employees who may or may not be Catholic. Compared to past eras of religious discrimination that included the burning of churches, denials of employment, forcing people to live in specific neighborhoods, and other subtle and not-so-subtle instances of abuse, this has not been an era marked by harsh or violent discrimination. America has, by and large, come to accept its religious diversity.

There are other examples as well. Six days after 9/11, for instance, when the nation might have turned toward bloody attacks on its Islamic minority, President George W. Bush went to the Islamic Center of Washington, DC, and spoke eloquently about the virtues of Islam, calling American Muslims "friends," "taxpaying citizens," and "doctors, lawyers, law professors, members of the military, entrepreneurs, shopkeepers, moms and dads" just like everyone else. Bush quoted from the Koran: "In the long run, evil in the extreme will be the end of those who do evil." He differentiated the terrorists from the faith on whose behalf they claimed to act: "The face of terror is not the true faith of Islam. That's not what Islam is all about. Islam is peace." And then he went on to plead for Americans to recognize the tradition of religious pluralism: "Women who cover their heads in this country must feel comfortable going outside their homes.

Moms who wear cover must be not intimidated in America. That's not the America I know."[4]

For the most part, his pleas were heard. There were some instances of anti-Islamic violence in the aftermath of 9/11. But they were few and far between. And when thornier ones did arise, such as the persistent attempt to outlaw the use of Muslim Sharia law in the United States by various state legislators and political activists throughout the south and the Midwest, they were laughed away, responded to with the argument that no religious laws are allowed to be consulted in the American legal system, or—most consistently—found to be unconstitutional.[5]

Another emblem of America's quiet acceptance of religious pluralism might be the successful work of Eboo Patel, an Ismaili Muslim of Indian descent who grew up in the Chicago suburbs. In 2002, Patel began the Interfaith Youth Core (IFYC) in order to ensure that conversations about diversity were inclusive of faith, as well as the country's more traditional diversity groups, defined by race, class, and gender. The IFYC has grown significantly since its founding, not because it has had much work to do in addressing instances of religious discrimination, but because the general acceptance of America's religious pluralism has led to an increased number of outreach and service efforts, of religious minorities working "better together," as the group's slogan has it. In 2009, Patel became a founding member of President Obama's Advisory Council on Faith-based Neighborhood Partnerships.

But perhaps nowhere is the acceptance of America's religious pluralism more profound than as witnessed by the open and unafraid proclamations of the increasingly large numbers of Americans who find no religious home in American society. As Matthew Hedstrom has shown in Chapter 15, those who were once called "freethinkers" and pilloried for holding values contrary to American life are now called the "nones," a moniker that always provokes laughs from Catholic students. Historically, the number of Americans claiming no religious affiliation has always been small—just 7 percent in 1972. But since the 1990s, the curve has shot upward, with nones now constituting somewhere close to 20 percent of the entire population. A small number of these nones are atheists or agnostics, with just more than 2 percent of Americans openly claiming to have no belief in God, and just more than 3 percent claiming to have no dog in the fight. This means that the rest of the nones—as much as 15 percent of the total population—believe in God or gods or the supernatural but have no interest in affiliating themselves with one faith or another.[6]

The best research on the nones shows them deriving from two primary sources. The first—a smaller tributary—are ex-Catholics. These are Catholics who have been demoralized by the Church's handling of the sexual abuse scandal and other perceived infractions. During the first decades of the twenty-first century, a full 11 percent of Americans considered themselves ex-Catholic. However, it is a smaller proportion of this 11 percent who claim to be among the nones. While there are scads of former Catholics across the country, former Catholics typically find it difficult to let go of the faith of their fathers. Catholicism seems to be among what sociologist Slavica Jakelic has called "collectivistic faiths," or religions that hold tightly onto the identity of their followers for reasons that extend beyond the institutional.[7]

The second and much larger collection of nones are young Americans, those who sociologists call millennials because they came of age during the turn of the millennium. One-third of millennials claim to have no religious affiliation. And among this third, nearly 90 percent say they aren't looking for a religious group to belong to.[8]

This isn't just a generational dispute. Instead, the youth are simply leading the way. With the exception of the "Greatest Generation," the percentage of nones has increased among every demographic group since 2007.[9] Rather than simple youthful rebellion, then, there are larger forces at work.

For our story, though, what is revealing is that as the nones have increased during the past decade, there have been almost no protests. Instead, major institutions have accommodated. One of the most vibrant pastoral offices at Harvard University, for instance, is the Humanist Chaplaincy, which was founded in 1974 but became a prominent national voice for the nones after Greg Epstein took over in 2005. Epstein has been featured widely in numerous public forums, and his 2010 book, *Good Without God*, spent several weeks on the *New York Times* bestseller list.

Meanwhile, the traditional voices opposing secularization within American life have not bothered to raise the cudgel, instead offering something of a truce. Most prominently, the Southern Baptist Convention, the largest denomination in the country, has appointed (by its standards) something of a political moderate, Russell Moore, to its most powerful position, president of the denomination's Ethics and Religious Liberty Commission. And on once-hot button issues like gay marriage, Moore has said things like this:

Above all, we [evangelical Christians] must prepare people for what the future holds, when Christian beliefs about marriage and sexuality aren't part of the cultural consensus but are seen to be strange and freakish and even subversive. If our people assume that everything goes back to normal with the right President and a quick constitutional amendment, they are not being equipped for a world that views evangelical Protestants and traditional Roman Catholics and Orthodox Jews and others as bigots or freaks.[10]

With words like this, Moore is recognizing not that his flock needs to stop fighting but that the ideals of pluralism have triumphed and his people must accept that fact. The Religious Right will continue to fight, but it can no longer think that the coming of the millennium is just around the corner. And, one might infer from Moore's words, neither is the apocalypse.

Perhaps surprisingly, this general acceptance of America's religious pluralism turns out to be more ideological than demographic; in this case, it's the ideas that matter, not the numbers.

Aside from the rise of the nones, for instance, there has not been any recent uptick in religious minorities in the United States. And when one looks at the numbers, it's clear the United States is still a profoundly Christian nation. Somewhere in the range of 76 to 78 percent of Americans identify as either Protestant or Catholic. Breaking this down a bit, roughly 25 percent of Americans identify as Catholic, while just over 50 percent identify as some Protestant denomination. Still, among nations of the world, the United States isn't all that religiously diverse. Indeed, a Pew study from 2012 ranks the United States the sixty-eighth most religiously diverse nation in the world, more diverse than Iran or Afghanistan but far less diverse than Vietnam, Nigeria, Suriname, or New Zealand.[11]

Some might suggest that the preponderance of America's religious diversity lies not in how we rank in majority-versus-minority comparisons but in the multiplicity among the quarter or so of Americans who are not Christian. On one hand, that's certainly true: practically every religion under the sun can be found on these shores. But on the other hand, these numbers must be viewed with considerable caution. Consider, for example, that most of America's non-Christian population claims to have no religion at all (almost 20 percent of the population), while all the other religious minorities—Jews, Muslims, Hindus, Buddhists, and all the rest—*all together* total just 5.3 percent of the population.[12]

Still others might argue that America's religious diversity lies not in faiths beyond Christianity but in the vast expanse of denominational differences within Protestantism itself. Sure, we might not have many Jews, Muslims, or Hindus, but we do have Southern Baptists, National Baptists, Methodists, Southern Methodists, Episcopalians, Churches of God, Assemblies of God, Vineyards, Lutherans, Presbyterians, pentecostals, African Methodist Episcopalians, Missouri Synod Lutherans, and more. And while that too is true, it has been a widely noted historical trend that the pull of denominationalism has declined considerably in the latter half of the twentieth century, with each denomination more or less aligning itself in one of two camps: evangelical or liberal Protestant. And what has divided these two camps? While there are many components to a complete answer to this question, it's clear that one vital factor is how a denomination weighs in on the question of religious pluralism. Does it accept the fact that other people might have legitimate religious claims and that those claims should not be summarily discounted when considering the good of the commonweal? Or should those claims be dismissed as false and therefore dangerous to the life of the nation?[13]

Nevertheless, if the United States can make little claim to being among the most religiously diverse nations in the world, and if even the diversity within American Protestantism has declined precipitously during the past fifty years, what has in fact changed is that Americans have become far more accepting of religious traditions that are not their own. Indeed, this acceptance of religious pluralism has been so successful that it has provoked a rearguard response from some evangelical Protestants actively seeking to "take their country back" to its supposedly Christian origins, although it is clear that, despite their fiery rhetoric, they're stuck fighting over the scraps, like whether or not a gigantic statue can sit on the lawn of a city hall somewhere or how school curriculums should be designed in one particularly religious state. Despite all the banter, pluralism has clearly carried the day.

What is the history of this acceptance of religious pluralism?

The story begins in the earliest years of the twentieth century. Before then, despite the fact the First Amendment meant religious majorities couldn't demand that other faiths become Protestant, Protestants did in fact operate what historian David Sehat has called a "moral establishment" in America. Beginning almost immediately after the nation's founding, American Protestants deliberately set the tone and tenor for the nation's moral life, helping determine right from wrong, legal from illegal, good from bad. As the early nineteenth-century jurist James Kent put it, this Protestant moral establishment came into existence "not because christianity was established by law, but because christianity was . . . the basis of the public morals."[14]

As Sehat explains, it was through the courts that this "moral establishment" took hold. When in 1811, a New York man named Ruggles, probably drunk, shouted in public, "Jesus Christ was a bastard and his mother must be a whore," he fought his subsequent arrest because New York did not have a blasphemy law and, even more to the point, the state's constitution guaranteed religious freedom. That didn't matter. The court found Ruggles guilty, somewhat remarkably citing the common law of the state. Because Protestant Christianity was part of the Anglo-American way of life, the court held that blasphemy was a punishable crime. To contend otherwise would be "to corrupt the morals of the people, and to destroy good order." The *Ruggles* case had a domino effect. By 1844, the US Supreme Court had signed on, codifying, outside legislative statute, Protestantism norms in America. From *Ruggles* onward, the United States lived with what Sehat calls a "proxy religious establishment" that ruled from the courts and bled into greater society at large.[15]

But this religious monism couldn't survive the first decades of the twentieth century. It was then, on the streets of industrial America, when Protestant ministers like Walter Rauschenbusch and Washington Gladden and Protestant laywomen like Jane Addams began what came to be called the Social Gospel movement. But as they were setting up their halfway homes and lobbying for better garbage collection in America's growing metropolises, the Social Gospelers encountered a collection of Catholic and Jewish charitable agencies doing much the same work. After all, a vast majority of the European immigrants who flooded to the United States during the final quarter of the nineteenth century were either Catholic or Jewish. The Catholic Church at first worked from afar to meet the social needs of the immigrants, for instance, by allowing each diocese to organize its own charitable work. By 1910, however, it became clear they needed greater organization, so the Church organized the National Conference of Catholic Charities, a loose organization of diocesan groups, which was strengthened during the First World War by the creation of the National Catholic War Council, which eventually became the National Catholic Welfare Conference (NCWC) when the war ended.[16]

American Jews were also there. They had a long history of communal service, especially through the local *landsmanschaftn*, or societies of immigrants originating from the same town or region and who offered services to new immigrants. In 1899, the National Conference of Jewish Charities combined many of these efforts into one national body. Joined by the likes of B'nai B'rith, the National Council of Jewish Women, the American Jewish Committee, Hadassah, the Anti-Defamation League, and the American Jewish Congress, the reach of Jewish charity groups extended widely.

Thus when Protestant Social Gospelers did their good work during the first years of the twentieth century, they ran headlong into Catholic and Jewish agencies doing much the same work. Eventually crises prompted the first bouts of cooperation between the three groups. In 1907, for instance, an economic recession in Pittsburgh led Protestant, Catholic, and Jewish groups to consolidate charitable efforts. A 1912 flood in Dayton, Ohio, led all the organizations in the Cincinnati and Dayton areas to come together to create a Community Chest. Interfaith Community Chests began popping up everywhere, and by the 1930s they operated in more than four hundred cities across the United States and Canada. By then, it was relatively common for figures within Protestantism, Catholicism, and Judaism to work together toward social ends.

Along with these civic needs, the other specter provoking interfaith cooperation was secularism. It was of course the forces of modernity that prompted Max Weber—at this exact same time—to pronounce his famous dictum that as society grows increasingly modern, the hold of religion steadily decreases. To prevent that from happening, mainline American Protestants created the Religious Education Association in 1908 to educate the youth about the dangers of secularism. In this effort they began to bring together what were rapidly becoming seen as the country's three central faiths—Protestantism, Catholicism, and Judaism. The effort wasn't terribly successful; fear of proselytization and historic rivalries were too prominent, and Catholics hardly participated at all. But it did signal a second flank in the acceptance of the idea of religious pluralism.

Still, this acceptance wasn't the norm in the 1920s and 1930s. Antisemitism and anti-Catholic vitriol persisted long into the twentieth century. Although discrimination against religious minorities was minimal compared to that confronted by racial minorities, Catholics were still widely suspected of seeking political control of the United States in an effort to kowtow to the Vatican line, while Jews were thought to yearn for financial control of the country, one business at a time. For their part, Protestants used their power to discriminate, having real estate agents shepherd Catholics and Jews to separate neighborhoods, preventing Catholics and Jews from joining business clubs and social fraternities, and even restricting Catholics and Jews from certain kinds of jobs.

It would take the Second World War for interfaith harmony to triumph. With the rise of Hitler, America's faith leaders (and others) worked hard to promote a vision that embraced America's pluralism. To do otherwise risked making America look no better than Hitler's Germany. Some of these attempts bordered on the saccharine. A priest, a rabbi, and a minister would travel the country together, for instance, putting on shows in theaters and calling themselves "The Tolerance Trio." Norman Rockwell's take on the America's "Four Freedoms" prominently showed a Catholic woman fingering her rosary, a Jew in a yarmulke, and several Protestants bowing their heads in prayer—all seemingly worshiping together. But other outcroppings were more substantive. Organizations like the National Conference of Christians and Jews would go to cities and set up satellite organizations to handle interfaith strife. Radio programs nationwide preached the importance of tolerance and goodwill. The Religious News Service (RNS) was crafted in this period to promote and report on interfaith activity. All were efforts to challenge the idea that the United States was in any way a Christian nation. In the face of Hitler, the national imagination had to change, and interfaith leaders sought to promote an image premised on what was then being called Judeo-Christianity.

With the Cold War, the image of a tri-faith America prevailed. Movies appeared throughout the 1940s and 1950s featuring interfaith tolerance as a central theme. *Gentleman's Agreement* (1948), *Big City* (1948), *Angels in the Outfield* (1951), and dozens more preached interfaith tolerance and amity among Protestants, Catholics, and Jews as exemplars of good Americanism. The newly founded Ad Council promoted the idea's virtues in its earliest campaigns. Brotherhood Days were held annually as national holidays, celebrating "making America safe for differences." Posters showed America populated by millions of people labeled "Protestant, Catholic, and Jew." In America, so the message went, tolerance for outsiders was a definitional trait, and pluralism had to reign.

The idea was lampooned too, of course. As Tom Lehrer sang in his 1965 song, "National Brotherhood Week":

> Oh, the Protestants hate the Catholics,
> And the Catholics hate the Protestants,
> And the Hindus hate the Muslims,

> And everybody hates the Jews.
> But during National Brotherhood Week, National Brotherhood Week,
> It's national everyone-smile-at-one-another-hood week.
> Be nice to people who
> Are inferior to you.
> It's only for a week, so have no fear.
> Be grateful it doesn't last all year.[17]

This doesn't mean the idea didn't have ramifications. Indeed, the fact that Catholics and Jews were now perceived as central partners in the American experience began to change the way Americans interacted with one another. Challenges emerged in schools and neighborhoods. Collegiate social fraternities had to alter discriminatory charters limiting membership to white Protestants. City councils had to ponder the once-taken-for-granted placement of crèches on city property. Public schools could no longer begin each day with a reading from the King James Bible. Protestant Christianity could no longer be normative.

Disputes often ended up in the courts—the same place that Protestant Christianity had become the moral authority in the land. And by the early 1960s, the US Supreme Court decided two landmark cases that limited the public role of religion in American life. In *Engel v. Vitale* (1962), which concerned reciting prayers in public schools, the Court found that "government in this country should stay out of the business of writing or sanctioning official prayers and leave that purely religious function to the people themselves and to those the people choose to look to for religious guidance." The next year, in *Abington Township School District v. Schempp* (1963), the Court outlawed Bible readings in public schools, declaring that the United States had to be officially neutral in matters of religion, "neither aiding or opposing religion."[18] The way that most people read these cases is that the acknowledgment of Catholics and Jews in American life had forced the government to work through the implications of religious pluralism, either sanctioning religious displays from every religious group who asked for it, or sanctioning none at all. To do anything else was to play favorites. And now that Protestantism had been demoted from its status atop the hierarchy, the Supreme Court was no longer going to allow favoritism. The United States, the Court declared, was a religiously pluralistic nation, and the people had to respect that.

That this all happened before 1965 is important because it was in that year that the United States relaxed its immigration laws. Whereas the laws from the 1920s sharply limited immigration from Africa, Asia, and Latin America, immigrants from those places came to the United States in substantial numbers after 1965. More Africans have immigrated to the United States since 1965, for instance, then during all of slave times. In 1960, Americans of Asian descent constituted just 5 percent of the foreign-born population; since then, the number has jumped to nearly 30 percent.

And of course they brought their religions with them. In her important 2001 book, *A New Religious America: How a "Christian Country" Has Become the World's Most Religiously Diverse Nation*, Diana Eck described her encounters with Buddhists, Muslims, Hindus, Sikhs, Jains, Zoroastrians, and dozens of other religious groups from around the world. And although she poses her book as a warning about the potential pratfalls of a new religious demography, it is clear that because of the work done earlier to embrace the notion of religious pluralism, most of the encounters are celebrations. In the 1990s, the US Navy commissioned its first Muslim chaplain and opened its first mosque. Religious celebrations are held throughout the country by millions of religious minorities, without repercussion or restriction. New friendships have formed, and the country has, by and large, accepted its new identity.[19]

Well, not entirely.

Beginning in the 1970s, a collection of politically conservative evangelical Protestants began to organize a counter-movement, one—as they put it—to "take their country back." Although racial segregation was certainly one motivating factor in the formation of the Religious Right (schools could be segregated if they were religious schools), it is also clear that members of the Religious Right were passionately eager to resist the rising tide of religious pluralism in the United States, which they blamed for liberalizing the culture by allowing easier divorce, more premarital sex, legalized abortion, and equal treatment of religious minorities in the public square.[20] Indeed, the whole crux of cultural authority seemed to be under attack in the 1960s and 1970s, and, for Protestants who once took for granted their predominance over American culture, this was a distinct loss of status. Protestors thus made noise when "family values" came under attack. Recognizing that the courts had codified religious pluralism in the 1960s, the Religious Right targeted the nation's legislators, ranking them by their adherence to supposedly Judeo-Christian principles and then publishing their rankings widely. Eventually, watchdog organizations began to prod businesses to broaden celebrations of Christmas to include other faiths by replacing "Merry Christmas" with

"Happy Holidays." Activists supported putting up crèches again, or even placing gigantic stone statues of the Ten Commandments outside several of the nation's courthouses.

While the political ramifications of the Religious Right are beyond the scope of this chapter, the effects of the Religious Right were two-fold, and both were unforeseen by the Religious Right itself. On the one hand, their battles helped amplify debates about how high the wall between church and state should be. As activists from the right fought over symbolic and monetary support for the public airing of their faith, other groups arose to counter them, creating pitched and partisan strug-gles that provoked questions of how much faith Americans wanted in the public sphere. In the Mount Soledad neighborhood of San Diego, California, for example, a cross on public land that was erected in 1913 came under attack in the 1990s and 2000s for prioritizing Christianity and thereby violating the First Amendment. Religious Right activists fought back, the American Civil Liberties Union (ACLU) got involved, and the case is still being litigated, with the ACLU hoping the federal government will simply sell the land to a ready buyer or move the cross to a nearby Episcopal Church. Neither option satisfies religious adherents who claim the presence of the cross affirms the country's commitment to Christianity. Similar debates are taking place over school curricu-lums, as Mark Chancy has shown in Chapter 10. Again and again, the courts have come down on the side of religious pluralism, upholding their inclination that the government should not play favorites when it comes to religious expression or belief.

The other unanticipated effect of the Religious Right was the dramatic increase of America's nones. In *American Grace*, a revealing portrait of America's religious landscape during the Obama years, sociologists Robert Putnam and David Campbell argue that it was the politicizing of religion by the Religious Right that turned the younger generation off faith. If that's what religion looks like, these millennials argued, then they wanted nothing to do with it. So they stopped going to church. The rise of the nones, especially the younger ones, can thus be attributed as a direct response to the Religious Right.[21]

Although in a subordinate role to greater societal trends, President Obama has played his part in this almost casual acceptance of American religious pluralism. In his January 2009 inaugural address, Obama became the first president to openly acknowledge the nones as important constituents in the American project. "We are a nation of Christians and

Muslims, Jews and Hindus, and non-believers," he said, before going on to honor the country's acceptance of the idea of pluralism:

> We are shaped by every language and culture, drawn from every end of this Earth; and because we have tasted the bitter swill of civil war and segregation, and emerged from that dark chapter stronger and more united, we cannot help but believe that the old hatreds shall someday pass; that the lines of tribe shall soon dissolve; that as the world grows smaller, our common humanity shall reveal itself; and that America must play its role in ushering in a new era of peace.[22]

Although critics have tried to distort the president's own religious commitments, as Rebecca Goetz describes in Chapter 5, hardly a peep has been murmured when he advocates American pluralism.

Obama also immediately (within a week of being sworn in) re-crafted President Bush's Office of Faith-based Initiatives, designed to funnel money to religious organizations providing social services to the hungry or the poor. While the roughly $2.2 billion per year set aside for the initiative was supposed to be dispersed to non-proselytizing efforts of recipients, the office quickly became a target for complaints that the money was being overwhelmingly sent to groups from the Religious Right who supported Bush's presidency. In 2004, the Freedom From Religion Foundation actually sued the federal government over the constitutionality of the office. One of Obama's first acts was to broaden the number of recipients, as well as establish an expansive advisory council to ensure there was no favoritism at play.[23]

But nowhere has this understanding of American pluralism shaped Obama's presidency then in his dealings with predominantly Muslim countries. As Andrew Preston describes in Chapter 11, Obama sought to reconcile relations with certain Middle Eastern countries a few months after his inauguration. At a joint press conference with the president of Turkey, Obama reflected on some of the similarities between the two nations, citing a common if contested tradition of religious pluralism. "Although," Obama said, speaking of the United States, "we have a very large Christian population, we do not consider ourselves a Christian nation or a Jewish nation or a Muslim nation; we consider ourselves a nation of citizens who are bound by ideals and a set of values."[24]

The conservative media, led by Fox News, tried to use the line to discredit the president. On the television program *Hannity*, former Speaker of the House of Representatives Newt Gingrich said he thought Obama was "fundamentally misleading about the nature of America. We are not a secular country." Sean Hannity wondered, "How insulted should the average American be? Because I'm offended," before going on to say Obama was "clearly not reading our framers and our founders, because they all refer to the Judeo-Christian ethic as the foundation of this country." Later, Hannity introduced a segment by former Bush deputy chief of staff Karl Rove, saying, "And as Christians celebrate their Holy Week, President Obama is busy out there telling the world this is not a Christian nation." Rove responded, "Yeah, look, America is a nation built on faith. I mean, we can be Christian, we can be Jew, we can be Mormon, we can be, you know, any variety of things. We're a country that prizes faith and believes that we are endowed by our creator with certain inalienable rights."

Of course, none of these comments actually suggested that Obama was wrong in what he said. Never mind that the "Judeo-Christian ethic" didn't exist until the early years of the twentieth century and therefore wouldn't have been available to the founders, nor that Obama never said the United States was a "secular country," whatever that might be. Indeed, despite the tacit angling for a way to discredit the president, all the comments on Fox News perhaps ironically confirmed the pluralistic nature of American religious life in the age of Obama. Before long, the ideologues on Fox discovered the issue didn't have legs and went after the president in other ways.

Closer to home, Obama endorsed American pluralism once again when, in 2010, he supported the right of New York City's Muslim community to build an Islamic community center two blocks from the site of the recently destroyed World Trade Center. "As a citizen, and as president, I believe that Muslims have the same right to practice their religion as anyone else in this country," he said, affirming American pluralism. "That includes the right to build a place of worship and a community center on private property in lower Manhattan in accordance with local laws and ordinances," he said, adding, "This is America, and our commitment to religious freedom must be unshakable."[25]

Plans for the community center continue to be debated, although the debate has shifted from whether or not the Islamic center should be allowed to be there to whether or not it is in good taste for it to be there. For most Americans, like Obama, have accepted the idea of religious pluralism. Indeed, perhaps the most revealing finding in Putnam and Campbell's sociology of American religious beliefs, *American Grace*, is that most Americans believe that people of faiths different from their own can still go to heaven, which is as casual an acceptance of religious pluralism as you're likely to find.[26] While there is always the risk that the rhetoric of tolerance that I've described will coincide with a rise in physical violence, akin to that suggested by Rebecca Goetz in Chapter 5 and Arlene Sánchez-Walsh in Chapter 9, the manner in which religious pluralism came to uncontested fruition—under the tutelage of numerous powerful groups including the predominant majority one—suggests that today's efforts to "take the country back" will be just as fictional as the history to which those cultural monists aspire.

Notes

1. See Charlie Savage, "Sotomayor Confirmed By Senate, 68–31," *New York Times*, August 6, 2009, A1; Charlie Savage, "Sotomayor Sworn in as Supreme Court Justice," *New York Times*, August 8, 2009, A12; Bill Donohue, "Sotomayor's Catholicism," *Catalyst* (July/August 2009), http://www.catholicleague.org/sotomayor%E2%80%99s-catholicism-2/.
2. Pew Research Center, *Religious Hostilities Reach Six-year High*, January 2014.
3. US Equal Employment Opportunity Commission, "Religion-based Charges FY 1997–FY 2013," http://www.eeoc.gov/eeoc/statistics/enforcement/religion.cfm.
4. George W. Bush, "Islam is Peace," remarks by the president at Islamic Center of Washington, DC, September 17, 2001, http://georgewbush-whitehouse.archives.gov/news/releases/2001/09/20010917-11.html.
5. See, for instance, Eric Eckholm, "Court Upholds Blocking of Amendment against Shariah Law," *New York Times*, January 10, 2012, A19.
6. Pew Research Center, "'Nones' on the Rise," October 9, 2012, http://www.pewforum.org/2012/10/09/nones-on-the-rise/; Pew Research Center, "Growth of the Nonreligious," July 2, 2013, http://www.pewforum.org/2013/07/02/growth-of-the-nonreligious-many-say-trend-is-bad-for-american-society/.
7. On Catholics, see Pew Research Center, "Faith in Flux," April 27, 2009 [rev. February 2011], http://www.pewforum.org/2009/04/27/faith-in-flux/. See also Slavica Jakelic, *Collectivistic Faiths: Religion, Choice, and Identity in Late Modernity* (Burlington, VT: Ashgate Publishing Co., 2010).
8. Pew Research Center, "'Nones' on the Rise."
9. Ibid.
10. Russell Moore, "Same Sex Marriage and the Future," *Moore to the Point* (blog), April 15, 2014) http://www.russellmoore.com/2014/04/15/same-sex-marriage-and-the-future/.

11. For the general demography of American religious life, see Barry A. Kosmin and Ariela Keysar, *American Religious Identification Survey (ARIS 2008)* (Hartford, CT: Institute for the Study of Secularism in Society and Culture, 2009), http://commons.trincoll.edu/aris/publications/2008-2/aris-2008-summary-report/. For the Pew Study, see Pew Research Center, "Global Religious Diversity: Half of the Most Religiously Diverse Countries are in Asia-Pacific Region," April 2014, http://www.pewforum.org/files/2014/04/Religious-Diversity-full-report.pdf.

12. Kosmin and Keysar, *American Religious Identification Survey.*

13. For these divisions, see Robert Wuthnow, *The Restructuring of American Religion* (Princeton, NJ: Princeton University Press, 1990).

14. David Sehat, *The Myth of American Religious Freedom* (New York: Oxford University Press, 2011), 63.

15. Ibid., 61.

16. This and the following few paragraphs derive from my book, *Tri-Faith America: How Postwar Catholics and Jews Forced America to Live Up to its Protestant Promise* (New York: Oxford University Press, 2011).

17. Tom Lehrer, "National Brotherhood Week," *That Was the Year That Was,* Reprise/Warner Brothers Records, 1965.

18. *Engel v. Vitale,* 370 U.S. 421 (1962) and *Abington School District v. Schempp,* 374 U.S. 203 (1963).

19. Diana Eck, *A New Religious America: How a "Christian Country" Has Become the World's Most Religiously Diverse Nation* (San Francisco: HarperSanFrancisco, 2001).

20. The best account of the argument that race was vital to the formation of the Religious Right comes from Randall Balmer, "The Real Origins of the Religious Right," *Politico,* May 27, 2014, http://www.politico.com/magazine/story/2014/05/religious-right-real-origins-107133.html#.VD2IOuevyRN, but Balmer proposed this thesis in early works, including *Thy Kingdom Come: How the Religious Right Distorts Faith and Threatens America* (New York: Basic Books, 2007), and *Redeemer: The Life of Jimmy Carter* (New York: Basic Books, 2014). For a nice counterbalance, see Steven P. Miller, *The Age of Evangelicalism: America in the Born-again Years* (New York: Oxford University Press, 2014).

21. Robert D. Putnam and David E. Campbell, *American Grace: How Religion Divides and Unites Us* (New York: Simon and Schuster, 2010), 120–122.

22. Barack Obama, "Inaugural Address," January 20, 2009, http://www.whitehouse.gov/blog/inaugural-address.

23. For the controversies, see, for instance, Diana B. Henriques and Andrew Lehren, "Religion for Captive Audiences, With Taxpayers Footing the Bill," *New York Times,* December 10, 2006, http://www.nytimes.com/2006/12/10/business/10faith.html?pagewanted=print&_r=0.

24. Barack Obama, "Joint Press Availability with President Obama and President Gul of Turkey," Ankara, Turkey, April 6, 2009, http://www.whitehouse.gov/the-press-office/joint-press-availability-with-president-obama-and-president-gul-turkey.

25. Barack Obama, "Remarks by the President at Iftar Dinner," August 13, 2010, http://www.whitehouse.gov/the-press-office/2010/08/13/remarks-president-iftar-dinner.

26. Putnam and Campbell, *American Grace*, 535.

Afterword

Amanda Porterfield

FOR READERS LOOKING for insight into religion's role in American politics today, one lesson emerges above all others from this rich collection of essays. Careful study of American history is indispensable. Not the same thing as idealizing the American past, historical understanding of religion's role in American politics requires attention to the historical contexts of religious meaning and political decision-making. Contexts are vital because, as historical situations change, the meanings of religious terms and the implications of political decisions change as well. We can best see continuities between past and present, and thus understand the history that makes American religion and politics what they are today, by situating past events in their own time and not simply projecting present ideas onto the past.

Related to the vital matter of context, historical understanding of religion's role in American politics requires attention to the quality and orientation of the sources that represent the past. The past is not something to be found and settled once and for all but is better conceived as layers of interpretation accumulating and continuing to influence one another over time. Consequently, sorting through accounts of religion and politics in American history involves trafficking in interpretation. Besides being fascinating in its own right, investigation into these layers of interpretation offers better understanding of ourselves—after all, the past has made us who we are. There may be no more effective way of gaining awareness of why we think and act religiously and politically as we do today, or any more effective way of achieving better understanding of why others think and act differently, than to carefully sort through religious and political interpretations of the past. With many good examples of careful sifting through interpretations about the past, the essays in this volume help us better understand who and where we are today.

Building on this basic point about history's importance for understanding religion and American politics today, this afterword identifies three important conclusions that readers might draw from this fine collection of diverse essays. The first conclusion is that religion has long been an active force in American politics, and the more one looks for religion in the political events of the past, the more religion one finds.

The second conclusion drives toward an ample understanding of religion that involves constellations of behavior and practical expression. Neither religion nor its influence on politics can be fully appreciated by defining religion simply and narrowly as a matter of belief. As several of the essays in this volume show, practices derived from religious contexts, and from efforts to protect religious worlds from criticism, may have affected American political life as much or more profoundly than any theological belief. This is not to say that everything about the past, or everything about politics, is somehow religious. But looking for religion in American politics is often productive in yielding deeper insight into the political decisions people make, and into political practices and movements that shape institutions.

The third conclusion attends to the fluidity of the terms under investigation—the meanings attached to "religion" and "politics" have changed over time, as have American understandings of where one stops and the other begins. In other words, religion and politics are socially constructed categories with definitions that shift from one historical moment to the next. Looking at religion and politics this way, as historical constructs, enables us to see that their relationship today is not the same as their relationship in the past. Among other benefits, this alertness to discontinuity between past and present clears the way to see underlying elements of continuity.

Many of the essays in this volume support the first conclusion, that historical investigation of religion's role in American politics yields plenty of it. To take a particularly clear example of this point, Charles Irons shows that Thomas Jefferson considered Jesus a moral guide and devoted considerable effort to studying the New Testament, even though he espoused a materialistic philosophy that rejected miracles. Jefferson may not have been a Christian—if that term means assent to supernatural revelation—but he was staunchly "Protestant" in his devotion to reading, individual conscience, voluntary associations, and reason. Though these devotions are not unique to Protestants, Protestants elevated their importance above other aspects of Christianity and fought to defend them in the sixteenth and seventeenth centuries. As a result of Jefferson's influence and that of other Protestant leaders, the American political system reflects Protestant devotion to the elevated importance of texts, conscience, voluntarism, and reason.

On a different topic, Darren Dochuk's essay on the history of political debates about the oil industry supports the same general conclusion, that if one looks for religion in politics, religion often emerges as a driving force. While Standard Oil founder John Rockefeller championed his company as an expression of God's providential design for America, journalist Ida Tarbell condemned its monopoly of oil production as un-Christian, and her arguments helped break up the company. Later American desires to convert the world to Christianity helped justify American efforts to control world energy, while today, religious voices within environmental movements shape efforts to minimize carbon footprints and restrain oil production.

Making a similar point about religion's influence on politics, Matthew Sutton examines the political consequences of dire warnings about the end of time promulgated by Protestant religious leaders. David Koresh's prediction of violent tribulation in the last days set the stage for the US government's role as the agent of destruction. Harold Camping's vision of tribulation generated hostility toward feminists and homosexuals. Most politically influential of all, Billy Graham's repeated efforts to identify signs of the end times in world affairs created a bridge between conservative evangelicals and Republican presidents that the GOP assiduously nurtured.

While Irons, Dochuk, and Sutton uncover examples of religion's role in politics, Anthea Butler looks at the political dimensions of religion. In Butler's analysis, conservative black evangelicals depend on their religious conservatism to make the political statement, aimed at white evangelicals, that they are respectable American citizens. Ironically, Butler argues, black investment in religious conservatism has the unintended effect of isolating black conservative evangelicals as a political minority. While Irons finds Protestant values translated into secular politics, Dochuk finds competing expressions of Protestant Christianity driving the politics of big oil, and Sutton finds religious visions of tribulation generating real political consequences. Butler's study of conservative black evangelicalism finds the dynamic relationship between religion and politics operating in the reverse direction, with political goals activating religious life. Nevertheless, it offers us yet another example of the porous boundary between religion and politics.

Turning from these examples of the interplay between religion and politics, another set of essays illustrates the second conclusion, that religious influence in politics is as much about practice as it is about belief or theology. For example, in his essay on Mormon religious politics, Spencer Fluhman argues that ritual behavior, including bodily practices involving diet and sex, have defined Mormon religious identity since the mid-nineteenth century. Political relationships with outsiders developed around the secrecy of these practices as Mormons attempted to shield themselves from abuse, ironically fueling suspicion of their religious deviancy and making secrecy itself a religious practice that Mormons must constantly negotiate.

While Fluhman's essay provides a clear example of how religion's role in politics can revolve around matters of ritual practice, Kate Carté Engel calls attention to religious practice in order to explain how conservative Christians read American political history. Avoiding critical analysis of sources, and abstracting events from their contexts in order to make a religious point, conservative Christians practice their religion by imposing it upon American political history, thereby proclaiming the truth of their religion through public education. Complementing Engel's analysis of how Christian conservatives practice their religion of American political history, Mark Chancey shows how Christian conservatives elected to the Board of Education in Texas used their political power to impose their religious will on standards imposed by the state for teaching American history. As a way to promoting their religion as a righteous challenge to Islam on one hand and secular liberalism on the other, these elected officials practice their religion by requiring textbooks used in Texas public schools to link the American Founding Fathers back to Moses, and the US Constitution back to the Ten Commandments.

In addition to this attention to the practice of religion in politics, many of the essays in this volume lead to the third conclusion, that both religion and politics are historically constructed categories that have changed over time. For example, in his essay on religious pluralism, Kevin Schultz shows that religious discrimination in the United States has decreased since 2009 as the result of long efforts to define religious traditions as complementary partners in a larger political consensus respectful of religion.

This embrace of religious pluralism marks a departure from political conflict over religious diversity in the past and reflects an underlying shift in the meaning of "religion" from something true to something broader and more nebulous, accommodating many truths. Matthew Hedstrom's essay on the rise of the "nones" develops a related argument. Hedstrom traces the values of Americans unaffiliated with religious institutions today back to the transcendentalists of the nineteenth century. Those earlier proponents of freedom from institutionalized religious authority pressed for a liberal political respect for the universal spiritual truths embedded in all religions, unlike more conservative Americans of their time who insisted that only particular forms of Protestant Christianity should be recognized as true. Like Schultz's essay, Hedstrom's points to the shift that has occurred in the meaning of "religion." While underlying political differences persist between religious liberals and religious conservatives today, and conservatives may seem to have the upper hand in political elections, liberal respect for spirituality has universalized the meaning of "religion" for everyone.

The reconstruction of religion in relation to politics is also the theme of Alison Greene's essay on the history of religion's role in public welfare. Legislative acts during the Great Depression marked transformations in the division of labor between religion and government, in interaction between religion and government, and in political recalibrations of the dividing line between them. Greene shows that as religious institutions proved incapable of meeting the challenges to public welfare, government agencies assumed more responsibility, eventually enlisting religious agencies as government subsidiaries. With respect to their contributions to public welfare, then, religion and government both operated very differently after the 1930s than before, and their relationship to one another changed profoundly.

Focusing on a more recent shift in the meaning of "religion" in relation to politics, Andrew Preston calls attention to the crossroads the United States currently faces with respect to religion's role in American foreign policy. In his discussion of the shift in President Obama's view, from his descriptions of America, early in his first term, as a faith-based democracy, to the absence of religion in his more recent descriptions of American political interests, Preston points to the divisiveness of religion at home as an increasing political problem for Obama after his first election, and one that forced him to discuss American democracy apart from religion. Preston's essay offers an important reminder that religious influence in politics is not necessarily a simple or straightforward process, and that religion may be ignored, resisted, deflected, or redirected. In the case of President Obama, endorsement for religion as an agent of political change became problematic as the political effects of the religious backlash against him increased.

Stephen Miller's essay on the upsurge of post-Christian hope in the 2008 presidential election—and its decline after that election—offers a fruitful complement to Preston's argument about Obama. Casting widespread enthusiasm for Obama in the 2008 campaign as a spiritual awakening akin to earlier religious awakenings in American history, Miller points to a strong and previously disorganized cohort of spiritual seekers opposed to conservative interpretations of Christianity within that evangelical revival. Fierce reaction to the election of Obama caused high-flying spiritual enthusiasm for Obama to dissipate, as did the hard political choices Obama had to make, and the new political coalitions that emerged among a broad range of religious conservatives to thwart his leadership.

As the essays by Greene, Preston, and Miller all illustrate, the boundary between religion and politics is often blurred and porous, and perceptions about where the boundary should be drawn change as historical actors recalibrate the meaning of religion in relation to politics. This fluidity of religion as a historical construct finally inseparable from politics is not a new phenomenon. Its can be traced back through medieval Christendom to ancient Rome. But in the United States, this fluid relationship between religion and politics is rendered more complex by the institutional separation of church and state and by efforts, on both the right and left, to keep religion out of politics. In many cases, those efforts might best be interpreted as efforts to keep bad religion out of politics for the sake of the future. Insofar as politics involves some appeal to moral values, and some vision of what the future should be, "religion" in the broad sense that includes disagreements about bad and good, can often be found in politics.

Because the meaning of religion changes over time, and in relation to politics, attention to historical change leads to criticism of simplistic interpretations. Beyond that, and perhaps even more important, attention to how religion and politics have changed reveals continuities with the past that otherwise would have been overlooked. Rebecca Goetz's essay on Muslims in America illustrates this point. Only when assertions about America as a Christian nation come to be seen as simplistic ideals laid onto the past can aspects of the past occluded by the imposition of those ideals come into view. Thus dispensing with claims, especially after 9/11, that Islam is essentially un-American, Goetz finds that Islam has been part of the fabric of American religious life since the earliest days of European colonization. With something like a million people in North America familiar with Islam by 1800, that religion is more deeply entrenched in American history than many of its detractors think.

Edward Blum's call to pay attention to the human bodies obscured by religious and political rhetoric offers another way of thinking about what it means to look underneath formulaic interpretations regarding religion's role in American political history. Blum argues that black bodies are often hidden by religious rhetoric about the American people. We should question how religion and politics affect human bodies, Blum argues, and give particular attention to bodies obscured by lofty claims about American freedom and opportunity. Looking for and listening to these bodies, he suggests, may reveal aspects of American political and religious history we might not otherwise have seen. Making a related point, Jennifer Graber points to stereotypes about bodies that turn attention away from what bodies actually have to say about the world and about themselves. American fixation on stereotypes about the bodies of women, Graber suggests, has obscured American understanding of foreign cultures, and women's lives within them.

Last but not least, Arlene Sánchez-Walsh calls attention to the apparent disconnect between religion and politics on the issue of immigration. While many religious organizations in the United States express compassion for immigrants and strongly support immigration reform, the Republican Party has blocked immigration reform and encouraged a flourishing of negative stereotypes about immigrants. At one level, GOP efforts to resist the pressure of religious organizations for immigration reform reflect the hardball realism of politics and fear of losing elections as a result of demographic trends favoring immigrant groups. At another level, as many of the essays in this volume suggest, religion is not always about compassion. Political resentment carries religious force as much as compassionate reform, and the division between religion and politics is never entirely clear-cut, with religious feeling all on the side of good against the harsh realities of politics. Political conservatives opposed to immigration reform are not immune to religion, or to religious visions of America as a nation of white European immigrants fallen away from its righteous path through world history.

But resistance to change and fear of people who might bring change is only part of the story. Conservative religious control over positive religious readings of American history is also a factor, along with distrust of students of American history who are willing to examine that history with a critical eye. Another reason for the strength of GOP politics may be more fundamental—the United States is a republic with a constitution that, in its original form, was conservative. Certainly, democratic elements can be found in the colonial era as well as in the nation's founding. But compared to the proclamation of human equality in the Declaration of Independence, the US Constitution is an exclusionary political document with respect to civil rights. Every single advance made in broadening civil rights since the ratification of that document has been a hard-fought battle. Conservatives today have the US Constitution—as it was first ratified—on their side.

On the other hand, the Constitution as it has evolved and been interpreted also provides checks that make huge religio-political victories difficult to manage and sustain. Muddling through with compromises may not be pretty, but it may be better than the alternatives. This difficult but useful political process, with all its conflicting religious forces embedded, may not be entirely dissimilar from writing good history.

Index